THE ISRAEL/PALESTINE QUESTION

The Israel/Palestine Question assimilates diverse interpretations of the origins of the Middle East conflict with emphasis on the fight for Palestine and its religious and political roots. Drawing largely on scholarly debates in Israel during the last two decades, which have become known as 'historical revisionism', the collection presents the most recent developments in the historiography of the Arab–Israeli conflict and a critical reassessment of Israel's past. The volume commences with an overview of Palestinian history and the origins of modern Palestine, and includes essays on the early Zionist settlement, Mandatory Palestine, the 1948 war, international influences on the conflict and the Intifada.

Ilan Pappé is Professor at Haifa University, Israel. His previous books include *Britain and the Arab–Israeli Conflict* (1988), *The Making of the Arab–Israeli Conflict, 1947–51* (1994) and *A History of Modern Palestine and Israel* (forthcoming).

Rewriting Histories focuses on historical themes where standard conclusions are facing a major challenge. Each book presents 8 to 10 papers (edited and annotated where necessary) at the forefront of current research and interpretation, offering students an accessible way to engage with contemporary debates.

Series editor **Jack R. Censer** is Professor of History at George Mason University.

REWRITING HISTORIES
Series editor: Jack R. Censer

Already published

THE INDUSTRIAL REVOLUTION AND WORK IN
NINETEENTH-CENTURY EUROPE
Edited by Lenard R. Berlanstein

SOCIETY AND CULTURE IN THE SLAVE SOUTH
Edited by J. William Harris

ATLANTIC AMERICAN SOCIETIES
From Columbus through Abolition
Edited by J.R. McNeill and Alan Karras

GENDER AND AMERICAN HISTORY SINCE 1890
Edited by Barbara Melosh

DIVERSITY AND UNITY IN EARLY NORTH AMERICA
Edited by Philip D. Morgan

NAZISM AND GERMAN SOCIETY 1933–1945
Edited by David Crew

THE REVOLUTIONS OF 1989
Edited by Vladimir Tismaneanu

THE FRENCH REVOLUTION
Recent debates and new controversies
Edited by Gary Kares

Forthcoming

HOLOCAUST: ORIGINS, IMPLEMENTATION AND
AFTERMATH
Edited by Omer Bartov

STALINISM
Edited by Sheila Fitzpatrick

THE
ISRAEL/PALESTINE
QUESTION

Edited by Ilan Pappé

London and New York

First published 1999
by Routledge
11 New Fetter Lane, London EC4P 4EE

Simultaneously published in the USA and Canada
by Routledge
29 West 35th Street, New York, NY 10001

Reprinted 2002

Routledge is an imprint of the Taylor & Francis Group

Typeset in Palatino by
The Florence Group
Printed and bound in Great Britain by
MPG Books Ltd, Bodmin, Cornwall

British Library Cataloguing in Publication Data
A catalogue record for this book is available
from the British Library

Library of Congress Cataloguing in Publication Data
The Israel/Palestine question/ [edited by] Ilan Pappé.
p. cm. – (Rewriting histories)
Includes bibliographical references and index.
1. Jewish–Arab relations – History – 1917–1948.
2. Israel–Arab war. 1948–9 – Historiography.
3. Palestinian Arabs–Israel.
I. Pappé, Ilan. II Series: Re-writing histories.
DS119.7.I82619   1999
956.04'2–dc21   98-36351 CIP

ISBN 0–415–16947–X (hbk)
ISBN 0–415–16948–8 (pbk)

CONTENTS

SERIES EDITOR'S PREFACE

Few fields can claim to be more energized than the study of the Arab–Israeli conflict. For decades after the founding of Israel, scholars associated with the fledgling state wrote works that defended its every aspect. For example, such historians claimed that Arab states encouraged Palestinians to evacuate the contested areas in 1948. Thus, in these versions, the Arabs caused the refugee problem. This volume focuses on the tremendous outpouring of recent studies that reinterpret the history of this struggle by depicting the Palestinians' perspective in a far more supportive light. Arguing that they have consulted the archives much more carefully, these scholars have shown, among many other findings, that efforts at solidarity among Arab and Israeli workers went awry because of limits on both sides. Likewise, the 1948 exodus relates significantly to Israeli policy. Throughout this work, responsibility is more equally shared, and the Palestinians receive more direct attention. Indeed, this volume collects a series of essays with which any serious student of the period will have to grapple before making conclusions.

ACKNOWLEDGEMENTS

All articles and extracts in this volume (except for Chapter 1) have already been published. We should like to thank the following copyright holders for permission to reproduce their work.

Chapter 1   New historiographical orientations in the research on the Palestine Question (written for this volume by Ilan Pappé).

Chapter 2   Reprinted from *Journal of Palestine Studies*, vol. 21/2 (winter 1992), no. 82, pp. 5–28.

Chapter 3   Reprinted from *The Palestinians and the Middle East Conflict*, Haifa University 1979, pp. 21–32.

Chapter 4   Reprinted from *Journal of Historical Sociology*, vol. 6 no. 3 (September 1993), pp. 327–50.

Chapter 5   Reprinted from Michael N. Barnett (ed.), *Israel in Comparative Studies: Challenging the Conventional Wisdom*, State University of New York Press, New York 1996, pp. 227–44.

Chapter 6   Reprinted from *Comparative Studies in Society and History*, vol. 35 no. 3 (July 1993), pp. 601–27.

Chapter 7   Reprinted from Albert Hourani, Philip S. Khoury and Mary C. Wilson (eds), *The Modern Middle East*, I. B. Tauris, London and New York, 1993, pp. 467–502.

Chapter 8   Reprinted from the *International Journal of Middle Eastern Studies* 27 (1995), pp. 287–304.

Chapter 9   Reprinted from *1948 and After: Israel and the Palestinians*, Clarendon Press, Oxford 1990, pp. 69–88.

Chapter 10   Reprinted from *Journal of Palestine Studies*, vol. 21/1 (autumn 1991), no. 82, pp. 90–7.

ACKNOWLEDGEMENTS

Chapter 11   Reprinted from Eddy Kaufman, Shukri B. Abed and Robert L. Rothstein (eds), *Democracy, Peace and the Israel–Palestinian Conflict*, Lynne Rienner Publishers: London and Boulder, 1993, pp. 163–88.

Chapter 12   Reprinted from Jamal R. Nassar and Roger Heacock (eds), *Intifada –Palestine at the Crossroads*, Praeger, New York, 1990, pp. 105–23.

1

INTRODUCTION

New historiographical orientations in the research on the Palestine Question

Ilan Pappé

This reader focuses on the history of the Palestine Question which is at the heart of the Arab–Israel conflict. This collection wishes to present, to students and experts alike, some of the most recent developments in the conflict's historiography. In doing that, this collection does not cover every aspect or historical chapter in the history of the conflict. Its mode of selection is contemporary and fed by the current and most recent areas of scholarly interest. It includes only works which have challenged previous conceptions and paradigms in the historiographical enterprise. As such, the collection does not represent a balanced view of the old and new scholarly interest in the conflict's history; it rather stresses the new at the expense of the old. It should be seen as a summary of a phase in the conflict's historiography – a phase characterized by challenges to the conventional and mainstream historiography. But even that categorization has proved to be too broad. The space given to a reasonable reader could not include all the challenges made in the last few years. I have been content with works which represent trends appearing in other similar works. All the contributions to this volume are slowly becoming part of the accepted literature on the conflict. In fact, one could easily say that it is impossible to teach or read about the conflict without referring to the points and challenges made by the contributors presented here.

The new scholarship displays several discernible characteristics. It provides a history of the conflict which is influenced by recent historiographical debates taking place around the academic world at large. Thus, the works here present a double-edged wish to introduce an interdisciplinary methodology into the research as well as to inject a more skeptical view towards historical narratives written under the powerful hand of nationalist elites and ideologies.[1]

A more skeptical view towards national elites as well as towards the history of elites, is part of an effort, following recent trends in European historiography, to rewrite into history the lives of peasants, workers, women and anyone else excluded in the past by hegemonic groups of historians. The field of Middle Eastern studies as a whole has only recently opened up to such views and the last few years saw the appearance of works reconstructing the history of non-elite groups in the area. Hence there was very little in the way of social or cultural history of the Middle East.[2] In the case of the history of the Palestine conflict these new subject matters appeared even later in the day. Here we are interested in works that could be termed the social history of the conflict. This new orientation is represented here through the works of Zachary Lockman, Ted Swedenburg and Islah Jad. Lockman deals with the life of Jewish and Arab workers in the early Mandatory period – examining the tension between class solidarity and national commitment as well as between colonialist and colonized workers and their respective trade unions. Ted Swedenburg examines the role of the peasant in the national Palestinian revolt in 1936–9. This analysis can be and will be used again for understanding the role of the peasants in the *Intifada*. The *Intifada*, in fact, triggered some of the most intriguing work in the field of social history. One such work is that of Islah Jad, which in this volume discusses the place and influence of women on national politics since 1919 and until the *Intifada*.

A second common and connected feature of the new works is that they seem to perceive the Palestine conflict as one fought between a strong ex-colonial party – Israel – and a weaker one – a colonized party, the Palestinians. A balance of power which dominated the previous historiographical phase – Israelis were determining the agenda and orientations of the historiographical enterprise – demonstrated that they did not only colonize the land but also its history. At that stage, by and large, Israeli historians conveyed the message that Israelis were the victims of the conflict and constituted the rational party in the struggle over Palestine, while the Palestinians were irrational if not fanatic, intransigent and immoral. To be fair, one should say that several, although not too many scholars, outside the area, attempted to write the conflict's history from a different perspective; they wrote under the assumption that both parties to the conflict should be treated as more or less equal in power as well as in guilt and justice.

The stronger party, and this of course may be a temporary state of affairs, has the power to write the history in a more effective way. In our particular case, it had formed a state and employed the state's apparatus for successfully propagating its narrative in front of domestic as well as external publics. The weaker party, in our particular case,

2

was engaged in a national liberation struggle, unable to lend its historians a hand in opposing the propaganda of the other side.

But things have changed. Palestinian historians succeeded in putting across a historical version which has, in the words of our first contributor, Beshara Doumani, brought Palestinians back into the history of Palestine. Here the two orientations we have described intertwine. The Palestinian historians challenged a major Zionist claim about the absence of any meaningful Palestinian existence before the arrival of the new Jewish immigrants in 1882 by reconstructing 'from below' the life of a Palestinian community in the pre-Zionist era. Thus, as Doumani shows in his article, rewriting the Palestinians into the history of Palestine was done first as a challenge to Israeli historiography, which had totally excluded them when writing about Palestine before the arrival of Zionism, and second as part of a more general historiographical trend – writing about a community as a whole with its elites and non-elite groups.

Butrus Abu-Manneh, our second contributor, long before this more conscientious trend began, researched the conditions in which a new geopolitical entity emerged in Palestine – the autonomous sanjak of Jerusalem. This structural and administrative reorganization, initiated by the Ottoman reformers in 1872, contributed to the emergence of a local Palestinian identity, focused around the city of Jerusalem and occurring before the arrival of the first Zionists. The importance of structural transformation in producing the circumstances ripe for the birth of modern nationalism is one of the main claims made in recent theoretical treatments of the phenomenon of nationalism.[3]

Other structural changes are described in full in books which have to be read as a whole and therefore I have decided not to include extracts from them in this reader. These are the books by Beshara Doumani, Rashid Khalidi, and the joint book by Baruch Kimmerling and Joel Migdal,[4] all of which give the impression that before the appearance of the Zionist movement, a local national identity had been in the making.

This view on the origins of Palestinian nationalism contrasts with the claim made by Israeli historians in the past about Palestinian nationalism being only a by-product of Zionism. It also contradicts the more romantic view taken by a small number of old Palestinian historians who argued that Palestine had existed from time immemorial (see for instance the Palestinian Encyclopedia).[5]

The new works are thus written from a sympathetic point of view towards the predicaments of the weaker party in the conflict – the Palestinians. A related consequence of this attitude is the inclusion of more Palestinian scholars among the producers of our historiographical knowledge about the conflict. In the past, Israeli historians working on the conflict's history were considered by the principal academic centers in the Western world as professionals, while Palestinian works were branded as sheer propaganda. The reversal in this situation occurred for several reasons, the most important of which was the appearance of Edward Said's seminal book, *Orientalism.* This work had a considerable influence on the scholarly world interested in the Middle East. Said's deconstruction of Western orientalism was easily applied to the Israeli academia and its treatment of the past. His works in general contributed to a more positive attitude towards the Palestinian historical narrative. Said also influenced several Israeli scholars who found his prism useful in deconstructing their society's attitude, particularly the local academia's approach, towards the Palestinians in the past and in the present.

The Saidian prism became useful when a chain of dramatic events in Israel in the 1970s and 1980s led a new generation of Israeli scholars to suspect the ideological bent of their predecessors and to adopt a more positive position towards their Palestinian counterparts. At that period, Israeli sociologists exposed the impact Zionist ideology had on what was widely considered hitherto as an 'objective' Israeli research on the conflict. The work of these sociologists is part of a more comprehensive trend in the Israeli academia, one I choose to name the post-Zionist scholarship. It began with the works of Israeli historians looking into the history of the 1948 war and portraying a historiographical picture of it which challenged the official Zionist historical version. The gist of this historiographical revisionism was the willingness of those historians to reassess, with a critical eye, their country's past. They became known as the 'new historians'. This collection, therefore, reflects some of their major contributions in the field. The self-criticism shown by Israeli historians has, on the one hand, delegitimized some of the principal claims made by mainstream Israeli historians and on the other hand, legitimized claims made in the past by Palestinian historians. This orientation has narrowed down the gap between the two respective national narratives of the conflict's history. One can see the emergence of a joint narrative, constructed by professional historians on both sides, which accepts major chapters in the Palestinian narrative, while rejecting principal ones in the Zionist narrative.

One good example of this rapprochement is what Uri Ram calls in his article in this volume the introduction of the colonialist paradigm into the Israeli historical research on Palestine. Ram summarizes for us the works which adopted this paradigm and analyses their effect. A prime example of such an introduction of the colonialist paradigm is the work by Gershon Shafir, who was one of the first Israeli scholars to examine Zionism as a pure colonialist phenomenon, while using both a deductive and a comparative approach. Zachary Lockman, whose article appears as well in this section on colonialism, has also chosen to analyse

4

the Zionist enterprise as colonialist conduct and especially its strategy *vis-à-vis* the local labor market. Viewing Zionism and the Jewish community in the past through the colonialist paradigm reflects similar claims made through the years by the Palestinians about the Israeli society. It also provides a different historical explanation for the present predicaments of the Israeli society.

The focus of the historiographical revisionism in Israel, as mentioned, has been the 1948 war. This is not surprising. This formative year epitomizes for the Israelis the most miraculous point in their national history, while for the Palestinians 1948 is the most tragic and catastrophic year in their history. Most of the Israeli foundational myths revolve around the war and its consequences. Challenging these myths is more than just a historical debate, it also casts doubt on some of the principal moral assumptions and perceptions dominating the Israeli national agenda. The major themes brought about by the 'new historians' are summarized in Avi Shlaim's article and are demonstrated through a chapter taken from Benny Morris's book, *1948 and After*.

The 'new historians' have narrowed the gap between the two historical versions of the 1948 war. But, as transpires from the critique launched by Palestinian historians against the 'new historians', there is still a long way to go. The section devoted to the 1948 war includes a critique by Nur Masalha on the 'new historians' and particularly on Benny Morris. So there are still differences of historiographical interpretation, but it seems clear that the 'new historians' have responded more favorably than the early generations of historians in Israel to the Palestinian historical version of the conflict. It is safe to say now that some, although not all, of the principal chapters in the Palestinian historical narrative have been adopted by professional Israeli historians.

This collection ends with two works which manifest the inevitable link between the historical research and present reality. Historians tend to focus on issues which reflect current interest in the reality of Israel and Palestine. One common feature troubling both conscientious Israelis and Palestinians is the fate of democracy in their respective societies. A particular group of Palestinians, the Palestinian citizens of Israel, are interested in the fate of democracy on both sides. They are the victims of the non-democratic aspects of the Israeli system and they share the democratic aspirations of many of their people living under Israeli occupation or under the authority of the PLO in the rest of Palestine. An analysis of their history and status, as part of a more general discussion on democracy in Israel, is given here by As'ad Ghanem and Nadim Rouhana.

The study by Islah Jad closes this reader. It reviews the *Intifada* in a historical and a comparative context. It displays a willingness to keep the historical research in constant contact with the agendas of the communities as a whole. By focusing on the role of women in the upris-ing, this article combines the value of contemporary research with another common feature of all the articles in this collection, the reconstruction of hitherto marginalized social groups within both communities.

To sum up, it seems that we can find some hints in the articles here as to the possible future avenues to be followed by the next generation of historians. It stands to reason that more works will appear analysing the social and cultural developments in Israel/Palestine and fewer concerning the political dramas of the country's history. The historians' despair of their political elites, the expertise in interdisciplinary approa-ches and a tendency not to stick to elite analysis have highlighted the history of women, workers and peasants in the conflict. Their lives in the past did not always revolve around the grand and dramatic events one can reconstruct with the help of diplomatic and political archives. Historians found different subject matters and discovered new non-political sources. The social history, not to mention the cultural history, of the conflict is still a barren land waiting for future scholars. The precur-sors of this vital history are already here and some of them are included in this volume.

Moreover, there will probably be, on both sides, a growing recogni-tion of the other side's historical version and a more critical view of each side's own history. This would need a common consent between histo-rians about the need to accept the weight that ideological constraints have on the writing of history in a conflictual situation. One can only hope that although peace does not seem to be coming soon to Israel and Palestine, these constructive orientations will continue none the less to develop and contribute to a better coexistence in the torn land of Palestine.

But even what we have so far is very impressive. A more common agenda on the past is in the making and it is one which can create a common agenda for the future. A new narrative is being constructed as a bridge which connects conflicting versions as well as leading into a possibly better future.

NOTES

1 This general trend is summarized and introduced in Quentin Skinner (ed.), *The Return of Grand Theory in the Human Sciences* (Cambridge: Canto, 1991).
2 A recent reader has summarized these works on the Middle East; see Albert Hourani, Philip Khouri and Mary Wilson, *The Modern Middle East* (London and New York: I.B. Tauris, 1990).
3 See the works of Ernest Gelner, *Nations and Nationalism* (Oxford: Blackwell, 1973), Eric Hobsbawm, *Nations and Nationalism since 1780* (Cambridge:

Cambridge University Press, 1990) and Benedict Anderson, *Imagined Communities* (London: Verso, 1990), for instance.

4 Beshara Doumani, *Rediscovering Palestine: The Merchants and Peasants of Jabal Nablus 1700–1990* (Berkeley: University of California Press, 1995); Rashid Khalidi, *Palestinian Identity: The Construction of Modern National Consciousness* (New York: Columbia University Press, 1997); Baruch Kimmerling and Joel Migdal *Palestinians* (New York: Free Press, 1995).

5 See for instance the Palestinian Encyclopedia (*Al-Mawsu'at Al-Filastinniya*) (Damascus: PLO Publications, 1982) asserting that Palestinian origins are in the Cananite civilization).

Part I

THE HISTORY OF
PALESTINE REDISCOVERED

2

REDISCOVERING OTTOMAN PALESTINE

Writing Palestinians into history

Beshara B. Doumani

In this article, Beshara Doumani draws our attention to the immense impact of ideologies and politics on the historiography of Palestine. He points out to us the underlying ideological assumptions determining the historiographical agendas of both the Zionist and Palestinian narratives. This deconstruction of both national narratives has not been done before, and Doumani's work is one of the first to stress the need to link the historiographical debate with the concrete historical research.

Doumani's analysis leads him to conclude that the historiographical agenda has been formulated in such a way as to exclude the Palestinians from the history of Palestine between the seventeenth and nineteenth centuries. This is the common picture of an empty Palestine, or at least a marginal Ottoman province, waiting to be redeemed by Western modernizers – a historical picture bowing to the dominance of Zionist interpretation in the research and suffering from the lack of Palestinian historiographical effort. Doumani calls for the rewriting of the Palestinian into the history of Palestine, not only in recharting the political history of the place, but more importantly, by reconstructing the economic as well as the cultural life of the community which will define itself as Palestinian in the twentieth century. His call for an empathetic view on the Palestinians as well as for writing history 'from below' is echoed in many articles in this collection.

* * *

A critical evaluation of historical works on Palestine and the Palestinians during the Ottoman period is a vast and varied topic.[1] This essay does not attempt a comprehensive overview, nor does it provide the outline for such a project.[2] Rather, it seeks to initiate a debate by making a number of tentative arguments in response to the following question: What are the underlying ideological assumptions and historical contingencies that have determined the contours of inquiry into the modern history of Palestine and the Palestinians, and what are the necessary first steps towards constructing an alternative history?

In dealing with the first part of this question, I argue that the seemingly irreconcilable traditions of historical literature on Palestine – Zionist versus Arab nationalist, Orientalist versus Islamicist – actually operate within a single discourse. While each camp reaches opposite conclusions and passionately promotes its own particular set of historical villains and heroes, they share similar assumptions about the Ottoman period, tend to have a narrow view of what constitutes history, follow similar periodization, and generally agree in their definition of active forces of change.

Consequently, our knowledge of Palestinian history is highly uneven, and the intersecting points of research present us with an almost surreal portrait. On the one hand, thousands of books and articles have focused high-powered beams on particular periods, subjects, and themes deemed worthy of study. On the other hand, entire centuries, whole social groups, and a wide range of fundamental issues remain obscured by dark shadows.

For example, many Israeli, Arab, and Western historians have long argued that the Ottoman period, particularly from the seventeenth to the early nineteenth centuries, was one of decline and stagnation until the coming of the West and the promulgation of Ottoman reforms from above. They posit such a sharp historical break between the "traditional" and "modern" periods that continuity is denied and the past becomes strangely irrelevant. Even Islamicists who speak of the "Golden Age" of Islamic justice under Ottoman rule agree that the "old" world was shattered, and that the modern history of Palestine began with the arrival of external elements whether in the shape of Napoleon in 1798, the "modernized" Egyptians of Muhammad Ali in 1831 or the first wave of European Jewish settlers in 1882. It should not come as a surprise, therefore, that there is not a single English-language monograph on seventeenth-century Palestine, and only two on the eighteenth century.

Similar generalizations can be made about the kind of history written. Despite the growing number of social and economic histories, the focus, by and large, has been on political events, personalities, and administrative structures. The latter are crucial areas of investigation, but in the paucity of bottom-up as opposed to top-down studies, the native

12

population has tended to be excluded from the historical narrative: the major lacuna in the historiography of Palestine during the Ottoman period is the absence of a live portrait of the Palestinian people, especially the historically "silent" majority of peasants, workers, artisans, women, merchants and Bedouin.

The second part of the above question deals with the construction of an alternative history. No doubt there is an urgent need to write the Palestinians into history, especially in light of the ongoing intifada, which has aptly demonstrated the collective power of ordinary people to precipitate changes of historic proportions. Furthermore, understanding key issues in twentieth-century Palestinian history, such as nationalism and class relations, necessitates a detailed investigation of the social, economic, and cultural changes in Palestinian society during the Ottoman era, particularly the so-called "dark ages" of the middle period. In addition, local sources that bring the voices of the Palestinians themselves to the fore – Ottoman court records, private family papers, and oral history – deserve greater attention from scholars than they have hitherto received.

Just as important as casting a wider net of research interests, however, is the need for a reconsideration of the way this history is theorized. Rediscovering the underlying connections between past and present and erasing the artificial lines between "external" dynamics and "internal" rhythms of change make it imperative to deconstruct the assumptions of modernization theory – heir of nineteenth-century Orientalism and the dominant paradigm informing most works on the history of Palestine – and to formulate an alternative approach.

The paucity of theoretical works in the field of Middle East history, the dearth of comparative studies, and the fact that the field of "new" Ottoman history is still in its early (though very vigorous) stages, make the task of outlining a new theoretical model for understanding the transformations in Palestine during the early-modern and modern periods a precarious one. This essay aims only at raising a number of questions that might focus debate and point to potentially fruitful lines of inquiry.

Biblical rediscovery of Palestine in the nineteenth century

Over the last hundred years, both Zionists and Palestinian nationalists have embarked on a process of historical (re)discovery of Palestine's past, a task fueled by an intense and unrelenting political drama. Projecting current nationalist feelings and aspirations backwards, both sought to create a nation through an historical "nationalist charter." But before embarking on a detailed consideration of the Palestinian/Arab nationalist and Zionist historiography of Ottoman Palestine, and the terms of reference they share, a brief word must be said about yet another process of discovery which set the stage for both – the European biblical rediscovery of Palestine.

For Europeans, the nineteenth century was the discovery century *par excellence*, for it witnessed the extension of (primarily) British and French economic, political, and cultural hegemony over the nonindustrialized world. Yet, the inhabitants of "other" societies rarely occupied a central place in the consciousness of nineteenth-century European historians, whose narratives, instead, were dominated by tales of brave conquests and enlightened rule by white Christian males. "Natives" – black, brown, and yellow – were portrayed either as resistors to the forces of progress, or romanticized as the pristine remnants of a passing traditional society.

The case of Palestine follows this basic trend, but its image in the eyes of nineteenth-century European historians was further complicated by this country's unique religious/symbolic significance to the West as the home of Judaism, the birthplace of Christianity, and the heartland of the Crusader adventure. Small in size and of unexceptional economic potential, the dominant image of Palestine was that of the "Holy Land," waiting to be reclaimed both spiritually and physically. Pilgrims, businessmen, government representatives, and tourists all landed on its shores in increasing numbers, but often with a single fervent wish in their hearts: to traverse an unchanged landscape where biblical journeys could be endlessly reenacted.

The combination of these factors resulted in a voluminous but highly skewed output of historical literature. More was written on this small region than any other in the Middle East with the exception of Egypt. Yet, the focus was extremely selective and the gaps glaring. One example is chronology: a graph of nineteenth-century books on Palestine according to the periods they cover would show two rather conspicuous spikes perching over the biblical and Crusader periods. These were the eras deemed most significant because they were the most directly linked to European history. The intervening and following centuries, mostly characterized by Arab/Muslim rule, were largely ignored despite the fact that it was precisely during these centuries that the basic structures of contemporary Palestinian society, economy, and culture were forged.

A second example is the preponderant number of works on Jerusalem. The religious, administrative, and symbolic significance of Jerusalem is such that in the minds of many the history of the Holy City was practically synonymous with the history of Palestine as a whole. This tendency has cast a shadow over the rest of Palestine, particularly the hill regions of Hebron, Nablus, and the Galilee for which, until today, we have few sources and even fewer interested historians. Furthermore, Jerusalem is a unique city and its experiences cannot be generalized, especially not to the rural areas where over 80 percent of the population lived.[3]

The third and most important example is the lack of interest in the history of the people who lived on that land. The dominant genres at the time – travel guides[4] and historical geography[5] – focused primarily on the relationship between the physical features of Palestine and the biblical events described in the Old and New Testaments.

The amazing ability to discover the land without discovering the people dovetailed neatly with early Zionist visions. In the minds of many Europeans, especially Zionist Jews, Palestine was "empty" before the arrival of the first wave of Jewish settlers in 1881–84. "Emptiness," of course, did not denote, except for the most ignorant, the physical absence of the native population. Rather, it meant the absence of "civilized" people, in the same sense that the Americas and Africa were portrayed as virgin territories ready for waves of pioneers. The famous Zionist slogan, "a land without a people for a people without a land" was, therefore, but a manifestation of a wider European intellectual network characterized by chauvinistic nationalism, racial superiority, and imperialistic ambitions. The political implications of the deep-rooted unwillingness to deal openly with the question of the native population were such that the fundamental political rights of the Palestinian people, not to mention their very existence, are still a matter of contention even today.[6]

Of course, the indigenous inhabitants were not entirely invisible. They regularly appeared in nineteenth-century photographs and postcards as decorations and icons of ancient times: the shepherd tending his flock, the woman drawing water from a well, the peasant plowing his field.[7] They also filled a variety of roles, often exotic stereotypes of the Orient – the pompous pasha, the harem girl, the devious merchant – in traveller books and the popular press.[8] Most importantly, perhaps, Palestinians were the subject of ethnographic studies on peasant society, custom, and religion.[9] More often than not, however, these valuable studies aimed not so much at investigating Palestinian society as it actually was, but rather at documenting an unchanging traditional society before its anticipated extinction due to contact with the West.

The image of European-inspired progress against a bland backdrop of Ottoman/Islamic decline combined with the very real discontinuities caused by the sharp intrusion of the Zionist movement and British occupation to obfuscate the crucial connections between Palestine's Ottoman past and its present. The burden for historical transformation was placed on outside forces, thus creating the crude dichotomies that informed, until recently, much of the literature on Ottoman Palestine: traditional/modern, internal/external, and passive/active.

Beginning in the 1950s, original research, based primarily on central Ottoman archives and local sources, has considerably blunted the sharp edge of these dichotomies and added a gradation of shades to the stark white/black images of the past. Nevertheless, the increasingly sophisticated debate between Israeli and Arab nationalist historians still takes place within the general framework of Ottoman decline and Western progress originally constructed by nineteenth-century European Orientalist scholars.

Palestinian historiography

Palestinians were the last to begin writing on the history of Palestine as defined geographically by the British Mandate. Why? The answer depends, in part, on the problematic of what is meant by "Palestine," and in whose minds, in what form, and at what time it was consciously articulated.

On the one hand, an administrative entity called Palestine did not exist during the Ottoman period, and before the balkanization of the Middle East following World War I, most Arab writers generally thought of Palestine as the southern part of *bilad al-sham*, or Greater Syria, and it was in this context that they discussed its history.[10] Moreover, a cohesive Palestinian intelligentsia was slower to develop and smaller in number than was the case in Mount Lebanon, Syria, and Egypt. This was due to the fragmented political culture of the period, among other factors.[11] Most importantly, nationalist ideology, which views the world through the prism of the territorial state was, in the nineteenth century, more developed in Europe than in the Arab East.

On the other hand, the formation of "Palestine" in the consciousness of the native population was not simply an automatic response to foreign encroachment and rule, or the uncritical absorption of European definitions of Palestine along biblical lines. The idea also had regional and local roots. It was not a coincidence, for example, that the central Ottoman government established an administrative entity with borders practically identical to those of Mandate Palestine on three brief occasions during the nineteenth century: 1830, 1840, and 1872.[12] Moreover, local economic networks that integrated the cities with their hinterlands; peasant mobility and clan relations; and commonly shared cultural practices, such as the annual Nabi Musa pilgrimage that enjoyed "national" participation, were some of the factors that contributed to a shared collective historical memory and sense of identity. Just as important were the economic, social, and kinship networks connecting the well-to-do merchants, religious leaders, tax farmers, and political elites of the various urban centers to their contemporaries both within Palestine and in other towns and cities of Greater Syria. In short, the existence of an Ottoman "Palestine" can neither be categorically denied for technical/administrative reasons nor uncritically assumed by nationalist fiat. Rather, the emergence of Mandate Palestine was a complicated historical process that combined European penetration, Ottoman rule, and indigenous social, economic, and cultural networks in ways that were to have grave implications for future developments.

In any case, there is no doubt that, among Palestinian intellectuals at least, the process of nationalist self-definition was well underway by the turn of the century. After the Young Turks came to power in Istanbul in 1908, the number of outlets for the growing intelligentsia multiplied, mostly in the form of newspapers, pamphlets, journals, and school text-books.[13] Quickly, these forums became the preserve of those writers concerned with the immediate political battle against foreign colonial settlement. In short, Palestinian writers joined numerous other historians in the Arab world and beyond who were involved in a globally perva-sive phenomenon – the nationalist rewriting of history.[14] The publication of historical monographs began in earnest in the early 1930s. The output was intense, variegated, and spontaneous; all the important trends in Palestinian historiography at the present can be traced to the Mandate period. The two most important genres, discrete but interconnected, I have labelled the "Call to Battle" and the "Affirmation of Identity."

These two genres do not represent the entire spectrum of Palestinian historiography, especially as it became more sophisticated with the crystallization of the Palestinian national movement under the leader-ship of the Palestine Liberation Organization (PLO) in the late 1960s. Rather, they codify the two major trends in the broad sweep of the field. In both genres, however, the majority of works published during the Mandate period were not written by trained historians, but by journalists, lawyers, politicians, and school teachers – all of whom were deeply affected by the intense political atmosphere, and motivated by the need to confront a sophisticated and resourceful adversary.

The Call to Battle

As one might surmise, the "Call to Battle" genre focused primarily on exposing the goals, strategy, and methods of the Zionist movement, the motivations of British policy, and the sources of Palestinian resistance, and thus paid little attention to the Ottoman period.[15] Nonetheless, authors of the genre did make a number of common generalizations that must be examined, if only because their works are widely read and because their views of the Ottoman period are pervasive among the Palestinian public.

The "Call to Battle" genre refers to narratives by authors such as Najib Nassar,[16] 'Issa al-Sifri,[17] Yusif Haikal,[18] and Wadi' al-Bustani[19] – all of whom were involved in the national movement, when they wrote detailed political monographs targeted at fellow Arab intellectuals eager to be informed about the complexities of this fast developing conflict. The same applies to those who followed them, including Emil al-Ghuri,[20] Muhammad 'Izzat Darwazah,[21] Subhi Yasin,[22] Akram Z'eitar[23] and 'Abd al-Wahab al-Kayyali (see below). The short shrift generally accorded to the Ottoman period by these authors stems not only from their preoccupation with countering British and Zionist claims, but also from their Arab nationalist approach to history: on the one hand, the Ottoman period was dismissed as backward and as having suppressed Arab culture, and on the other hand, the existence of Palestine and a Palestinian national consciousness was assumed a priori. What is interesting in their treatment of the Ottoman period – generally confined to brief descriptions of the administrative and demographic structures of Ottoman rule circa 1880, projected backwards to stereotype four centuries of rule – is that their frame of reference is basically the same as that formulated by their adversaries in terms of causality, periodization, and the Ottoman legacy. As with the Europeans and the Zionists, the interpretation centers on the idea of Ottoman decline and views local history as stagnant and inconsequential until the arrival of the Europeans.

'Abd al-Wahab al-Kayyali's well researched and tightly organized *Tarikh Filastin al-hadith* (The Modern History of Palestine) (1970) is the quintessential example of the genre and easily the most widely circulated political narrative on the subject.[24] Like the other authors of the genre, Kayyali begins his actual narrative in 1882, and the brief chapter on the geography and history of Palestine from the Canaanites to 1882 is devoted primarily to a history of the Zionist movement and the "imperialist ambitions" of Britain. The history of the land and its people, especially during the thirteen centuries between the Islamic conquest and the first wave of Jewish settlement, is hardly mentioned.

The following chapter, "Arab Resistance to Zionism before the First World War," begins with a mixed review of the Ottoman legacy: He reproduces the standard Arab nationalist assertions that the Ottoman state was feudal, backward, and oppressive, yet he stresses the prosperity of Palestine before the first Jewish *aliya* (pp. 37–38). He argues, for example, that Palestine during the Ottoman period was characterized by a feudal regime in which a few landowning families, controlling extremely large estates, ruled over an undifferentiated, impoverished, and backward peasantry (p. 38). He credits the 1858 Ottoman Land Code with establishing private property and large land ownership practically overnight, and accuses the Ottoman state of heavy taxation. He also blames its land codes for allowing Palestinian property to pass into the hands of foreigners, such as the Lebanese Sursuq family, who in turn sold it to the Zionists.

In fact, these statements are inaccurate and misleading. First, the 1858 law's primary concern was to protect state property and small peasant holdings, and was actually biased against the formation of large estates.[25] That its consequences often contradicted its aims can only be explained by studying changes on the ground, not laws imposed from above. Second, small peasant landholdings characterized the majority of agricultural land ownership then, and still do till this day, especially in the hill areas. There were regional differences, but those are never addressed in this genre, even though an understanding of them is crucial to explaining why the pattern of Zionist settlement and the borders of the 1947 partition plan took the shape that they did.

Third, the emergence of a market in land and the rise of an urban-based large landowning class were rooted in long-term transformations that *preceded* the promulgation of the 1858 Land Code. Indeed, recent evidence shows that the purchase and sale of nominally *miri*, or state land, was taking place as early as the late 1830s.[26] Moreover, the lands that the Sursuqs and others purchased from the Ottoman government were not arbitrarily chosen. Rather, their availability was determined by a number of interconnected factors such as expansion in cultivation due to increased commercialization of agriculture, population growth, centralization of Ottoman rule, improved access of urban merchants to the rural surplus, and the massive indebtedness of peasants.

Fourth, taxation under the Ottomans was never as heavy nor as efficiently and regularly collected as under the British. On the contrary, much of the surplus expropriated from peasants in the form of taxes in cash and kind went into the coffers of local leading families, not the Ottoman state. Fifth, until the late nineteenth century, most Palestinians enjoyed a great degree of self-rule. The Nablus region, for example, was governed by native families continuously for most of the Ottoman period. This is only one of many unexamined long-term factors that explain Nablus' central role in the 1834 rebellion against Egyptian rule, in the 1936–39 rebellion against the British Mandate over Palestine, and in the ongoing intifada against Israeli occupation. Finally, the integration of Palestine's economy into the European-dominated, capitalist world market was not a result of Jewish immigration or British imperial actions. Indeed, if one criterion was vigorous economic growth in agricultural production for export to Europe, Alexander Schölch has convincingly shown that the takeoff period preceded Jewish immigration by at least three decades.[27] In fairness to Kayyali, however, it should be recalled that, like other authors of this genre, he did not set out to examine the Ottoman period in detail. In addition, when he wrote this book, little was known about the social and economic transformation of Palestine during the last century of Ottoman rule, and even less on the dynamics of peasant production. Indeed, most of the above issues have yet to be systematically addressed in history books on Palestine.

Nevertheless, Kayyali's generalizations continue to resonate widely, despite the fact that they suffer from a serious contradiction: conditions under Ottoman rule are described in extremely bleak terms while at the same time the reader is presented with a rather ideal portrait of a prosperous Palestinian society before Zionism. Kayyali's solution is a romanticization of peasant society, yet another strong tendency in nationalist Palestinian historiography. In his words:

> ... despite the backward and oppressive conditions that limited the productivity of the Palestinian peasant ... his energy and competence were an object of praise by visitors to Palestine from travellers, historians, tourists, and artists. [Furthermore] concrete indications prove that Palestine, before the Zionist invasion, flowed with resources and profits.[28]

Kayyali's portrayal of pre-1882 Palestine as a satiated and prosperous society is not based on careful study, but rather on a nostalgic and defiant vision of the past that is typical of nationalist historians. Similarly, his portrayal of Palestinian resistance to Zionist settlement and British occupation does not delve into the roots of Palestinian nationalism, because his framework of analysis assumes that Palestinian nationalism is but a hybrid of Arab nationalism and a response to Zionist colonization. Despite some recent studies, this view remains largely unchallenged even though it cannot begin to explain the economic forces, social character, or deeper cultural underpinnings of Palestinian solidarity and identity that have sustained the hundreds of thousands of refugees living in exile, and that have contributed to the emergence of a national movement under the umbrella of the PLO.[29]

With few exceptions, the "Call to Battle" genre blames Ottoman rule for setting the stage for disaster, presents the Zionist movement as the dynamic actor, and portrays Palestinian resistance as inevitable, self-explanatory, and passive, with the possible exception of the 1929 uprising and 1936–39 rebellion. Throughout, the 1880s is the standard starting point, with the next punctuation mark being the British occupation in 1917.

As with any genre whose primary goal is to justify a nationalist struggle by mobilizing against an enemy, the "Call to Battle" genre's primary concern is with the "Other." Internal contradictions, differences, and developments are glossed over. In one of those ironic moments of intellectual history, a single idea – Ottoman decline and Western-initiated modernization – provides the indispensable foundation for competing and seemingly irreconcilable traditions of Palestinian and Israeli historical literature. Consequently, we are not much closer to understanding the modern origins of Palestine and the Palestinian people.

Affirmation of Identity

The "Affirmation of Identity" genre is the more important for rediscovering the roots of Palestinian history. Faced with a denial of their right to self-determination – in essence, their history – many educated Palestinians during the Mandate scavenged for every scrap of information that would prove the Arabness of Palestine, indeed, their existence as a people. By turning inward in their search for self-definition, in contrast to the "Call to Battle" genre's outward thrust, authors such as 'Umar Salih al-Barghuthi,[30] Khalil Totah,[31] Ahmad Samih al-Khalidi,[32] As'ad Mansur,[33] Ihsan al-Nimr,[34] Augustine al-Marmaji,[35] Abdullah Mukhlis,[36] and later on, Mustafa Murad al-Dabbagh,[37] Muhammad 'Izzat Darwazah,[38] and 'Arif al-'Arif, [39] produced a diverse collection of historical works ranging from city narratives (often the author's hometown), to multi-volume biographical dictionaries and historical geographies.

Many of these authors were descendants of old landowning, notable, or conservative merchant and religious families who achieved positions of power, status, and wealth during the Ottoman period. This tended to give them a more sympathetic view of the Ottoman legacy, in contrast to the authors of the "Call to Battle" genre who were frequently members of the emerging modern middle class. They also drew on indigenous traditions of scholarship (biographical dictionaries, local histories, and so on). Finally, their background gave them familiarity with local Palestinian archives, because their families' positions and properties were registered in letters of appointment, *waqf* charters, bills of sale, *hasr irth* (inheritance estates), and other documents shedding light on the administrative, social, religious, and cultural institutions of the early-modern and modern periods.

It was thus that, in their search for the Arab roots of Palestine, they pioneered the use of long-ignored local sources, such as the Ottoman court records and family papers, now recognized as indispensable to any study of Ottoman Palestine. They also tapped the collective memory of their compatriots through oral history, documented the rituals of daily life through first-hand observation, and made invaluable comments on the physical and cultural environment of the urban centers. Finally, it is in their works that we meet Palestinians from all walks of life: rural clan *shaykhs*, urban notables, merchants, artisans, peasants, and other social elements whose histories have long been marginalized. Indeed, by going beyond political narrative to delve into the rich details of Palestinian life and culture during the Ottoman period, this genre has laid the foundations for a rethinking of the modern history of Palestine.[40]

Given their perspective, it is not surprising that many members of this genre effectively turned Orientalist assumptions on their head: decline and oppression was associated with the coming of the "West," while justice and peace were attributed to the period of Islamic rule. For example, in his four-volume study *Tarikh Jabal Nablus wa al-Balqa'* (History of Nablus Mountain and al-Balqa'), published between 1937 and 1975, Ihsan al-Nimr argued passionately that the eighteenth and early nineteenth century constituted what he called "the golden age" (vol. 1, p. 139). Nablus, he insisted, was prosperous and ruled by noble, just, and protective native sons, including, as he frequently pointed out, some of his own ancestors.

The power, wealth, and status of the Nimr family – which was based, among other things, on leadership of the local *sipahis* (Ottoman cavalry) and *timar* holders (fiefs granted by the Ottoman state) – declined precipitously as a result of Egyptian rule, the *Tanzimat*, and British occupation. It is not surprising, therefore, that as far as Nimr was concerned, Ottoman reforms and British rule, far from ushering in modernity, stability, and prosperity, actually brought chaos, civil strife, exploitation, corruption, and stagnation.[41] Indeed, he specifically challenged the dominant view that Palestine was in a backward state until the 1831 Egyptian invasion, which is widely credited with ushering in the modern period.

To support his argument, Nimr utilized oral histories, Ottoman court records, archives of the Nablus municipality, and an extensive knowledge of genealogies, people, and places. He also compiled a large number of private family documents ranging from letters of appointments and contracts with peasants to business and personal correspondence. His original research on all aspects of the Nablus region – politics, economy, culture, social life, and the physical environment – brought to light a wealth of information, and preserved the collective memory of an entire generation that experienced the transition from Ottoman to British rule. The key to his contribution, one can easily argue, was not the merit of his historical arguments, which were often weak, but rather his imaginative and resourceful utilization of a wide range of sources; just as important was his concern for details about all aspects of daily life. Moreover, Nimr was correct in proposing that Nablus, a town of the interior, witnessed a decline in power, prosperity, and independence after the Egyptian invasion – at least in contrast with the growing size and commercial importance of Beirut, Jaffa, Haifa, and other coastal cities connected to the spiraling trade with industrialized Europe.

'Arif al-'Arif, whose *al-Muffassal fi tarikh al-Quds* (The Detailed History of Jerusalem) (1961) early on became a basic reference, also waxed poetic about the past, lamenting the days of a golden Islamic era untainted by foreign influences. His book, like Nimr's, effectively utilized local sources to present a rich tapestry of life in Ottoman Jerusalem. But 'Arif's nostalgia for a pure Islamic past, unlike Nimr's, was not based on concrete historical arguments. Rather, it rested on his distaste for the ideological uncertainties and popular politics of modern life, and, more importantly, on his exaggerated notion of the role of the al-*mahkama al-shari'ah* (Islamic law court) in Islamic society:

> Generally speaking, the people lived in prosperity, comfort, and security. There was nothing to disturb the even tenor of their existence in Jerusalem or in the other towns of Palestine. There was no radio or television, nor were there newspapers, and people heard very little news, and then only occasionally. . . . They held their heads high, and the entire administration was in the hands of Muslims and their *qadi*, who . . . wielded unlimited power.[42]

In reacting to Western claims about the inferiority of the East by simply reversing the value judgement on the modern period, 'Arif and a multitude of other similarly minded historians only reinforced the basic Orientalist assumption: the old world was shattered by external forces. In that sense, Islamicist and Orientalist paradigms are but two sides of the same coin. Both draw a clear and inviolable line (as do many Zionist historians and Palestinian authors in the "Call to Battle" genre) between past and present, glossing over historical continuities. This is not to say that there were no discontinuities, for few regions in the Middle East have been as shaken by historical earthquakes as Palestine. Rather, the intent here is to emphasize that the legacy of the Ottoman period is much more problematic, subtle, and deeply rooted than the above dichotomies would allow.

The works of Ihsan al-Nimr and 'Arif al-'Arif also demonstrate what has remained till today one of the earliest and most vital trends within this genre – the large number of works on specific cities and towns. This trend's importance is twofold. First, it has illuminated the histories of areas central to the Palestinian experience but long neglected by Eurocentric historians concerned primarily with Jerusalem and the commercial coastal cities. This does not mean that Palestinian authors do not share these priorities; in terms of numbers of publications by Palestinians, Jerusalem has received the lion's share because of its symbolic significance,[43] and the coastal cities of Jaffa and Haifa[44] are the next most frequently studied. All three cities grew the fastest since the mid-nineteenth century, were the first to feel the brunt of large foreign communities, and were home to most of the Palestinian intellectuals during the Mandate period. Nevertheless, Palestinian authors have also pioneered the study of other, less academically popular places, such as the two declining coastal cities, Gaza and Acre,[45] as well as the interior cities and towns of Safad,[46] Nazareth,[47] Jenin,[48] Nablus,[49] Ramallah,[50] Hebron,[51] and Bethlehem.[52] In fact, the number of city and town histories has been quickly growing over the past two decades.

Second, this trend, fed and sustained by the strong local identification of many of the authors, has forcefully posed the question of whether the history of Ottoman Palestine should begin with the premise of difference rather than homogeneity. This is not to imply that Palestine was composed of isolated, self-sufficient communities, for that was not the case. Rather, the decentralized nature of Ottoman rule, the remarkable continuity of both rural and urban ruling families, and geographical and agricultural peculiarities giving rise to varied rituals of everyday life were some of the factors that combined to impart a distinct cultural flavor, mythology, and historical memory to each village, town, and city and, at the larger level, to clusters of villages and entire regions. While outside observers may see these differences as largely irrelevant, they were very real for those who experienced them on a daily basis.

The importance of local bonds can be seen in the recent attention being paid to village histories, which have proliferated since the early 1980s. Ironically, just as these local bonds were being seriously undermined by deepening nationalist loyalties and the urbanization of rural life, spontaneous and uncoordinated individual and collective efforts were marshalled to preserve local memory and pride through the production of dozens of monographs on such places as Jericho,[53] Birzeit,[54] al-Bassa,[55] Sa'ir,[56] Bani Na'im,[57] al-Rama,[58] 18 al-Dawaymeh,[59] and al-Taybeh.[60] Many of these "hometown" studies are amateurish works, often printed at the author's expense. Almost all paint a romantic and idealist portrait. Yet, while the authors' training and objectivity might be impaired, their intimate knowledge of their immediate environment and ability to tap the collective historical memory of the town's elders have made accessible, for the first time, that most elusive sphere of Palestinian history: the rural experience.

Another early trend in the "Affirmation of Identity" genre, albeit a less vigorous one, was the production of multi-volume reference works, often covering all of Palestine from ancient times to the present. Some were biographical dictionaries listing the important men of Palestine, especially during the Ottoman period. The majority, however, can be loosely described as historical geographies. The best known and most frequently used of the latter type is Mustafa Murad al-Dabbagh's monumental eight-volume work, *Biladuna Filastin* (Our Country Palestine) (1947–1966), which documents in zealous detail the landscape of Palestine in effort to prove its Arab character. The major drawback of this and similar works produced prior to the 1960s,[61] is their overly ambitious comprehensiveness, fetish with documentation, and most importantly, weak historical context. Much of the information is collapsed into an unyielding mass with little regard to change over time, as if the more information stuffed between the pages, the weightier the argument. Nevertheless, these reference works have been invaluable to multitudes of students and scholars who turn to them on a regular basis. This type of work is no longer produced by individuals. Rather, various research centers – such as the PLO Research Center (Beirut), the Institute for Palestine Studies (Beirut, Washington, D.C., and Paris), and the Arab Studies Society (Jerusalem) have taken over the task of generating multi-volume works ranging from encyclopedias and city histories to compilations of documents.

While these collective enterprises are professionally done and extremely useful, the major problem Palestinian historians face today is not in locating evidence testifying to their existence as a people, or to the justness of their cause, but in regaining the initiative in interpreting their own history. The "Affirmation of Identity" genre has pioneered the expansion of subject material and sources relevant to a rediscovery of Palestinian history during the modern period. Since the 1960s, however, the initiative for the rediscovery of Ottoman Palestine has shifted from Palestinian authors to their Israeli counterparts.

Israeli historiography of Ottoman Palestine

Both in terms of quantity and quality of output, Israeli historians now dominate this field. The reasons for this shift have to do with differing objective circumstances, and the divergent agendas of both peoples in the post-1948 period. The overwhelming majority of Palestinian intellectuals found themselves outside Palestine after the 1948 and 1967 wars. Adjustment to life in exile, preoccupation with daily survival, inaccessibility of key local sources, and the lack of indigenous and stable academic institutions were compounded by the consuming task of rebuilding a new national movement, not to mention the increasing ideological pull of Arab nationalism, which downplayed and stereotyped the Ottoman period altogether.

The young Israeli state, meanwhile, already had in place an extensive system of academic institutions. Moreover, well-established historians – mostly European immigrants steeped in the German Orientalist tradition – were in the process of training the post-1948 generation. Izhak Ben-Zvi, the second president of Israel and himself an amateur historian, established the Yad Izhak Ben-Zvi Institute for the Study of Eretz Israel, the only research institution devoted to the study of Palestine before the establishment of the Israeli state.

The major focus of Israeli historiography, of course, is not the Palestinians but the Jews. Specifically, Israeli historians were busy creating their own nationalist historical charter and trying to prove the undying connection between Jews and the land they called their own. Even before the establishment of the State of Israel in 1948, many Zionist scholars were studying Ottoman Palestine. The basic motivation was the practical realization that understanding the Ottoman legacy was crucial to the successful establishment and expansion of a state infrastructure. One of the most pressing tasks, or example, was transforming the old system of land relations. This was the topic of Avraham Granott's important study *The Land System in Palestine: History and Structure* (1948).[62] Granott was the managing director of the Jewish National Fund and an expert on land purchases. His study of land ownership and organization from the mid-nineteenth century onwards remains a primary reference for those interested in the defining key features of Palestinian society and economy. In Granott's words,

> ... a knowledge of conditions prevailing before the establish-ment of Israel is vital to anyone interested in the history of our country, and is essential for all those concerned with its future – the man of action helping to develop Israel's economy, the legislator who works out a new code of land laws, and anyone who has a part in shaping the agrarian economy of the new state. All these must trace earlier developments and follow the roots into the past (p. viii).

Another legacy of the past with profound implications for the successful colonization of Palestine was the indigenous inhabitants' pattern of settlement. In a series of three influential articles, another government official, D.H.K. Amiran, asked why Palestinians historically concentrated in the hill areas even though the coastal regions were more fertile.[63] In formulating an answer, he glossed over the social structure and historical development of the local population and focused instead on the "lack of security," which he ascribed to Bedouin raids and "Palestinian backwardness" (specifically, the inability of Palestinians and the Ottomans to use modern means of agricultural production and to deal with malaria). His conclusion that "it was not the land that was bad, but the fact that it was occupied by people or administered by governments who did not make proper use of it" (p. 260) does not do justice to his overall contribution to this subject. It does, however, reveal a common underlying assumption and a key ideological argument: Palestine was a neglected land rescued by Jewish colonization.

It is important to discuss further the "lack of security" argument advanced in Amiran's articles because it is central to most Israeli histo-ries of Ottoman Palestine. Moshe Ma'oz's often quoted work, *Ottoman Reform in Syria and Palestine, 1840–1861*, begins with the assumption that the law and order imposed by the Egyptians when they occupied Palestine in 1831 " ... brought about an end to centuries of confusion and backwardness and opened a new stage of stability and moderni-zation."[64] He goes on to say that Ibrahim Pasha, son of Muhammad Ali and the commander of the Egyptian forces, was able to " . . . alter the social structure of the country" by undermining the old feudal order, opening Syrian society to the West, and centralizing the apparatus of government and administration (p. 19).

Ma'oz's narrative of Palestine as a passive victim of Ottoman decline whose modern beginnings were a result of external events – beginning with the Egyptian invasion in 1831, continued by European-imposed Ottoman reforms, and capped by Jewish settlement – is based on assertions about the "lack of security," the "absence" of strong central control and rational state bureaucracy, "ignorance" of the concept of citizenship for all, and "disinterest" in public works. The obstacles to modernization, in his opinion, were also internal: "Bedouin pillage," "rapacious pashas" (Ottoman governors), "bloody factionalism," and the incompatibility of Islam with Western forms of government and administration (pp. 8–10).

A detailed critique of these generalizations lies beyond the scope of this essay. Suffice it to say that they are based on two paradigms that were quite accepted at the time: Ottoman decline and modernization theory. The first assumes that the growing weakness of the center vis-à-vis Europe necessarily meant that the periphery was also in decline, hence the "dark ages" of the middle period of Ottoman rule. The latter, likewise based on a Eurocentric assumption, is that all societies must proceed along a universal, linear path of development identical to that of the "West." Both paradigms gloss over the complexity, dynamics, and historical development of the indigenous society, and both posit a sharp break with the past.

Just as important, neither paradigm is based on concrete evidence. For example, Ma'oz, echoing the unmitigated hostility towards Bedouin evident in much of the literature, accuses them of being

> . . . the chief cause of the destruction of the countryside and the subsequent ruin of agriculture and commerce. These powerful nomads *infested* the Syrian provinces, *pillaged* caravans and travellers along the roads, *ravaged* large pieces of cultivated land, and even *dared* to raid villages that were situated on the outskirts of big towns (p. 9, emphasis added).

Aside from the obviously negative value judgements, this view completely ignores the multitude of economic, political, and cultural connections that linked the Bedouin with the settled regions. The Bani Sakhr and Huwaytat tribes, for example, have for generations sent thousands of camel loads annually to Nablus, supplying the city's merchants and soap manufacturers with *qilli*, a raw material crucial to the city's soap industry.[65] They also provided raw wool, *samn* (clarified butter), horses,

Eurocentric value judgements)

camels, and other primary products in return for iron, textiles, and other manufactured items. A network of political agreements further tied the Bedouin to the urban centers, which were keen on safeguarding the *hajj* procession and routes of trade. The interruption of these activities, it must be stressed, was the exception, not the rule. Besides, the distinction between Palestine's Bedouin, the majority of whom often engaged in various forms of agriculture, and peasants who were highly mobile at the time, is often too blurred to allow for uncomplicated analysis. All of the above gives credence to Talal Asad's argument, which views the Bedouin as part of an overall economic system, unified by a structure of domination based on the extraction of surplus.[66]

Other important driving forces that have sustained the interest of Israeli historians in Ottoman Palestine are revealed by the research trends evident in the many anthologies of their works over the past two decades.[67] *Studies on Palestine During the Ottoman Period*, edited by Moshe Ma'oz, is the first and most comprehensive.[68]

One overall set of concerns in this anthology involves understanding the demographic and political terrain which existed before Jewish colonization. How many Arabs were in Palestine? Who were their leaders? How did they relate to political authority? What were the fiscal and administrative structures of Ottoman rule? How did Arab Muslims deal with Christians and Jews? How did foreign rule shape political attitudes? These issues were, and remain, clearly relevant to decision makers in the Israeli state who have the responsibility of drafting government policy *vis-à-vis* the substantial Palestinian community under their control. Not surprisingly, many of the scholars published in this and subsequent anthologies also doubled as "Arab experts" employed by the state in official capacities as advisors on Arab affairs. In addition, many scholars of Arab and Islamic history, especially the more nationalist post-1948 group of Israeli Ottoman historians – such as Moshe Ma'oz and Amnon Cohen – also wore another academic hat, that of the political scientist, authoring books on such current topics as contemporary Palestinian political organizations and Syrian politics under the Asad regime.[69]

The second set of concerns evident in that first anthology deals with the history of Jewish communities in Ottoman Palestine and, by extension, of urban life in Jerusalem, Safad, Tiberias, and Hebron – the four cities in which they lived. Although the Jewish communities constituted but a fraction of the entire population, we know much more about them at this point than about any other group that lived in Palestine during the Ottoman period. Indeed, a significant portion of what we know about the "non-Jewish" residents is a direct result of research on the Jewish community.[70]

This first anthology also reflected a deep concern with sources. In fact, Israeli scholars were the first to systematically mine the central Ottoman archives, opened to researchers in the late 1940s, for the study of Palestine. Uriel Heyd[71] pioneered these efforts, and he was quickly followed by Moshe Ma'oz, Amnon Cohen, Haim Gerber,[72] and a host of other Israeli researchers. Their collective work greatly increased our knowledge of the administrative, fiscal, and political superstructure of Ottoman Palestine, but paid little attention to social and cultural issues, and largely failed to deal with the indigenous population except for the notables. This top-down strategy of historical narrative on Ottoman Palestine was partly due to the nature of the sources themselves. The central Ottoman archives reflected the concerns of the administrative center, and presented a largely bureaucratic vision as to what should, instead of what actually did happen. Another factor was the pervasiveness of the institutionalist approach that characterized most of the literature on Ottoman history. It is no coincidence, for example, that regardless of differences in opinion about historical villains and heroes, the writings of Arab historians who worked with the central Ottoman archives at the same time shared a similar approach.[73]

More recently, Israeli Ottomanists have been paying greater attention to local Palestinian archives. This trend was motivated both by the desire to historicize the *yishuv* (Jewish community in Palestine), and by the growing popularity of social and economic research in the field of Middle East studies in general.[74] Local archives, rich in data about property transfers, lawsuits, and matters of personal status, lend themselves greatly to both objectives. Ottoman court records are particularly valuable because the court served all residents regardless of religion, class, or gender, and maintained detailed records of all the cases brought before it daily. The court also served as a public records office of sorts, in which copies of administrative correspondence, *waqf* charters, and accounts of the various affairs of mosques and other religious institutions were kept. Amnon Cohen was the first of the Israeli Ottoman scholars to look into Jerusalem's Ottoman Islamic court archives while researching the city's sixteenth-century Jewish community in the early 1970s. Since then, a number of his colleagues and students have followed suit. For the historian with patience, such records provide detailed and intimate snapshots of urban life during Ottoman times, and even reveal long-term trends in social, economic, and cultural transformations.[75]

Over the past two decades, many Arab scholars have also delved into central and local Ottoman archives, particularly historians connected with 'Ain al-Shams University (Cairo), Damascus University, and the University of Jordan.[76] Currently, the most dynamic Arab center for the study of Ottoman Syria is the University of Jordan.[76] Specifically, Muhammad Adnan al-Bakhit and his colleagues, in addition to training a large number of students, have established the Center for Documentation and Manuscripts, which houses an impressive archival collection, including microfilm copies of all the Ottoman court records of Palestine. The fact remains, however, that most of the basic reference works on Ottoman Palestine have been, and continue to be, produced by Israeli scholars. This has proved to be a double-edged sword for those interested in rediscovering modern Palestine and writing Palestinians into history. On the one hand, the generally high academic standards and pioneering field work have greatly increased our knowledge. On the other hand, Israeli domination of the field has served to reinforce categories of knowledge and particular lines of research that shed light on some aspects of the Ottoman past and neglect others. The entire middle period of Ottoman rule has received scant attention, and the social groups that constitute the majority of the population have been largely ignored. Hence, the need to reconstruct the history of Ottoman Palestine.

Writing Palestinians into history

As with all forms of intellectual production, the writing of history is organically linked to and affected by the ideological environment and historical context of the author, often shedding more light on the times of the writer than on the intended subject. The historiography of Palestine is a classic example of this phenomenon. As a land of great symbolic significance to adherents of the world's three monotheistic religions, and as the common objective of two competing national movements, its past has been subjected to multiple and, at least on the surface, contradictory traditions of historical interpretation. Throughout this century, the interplay between power and knowledge has produced a series of tunnel visions, each of which questions the legitimacy of the other. Yet, and as far as the Ottoman period is concerned, these tunnel visions, far from resembling parallel highways that never meet, actually intersect, in that they generally agree as to what is important to study and what is not.

Writing the indigenous population into the history of Ottoman Palestine is called for not only as a worthwhile academic project in its own right, but also because it is a prerequisite for a fuller understanding of present realities and a necessary element in the process of empowerment through knowledge. This project must operate simultaneously on three interdependent levels. First, systematic interrogation of the hitherto under-utilized primary sources that have preserved the voices of the inhabitants: Ottoman court records, family papers, physical evidence, and oral history. Second, the casting of a wider research net that takes into account the middle period and the disenfranchised social groups long excluded from historical discourse. Finally, the development of theoretical research frameworks based on the organizing principles of political economy and recent advances in cultural history, as opposed to Orientalist and modernization theory paradigms.

For example, one of the major debates that has dominated works on Ottoman Palestine revolves around the question: when did the modern period begin? Most scholars have settled on the Egyptian period (1831–40) as the turning point. Ibrahim Pasha, we are told, restored law and order, gave minorities equal rights, established a unified "rational" state structure, advanced commercial and political relations with the West, and paved the way for the reassertion of central Ottoman control. Alexander Schölch added another dimension to the debate when he argued that, in addition to the political and administrative changes brought about by the Egyptian occupation and Ottoman reform, the key factor was the integration of Palestine into the capitalist world economy, a process which he located in the 1856–82 period.[77]

Yet one can raise serious questions about all the above generalizations. The Egyptian period, far from ushering in law and order, was punctuated by violent uprisings and followed by decades of bloody internecine conflicts, for the Ottoman government was not able effectively to centralize its rule until the 1860s. Moreover, most of the institutional changes that the Egyptians tried to effect were either abandoned or had no chance of succeeding due to fierce resistance and the short period of their rule. True, the Egyptian period witnessed the demise of some ruling families and the rise of others, and it also marked a turning point insofar as it created new means of controlling the population – conscription, a head tax, and generic administrative councils. But none of these "achievements" sprang from a vacuum. What the Egyptian period accomplished, it did by crystallizing a series of long-term developments that were already taking place.

The same holds true for economic integration. As recent research on Syria, Iraq, and Egypt has shown, if modernity is to be defined by changes in agrarian and urban–rural relations due to the growth of commercial agriculture, development of private property in land, and the emergence of a new ruling class based more on wealth than political office, then one can trace this process at least as far back as the eighteenth century, and not to some overnight transformations resulting from foreign occupation or top-down reforms.

The key point here is that some aspects of "modernity" surfaced long before they were "initiated" by outside stimuli, while "traditional" modes of organization survived much longer than is usually admitted. The social formations in the Arab East, including Palestine, were not houses of cards easily collapsed from the outside. On the contrary, they were deeply rooted though flexible and dynamic networks that interacted with externally imposed changes and filtered them into the rhythms of everyday life. Hence, there is a need for a more flexible periodization of Ottoman Palestine that would take into account not only the long-term socioeconomic and cultural changes, but also the fact that these changes were often felt in an uneven and contradictory manner depending on factors of class, gender, and geographical location.

Equally important is the need for detailed study of such basic issues as: the local mechanisms governing the commercialization of agriculture and development of a market in land; the material base of the "politics of notables;" Bedouin-rural-urban relations and power structures; new patterns of capital investments in the countryside by merchants; peasant indebtedness, and the rise of a new ruling class composed of merchants, landowners, tax farmers, and office holders; shifting attitudes towards a centralizing state; changing notions of justice, authority, and knowledge; increasing differentiation among the peasantry and the spread of urban religious and legal systems into village life; the concentration of wealth and its effect on family relations, such as the increasing disenfranchisement of women; the spread of a money economy and erosion of clan solidarity, local and regional trade networks, and the way merchants, tax farmers, and ruling families carved the hinterland into spheres of influence; varying attitudes to foreign economic and political penetration, and escalating religious and ethnic tensions; labor migration and the growth of cities; and intermarriage and social interaction among urban elites in Greater Syria.

Without further research into these and other crucial areas, the bare outlines of the political economy and cultural history from below will elude us, especially for the seventeenth century, for which, as was mentioned before, we do not have a single English monograph. Until Palestinians are written into the history of Palestine, it will be difficult to answer key questions about the nature of Palestinian society on the eve of the twentieth century, much less understand why its members took the decisions that they did during the Mandate period and beyond.

NOTES

Beshara B. Doumani teaches history at the University of Pennsylvania and is on the editorial committee of *Middle East Report*. He would like to thank George Atiyeh and his staff at the Library of Congress for facilitating access to Arabic material, as well as Salim Tamari, Zachary Lockman, and two anonymous readers whose comments considerably strengthened this essay.

Source Journal of Palestine Studies XXI, no. 2 (Winter 1992), pp. 5–28

1 The phrase "historical works" is used here to refer strictly to studies which primarily provide an historical narrative. Travel books as well as ethnographic, sociological, or cultural studies are not included.

2 Essays on Palestinian historiography include Tarif Khalidi, "Palestinian Historiography: 1900–1948," *Journal of Palestine Studies* X, no. 3 (spring 1981), pp. 59–76; and Yehoshua Porath, "Palestinian Historiography," *Jerusalem Quarterly* 5 (1977), pp. 95–104. Also of interest is Chapter Five in Adnan Abu Ghazaleh, *Arab Cultural Nationalism in Palestine* (Beirut: Institute for Palestine Studies, 1973); and K.W. Stein, "A General Historiographic and Bibliographic Review of Literature on Palestine and the Palestinian Arabs," *Orient* (Opladen) 22 (198 1), pp. 100–112.

3 Socially and culturally, Jerusalem is much more diverse. Politically and economically, moreover, its connections to the surrounding hinterland were considerably weaker than other Palestinian urban areas, for as an administrative and religious center, it enjoyed substantial external sources of income.

4 Baedeker's 1894 edition of *Palestine and Syria: A Handbook for Travellers*, focuses on the Jewish and Christian biblical period and the Crusades. The intervening centuries of Arab/Muslim rule are described as "... a continuous scene of war and bloodshed, accompanied by an interminable series of internecine dissensions, intrigues, and murders." (Leipzig: Karl Baedeker Publishers, 1912), p. LXXXII.

5 The best known was George Adam Smith's *Historical Geography of Palestine* (1894). Meticulous, thorough, and based on extensive travel and personal observation, it was reprinted over thirty times. Smith, then Principal and Vice-Chancellor of the University of Aberdeen, provided maps so accurate that they were consulted by the British government in defining the borders of Mandate Palestine during the Versailles Conference in 1919.

   Smith used the Bible and archaeological remains to illustrate, in great detail, the religious significance of the "Holy Land." As far as he was concerned, the history of Palestine stopped in A.D. 634 with the Arab conquest, and did not resume until Napoleon's invasion in 1798 except for the brief interlude of the Crusades. Thirteen centuries of continuous settlement by an Arabized Palestinian population are barely mentioned, and then only to stress the inferiority and irrationality of the Orient as compared to the Occident.

6 One example is Joan Peters' *From Time Immemorial: The Origins of the Arab–Jewish Conflict Over Palestine* (New York: Harper and Row, 1984). Though not a historian, her work was hailed by the major press as an authoritative revisionist account, despite the fact that the book has been thoroughly discredited. See articles by Edward Said and Norman Finkelstein in Edward Said and Christopher Hitchens (eds.), *Blaming the Victims: Spurious Scholarship and the Palestinian Question* (London; New York: Verso, 1988). For the best work on the population of Palestine starting in the late Ottoman period, see Justin McCarthy, *The Population of Palestine* (New York: Columbia University Press, 1990).

7 See Sarah Graham-Brown, *Palestinians and Their Society, 1880–1946: A Photographic Essay* (London; New York: Quartet Books, 1980), and *Images of Women: The Portrayal of Women in Photography of the Middle East, 1860–1950* (New York: Columbia University Press, 1988). Also see Annelies Moore and Steven Machlin, "Postcards of Palestine: Interpreting Images," *Critique of Anthropology* 7, no. 2, pp. 61–77.

8 Many traveller accounts, of course, provided insightful information about economic, social, and cultural life. The best known in this regard, are C.F. Volney, *Travels in Syria and Egypt in the Years 1783, 1784, and 1785*, 2 vols. (London, 1787); and John Lewis Burckhardt, *Travels in Syria and the Holy Land* (London, 1822).

9   See, for example, Ermete Peirotti, *Customs and Traditions of Palestine* (London, 1864); Elizabeth Ann Finn, *Palestine Peasantry, Notes on Their Clans, Warfare, Religion, and Laws* (London, 1923); Rev. F.A. Klein, "Life, Habits, and Customs of the Fellahin of Palestine," *The Palestine Exploration Fund* 12 (1881), pp. 110–18, 297–304, and vol. 13 (1883), pp. 41–48.

10 See for example, Yusif al-Dibs, *Tarikh Suriya*, eight vols. (Beirut, 1893–1902); Muhammad Kurd 'Ali, *Khitat al-Sham*, six vols. (Damascus, 1963); and Rafiq al-Tamimi and Muhammad Bahjat, *Wilayat Beirut* (Beirut, 1916).

11 Syria and Egypt, with their large cities, were bound to produce many more chroniclers than Palestine. But why was the smaller region of Mount Lebanon much more productive? The presence of many private educational missions, and the early development of a single, centralized emirate ruled by one family over a long period of time, are the two major factors, for most contemporary historical narratives revolve around rulers who managed to pull together a centralized state within a state.

12 See Alexander Schölch, *Palästina im Umbruch, 1856–1882: Untersuchungen zur Wirtschaftlichen und Sozio-Politischen Entwicklung* (Palestine in Reconstruction, 1856–1882: Studies on Economic and Socio-Political Development) (Stuttgart: Franz Steiner Verlag Wiesbaden GmbH, 1986). Citations are taken from the Arabic translation by Kamil al-'Asali, *Tahawulat jad-hriyya fi Filastin, 1856–1882: Dirasat hawl al-tatawur al-iqtisadi wa al-ijtima'i al-siyasi* (Amman: University of Jordan Press, 1988), pp. 19–28. An English translation is currently being prepared by the Institute for Palestine Studies, Washington, D.C.

13 Rashid Khalidi, "The Press as a Source for Modern Arab Political History," *Arab Studies Quarterly* 3, no. 1 (winter 1981), pp. 22–42; and "The Role of the Press in the Early Arab Reaction to Zionism," *Peuples Mediterranéens* (July–September 1982). For a general overview on the development of Arab Palestinian intellectuals during this period, see Muhammad Muslih, *The Origins of Palestinian Nationalism* (New York: Columbia University Press, 1988). For detailed information on all the Arabic press organs during the late Ottoman and Mandate periods see Yusif Khury, *al-Sahafa al-'Arabiyya fi Filastin, 1876–1948* (Beirut: Institute for Palestine Studies, 1976).

14 Many Jewish nationalist historians, for example, were simultaneously producing historical works which tried to prove a continuous and unbroken Jewish presence in the ancient land of Israel from biblical times to the present. See David Myers, "History as Ideology: The Case of Ben Zion Dinur, Zionist Historian 'Par Excellence'," *Modern Judaism* (May 1988), pp. 167–93.

15 A sub-category within this genre includes books written in the English language by Western-educated Palestinians such as George Antonius, Michael Abcarius, Frank C. Sakran, Henry Cattan, Sami Hadawi and Wasif Abbushi. I labeled this sub-category "A Plea for Justice," because the authors specifically targeted European and American audiences in arguing the merits of the Palestinian case. While deserving of greater study, this sub-category will not be discussed, because it shares the major assumptions of the "Call to Battle" genre, and like it, it also focuses primarily on the Mandate period.

It must be pointed out, however, that in targeting Western audiences, particularly the liberal elements of the intelligentsia and civil service, and calling upon them to live up to their professed democratic and humanitarian ideals, writers in the "Plea for Justice" subcategory faced a dilemma: they affirmed these liberal values, but were at a loss to explain how a society based on such values can behave in the imperialistic and exploitative manner that it did. The feelings of bitterness and disillusionment are most evident in George Antonius, *The Arab Awakening* (1938), and T. Canaan, *The Palestine Arab Cause* (1936). Most of these writers have attempted to resolve the contradiction by blaming unjust policies on ignorance and/or the machinations of individuals and the Zionist lobby. Consequently, the long-term material determinants of British or United States foreign policies are frequently glossed over. Few books break decisively from this tradition. Nevertheless, and in the increasingly important battle for U.S. public opinion, this sub-category within the "Call to Battle" genre has spearheaded the drive to challenge the prevalent Zionist constructions of history, and to present a positive Palestinian perspective.

16 *Al-Sahyuniyya* (Zionism), (1911).

17 *Filastin al-'Arabiyya bayn al-intidab wa al-Sahyuniyya* (Arab Palestine between the Mandate and Zionism), (Jaffa, 1937).

18 *al-Qadiyya al-Filastiniyya: tahlil wa naqd* (The Palestine Cause: Analysis and Criticism), (Jaffa, 1937).

19 *al-Intidab al-Britani batel wa mahal* (The British Mandate: Null and Void), (1936).

20 *al-Mu'amara al-kubra wa ightiyal Filastin* (The Great Conspiracy and the Liquidation of Palestine), (1955); and *Filastin 'abra sittin 'aman* (Palestine Over Sixty Years), two vols. (Beirut, 1971, 1973).

21 *Hawla al-haraka al-'Arabiyya al-haditha* (On the Modern Arab Movement) (1950); and *ma'sa Filastin* (The Tragedy of Palestine), (1960).

22 *Al-Thawra al-'Arabiyya al-kubra fi Filastin, 1936–39* (The Great Arab Revolt in Palestine, 1936–39), (Cairo, 1967).

23 *al-Qaddiyya al-Filastiniyya* (The Palestine Cause), (1956).

24 Originally a Ph.D. dissertation submitted to the School of Oriental and African Studies in London. First published in 1970, it has been reprinted a number of times, and translated into English and French. Taught in many Arab universities, it is the only book of its kind to be published and distributed by a major Western commercial publishing firm (Croom Helm). The following parenthetical citations are taken from *Tarikh Filastin al-hadith*, ninth Arabic edition (Beirut: al-mu'asasa al-'Arabiyah li al-dirasat wa al-nashr, 1985).

25 For an outline of the debate on the 1858 Land Code, see Peter Sluglett and Marion Farouk-Sluglett, "The Application of the 1858 Land Code in Greater Syria: Some Observations," in Tarif Khalidi, ed., *Land Tenure and Social Transformation in the Middle East* (Beirut: American University of Beirut, 1984), pp. 409–24.

26 For details, see Beshara Doumani, "Merchants, Socioeconomic Change, and the State in Ottoman Palestine: Jabal Nablus, 1800–1860," (Unpublished Ph.D. dissertation, Georgetown University, 1990).

27 See his "European Penetration and the Economic Development of Palestine, 1856–82," in Roger Owen, ed., *Studies in the Economic and Social History of Palestine in the Nineteenth and Twentieth Centuries* (Carbondale and Edwardsville: Southern Illinois University Press, 1982), pp. 10–87. For further discussion, see his book, *Palästina im Umbruch*.

28 *Tarikh Filastin*, p. 38. My own translation.

29 Only recently are partial answers being put forth. Rosemary Sayigh's *Palestinians: From Peasants to Revolutionaries* (London: Zed Press, 1979) points to the importance of family, clan, and village solidarity as well as a collective historical memory as bases of social organization and sources of self-identity. Her data, however, is limited to refugee camp dwellers in Lebanon. Muhammad Muslih's *The Origins of Palestinian Nationalism* (New York: Columbia University Press, 1988) is one of the first to search for

Ottoman roots, looking for the social basis of Palestinian nationalism among elements of the nineteenth-century ruling elite, which he dubs "office-holding urban notables." Although informative and well researched, the first part is marred by uncritical acceptance of the reductionist generalizations common to the field of Ottoman history. Moreover, by focusing only on one small social group, he presents too narrow a view of what constitutes nationalism.

30 His best known work, *Tarikh Filastin* (History of Palestine), (Jerusalem, 1922), was coauthored with Dr. Khalil Totah. Others works include articles on Palestinian customs and folklore published in the *Journal of the Palestine Oriental Society*.

31 Coauthored *Tarikh Filastin* with al-Barghuthi. He also coauthored *Tarikh al-Quds wa daliluha* (History and a Guide of Jerusalem), (Jerusalem, 1920), with Bulus Shehadeh.

32 *Rijal al-hukum wa al-idara Filastin* (Political and Administrative Figures in Palestine); *Rahlat ahl al-'ilm wa al-hukum fi rif Filastin* (Learned and Government Figures of the Palestinian Countryside), (1968).

33 *Tarikh al-Nasira min aqdam azmaniha ila ayyamina al-hadira* (History of Nazareth From Ancient Times to Our Present Days), (Cairo: Matba'at al-Hilal, 1923).

34 *Tarikh Jabal Nablus wa al-Balqa'* (History of Nablus Mountain and al-Balqa'), four vols. (Nablus: 1937–1975).

35 *Buldaniyat Filastin al-'Arabiyya* ([Topographical Historical Dictionary] of Arab Palestine), (Beirut: Jean d'Arc Press, 1948).

36 His works appeared in dozens of articles in various Arab journals and newspapers during the Mandate period. A collation of many of these works along with a biography of the author was compiled by Kamil al-'Asali, *Turath Filastin fi kitabat 'Abdullah Mukhlis ma'dirase muffassala 'an hayatahu wa shakhsiyatahu al-'ilmiyya* (The Heritage of Palestine in the Writings of Abdullah Mukhlis Along with a Detailed Study of his Scientific Life and Personality), (Amman: Dar al-Karmil-Samid, 1986).

37 *Biladuna Filastin* (Our Country, Palestine), eleven vols. (Beirut: Dar al-Tali'a, Fourth Edition, 1988).

38 *Tarikh al-jins al-arabi fi mukhtalaf wa al-atwar* (History of the Various Roles and Circumstances of the Arab Race), seven volumes. (1959–1964); *Khamsa wa tisun 'aman min al-hayat: mudhakarat wa tasjilat: 1305/1887–1332/1918* (Ninety-five Years of Life: Memoirs and Writings), (Damascus: al-Jam'iyya al-Filastiniyya li al-Tarikh wa al-Athar wa al-Markaz al-Juyughraphy al-Filastini, n.d.)

39 His best known work is *al-Muffassal fi tarikh al-Quds* (The Detailed History of Jerusalem), (Jerusalem: Matba'at al-Andalus, 1961). Other works include: *Tarikh Bir al-Sab' wa-qaba'iliha* (History of Beersheba and its Tribes), (Jerusalem: Matba'at Bayt al-Maqdis, 1934); *Tarikh Ghazza* (History of Gaza), (Jerusalem: Matba'at Dar al-Aytam al-Islamiyah, 1943); and *al-Mujaz fi tarikh 'Asqalan* (Brief History of Asqalan) (Jerusalem, 1943).

40 A sub-category within this genre includes social and ethnographic studies by Tawfiq Canaan, Nimr Sarhan, and Ibrahim Muhawi, among others, on peasant folklore, religious practices, use of houses, and manners of dress. I labelled this sub-category "Preservation of Culture," because most of these works were written to counteract the negation of Palestinian culture due to occupation and dispersal. Many of these works can be found in the pages of journals such as *al-Mujtama' wa al-turath* (Journal of the Society for the Preservation of the Family, al-Bireh), and the *Journal of the Palestine Oriental*

Society. This sub-category will not be discussed because, strictly speaking, these works neither are nor were intended to be historical studies.

41 This is a constant theme throughout. For an idealized portrait of life under Ottoman rule see vol. 2, pp. 343–59. For his opinion on reasons for decline, see vol. 3, pp. 44–60.

42 The Closing Phase of Ottoman Rule in Jerusalam," in Moshe Ma'oz ed., *Studies on Palestine During the Ottoman Period* (Jerusalem, 1975) p. 339

43 For example, Khalil Baydas, *Tarikh al-Quds* (History of Jerusalem), (1922); Muhammad Adib al-'Amin, *al-Quds al-'Arabiyya* (Arab Jerusalem), (1971); Ishaq Musa al-Husayni, *'Urubat bayt al-maqdis* (Arabness of Jerusalem), (1967); and Ahmad Samih al-Khalidi, *Tarikh bayt al-maqdis* (History of Jerusalem), (Unpublished, n.d.).

44 For example, A.S. Marmaji, *"Nadhra fi tarikh Yafa"* (A View of the History of Jaffa), *al-Mashriq* XXVI, nos. 10 and 11 (1928); Jamil al-Bahri, *Tarikh Haifa* (History of Haifa), (Haifa; 1922).

45 Mahmud 'Ali 'Attalah, *Niyabat Ghazza fi al-'ahd al-Mamluki* (The Province of Gaza in the Mamluk Period); Salim 'Arafat al-Mbayyid, *Ghazza wa qita'iha* (Gaza and its District), (Cairo, 1987). Naji Habib Makhkhul, *'Akka wa quraha min aqdam al-azman ila al-waqt al-hadir* (Acre and its Villages from Ancient Times until the Present), (Acre, 1979).

46 Mahmud al-'Abidi, *Safad fi al-Tarikh* (Safad in History), (Amman: Jam'iyat 'Ummal al-Matabi' al-Ta'awiniyah, 1977).

47 In addition to Mansur's work see a rebuttal by Jusayn 'Umar Hamadeh, *Tarikh al-Nasira wa qadaha* (History of Nazareth and its Districts), (Amman, 1982). Also Mahmud 'Abd al-Qadir Kan'ana, *Tarikh al-Nasira* (History of Nazareth), (Nazareth, 1964).

48 Harb Hnayti, *Qissat madinat Jenin* (Story of the City of Jenin), (Tunis, n.d.).

49 Arif 'Abdullah, *Madinat Nablus* (Unpublished M.A. thesis, Damascus, 1964); Akram al-Ramini, *Nablus fi al-qarn al-tasi' 'ashar* (Nablus in the Nineteenth Century), (Amman, 1978); Said Bishtawi, *Nablus wa dawriha fi al-sira' al-Islami al-Salibi, 1099–1291 A.D./492–690 Hijri* (Nablus and its Role in the Muslim-Crusader Struggle 1099–1291 *A.D./492–690 Hijri*) (Unpublished M.A. thesis, Alexandria University, 1984), *Massallam al-Hilu, Qissat madinat Nablus* (Story of the City of Nablus), (Tunis, n.d.).

50 For example, Yusif Qaddura, *Tarikh madinat Ramallah* (History of the City of Ramallah), (New York, 1954); and 'Aziz Shahin, *Kashf al-niqab an alk-judud wa al-ansab fi madinat Ramallah* (Ramallah, Its History and Its Genealogies), (Birzeit University, 1982).

51 Taysir Jabara, *et al.*, *Madinat Khalil al-Rahman: dirasa tarikhiyya wa jughrafiyya* (The City of Khalil al-Rahman: An Historical and Geographical Study), (Hebron, 1987).

52 See Hanna 'Abdullah Jaqaman, *Jawla fi tarikh Bayt Lahm min aqdam al-azmina hatta al-yawm* (An Overview of the History of Bethlehem from Ancient Times until the Present), (Jerusalem, 1984); Jiryis al-'Ali, *Bayt Lahm: al-madinaah al-khalidah* (Bethlehem: The Eternal City), (Bethlehem, 1990); and Tuma Bannurah, *Tarikh Bayt Lahm, Bayt Jala, Bayt Sahur "Afratan" al-Quds* (History of Bethlehem, Bayt Jala, Bayt Sahur "Afratan" of Jerusalem), (Jerusalem: Matba'at al-Ma'arif, 1982).

53 Fawziyah Sheadeh, *Ariha, dirasa hadariyah* (Jericho, a Civilization Study), (1985). This book, originally an M.A. thesis submitted to St. Joseph's University in Lebanon, best illustrates the idealization of the past and other drawbacks of this genre.

54 For example, *Tarikh 'ashirat al-'aranikah fi Birzeit* (History of the 'Aranikah Clan in Birzeit) by Shehadeh Khury (unpublished manuscript written in the first half of this century), and Musa 'Allush, *Tarikh madinat Birzeit* (History of Birzeit City), (Birzeit, 1987)

55 Yusif Haddad, *al-Mujtama' wa al-turath fi Filastin: qaryat al-Bassa* (Society and Folklore in Palestine: al-Bassa Village), (Acre: Dar al-Eswar, 1985).

56 Muhammad 'Awad and Idris al-Jaradat, *al-Tariq al-munir ila tarikh Sa'ir* (The Shinning Path to the History of Sa'ir), (Hebron: Hebron University, 1987); Hebron Alumni Society, *Qaryat Sa'ir: dirasah maydaniyyah* (The Village of Sa'ir: A Field Study), Village Studies Series: 1 (Hebron, 1987).

57 Taysir Mas'udi and Sulayman al-Manasrah, *Qaryat Bani Na'im: dirasah maydaniyya* (The Village of Bani Na'im: A Field Study), Village Studies Series: 2 (Hebron: Hebron Alumni Society, 1987).

58 Jorjet 'Ukian, *et al.*, *al-Rama: Qindil Jalili* (al-Rama, A Galilean Lamp) (Acre: Matba'at Abu Rahman, 1989). This book was produced by al-Rama Local Council.

59 Musa 'Abd al-Salam Hdeib, *Qaryat al-Dawaymeh* (The Village of al-Dawaymeh), (Amman, 1985).

60 Muhammad 'Aql and Jawwad Masarweh, *Taybat Bani Sa'b bayn al-madi wa al-hadir* (Taybat Bani Sa'b Between the Past and the Present), (al-Rama; Matba'at al-Rama, 1989).

61 *Buldaniyat Filastin*, by Marmaji, preceded al-Dabbagh's work. A different kind of project, but one which also aims at wide scale documentation, is 'Arif al-'Arif, *al-Nakba* (The Disaster), six vols. (1956–1960).

62 The English edition was published in London by Eyre and Spottiswoode Press, 1952.

63 D.H.K. Amiran, "The Pattern of Settlement in Palestine," *Israel Exploration Journal* 3 (1953), pp. 65–78, 192–209, 250–60.

64 Oxford: Clarendon Press, 1968, p. v.

65 For a detailed discussion of the role of Bedouin in the soap industry, see Beshara Doumani, "Merchants, Socioeconomic Change, and the State in Ottoman Palestine: Jabal Nablus 1800–1860," (Unpublished Ph.D. dissertation, Georgetown University, 1990), pp. 327–34.

66 Talal Asad, "The Bedouin as a Military Force: Notes on Some Aspects of Power Relations Between Nomads and Sedentaries in Historical Perspective," in Cynthia Nelson, ed., *The Desert and the Sown: Nomads in a Wider Society* (Berkeley, 1974) pp. 61–74.

67 In chronological order of publication they are: Moshe Ma'oz, ed., *Studies on Palestine During the Ottoman Period* (Jerusalem: The Hebrew University and Yad Izhak Ben-Zvi, 1975) Amnon Cohen and Gabriel Baer, eds., *Egypt and Palestine: A Millennium of Association, 868–1948* (Jerusalem: Ben-Zvi Institute for the Study of Jewish Communities in the East, and Yad Izhak Ben-Zvi Institute for the Study of Eretz Israel, 1984); Gabriel Warburg and Gad Gilbar, eds., *Studies in Islamic Society: Contributions in Memory of Gabriel Baer* (Haifa: Haifa University Press, 1984), David Kushner, ed., *Palestine in the Late Ottoman Period: Political, Social, and Economic Transformation* (Jerusalem: Yad Izhak Ben-Zvi Press, 1986); Gad Gilbar, ed., *Ottoman Palestine, 1800–1914: Studies in Economic and Social History* (Haifa: Gustav Heinemann Institute of Middle Eastern Studies, 1990); Ruth Kark, *The Land That Became Israel: Studies in Historical Geography* (Jerusalem: The Magnes Press, 1990). All of these works, except for the first and the last, are distributed by E.J. Brill, Leiden, Holland and New York.

68 The anthology is divided into six parts: "Geography and Population" (six articles); "The Jewish Communities" (eight articles); "The Central Government and Political Change During the Last Century of Ottoman Rule" (six articles); "Foreign Activities" (seven articles); "The Impact of Western Culture and Technology on Traditional Society in the Nineteenth Century" (four articles); and "Archival Sources for the History of Ottoman Palestine" (nine articles).

69 See, for example, Amnon Cohen, *Political Parties in the West Bank Under the Jordanian Regime, 1949–1967* (Ithaca, NY and London: Cornell University Press, 1982). This book is based on Jordanian Security Services archives which were left, intact, in Jerusalem after the Jordanian army's withdrawal from the city in 1967. See also Moshe Ma'oz, *Palestinian Leadership in the West Bank: The Changing Role of the Arab Mayors Under Jordan and Israel* (London; Totowa, NJ: Frank Cass, 1984); *Syria Under Asad: Domestic Constraints and Regional Risks* (London: Croom Helm, 1986); and *Hafiz Asad, the Sphinx of Damascus: A Political Biography* (New York: Weidenfeld and Nicolson, 1988).

70 For example, Amnon Cohen's *Economic Life in Ottoman Jerusalem* (Cambridge: Cambridge University Press, 1989) followed two earlier monographs on the Jewish community of Jerusalem in the same period: *Ottoman Documents on the Jewish Community in Jerusalem in the Sixteen Century* (Jerusalem: Yad Izhak Ben-Zvi Institute, 1976); and *Jewish Life Under Islam: Jerusalem in the Sixteenth Century* (Cambridge, MA and London: Harvard University Press, 1984).

71 See his meticulously researched book, *Ottoman Documents in Palestine, 1552–1615: A Study of the Firman According to the Muhimme Defteri* (Oxford: Clarendon Press, 1960).

72 Amnon Cohen is the most prolific of these authors. His first book – *Palestine in the Eighteenth Century: Patterns of Government and Administration* (Jerusalem: The Magnes Press, The Hebrew University, 1973) – was based primarily on central Ottoman archives, and remains our major secondary source for that period. In addition to his monographs on sixteenth-century Jerusalem, he coauthored, with Bernard Lewis, *Population and Revenue in the Towns of Palestine in the Sixteenth Century.* (Princeton, NJ: Princeton University Press, 1978). Gerber's major work on Palestine is *Ottoman Rule in Jerusalem, 1890–1914* (Berlin: Klaus Schwarz Verlag, 1985).

73 See for example, 'Abd al-Karim Ahmad, *al-Taqsim al-Idari li Suriya* (The Administrative Division of Syria), (Cairo, 1951); 'Abd al-Karim Gharaybeh, *Suriya fi al-qarn al-tasi' 'ashar* (Syria in the Nineteenth Century), (Cairo, 1961); 'Abd al'Aziz 'Awad, *al-Idara al-'Uthmaniyah fi wilayat Suriya* (Ottoman Administration in Syria), (Cairo, 1969); Muhammad 'Adnan al-Bakhit, *The Ottoman Province of Damascus in the Sixteenth Century* (London, 1972); and 'Abd al-Karim Rafeq, *al-'Arab wa al-'Uthmaniyun, 1516–1916* (The Arabs and the Ottomans), (Damascus, 1974); Bahjat Husayn Sabri, *Liwa' al-Quds taht al-hukum al-'Uthmani, 1840–1873* (The Province of Jerusalem Under Ottoman Rule, 1840–1873), (Unpublished M.A. manuscript, 'Ain al-Shams University, Cairo, 1973).

74 The latter point is reflected by the titles of two recent anthologies – David Kushner, ed., *Palestine in the Late Ottoman Period: Political, Social and Economic Transformation,* and Gad Gilbar, ed., *Ottoman Palestine, 1800–1914: Studies in Economic and Social History.*

75 For a survey of extant court archives and an analysis of how they have been used, see Beshara Doumani, "Palestine Islamic Court Records: A Source of Socioeconomic History," *MESA Bulletin* 19, no. 2 (December 1985), pp. 155–72.

76 The University of Jordan, since 1974, has organized and hosted four meet-
    ings of The International Conference on the History of Bilad al-Sham. For
    information on participants and the papers presented, see Muhammad Adnan
    al-Bakhit, *et al.*, *The International Conference of Bilad al-Sham; Collective Index*
    (Amman: University of Jordan, 1990).
77 Alexander Schölch, *Palästina im Umbruch*. Haim Gerber, in his *Ottoman Rule
    in Jerusalem, 1890–1914* (1985), explicitly argues that economic growth in
    nineteenth-century Palestine, long credited to European immigrants, was for
    the most part organized by the local population. He also raises serious reser-
    vations about the pervasive view that Palestine was depopulated and overrun
    by lawlessness, corruption, and insecurity. See his articles, "Modernization
    in Nineteenth-Century Palestine: The Role of Foreign Trade," *Middle Eastern
    Studies* 18, no. 13 (July 1982), pp. 250–64; and "The Population of Syria and
    Palestine in the Nineteenth Century," *African and Asian Studies* [Jerusalem],
    13, no. 1 (March 1979), pp. 59–80.

3

THE RISE OF THE SANJAK
OF JERUSALEM IN THE LATE
NINETEENTH CENTURY

Butrus Abu-Manneh

Modern theories of nationalism are full of contradictory and intriguing expla-nations for the birth of nations. On one point they all seem to agree – one should look for a set of complicated and measured socioeconomical and politico-cultural processes which have forged a new identity and novel interpretation of the human reality. One of the important features is the restructuring of a community's boundaries in a way that corresponds to a shared history as well common language and customs, which together can be the precursors of the new national identity.

A major task of a new Palestinian historiography is to find these early trans-formations which led later to a clear sense of identity and solidarity. This is an important effort against the Israeli claim that only Zionism gave birth to Palestinian identity; otherwise the local Arab population would have been inte-grated into one of the neighboring Arab national movements.

In this article, Butrus Abu-Manneh, a Palestinian historian from Israel, describes the rise of the sanjak of Jerusalem in 1872. This administrative act taken by the Ottomans, which helped to formulate a clearer sense of boundaries and belonging in the land of Palestine, centered around the city of Jerusalem. As Abu-Manneh shows, this move also enhanced the social position of the leading family in Jerusalem, the Husaynis, who formed the core of the national movement during the British occupation of Palestine. The failure of the Husaynis later on to mobilize the rest of the notable families, and with them the whole of Palestinian society, is part of the self-criticism expressed by Palestinian historians who are not content with just blaming Israel for the Nakbah. The historical roots of this event – the essence of which is now the focus of Palestinian historiographical research – can be traced in this article.

* * *

Throughout the Ottoman period and until the early decades of the nineteenth century Jerusalem was regarded as an ordinary sanjak.[1] On the whole, it was part of the province of *Sham* (Damascus) and subject to its governor. Its jurisdiction was limited to the Judean hills.[2] The coastal plains from Jaffa to Gaza formed administrative units of their own: the sanjaks of Gaza and Jaffa.[3] Indeed, the sanjaks of central and southern Palestine were, until the nineteenth century, of marginal importance to the Ottomans; they contributed a small share to the expenses of the *Haj* caravan of Damascus.[4] While the coastal areas functioned also as a bridge connecting Anatolia and Syria with Egypt, their governor was responsible for the safety of that part of the route. In the eighteenth century, due to the decline of law and order in the empire, those sanjaks were neglected and went through a period of substantial decline.[5] In the nineteenth century, however, this situation changed radically. New challenges facing the Ottoman Government during that century aroused the need for reinforcement of Ottoman rule in the area. Consequently, the sanjaks of Jerusalem and Gaza acquired a renewed importance for the Ottoman authorities.

First of all, the international status of Jerusalem and indeed of Palestine as a whole began to rise. Religious revivals in England and America since the early nineteenth century, archaeological enthusiasm and a desire to study ancient and biblical history led to a stream of scholars and travellers who exposed the Holy Land to the Western reader. The use of steamers, moreover, made sea travel shorter and safer and travelling became easier and cheaper. Consequently, curiosity and devotion brought yearly a constantly increasing number of pilgrims and visitors from many Christian countries.[6]

In other words, the interest in Palestine grew substantially among the Christian peoples in the course of the nineteenth century. This interest manifested itself in the erection of new churches or in restoration of the old ones; in the building of convents and especially in missionary activities which led to the establishment of schools and hospitals in Jerusalem and other towns. Almost all the European powers took part in the drive to establish "a presence" in the country – perhaps, we might suggest, not without Ottoman blessing.[7] Moreover, towards the end of the century, British commercial interests grew substantially as well as French economic investments.

Modern historiography points to a connection between the rise of European presence and interests in the country and the decision of the Ottoman Government to separate the sanjak of Jerusalem from the province of Syria and to constitute it as an independent sanjak subject directly to Istanbul.[8] Thus Tibawi wrote: ". . . the complicated religious character of the city and the increased foreign interests in it . . . [were] among the considerations which brought about the change."[9] Porath, on the other hand, saw this administrative measure as "rooted in the international interest in Jerusalem and the dispute between various Christian sects over rights to the holy places."[10] Parkes regarded it as due to the "increasing European population drawn to the country which in 1889 included the first Jewish colonies."[11]

Though there is a great deal to say in favor of these arguments, they are not fully convincing as the only, or the decisive causes which led the Porte to decide upon direct control over the sanjak of Jerusalem and southern Palestine. Such arguments err in regarding nineteenth-century regional history as simply a reflection of European interests and politics. Were this the case, then why was not the sanjak of Acre included? To state that the Porte established direct control over Jerusalem owing to considerations connected with European interests is only half the truth at best. These statements ignore the new political set-up which emerged in the area during the first half of the nineteenth century and which, it is believed, was equally decisive in the formulation of Ottoman policy towards the sanjak of Jerusalem in the last few decades of the century.

An early facet of this policy could be illustrated by the special interest that Sultan Mahmud II showed in Jerusalem, its Muslim inhabitants and its sacred shrines. Extensive repairs and restorations were undertaken by the sultan in the Muslim holy places.[12] He tried, moreover, to foster ties with local notables. For instance, in 1813 he invited a Muslim dignitary of Jerusalem to Istanbul and received him as an honored guest.[13] Perhaps this was an attempt on the part of the Sultan to improve his image in Muslim eyes. At a time when the Sultan was trying to have his assumption of the Caliphate widely accepted, such acts were, it seems, deemed necessary – especially since the holy places in the Hijaz had fallen to the Wahhabis and, after their reoccupation by Muhammad Ali Pasha of Egypt, had been kept under his control for almost thirty years. This special interest which the Ottoman sultans showed in Jerusalem continued under Mahmud's successors and indeed reached a climax in the later days of Abdulaziz and especially under Abdulhamid II.

But if the city of Jerusalem and its holy places started to acquire a prime importance in Ottoman eyes, the occupation of Syria by Muhammad Ali was a turning point in Ottoman policy towards Syria as a whole and towards the sanjak of Jerusalem in particular. Already in 1830, on the eve of Muhammad Ali's invasion, the sanjaks of Jerusalem and Nablus were transferred to the control of Abdullah Pasha, the governor of Acre.[14] By this act, the whole of Palestine was united under Acre,[15] which suggests that the Porte was working to reinforce the Syrian front in face of Muhammad Ali's ambitions.[16]

With the Ottoman restoration in 1841, the sanjak of Jerusalem began to enjoy a special status among the Palestinian sanjaks – long before foreign interests in Palestine became substantial. Its jurisdiction was widened to include the districts of Gaza and Jaffa (permanently) and the sanjak of Nablus (until 1858).[17] Thus, for the first time in its history under the Ottomans, Jerusalem became the administrative center of central and southern Palestine. In the same year, the new sanjak was separated from the province of Damascus and put directly under Istanbul; a governor of high rank was nominated to govern it.[18] But this arrangement was short lived. Again in 1854 at the time of the Crimean War, Jerusalem became an independent sanjak, and even was raised temporarily to the status of a province.[19]

In spite of the fact that Jerusalem became an important administrative center after 1841, the tendency at the Porte during the Tanzimat period was to keep it and its sanjak within the framework of the province of Damascus. Due to the struggle with Muhammad Ali, the leading Tanzimat statesmen gave priority, it seems, to the strengthening of Ottoman rule in Syria as a whole, including Jerusalem. Much of their policy in Syria after 1841, and indeed the intensity and nervousness which marked the application of the Tanzimat reforms, were apparently due to this intention.[20] But the events of 1860 in Damascus had shown them that to secure stronger Ottoman control over the country was in itself not enough. They felt that there was a need to reinforce internal consolidation and to lay the basis of social integration. Thus, with the application of the *vilayet* law of 1864, 'Ali and Fuad decided to unite the provinces of Damascus and Sidon (which included the former province of Tripoli) into one. The new province – called "Syria" – extended from south Aleppo to Akaba and from the Mediterranean Sea to the desert (Mt. Lebanon excluded). 'Ali appointed as its governor his protege, the capable and enlightened Mehmet Rāshid Pasha, who – for five and a half years – worked indefatigably for the internal integration of the provinces.[21]

However, the death of 'Ali in September 1871 brought a basic change in this policy, as it did in much of what the Tanzimat statesmen represented. Mahmud Nedim, his successor as Grand Vezir, had his own ideas about reform, and about what policies were best needed to preserve the integrity of the empire.[22] One of his first acts after his rise to power was to dismiss Mehmet Rāshid Pasha from the governorship of Syria. Later, in the summer of 1872, Nedim separated the sanjak of Jerusalem from the jurisdiction of Damascus, under which it had been for centuries, and constituted it as an independent sanjak subject directly to Istanbul.[23] For about two months even the sanjaks of Balka (Nablus) and Acre were added to it, and the three formed a province officially called "Kuds-i Şerif Eyaleti."[24]

This measure moved the British consul in Jerusalem to report of "the recent erection of Palestine into a separate eyalet."[25] But no sooner did

Mustafa Surayya Pasha, the new Vali, arrive in Jerusalem than he received a telegram that the two sanjaks of Nablus and Acre were rejoined to the province of Syria.[26] Thus Jerusalem with the districts of Gaza, Jaffa and Hebron only formed the "sanjak of Kudus."[27] It stayed so until World War I.

No official explanation could be found as yet for this measure. We might assume, however, that Nedim sought means to reinforce Ottoman rule in the areas bordering Egypt. He apparently saw that, as an outpost on the border of Egypt, it would ultimately better serve Ottoman interests than to create an entity of Syria – for the emergence of Egypt as an autonomous state under a dynasty of its own brought with it, according to Bernard Lewis, a "rivalry between Ottoman Istanbul and Khedival Cairo which throughout the nineteenth and early twentieth centuries was an important element in Middle Eastern political life."[28]

Unable to undermine Egypt's autonomy or install a friendly Khedive, the Porte prudently chose to strengthen its hold over the neighboring provinces.[29] Indeed, the Porte had more reason to do so in light of the (sometimes unveiled) ambitions of the Khedives to restore their influence in the adjacent areas lost by Muhammad Ali in 1841.

Sultan Abdulhamid II (1876–1909) was, it seems, of similar opinion to Nedim concerning the sanjak of Jerusalem, which he kept separate and subject directly to Istanbul. He took care, moreover, to choose honest, earnest and capable Ottoman governors to govern it.[30] By the late 1890s the Sultan started to suspect the intentions of Abbas II towards him. By then, indeed, the Sultan and the Viceroy were not at all on the best of terms.[31] Thus, by the autumn of 1897, Abdulhamid began to send governors to Jerusalem from his own immediate entourage, in whom he apparently had more confidence.[32]

In February 1898, three notables of Gaza, the mufti Hanafi Effendi al-Husayni, his brother Abdulhai and his son 'Arif, were arrested and sent into exile in Anatolia. The British Consul in Jerusalem reported the possible connection between this act and the intended visit of the Viceroy to al-Arish:[33] "For fear of intrigue they were sent out of the way as the mufti has influence over a large section of the Arabs (Beduins)," he added.[34]

A year later (1899) an *irade* was issued by the Sultan authorizing the establishment of the district of Beer Sheba into a *qadā'* to be governed by a *kaim-makam* (a district officer).[35] The intention of the government, wrote an authority on Beer Sheba, was "to establish an administrative center on the Egyptian borders."[36] In this way, the Sultan evidently intended to prevent intrigue and to put the Beduins of the Negev under tighter control. A new township (Bi'r al-Sabi') was founded for that reason and its *kaim-makam* was raised to the rank of deputy *Mutassarreif* (governor of a sanjak).[37]

The existence of the sanjak of Jerusalem for almost two generations as a separate entity from the other regions of Syria was of tremendous importance for the emergence of Palestine about fifty years later. It also did much to determine the character and future of Palestinian politics, and contributed to the emergence of Palestinian nationalism as distinct from Syrian–Arab nationalism.

But to be a separate administrative unit is not in itself sufficient to create an image with which the people identify more than with a greater pan-Syrian entity. This image emerged as a result of a combination of factors – partly religious (both for Christians and Muslims) as has been analysed by Yehoshua Porath.[38] But, above all, it came about due to the character of the administrative reforms applied by the Ottomans in the Tanzimat period, to social changes and other factors.

First of all, the Tanzimat reforms imposed a centralized system of government where formerly the shaikhs and chieftains of the Judean hills enjoyed a *de facto* local autonomy each in his own district. The new Ottoman administrative system brought about the destruction of their power and opened their districts, perhaps for the first time in many centuries, to government institutions run by officials who applied new laws and rules. Centralization not only brought uniformity but above all it established the domination of the city, especially of Jerusalem, over its hinterland. The countryside became more than ever dependent upon the city.

Now, in the city itself, the Tanzimat opened the way for the local notables and dignitaries to enhance their power and influence. They succeeded in dominating the provincial government to a considerable degree and through it the entire sanjak. Thus where formerly the notables of Jerusalem had not enjoyed any power over the countryside except perhaps a moral one,[39] in the course of the century they acquired great power and influence.[40] What has been said about Jerusalem could also be said about Gaza, Jaffa and Hebron.

Consequently, a small number of families in the urban centers of the sanjak, headed by those of Jerusalem, became the new political and social elite of the country and utilized the power put in their hands. The new Tanzimat laws eased their way to acquire lands or even whole villages cheaply. Their sons were sent to the higher institutions of learning in Istanbul. Returning half-Ottomanized, they held offices in the sanjak or in the neighboring districts, such as *kaim-makams*, judges, officials, police officers, inspectors, etc. For a hundred years this new elite dominated the country and held its fate in their hands.

It was perhaps unfortunate from the Palestinian point of view that this elite was divided into two rival factions – led by the Khalidis on the one hand and the Husaynis of Jerusalem on the other, with their respective followings throughout the urban centers of the sanjak.[41] This division was not just competition for office, influence or gains, but above all had an ideological background – and, indeed, was part of the split which divided the Ottoman elite in the 1870s into two hostile camps over the system of government of the state. Broadly speaking, the former – the Tanzimat supporters – regarded the ending of the Sultan's arbitrary rule, the establishment of orderly government and the social and political integration of non-Muslims, as an absolute necessity for the preservation of the integrity of the empire; the latter believed that nothing should be done which might weaken or limit the powers of the Sultan and the domination of the Muslim element in the state.[42]

The Khalidis of liberal outlook supported the first trend, represented in the 1870s by Midhat and Rāshid Pasha and others. Shaikh Yasin, a senior member of the family, represented Jerusalem in the General Council of the province of Syria during the governorship of Rāshid Pasha. When Rāshid was dismissed in 1871 "the position of most of his supporters who belonged to the Reform Party (*Hizb al Islah*) was shaken."[43] But the ousting of Mahmud Nedim from his second Grand Vezirate in 1876, and the deposition of Sultan Abdulaziz shortly there-after by Midhat and his friends, resulted in the improvement of the position of the Khalidis. Yusuf Diyā',[44] a brother of Yasin, was elected as the representative of Jerusalem in the first Ottoman parliament and, along with Nafi' al-Jabiri of Aleppo and others, led the opposition to Sultan Abdulhamid's government. Consequently, when parliament was suspended in 1878, he was among those ordered to leave Istanbul without delay.[45] In the early 1880s we find him in Vienna, teaching Arabic, and at the end of the decade as a governor of a Kurdish district in the *vilayet* of Bitlis. Having learned Kurdish, he wrote, significantly enough, a Kurdish–Arabic dictionary.[46] Yusuf Diyā's brothers and other members of the family were also employed throughout the Hamidian period in various provinces of the empire. In spite of a temporary restoration of some prestige to the Khalidis in the late 1890s,[47] it could be safely assumed that their power in Jerusalem declined with the fall of the Tanzimat statesmen at the end of the 1870s.[48]

While the base of Khalidi power in Jerusalem was the *shar-'ïa* court – the chief clerkship of which passed through the family for a number of generations – the Husainis held the posts of the *Hanafi Mufti* and *Naqib al-Ashraf* of Jerusalem almost uninterruptedly (especially the former) from the late eighteenth century.[49] By virtue of this they supervised Muslim religious life in the city. Having been in disfavor during Ibrahim Pasha's rule, the Husainis managed to preserve their position, if not to strengthen it, in the Tanzimat period.[50] Generally of a conservative outlook, the Husainis, it seems, supported Sultan Abdulhamid and his policies. Consequently, they improved their fortunes and increased their power in the sanjak. During this period, they held two very influential posts in the city: that of the *Hanafi Mufti* and the head of the municipality. According to an observer, Selim Effendi al-Husayni – mayor for almost two decades – "occupies a high position in this city and exercises considerable influence over the mutessarif ... [and had] a considerable influence at Constantinople."[51] Many other members of the family filled key posts in the administration of the sanjak. The twentieth century found the Husayni family in a dominant position – though not without rivals, particularly among the Nashashibis. The latter family started to gain prominence following the weakening of the Khalidis, and especially after the rise of the Young Turks.

To sum up: in the course of the forty to fifty years that preceded World War I, Jerusalem was emerging both as an administrative and a political center, similar to those of Damascus and Beirut. Indeed, the separation of Jerusalem and its sanjak from the rest of Syria led the way for the emergence of a new polity. This development happened due to Ottoman policies in the area rather than as a result of advance planning. Even after the establishment of Mandatory Palestine through the joining of the sanjaks of Jerusalem, Nablus and Acre, Jerusalem held its primacy; yet, for a long time, there existed another two centers, Nablus and Acre (or Haifa), the notables of which were not always ready to take the lead of those of Jerusalem.

NOTES

Dedicated to the memory of the late Professor Uriel Heyd of Jerusalem.
I gratefully acknowledge the financial help rendered me by the University of Haifa for my research of this paper.

1 Sanjak was the traditional title of a subprovince in the Ottoman Empire. In the last few decades of the nineteenth century, the term *mutasarriflik* (Arabic *Mutasariffiyya*) was alternately used to denote the same administrative division. For the sake of convenience, we shall use in this paper the term sanjak only.
2 See A. Cohen, *Palestine in the Eighteenth Century* (Jerusalem 1973), p. 169.
3 Ibid., pp. 144ff.
4 Ibid., pp. 150f.
5 Cf. C. F. Volney, *Travels through Egypt and Syria* (New York 1798) II, pp. 183ff., 203f.; Cohen, pp. 171f.
6 D. S. Margoliouth, *Cairo, Jerusalem, and Damascus* (New York 1907), pp. 362ff.
7 Consul Moore, British Consul for about three decades in Jerusalem (see F.O. List of 1880, p. 150) expressed his astonishment "that the Russians and French should be able to obtain permission to build edifice after edifice (in Palestine) in rapid succession. ..." Moore-White, F.O. 195/1690, desp. 3, Jerusalem, 15 February 1890.
8 See below, note 23.
9 A. L. Tibawi, *A Modern History of Syria* (London 1969), p. 181.

10 Y. Porath, *The Emergence of the Palestinian–Arab National Movement* (London 1974), p. 16.

11 J. Parkes, *A History of Palestine From 135 A.D. To Modern Times* (London 1949), p. 221.

12 M. Kurd Ali, *Khitat al-Sham*, 6 vols. (Damascus 1925–1928), V, p.269; 'A. al-'Arif, *Tarikh al-Haram al-Qudsi* (Jerusalem 1947), pp. 28f and 52; see also by al-'Arif, *al-Mufassal fi Tarikh al-Quds* (Jerusalem 1961), pp. 306f and 504 (hereafter 'Arif, *al-Mufassal*).

13 A. Cevdet, *Tarih-i Cevdet*, 12 vols., 2nd impression (Istanbul A.H. 1309), X, 111. That dignitary was shaikh Abu al-Su'ūd Effendi, after whose arrival in Istanbul the Sultan himself paid him a visit first because of the fatigue and old age of the shaikh; he died in Istanbul a few weeks later. (Ibid.)

14 I. al-Nimr, *Tarikh Jabal Nablus Wa'l balqa'*, vol. 1, 2nd impression (Nablus 1975), p. 310; see also an appendix by B. B. Hubaish in Shihabī, *Tarikh alUmara' at-Shihabiyeen*, ed. A. Rustum and F. A. al-Bustani, 3 vols. (Beirut 1933), p. 800; A. Rustum, *al-Usul al 'Arabiyya*, 5 vols. (Beirut 1930–1933), 1, pp. 23, 24f., and 30f.; Spyridon, ed., *Annals of Palestine 1821–1841* (Jerusalem 1938), p. 55 (stated mistakenly as 1831 instead of 1830); cf. also G. J. Koury, *The Province of Damascus 1783–1832*, a dissertation submitted to the University of Michigan in 1970, p. 188.

15 The districts of Jaffa and Gaza were then within the jurisdiction of Acre, the seat of the province of Sidon. See Ib. al-'Awra, *Tarikh Wilayat Sulaiman Pasha al-'Adil* (Saida 1936), pp. 388f.

16 In addition, the Ottomans were, since about 1827, reorganizing the fief holders in Syria and Palestine which constituted the local military forces. See Khoury, pp. 182f.; Rustum, *al-Mahfuzat at-Malakiyya al'-Misriyya*, 4 vols. (Beirut 1940–1943), 1, pp. 74ff; al-Nimr, *op. cit.*, I., pp. 304; 11, pp. 210f. and 249ff.

17 Nimr, 1, p. 343; J. Finn, *Stirring Times*, 2 vols. (London 1878), 1, 161 f.

18 See a firman dated *Awasit Jumada al- Ula* 1257/1841 – copy in register (*sijill*) no. 283 of the *Shari'a* court of Jerusalem, p. 36; see also M. Maoz, *Ottoman Reform in Syria and Palestine* (Oxford 1968), p. 33 n. 6.

19 Ibid., pp. 122f.

20 For the application of the Tanzimat reforms in Syria between 1841–1861, see M. Maoz, *Ottoman Reform*.

21 For two short biographies of Rāshid Pasha, see *Sicill-i Osmani*, II, pp. 356–357; S. Faris (ed.), *Kanz al-Raglia'ib fi Muntakhabāt al-Jāwaib*, 7 vols. (Istanbul A.J. 1288–98), V, pp. 332–334. I am engaged at present in a study of Rāshid's rule in Syria.

22 On Nedim's Grand Vezirate, see R. Davison, *Reform in the Ottoman Empire* (Princeton 1962), pp. 280ff.

23 Some Arabic sources stated that this act took place in 1870. See, for example, Kurd Ali, *Khitat III*, p. 236; or in 1871, see *al-Muqtataf LII* (1918), p. 35; 'Arif, *al-Mufassal*, p. 311; or simply "after 1870" as with Sarkis, *Tarikh Urshalim* (Beirut 1874), p. 192. However, the above date is based upon Moore-Elliot F.O. 195/994, desp. 6, Jerusalem, 27 July 1872; *Sicill-i Osmani*, 11, p. 621; ha-*Havatzelet* (a Hebrew weekly that appeared in Jerusalem), II, no. 37 dated 12 July 1872; cf. M. A. Awad, *al-Idarah al-'Uthmantyya' fi wilayat Suriyya 1864–1914* (Cairo 1969), p. 339. Modern historians such as Tibawi (p. 181) and Parkes (p. 221) stated without giving evidence that the act of separation took place in 1887 or 1889 respectively. This, it seems, is a common error as it is mentioned in other publications; see, for instance, the *Hebrew Encyclopedia* (Heb.), VI, p. 503. But the fact that it is repeated may give rise to the idea

that the edict of 1872 was later cancelled and finally reimposed in 1887. It was not so. The *Salnames* (year books) of the central government of the following years which it was possible to check stated unequivocally that Jerusalem was "independently administered"; thus, the edict of 1872 was never cancelled. See the *Salnames* of A.H. 1291 (1874–75), 1292 (1875–76), 1296 (1878–79), 1297 (1879–80), 1299 (1881–82), 1301 (1883–84), 1302 (1884–85), 1303 (1885–86), 1304 (1886–87), 1305 (1887–88).

24 See Register no. 348 of the *Shari'a* court of Jerusalem, pp. 211–12, an edict to the "Vali" of "Kuds-i Şerif eyaleti" dated 4 Jamada 1 1289; see also pp. 218 and 231.

25 Moore-Elliot, ibid.

26 See *Sicill-i Osmani* 11, p. 64.

27 The boundaries of the sanjak according to a dispatch of the British Consul in 1900 were defined as the following: It was bounded on the north by a line which may be said to run from the coast of the Mediterranean near the mouth of the river Auja [Yarkon] eastward ... to the bridge over the Jordan near Jericho; on the south by a line drawn from the Mediterranean midway between Gaza and al-Arish to the town of Akaba; on the east by the river Jordan, the Dead Sea, and the valley running south ... to Akaba and on the west by the Mediterranean. He added that it very nearly corresponded to the Roman province of Judea as distinguished from Samaria and Galilee. See Dickson-O'Conor, F.O. 195/2084, desp. 15, Jerusalem 11 May 1900.

28 B. Lewis, *The Middle East and the West* (London 1968), p. 52.

29 In addition to Jerusalem, the sanjak of Bengazi on the western border of Egypt was also made, according to one source, an independent sanjak at about the same time. See A. S. al-Dajani, *Libya Qabl al-lhtilāl al-Itāli* (Cairo 1971), p. 199.

30 Such were Rauf Pasha who governed Jerusalem for almost 13 years (1877–1889) and Ibrahim Hakki Pasha (1890–1897), see Moore-White F.O. 195/1648, desp. 10, 6 May 1889; and Dickson-Currie, F.O. 195/1984 desp. 55, 8 November 1897.

31 L. Hirszowicz, "The Sultan and the Khedive 1892–1908" in *Middle Eastern Studies* VIII (1 972), pp. 287–311.

32 *Thamarāt al-Funuñ*, no. 1154, 8 November 1897, p. 3; Dickson-Currie, ibid.; Dickson-O'Conor, F.O. 195/2106, desp. 29, 15 May 1900; Dickson-O'Conor, F.O. 195/2175, desp. 46, 12 August 1904. This change took place two months after the first Zionist Congress in Basel in which it was decided upon "establishing for the Jewish people a publicly and legally assured home in Palestine." Whether there was a correlation between the two events is a matter for investigation.

33 Abbas II visited al-'Arish early in March 1898 and reached up to the border marks near the township of Rafah. See N. Shuqair, *Tarikh Sinā* (Cairo 1916), p. 555.

34 Dickson-Currie, F.O. 195/2028, desp. 10, 1 March 1898 and enclosure. This story was confirmed to me by Mr. Hamdi al-Husayni whom I met in Gaza on 10 February 1977. He added that they were taken to Ankara where they spent 8 years during which Hanfi Effendi died and was buried there.

35 *Thamarāt al-Funuñ*, no. 1236, 26 June 1899, p. 3.

36 'A. al-'Arif, *Tarikh B'ir al-Sabi' wa Qabailiha* (Jerusalem 1934), p. 244. Dickson-O'Conor, F.O. 195/2062, desp. 43, 30 November 1899.

37 M. M. al-Dabbagh, *Biladuna Filastin*, vol. 1, part 2 (Beirut 1966), p. 382.

38 See Y. Porath, pp. 6ff.

39 Nimr, comparing between the positions of Nablus and Jerusalem *vis-à-vis* their countryside in the pre-Tanzimat period, stated that the Nablus families held the governorship, over the district but the Jerusalem notables *"Effendies"* – i.e., office holders such as *Qadis, Muftis,* and *Naqibs,* etc., had no power over the countryside but were divided among themselves along with the factional division in the district. See T*arikh Jabal Nablus wa al-Balqā'*, vol. II (Nablus 1961), pp. 386ff.; p. 405 n. 1, and vol. I, p. 343 n. 1.

40 See report of Ekrem Bey, Governor of Jerusalem between 1906–1908 in Israel State Archives (ISA), 83/11, undated.

41 Moore-Jocelyn, F.O. 195/1153, desp. 10, 14 April 1877; Dickson-Currie, F.O. 195/1984, desp. 7, 8 February 1897. See also G. Frumkin, *Derekh Shofet bi-Yerushaleim* (Heb.) (Tel Aviv 1954), pp. 282ff.

42 A. H. Hourani, *Arabic Thought in the Liberal Age* (London 1962), pp. 105 and 262.

43 Ruhi al-Khahdi, *al-Muqaddima fi al-Mas'alah al-Sharqiyya* (Jerusalem n.d.) p. i; on the outlook of the Khalidis, cf. 'Arif, *al-Mufassal,* p. 274.

44 On Diyā', see Zirikh, *al-A'lam*, 10 vols., 2nd ed. (Cairo 1954), IX, pp. 310–11 and X., p. 254; R. Devereux, *The First Ottoman Constitutional Period* (Baltimore 1963), p. 267 n. 40.

45 Ibid., pp. 148, 156, 166–7, 247–8.

46 *Al-Hadiyya al-Hamidiyya fi al-lugha al-Kurdiyya* (Istanbul A.H. 1310). See Kahhala, *Mu'jam al-Muallifin,* 15 vols. (Damascus 1957–61), XIII, pp. 330–1.

47 As a sign of that we find that Shaikh Yasin served in the late 1890s as a mayor of Jerusalem for a short while between two terms of a Husaini mayor. (See *Thamarāt al-Funūn*, no. 1204, 31 October 1898, p. 5); cf. Dickson-Currie, F.O. 195/1984, desp. 7, Jerusalem 8 February 1897.

48 On the Khalidi family in general, I had two fruitful talks in December 1976 with Mr. Haydar Kamil and Mr. Hazim Mahmud, two senior members of the Khalidis presently living in Jerusalem. To both of them my thanks are due.

49 According to the family tree of the Husainis, a copy of which is possessed by Mr. S. I. al-Husaini, presently living in Jerusalem.

50 The senior member of the family 'Umar, the *shaikh al-Haram* and a previous *Naquib al-Ashraf,* and *Tahir Effendi,* the Mufti, were exiled to Egypt in 1834 by Muhammad Ali. See Rustum, *al-Mahfuzat,* I, pp. 171, 188–9; 'Arif, *al-Mufassal,* pp. 281 and 284; Spyridon, p. 93; cf. also *Mahfuzat,* 11, p. 489.

51 Dickson-Currie, F.O. 195/1984, desp. 7, 8 February 1897. See also Frumkin, p. 283; Porath, pp. 13f.

Part II

THE ORIGINS OF ZIONISM IN PALESTINE RECONSIDERED

4

THE COLONIZATION
PERSPECTIVE IN
ISRAELI SOCIOLOGY

Uri Ram

The revisionist historiographical outlook in Israel centered on three issues: early Zionism, the 1948 war and the early years of statehood. Of the three, the first issue touched upon the very essence of Zionism. A new look at the early years of the Zionist project in Palestine meant adopting a colonialist perspective and abandoning the purely national one adhered to, hitherto, by mainstream Israeli scholars.

In this article, Uri Ram shows how a colonialist perspective on Zionism became an academic tool and not merely a political statement against Zionism. This transformation necessitated a fresh theoretical and methodological approach to the Zionist reality in the past and in the present, a precondition which explains why sociologists, and not positivist historians, were able to embark on such a ground-breaking road into history. As Ram explains, it took more than just a different paradigmatic approach to produce such an examination. Several catalyctic events in the sociopolitical history of Israel generated this new perspective as well. This trend of viewing history as part of our sociology of knowledge is very much in line with Doumani's realization of the role of ideology in Palestine's historiography and provides a possible common ground for future joint research on the country's history.

* * *

Abstract   Though the characterization of Zionism as a colonial project is probably as old as the Zionist movement, as a specific scholarly sociological perspective in Israeli academia it was formulated only lately, in the wake of the Six Day War of 1967. This article outlines the contours of this new perspective, its theoretical assumptions and its political implications. It examines the historical circumstances which propelled its emergence, and then discerns two distinct sub-trends in it: Weberian and Marxist. Throughout are explored three distinct comparative issues: a comparison of the colonization perspective to other perspectives in Israeli sociology, especially the "dualist perspective": a comparison of the case of Israel with other colonization cases, such as the U.S.A.; and a comparison of the two sub-trends in the perspective itself to each other.

The reopened frontier and the emergence of the new perspective

The notion that Israel is a settlement-colony type of society became a staple of Arab and Palestinian thought, and from there disseminated to Western radical circles, in the late 1960s and early 1970s, against the background of the new sensitivity to Third-World and post-colonial issues. One publication that gave wide circulation to the idea was a book length essay published in 1973 by the French Marxian (later turned Moslem) scholar, Maxime Rodinson, titled *Israel: A Settler-Colonial State?* The gist of the book's argument is that:

> [T]he creation of the State of Israel on Palestinian soil is the culmination of a process that fits perfectly into the great European–American movement of expansion in the nineteenth and twentieth centuries, whose aim was to settle new inhabitants among other peoples or to dominate them economically and politically.

The consequences of this process, the essay proceeds, were determined by an inexorable historical logic:

> Wanting to create a purely Jewish, or predominantly Jewish, state in Arab Palestine in the twentieth century could not help but lead to a colonial-type situation and to development (completely normal, sociologically speaking) of a racist state of mind, and in the final analysis to a military confrontation. ... [1]

Another illustration of the circulation of this perspective at that time is a collection of articles drawn from an annual convention of the

Association of Arab–American University Graduates, published in 1974, titled *Settler Regimes in Africa and the Arab World*. A theme which runs through the essays in the volume is, as the editors describe it, the tendency of settler regimes to move towards exclusivism, exploitation, oppression, and racism. This, they maintain, "is as much true of the Afrikaner regime in South Africa as the Israeli regime in Palestine; of the former French regime in Algeria as the current Portuguese regime in Angola and Mozambique."[2] It was this spirit which precipitated in 1975 a resolution of the United Nations Assembly which condemned Zionism as a "form of racism."[3]

In Israel, however, the identification of Zionism as a colonial movement is usually regarded as slanderous. The consideration of Israel as a colonialist society, implying that the Jews conquered and expropriated a settled land and exploited or expelled the native dwellers, goes against the grain of the Zionist self-portrayal as a movement of a people without land returning to a land without people.[4] It is considered repugnant by Israel's Zionist left wing, which traditionally has professed self-liberation and redemption of a wasteland through toil, and by Israel's right wing, which traditionally has advocated that the "Whole Land of Israel" is an incontestable asset of the Jewish people by "historical rights" and providential covenant.

The emergence of the colonization perspective in Israeli sociology is a late fallout of the Six Day War's aftermath. The new circumstances of post-1967 Israel, especially the Israeli attempt to create "facts on the ground" in the occupied territories, threw a retrospective light on the historical process of Israeli nation-building and state formation, which was never so graphically visible before.

In this respect the settlement activity trailed by the nationalist religious *Gush Emunim* movement induced, inadvertently of course, the emergence of the most radical trend in Israeli sociology. The settlement initiative had begun right after the Six Day War with the entry of a group of religious zealots to Hebron and with the Labor government decision to establish the Jewish city, Kiryat Arba, in Hebron's outskirts. Since then Israel has established in the occupied areas more than a hundred settlements populated by more than a hundred thousand settlers.

The newer Israeli settlement movement (post-1967) differs from the older one (up to 1948, Israel's independence year) in two important respects: it is supported by a strong coercive force (the Israeli government and military) and its legitimating discourse is religious (rather than socialist). Yet despite these differences, it is obvious that this movement captures the ethos of the pioneer settlers of the Labor Movement which constituted the Israeli political elite up to the political "upheaval" of 1977, when the right wing Likud won the election. This resemblance indeed so embarrassed the ideologues of the Labor Movement that they hastened to invent a distinction between their own *"hityashvut"* (settlement) and the *"hitnachlut"* of *Gush Emunim*, a term used in the Bible to describe the Israelite conquerors-settlers of Canaan in antiquity.[5]

Since 1967 the Palestinian problem gained such salience that it could not be ignored for much longer. The occupation of the territories brought Israel, at long last, face to face with a large and mobilized Palestinian population. The activities of the Palestinian Liberation Organization made it, and its claims, recognized world-wide. In a short time it has mustered solidarity throughout the Third World, and in due course gained somewhat more reserved support from Western states and from the United Nations. Israel's invasion of Lebanon in 1982 was the first war waged by it directly against the Palestinians (rather than any Arab state) and likewise the Palestinian resistance which broke out in 1987, the *Intifada*, is the first mass mobilization of Palestinians against Israel since the 1940s. Israelis could not avoid being affected by this ever intensifying encounter, and Israeli consciousness became more and more exposed to the possible repercussions of the national conflict upon Israeli society itself.

Inside Jewish Israel the notion of Israel as a colonial society struck a chord in the 1960s only in marginal intellectual groups, such as *Matzpen* and *Etgar*.[6] The agenda of the *Matzpen* group exemplifies the first articulation of an explicit colonization outlook in Jewish–Israeli society. *Matzpen* was an offshoot of the Communist Party of Israel, formed in 1962 by a group of young radicals who splintered from the party, and later enlisted with the Trotskyist Fourth International.[7] Its conception of Israel anticipated in a rudimentary form the main staples of the colonization perspective. The principal points of this conception were the following: Israel represents a unique case of settler-colonialist and capitalist society. Though the colonization of Palestine was unusual in not being brought about by an imperial power, but rather by a nationalist movement, this movement nevertheless allied itself with imperialist powers against the progressive forces of the region. In Israeli politics the project of colonization overshadows any other concerns including class concerns, therefore the real assignment of the Israeli Labor Movement is not the protection of workers or the attainment of socialism, but rather "to organize Jewish labor for the Zionist cause".[8] The Israeli economy is unique in that it does not rest either on a profit economy or on the accumulation of debt, but rather on unilateral capital transfers. This enables the Israeli ruling bureaucracy to maintain an enormous military establishment and simultaneously to guarantee a reasonable standard of living to the population. Culturally and institutionally the colonial nature of Israel makes it inherently racist and oppressive, giving a privileged position to Jews over the native population.

It was the aftermath of the 1967 War which brought issues that had been submerged under layers of Israeli official historiography and sociography to the consciousness of a wider Israeli public, namely, the nature of the appropriation of territories, the relationships with the Palestinian inhabitants of these territories, and the implication these issues might have on Israeli society itself. This period saw a sort of replay of an anterior (pre-1948) history, secluded from public awareness by official Zionist historiography, and it provided a blunt demonstration of the applicability of the colonization argument.

That the recent emergence of the colonization perspective in Israeli sociology was induced by post-1967 circumstances is attested to by one of its leading practitioners, sociologist Gershon Shafir, formerly of Tel Aviv University and presently of the University of California at San Diego. Shafir concedes that for him:

> [T]he aftermath of the Six Day War revealed the gap between the evidence of Israeli society's gradual but definite transformation through its manifold relationships with the Palestinian Arabs who came under Israeli occupation, and the Palestinians' invisibility in historical and sociological accounts of the early formation of Israeli society. Although throwing off mental habits is always a slow process, I came eventually to the conclusion that, during most of its history, Israeli society is best understood not through the existing, inward-looking, interpretations but rather in terms of the broader context of Israeli–Palestinian relations.[9]

The new scholarly perspective is still an outcast in mainstream academia. It threatens to bestow an academic credibility on arguments which are used by Arabs in general and Palestinians in particular to dispute the legitimacy of Israel. We shall return to the political implications of the perspective at a later stage. For now it is important to perceive that this point of view expedites the examination of Israeli society in its geopolitical context and in interaction with the Palestinian society. While the mainstream perspective in sociology considers Israel "from the inside" as a discrete unit, it is the distinctive uniqueness of the colonization perspective that it takes the Israeli–Arab binational set of relations as its vantage point from which to examine Israeli society.

The essential insight advanced by the colonization perspective, as the label suggests, is the consideration of Israel as a colonial society or, more precisely, a settler-colonial society. This entails a drastic shift in the conceptual and comparative analytical framework employed to interpret Israel. Rather than being compared to Western democracies, as is usually preferred by mainstream, especially functionalist, sociologists, or to Eastern party-autocracies, as is implied by a conflict trend which targets Israeli Labor oligarchy, in the colonization perspective Israel is considered in the company of social formations such as Algeria under French rule or Kenya and Rhodesia under British rule, and mostly – and most distressing to liberal Israelis – the South African apartheid state. Historically speaking, the category of colonies of settlement also included the formative periods of nation-states as the U.S.A., Canada, Australia, and New Zealand.

The term "colonization" – compared to "imperialism" and "colonialism" – requires clarification. D.K. Fieldhouse maintains that in current usage "imperialism" refers to the dynamics of empire-building, and "colonialism" refers to the subjugation of a (non-European) society which is the product of imperialism. "Colonization" describes "the movement and permanent settlement of people from one country in another" where "the immigrants intended to establish societies as similar as possible to those they had left behind: they were not primarily concerned with the indigenous people they found overseas." The special feature of "colonization," he summarizes, "was thus the creation of permanent and distinctively European communities in other parts of the world," though these communities have included a portion of indigenous population and in many cases also adjunct sections of a non-European labor force.[10]

From the angle of the colonization perspective Israel is considered as a colonizing and a belligerent society. Sociologist Gershon Shafir claims that "At the outset, Zionism was a variety of Eastern European nationalism, that is, an ethnic movement in search of a state. But at the other end of the journey it may be seen more fruitfully as a late instance of European overseas expansion."[11] Likewise sociologist Avishai Ehrlich characterizes Israel as a "permanent war society," and claims that:

> The Israeli–Arab conflict has at its core the efforts of the Zionist settlers to create an exclusivist Jewish society in Palestine and the resistance, first of the native Arab Palestinians, and later of states, Arab and other, to this colonization project. . . . The social, national and state-building processes of Israel are seen by the Arabs as processes of destruction, dispersion and destructuration of Palestinian–Arab society.[12]

The dualist approach: blinders of national sociology

For a long time Israeli sociology simply evaded the specific geopolitical context which encases Israeli society. This is true with regard to Israeli–Arab relations in general, but even more so with regard to Israel–Palestinian relations in particular. This posture, not surprisingly, echoes the longstanding official Israeli refusal to recognize the national existence of the Palestinians, who were labelled in Israeli idiom as "Arab refugees," and the still persisting refusal to recognize their leadership, the Palestinian Liberation Organization. Mainstream sociology simply drew the boundaries of "Israeli society" around the territorial and ethnic Jewish presence, or what sociologist Baruch Kimmerling has named a "Jewish bubble."[13] It assumed a "duality" in which two societies, Israeli and Arab, exist separately side by side. While focusing its attention inside Israeli society, mainstream sociology completely overlooked the geopolitical parameters of this society, most fundamentally the impact on it of the international set of relations.[14]

An explicit acknowledgment – for the sake of rejecting it – of the colonization position was made by sociologist Sammy Smooha in a book on Israeli society from 1978. He depicted the "colonial perspective" as an antithesis to the "nation building perspective" on Israel and than set forth to reject both. For him the authenticity of Jewish nationality and the absence of a supporting colonial power behind it were sufficient arguments to dispel the case of colonization. He maintained that "Zionism is a liberating rather than a colonial movement" though simultaneously conceded that it is "imbued with some traces of the colonial spirit."[15] Sociologist Shlomo Swirski set forth, in an article from 1979, the basic premise of the colonization perspective. He maintained that the Jewish society in pre-state Palestine cannot be studied as a separate unit, but should rather be considered in its total context, which includes the relations between it and the British administration, the Jewish people outside Palestine, and the local Arab society. The categorization of the Arab population as an "external" factor, he maintained, and the characterization of the pre-state situation in terms of "dual society" did not stand historical scrutiny: "Jewish capital linked processes which took place in both groups and this linkage had a far reaching impact upon the form and content of the social institutions which were constructed in this period by both groups."[16]

A programmatic plea for an approach which would pivot around Jewish–Arab relations was made by sociologist Avishai Ehrlich in an article from 1987. Ehrlich, formerly of the Middlesex Polytechnic and currently an instructor at Tel Aviv University, was on the editorial board of the journal *Khamsin*, a European publication by *Matzpen* activists.[17] He observes that, despite the obvious impact that the protracted Israeli–Arab conflict had on the Israeli social formation, it is still a marginal area of research in mainstream Israeli sociology. Surveying the existing literature reveals:

economics and stratification, politics, culture and values, socialization and the family. Even fewer are researches which deal
with consequences of the conflict on Israeli social structure from
a macro-societal point of view using a historical-comparative
method or trying to establish connections between the dynamics
of the conflict and the process of social change in Israel. There
does not exist yet in Israeli sociology, and not due to its underdevelopment, a trend or school which takes the conflict and its
multiple aspects as a starting point for the explanation of the
specificity of Israeli society.[18]

The absence of a systematic and comprehensive treatment of these issues
by Israeli sociologists is regarded by Ehrlich as a result of a conceptual
blinder stemming from the sociologists' political commitment to Jewish
exclusivism and their adhesion to the hegemonic political consensus
which is based on the conception of separatism between Jewish and
Arab societies. Due to this blinder no trend in Israeli sociology had satis-
factorily integrated into a unified perspective the three major components
constituting the Israeli–Arab conflict, namely: Israeli society; Arab society;
and the conflict itself. The major trends of Israeli sociology have simply
managed to focus on Jewish society while conspicuously omitting the
other components which the colonization perspective requires: the Arabs
and the conflict. Alternatively they have addressed the Arabs, and separately the conflict, but without linking either to broad societal issues.

As Ehrlich complains, the Israeli–Arab conflict "is not taken as an
inherent aspect of the Zionist project":

> [I]t is not taken as a major condition which Jewish settlement
> instigated and to which it had to adapt and to respond as it
> evolved. The conflict is not perceived as a continuous formative
> process which shaped the institutional structure and the
> mentality of the Israeli social formation (as well as that of
> the Palestinian Arab society). At best, if at all, the Arabs and the
> conflict are regarded as an external addendum, an appendix
> to an internally self-explanatory structure: an appendix that
> erupts from time to time in a temporary inflammation. The Arabs
> and the conflict are thus viewed as external to the structure and
> process of Israeli society.[19]

An alternative perspective, offsetting the "dualism" of mainstream sociology and exploring the insights of the colonization perspective, emerged
only lately in Israeli academic sociology. In what follows, two versions
of the colonization perspective are examined. One, articulated by sociologist Baruch Kimmerling, focuses on the acquisition of territory and

imposition of control over it, as well as on the ensuing legitimatory edifice, and may thus be classified as a Weberian approach. The other, articulated by sociologist Gershon Shafir, focuses upon the land- and labor-market relations between Arabs and Jews and may thus evidently be classified as a Marxist approach.

As leverage for their theorizing about the Israeli colonization process and its offshoots, both employ the "Frontier Thesis" of the American historian Frederick Jackson Turner. The crux of this thesis is that much of American national and political culture, such as rugged individualism and popular democracy, had resulted from the ongoing encounter of Americans with the Western expanding frontier.[20] The Israeli applications modify the original thesis in a number of ways, and draw different conclusions about the effect of the frontier on this society.

Frontier and territory: a Weberian variation

Sociologist Baruch Kimmerling, of the Hebrew University in Jerusalem, refrains from the usage of the loaded term "settler-colonial" society and prefers instead the more neutrally sounding "immigrant-settler" society. And yet Kimmerling is probably the first established academic Israeli sociologist to address in a book length study the formation of Israeli society in terms of colonization, and to draw a direct comparison between the colonization of America and its impact upon the native Americans, and Israeli colonization and its repercussions for the Palestinians.[21]

Kimmerling proposes to refine Turner's thesis by a comparative and inter-social broadening of it. He accomplishes this by substituting the two fixed variables offered by Turner, frontier and democracy (or individualism), with two dynamic dimensions: a scale of "frontierity," measuring the degree of availability of free land for the settlers (low frontierity equals scarcity of territorial resources which is expressed in the high price of land) and a scale of "polity," which taps the extent of exclusion or inclusion of the indigenous inhabitants in the settlers dominant institutions. In the case of the United States it was in Kimmerling's terms the high degree of frontierity – that is, the abundance of "free" territorial resources – which generated the individualistic effects Turner attributes to it. In the case of Israel, argues Kimmerling, different conditions generated quite the opposite result. The situation which prevailed there was rather of a low frontierity – the entire territory targeted for Jewish settlement was possessed by someone else[22] – and hence only a collective endeavor could manage to acquire it. It is thus *low* frontierity

The *low*-frontierity in the case of Israel caused the emergence of a collectivist (rather than an individualist) dominant structure and ethos:

> From the end of the first decade of the century, the settlement
> activity, one of the central collective tasks, was undertaken by
> the left wing of the Zionist organization, which in exchange
> received the lion's share of the land and capital for the devel-
> opment of settlements which flowed from outside the system.
> As a result the left succeeded in creating power foci which
> enabled it to achieve the predominant position within the
> *Yishuv*'s structure – as the bearer of the power controlling
> the allocation of resources (national capital, immigration certi-
> ficates, etc.), and political decisions and, as a result, recognition
> as the symbolic bearer of the central collective goals.[23]

This is characterized by Kimmerling as "[T]he Turnerian hypothesis in
reverse: an analysis of what happens in a situation where there is no
frontier."[24] What happened was that the acquisition of land, the basic
requirement for colonization, consumed most of the resources of the
settler society, became the axis of the conflict between it and the indigenous population, and shaped the structure of the emerging Israeli society.
Thus, to recapitulate. while *high*-frontierity may explain the American
individualistic ethos, it is precisely *low*-frontierity which explains the
Israeli *collectivist* ethos.

In order to analyse the patterns and stages of the colonization process,
Kimmerling developed a typology of forms of control over territory.
The basic categories are presence (*de facto* residence form), ownership (a
de jure and economic form), and control (a coercive form). Different
combinations of the three yield several control patterns, starting with a
virtual absence of control, and ending with a full tri-patterned control,
which means an end to the frontier situation.[25] Hypothetically the Zionist
settlers could have gained possession over lands in three ways: force,
governmental compulsion, and purchase. Up to 1948, they only had at
their disposal the third option. Since then they resorted to power and
conquest.

The centerpiece of Kimmerling's thesis is that the need to purchase
land in conditions of low frontierity caused the formation of institutions
and the formulation of an ethos which shaped the character of
the emerging society as a whole.[26] Among the many ways in which the
activity of land acquisition was institutionalized, especially noticeable
were the Jewish National Fund (JNF) and the collective agricultural
settlements. The JNF was assigned a specific task. It had to transfer
land (by purchase) from Arab to Jewish ownership, and in order to guarantee that it would not be returned (by sale) to Arab hands, to remove

it out of the free market (where it was acquired originally) and retain it in a national trust (JNF lands are rented – not sold – and only to Jews). Thus the transfer of land from Arab nationals to Jewish nationals meant simultaneously its removal from capitalist to nationalized ownership. In other words, the particular pattern of colonization produced a collective effect.

In the context of the social and national conditions prevailing in Palestine, in order to be effective the purchase of land (*de jure* control) had to be complemented by its settlement (*de facto* control). With the method of private farming nearing bankruptcy the only potential settlers were the workers' groups. To be more precise, by exerting enormous pressure on the national institutions to exclude Arab workers, and thus undermining even further the profitability of private farming, these groups dispensed with their competitors and turned themselves into the only potential settlers. Thus emerged the complementary component to the nationalization of land – a collective pattern of settlement. Hence not only the pattern of acquisition but also the pattern of allocation of land was imperative for the rise of the Israeli collectivist social structure and ethos.

A symbolic episode reported by Kimmerling sheds light on this analytical insight. In 1908 the JNF began work on its first project in Palestine, the planting of a forest in the memory of Theodor Herzl, the founder of the Zionist movement. To do the work Arab laborers were hired from a nearby town. This was perceived by Jewish workers as a violation of the JNF charter and an insult to the memory of Herzl. A group of Jewish workers pressed the JNF to dismiss the Arab workers and hire them in their stead. The pressure bore fruits: the saplings planted by the Arabs were uprooted and replanted by Jewish workers who then completed the planting.[27] The rest is history. Of 272 Jewish settlements in 1944, 193 were on JNF lands; of these 152 were affiliated with the Labor Movement.[28]

In the given circumstances purchase of land and its settlement must have led to the next pattern in the land-control typology, that of coercion, which in its elemental forms meant armed defense. In the remote, small and communal settlements, the roles of laborer and watchman almost fused, and subsequently a national-collectivist defense component was added to the two other collectivist components of the nation-building and state formation processes (acquisition and settlement of land). As early as the 1920s the Zionist left started to redefine its self-image and perceived role in the nation-building process, and to undertake responsibility for the defense problems which resulted from the Jewish–Arab encounter.

With independence and the winning of the 1948 base of Israel was expanded far beyond the land that by Jews up to this point by purchase and settlement. Now Israel could impose sovereignty on all lands within its borders, what Kimmerling calls the "Israelification" of the land. In 1962 about 75 percent of all lands in Israel were owned by a state-formed authority, and close to 18 percent by the JNF. Only about 7 percent of land ownership was private. A basic law prohibits the transfer of ownership over the public land by sale or any other means.[29]

The emergence of social and institutional structures pertaining to the need to acquire, maintain and control territory inhabited by a hostile population also caused the creation of mechanisms of legitimation which had a decisive influence upon the Israeli collective identity. They propelled the pre-eminence of those cultural components which linked the settlers with the land. In this multifaceted phenomenon Jewish socialism, Jewish religion, youth culture, geography, archeology and every other conceivable resource, were mobilized to vindicate the right of the Jewish community over the territory.[30]

To sum up, Kimmerling posits that the most determining factors in shaping Israeli society were the geopolitical conditions of its emergence, that is, Arab–Israeli relations. More specifically, he maintains that the pattern of acquiring land by national funds, maintaining a presence over them by collective settlement, and defending them by a collective proto-military force, shaped the peculiar collectivist hegemony in Israeli society. In his own words:

> The need to acquire land and to establish presence on it had a considerable impact on the shape of the institutions of the *Yishuv* and to a certain extent on the social and political processes in the Jewish collectivity from its formative stages to the present day ... [it] brought about a societal institution comparable to the frontier settlements in North and South America and South Africa. The character of this type of settlement was not determined by economic considerations or social needs, but by its geo-political location. .... [31]

The role of economic consideration and social needs is exactly the issue where the Weberian and Marxian versions of the colonization perspective part ways.

Colony and labor: a neo-Marxist variation

Shafir, like Kimmerling, employs an amended version of Turnerian frontierism. He proposes to enhance the original thesis in two ways. First, he adds to it a comparative perspective. A comparison with, say, South Africa or Australia, easily demonstrates that, even granting Turner's thesis on the effect of the frontier, it does not provide a sufficient explanation for the variety of observed consequences, and hence additional factors must be brought in. Second, Shafir suggests that Turner's original insight is "Indian-ignorant," i.e., it does not perceive the local populace as affecting the process, or the effect of the process on it. In Shafir's view this ignorance omits the most essential feature of a frontier situation, that a frontier "is not a boundary line, but ... a territory or zone of interpretation between two previously distinct societies ...".[32]

Shafir's own point of departure is a critique of two of the leading trends in the Israeli sociological discourse, functionalism and elitism, which he faults on three charges: idealism, teleologism, and Jewish exclusivity. His own alternative account would thus be materialistic, historical and international.

For almost two and a half decades, from the 1950s to the mid-1970s Israeli sociology was dominated by the functionalist school. The hallmark of its nation-building analysis was the depiction of the immigrants of the Second- and Third-*Aliya* (waves of Jewish immigration to Palestine, 1903–1914 and 1919–1923 respectively), which established the Labor Movement, as idealistic devoted pioneers.[33] Shafir rejects this depiction which "never views the agricultural workers ... as having had to labor under economic constraints or in pursuit of economic interests of their own."[34] It is these economic constraints and interests, rather than social values, which are pivotal from his point of view. A critical school which emerged in Israeli sociology in the early 1970s adhered to the tenets of conflict-sociology and depicted the same groups of immigrants as an oligarchy in the making.[35] While lauding the basic premises of this school regarding the role of power and conflict in the nation-building and state formation processes, Shafir is critical towards its narrow rendition of politics as a tool of amassing power by leaders and organizations, rather than as a tool for the articulation of economic interests.[36] In his view:

> Both perspectives [functionalism and conflict] neglect the impact of economic interests and the structure of production as phenomena in their own right. They see the participants in the process of state and nation formation as possessing greater freedom in the pursuit of their intrinsic designs than the study of the economic conditions under which they operated would lead us to believe.[37]

Both functionalist and conflict sociology err in a teleological conception of the Second *Aliya*. While they are correct in regarding this *Aliya* as crucial, they are wrong to consider it retrospectively, starting with its elite position, rather than to consider prospectively the origin of its success. This entails another common error, an obliviousness to the

Palestinians, i.e., a consideration of the Jewish community as an intra-Jewish process, and the employment of a "dual" conception of the separate co-existence of two societies in Palestine/Israel. Shafir's own self-assignment, then, is to provide an interpretation which would account for the nation-building and state formation processes of the Jewish settlers in Palestine as an outcome of material strategies employed by them in conditions of a colonization of an already populated country. To view the Labor elite before it was an elite, and to view the colonization process before there was a separate Jewish society, Shafir suggests a thematic and periodic shift: a focus on the employment strategies of the Jewish workers in the First *Aliya* period, the root of the whole process.

Settler-colonial societies are propelled by the need to acquire land and settle it. This forms the basic prerequisite for their persistence in the new territory they target. The methods employed by them in the pursuit of this goal – their "land allocation" regimes – are configured by the combination of three variables: a "demographic ratio" between the settler and the indigenous population: the economic potentiality of the physical environment; and the measure of the settlers' coercive power.[38] Another inherent need of settler-societies is a large unskilled labor force to make use of the newly acquired land. In the pursuit of this need three labor regimes are possible (pertaining to three types of colonies): 1) the incorporation of native people (mixed colonies); 2) the "import" of enslaved or indentured workers (plantation colonies); or 3) a labor force composed of poor white settlers (pure colonies).

In analysing the evolution of the early Israeli labor regimes, Shafir merges a Weberian status analysis with Marxian class analysis. From Frank Parkin he adopts the concept of "social closure" to characterize the major mechanism of stratification not as free competition (functionalism) or class struggle (Marxism), but rather as the maximization of rewards by "restricting access to resources and opportunities to a limited circle of eligibles."[39] This concept accounts for both class and intra-class conflicts which involve ethno-cultural divisions. Edna Bonachic's concept of a "split labor market" further specifies the circumstances of such "enclosures", tying them to different bargaining powers and strategies exercised in a labor market composed of distinct groups – usually ethnic (and gender) ones – in possession of different resources (skills, trade union experience, etc.).

Shafir employs these theoretical blocks – the land allocation regimes and labor enclosure regimes in a colonial setting – to construct a penetrating argument about the core process of the early Israeli nation-building and state formation. The socio-economic rationale is briefly as follows: In a typical colonization process there are three social sectors which create a triangle of relations – capitalist settlers, non-capitalist settlers (workers), and an indigenous or imported labor force. Since capital gravitates towards the employment of the cheaper labor (the non-settler labor force), the higher paid workers (settler workers) are threatened with displacement. To protect themselves, rather than launching a struggle against the capitalists (who seem to be more formidable opponents) they resolve to exclude the lower paid workers from the market and – and this is a major point in Shafir's argument – they couch their economic struggle in ethnic or national terms. To perform successfully this switch from class to national idiom there must be a prior (extra-economic) closure practice. This prior exclusion is practiced by the capitalists, who construct from the outset a sector of workers excluded from equal access to rights and resources. Hence the settler-workers' own closure is a response ("secondary closure") to an initial split of the labor market caused by capitalist closure. Now – and this is a second major point – to administer their own closure the higher paid workers require the intervention of the state in their favor, to prevail over the capitalists (and also to subsidize the higher labor price so that the produce remains competitive). To secure this they resort to collectivistic ideologies.

The gist of Shafir's historical argument is as follows: the capitalist Jewish settlers of Palestine tended to employ the cheaper local Arab work force. The Jewish workers, determined to secure a quasi-European standard of living, resolved to forestall the employment of their competitors by excluding them from the labor market through the use of the nationalist argument. Thus they ushered in the struggle for the "conquest of labor" or for "Hebrew labor."[40] One tactic to which the capitalist settlers resorted in response was the importation of cheap Jewish labor from an Arab country – Yemen. This proved to work only partially.[41] Finally, the workers developed another strategy, the "conquest of land," i.e., cooperative settlement on national lands, which would become the backbone of Israeli nation-building and state formation.[42]

More specifically, in the period of the three decades he analyses, from the 1880s to the 1910s, Shafir discerns six essential land and labor regimes which were experimented with by the Jewish settlers until the final winning formula was designed.

First stage: This began with the arrival of the First *Aliya* immigrants (of the Jewish East European *Hovevei Zion* movement) in 1882. They established the first Jewish agricultural settlements, the *Moshavot* (Rishon Lezion, Zichron Yaacov, etc.), and created a smallholder farmer stratum. Yet in a very short time the farms floundered economically and were put under the auspices of the French–Jewish Baron Rothschild.

Second stage: Under the Baron, the *Moshavot* were turned into typical colonial plantation farms relying on the employment of a large, unskilled, seasonal Arab labor force.

Third stage: By 1900 the Baron's system became non-viable financially. The *Moshavot* were once again put under new sponsorship, this time of the Jewish Colonization Association.[43] A ruthless economic rationalization policy almost entirely displaced the Jewish labor force.

Fourth stage: This stage began in 1903 with the onset of the Second *Aliya* – an entry into the labor market of a wave of propertyless Jews. This short phase is characterized by their attempt to compete with Palestinian Arab workers by lowering their own standard of living.

Fifth stage: This stage started in 1905 with the launching by Second *Aliya* workers of the struggle to "conquer the labor," – that is, to maintain a high(er) level of wages by the exclusion of the Arab workers from the Jewish (*Moshavot*) labor market. One response by the planters was the attempt to "import" Jewish Yemenite laborers who were expected to work for "Arab wages."

Sixth stage: This stage began in 1909 and determined the future fate of the workers' movement. In this period a new concept emerged which integrated solutions for the land and labor issues of the Zionist colonization: the idea of cooperative settlements. The materialization of this idea would create the peculiar blend of the farmer and of the worker – of the landowner without labor power and of a labor force without land – into the "laboring settlement." This stage forged the unique Israeli format of nation-building and state formation: A collectivist national identity centered on the *Ashkenazi* (Jews of European origin) Labor Movement, excluding Arabs and including *Mizrachi* Jews (of Oriental origin) in a secondary status.

Thus between them the first two *Aliyot* tilted the Jewish community between two alternative courses of colonialist nationalism, capitalist and collectivist:

> [T]he first stages in the lives of the First and Second *Aliyot* were based on embracing, respectively, Arab agricultural methods and Arab standard of living. These attempts were abandoned, in both cases, within months. While the inadequacy of the First *Aliya's* original design enhanced the transition toward a capitalist plantation system that was aimed at the international market, the frustration of the Second Aliya's initial strategy intensified the nationalist dimension of its aims.[44]

The idea behind the "conquest of land" campaign was simple: if the workers cannot find suitable rewarding employment on the Jewish farms, they should become their own employers – collective autonomous farmers. To execute this program they had to acquire land, which under the prevailing conditions meant to purchase it. But the financial resources necessary were beyond their capacity. To their aid came the World Zionist Movement, which at the same time realized that private holdings could not attract large-scale Jewish immigration and provide it with a means of livelihood. Thus the two parties discovered a mutual interest and struck a deal: the Zionist Movement would provide the land, the workers would settle it and work it. The market forces were thus circumvented. Hence, the most significant features of Socialist Zionism evolved as a direct response to territorial and demographic constraints. These constraints stemmed from the presence in Palestine of a native population which possessed the land and from the lack of coercive power on the Jewish side. The separatist character of the Jewish national development, the leading role of the Labor Movement in the nation-building process, and the inclusion of *Mizrachim* in the national domain but in an inferior position – all are neatly explicable from the colonization perspective.

To sum up, Shafir maintains that due to the weakness of the settlement institutions (no imperial state power was at their disposal) and because of the relatively developed social conditions in Palestine (land had to be purchased for money, workers were sedentary peasants, etc.) to turn Palestine into a colony of the pure type (i.e., based on Jewish labor) Jewish settlement institutions could *not* rely on the workings of the market. They had to circumvent the market and to set up what Shafir terms "greenhouse conditions,"[45] that is to say, an environment doubly shielded from the competitiveness of the market: first, land, once purchased, was removed from the market and nationalized, and second, workers were allotted land collectively, thus relieved of the need to sell their labor in the market. The Zionist colonization process was carried out by two supporters: the national arm bought the land and the socialist arm tilled it.

A prime example of the far-reaching implications of this analysis is provided by Shafir's account of the origins and significance of the *kibbutz*, that most Israeli of all social institutions. He tears down two staples of mainstream analysis (and Labor's myth): that the *kibbutz* represents the Second *Aliya*'s institutional innovativeness and that it epitomizes Zionist socialist ideals. He maintains that the cooperative settlement type was not envisaged by the workers' political parties (and was even opposed by some of their leaders) and that it was rather "an unintended means and consequence of Jewish colonization."[46] Once the Zionist movement realized that Palestine could not attract enough private investment

71

or capitalist settlers it resolved to use as a vehicle for colonization the agricultural workers. These workers, more than carrying out some utopian socialist plan, have materialized the "pure settlement" model of colonization, i.e., colonization not based on an indigenous labor force. By this interpretation the socialist component of the *kibbutz* ideology was just a retrospective legitimation of what originally was a "pure colony" strategy. While the first *kibbutz* experiments started around 1905, the "inchoate cooperativism was reinterpreted as ideologically grounded collectivism" only retrospectively.[47] The *kibbutz* had become the trail blazer of colonization due to its success in bypassing the threat of labor market competition by Palestinian Arab workers and due to its function in the realization of the national possession of the land. It provided its members with a (relatively) high standard of living, with a level of cultural homogeneity, with the ability to rationalize the use of economic resources, and with enhanced dedication to the national cause. In short, the success of the collective settlement in Israel seems to Shafir not to attest to its attractiveness as an alternative social model, but rather to its function as a spearhead of the project of national colonization.

Another significant example of the far-reaching implications of the analysis is the case of the Yemenite workers. Shafir maintains that the status of the small Yemenite immigrant community in the *Yishuv* labor market divulged the future of ethnicity and class relations in Israel in embryo. In his account the Yemenites were brought to Israel not due to the Zionist commitment of the *Yishuv*, but in an attempt by the employers (planters) to force down the level of wages paid to Jewish workers to a level much closer to the wages paid to local Arab workers. This is the ultimate explanation for the inferior position of Yemenites, and later, by extension, of other *Mizrachi* immigration in the Israeli social structure, and it has very little to do with cultural differences or any alleged "primordial" differences (which in mainstream sociology were considered as the reasons for the "ethnic gap"). Shafir supports this contention with the argument that the most intense social conflict in the period he studied was waged between the only two groups sharing a common culture and language: employers and workers, both groups of Yiddish-speaking East European Jews. Cultural distinctions (or similarities) acquire their true significance only in the context of social relations, which for him means first and foremost labor market relations in the context of colonization. A major factor in defining the separate identity of the Yemenites and other *Mizrachi* groups, was not the specificity of their culture (traditional or otherwise), but rather the secondary status allotted to them in the labor market and the discriminatory allocation practices of the Zionist movement. Hence a split labor market has created a split national movement.

In sum, the colonization perspective in Shafir's version proposes a novel explanation for the cardinal features of Israeli society:

> [T]he Palestinian–Israeli conflict . . . gave shape precisely to those aspects of their society which Israelis pride themselves on being most typically Israeli: the protracted hegemony of the Labor Movement, the close association of soldier and farmer, the cooperative forms of social and economic organization – but also the secondary status of Middle Eastern and North African Jews.[48]

Political underpinnings: the territorial partition option

What is the immanent political agenda of the colonization perspective? Let us start again with *Matzpen*, this time to draw a line of distinction rather than an arrow of continuation. The sociologists of the 1980s who promulgate the colonization analysis do not share *Matzpen's* views on the desirable (or attainable) political solution to the Israeli–Arab conflict.

Matzpen projected a two-step revolutionary program: first, the elimination of Zionist ideology and institutions, or "de-Zionization" of Israel, and second, the formation of a regional transnational proletarian front against repressive and exploitative imperialist and capitalist regimes, and for the construction of a socialist Middle East.[49] While the colonization perspective certainly shatters basic Zionist convictions, it does not lead of necessity to the solution proposed by *Matzpen*.

Recognition of the colonial origins of Israel does not entail a wholesale de-legitimation of the state of Israel. What it does entail, however, is a moral recognition of wrong done to the Palestinians and a political recognition of their right to self-determination. The bottom line of such reasoning cannot be anything but a support for a compromise between the two competing claims over the territory of Israel/Palestine.

Shafir, for one, recognizes the justified desire of the Jews for a "political normalcy" which in the contemporary world means a territorial nation-state of their own. He even goes further and observes that in the pursuit of nationhood and sovereignty in the given circumstances not much could have been carried out significantly differently. Nevertheless, he argues, "we should also recognize that the epic of Zionism, in addition to the necessary and the heroic, was not devoid of a tragic dimension: the creation of Israel through the encroachment on, and, subsequently, displacement of the majority of the Arab residents of Palestine."[50] He calls for the abdication of the "ethics of conviction" – adherence to historical or transhistorical goals – on the part of both Israelis and Palestinians, and a resort to an "ethics of responsibility," that is consideration of the consequences of politics for living human beings. He thus supports a partition solution.[51]

Though Shafir's major work addresses the origins of the Israeli–Arab conflict, it ends with reflection about the nature of later Israeli neo-colonialist policies. In the post-1967 era Shafir identifies three stages: the military stage exercised by the Labor Movement while still in power (up to 1977), in which moderate colonization was justified by security considerations; the religious stage exercised by the *Gush Emunim* movement as the spearhead of the wider national-religious bloc, in which a radical Messianic justification was evoked; and an economic stage, exercised by later *Likud* governments, in which an attempt has been made to attract lower middle class Israelis to the occupied territories by economic incentives.

He maintains that Israeli colonization might have been, and still may be, exercised in two ways: "maximalist territorial exclusivism, the logical conclusion of which is the removal of the Palestinian Arabs; and the territorial partition of Eretz Israel/Palestine, leading to separate Israeli and Palestinian national development."[52] The first option represents the political agenda of the Israeli right, the second the agenda of the Israeli left. The historical significance of the hegemony of the Labor Movement was, from this perspective, that it had been inherently disposed to a territorial partition: "[P]recisely because it was militant in its demand for *exclusive* Jewish employment, the Labor Movement could eventually bear to be more *modest* in its demand for territorial expansion."[53]

Shafir considers this moderation an asset to be exploited today in order to reach an end to the century's long struggle over the land of Palestine/Israel. Yet his analysis leads him to the conclusion that the occupation of the territories in 1967 severed the nexus between territory and demography, and hence between economic and nationalist consider-ations, which in the past propelled the Labor Movement to choose a strategy of preferring a more exclusive and autonomous Jewish presence on a smaller territorial space. In the post-1967 situation, Israeli state and military power facilitates the redefinition of the colonization project in maximalist territorial terms. He warns that this approach can only lead to a moral and political catastrophe and concludes his book with a plea "[to] re-learn in altered circumstances, the hard lessons drawn by the Labor Movement from the early phase of the Israeli–Palestinian conflict: the necessity to combine militancy on the fundamental issues with realism and moderation."[54]

Kimmerling's is a very similar position. He discerns that more than two decades of Israeli control over territories which are included in the polity militarily, symbolically and emotionally, and even economically, but not legally and politically, have created a deep transformation in the Israeli political culture. This is a transition from a civil definition of the collectivity, focused on the *state* of Israel, to a primordial definition of the collectivity, focused upon *Eretz* Israel, i.e., the *land* of Israel. In the civil definition the boundaries of the collectivity are defined by universal citizenship; in the primordial by ascriptive nationality.

The political implications are, needless to say, far-reaching. In the citizenship concept individuals are linked to the collectivity by a set of legal rules, and the collectivity is supposed to be the sum total of the individuals, or to represent their common will. In the primordial concept, individuals are bound to the collectivity in a diffuse manner and are considered as organs of some larger spiritual whole (the nation, the community, etc.). The citizenship concept is congruent with a parliamentarian and liberal regime, while the primordial notion is congruent with a *Halachic* (religious Jewish law) particularistic and authoritarian regime.[55]

Analysing the political options facing Israel with regard to the Palestinian territories, Kimmerling warns that an annexation of the territories or even the continuance of the enforced status quo is bound to bring about a mass expulsion of their population. Israel is not willing to integrate the Palestinians into its political system, neither is it able to keep them for long under its dominion as non-citizens. Thus any solution other than the withdrawal of Israel from the territories is liable to bring an attempt at mass expulsion of the Palestinian population there.[56] The transformations that have already taken place and the ones he anticipates lead Kimmerling to raise a somber concern: "Can the Jewish nation-state, founded in 1948 as a civil and democratic state based on Western states' and societies' premises, still be said to exist?"[57]

Conclusion: a new sociological agenda

The colonization agenda in Israeli sociology was anticipated in the 1960s by dissenting intelligentsia on the margins of the left. It re-emerged as a mature sociological perspective in the wake of the 1967 War due to the high visibility which the processes of colonization and settlement gained since the reopening of the 1948 borders.

The colonization agenda surfaced in the early 1980s, and is still not fully legitimized in the sociological discourse. Shafir writes from abroad (though he began his work in Tel Aviv University), Kimmerling writes quite cautiously, Swirski writes from outside academia, and Ehrlich's academic career is strained. The dominant trend is still either to ignore the perspective or to condemn it. Yet the more salient the effect of the Israeli–Arab conflict becomes on Israeli society itself, the more the Palestinian perspective on Israel is being attended to inside Israel, and the more the political schism in Israel sharpens, the more the colonization perspective must penetrate the sociological discourse.

The major paradigmatic claim of this agenda is that Israel is a settler-colonial type society, and hence it is comparable to societies which emerged in analogous circumstances, such as the American colonies or South Africa. Both exemplars studied in this article employ Frederick Turner's frontier thesis, but significantly alter it. Kimmerling's Weberian concern is with patterns of territorial control and legitimation issues; in the case of Shafir, a Marxian concern with the labor market in a multi-ethnic situation is added to the emphasis on the colonial, rather than the frontier, aspects.

The major analytical insight advanced by the colonization perspective is that the colonization process – the acquisition of land and the gaining of employment in an already settled territory – and the ensuing national conflict had a formative influence upon the structure and ethos of Israeli society and accounts for its major peculiarities. In particular, both analyses discussed here concluded that the special role and status of the Labor Movement in the nation-building and state formation processes of Israel is attributable more to the logic of colonization than to any intrinsic social or idealogical characteristic of the movement.

Specifically, Kimmerling argues that the pattern of land acquisition by national funds and of land allocation to workers' cooperatives, deter-mined the hegemony of the collectivist movement. Likewise, Shafir argues that the segmentation of the labor market by the exclusion of Arab competition determined the separate Jewish identity of the evolving nation, and the unequal inclusion of the Yemenite workers in the labor market determined the relative status of distinct ethnic groups in the emerging nation.

The attribution of formative social processes to the logic of coloniza-tion is the strong denominator of both the Weberian and Marxian versions of the colonization perspective we discussed here. Yet a significant discrepancy between the two ought to be noted. Shafir's Marxist interpretation casts a doubt on the presence of distinct "nations" (Jewish/Israeli and Arab/Palestinian) prior to their encounter in a common territorial arena (Palestine/Israel). In his view the socio-economic categories – such as settler-employers or settler–workers – take precedence over the presumed national categories. The latter are thus considered as effects of the process of splitting the labor market and the ensuing logic presented above. National solidarities based on common culture or language are presented by him basically as ploys in the struggle between segments in the labor market. It is not entirely clear however how far can this suggestion be sustained, and whether Shafir himself makes a radical historiosophical argument about the meaning of Jewish and Israeli national identities as such, or whether he just offers an explanation for some contingent characteristics of them. Clearly this latter alternative is what Kimmerling suggests. His Weberian frame does not problematize the presence of political-cultural units such as nations, and does not have to attribute their presence to factors other than political and cultural. He thus takes it for granted that the colonial encounter took place between two distinct national units. This difference and its implications are not fully articulated by the protagonists discussed above.

Though the ideological underpinnings of versions of the colonization perspective may vary, we saw that the unequivocal tendency of the sociologists is to recognize the *post factum* rights of both the Israeli and the Palestinian nations to self-determination, and thus to support a partition of the contested land. While they candidly perceive the colonial history of Israel, they do acknowledge the right of the state of Israel to exist. They thus accept the boundaries that prevailed in the period of 1948–1967 as legitimate, yet consider the "second round" of colonization issued by the re-opening of the frontier in 1967, not only as mutilating Palestinian rights and obstructing peaceful resolution to the conflict, but also as endangering the very fabric of democratic political culture in Israeli society itself.

While the crux of Turner's thesis is the argument about the democratic influence of the frontier on American society, it turns out in the case of Israel that the frontier threatens to exert the antithetical effect, namely, the erosion of democratic structures. As an indication of this, Shafir cites the existence of a dual legal system for Jewish settlers and Palestinians and informal, but nonetheless pervasive, disparity in the enforcement of law and order on Arabs and Jews. This raises a worry that today unites Israelis and Israeli sociologists from the left to center: "Can the Israeli personality, institutions and forms of domination created in the West Bank, be prevented from filtering through into the mainstream of Israeli society, and subverting the spirit, even if not necessarily the formal expressions, of its democracy?"[58] The question mark may by now be redundant.

Various aspects of the colonization perspective may be questioned and various arguments of it still require further theoretical and historical articulation. The full study of the Israeli polity, economy, social structure and culture from this perspective still awaits its authors. Yet the contribution of the perspective cannot be overestimated. This perspective brought back something which all other scholarly perspectives in Israeli academia lost sight of – geopolitical and political-economic considerations. It justly underscores the indubitable centrality of colonizing a frontier in the nation-building and state formation processes; a "gestalt" switch which instantaneously exposes a different image of Israeli society from those portrayed by other sociological perspectives. Developments which functionalists understood as effects of underlying pioneering values, and conflict sociologists understood as sheer power contestation inside the Jewish elite, are recast from this perspective and made to be considered decisively overdetermined by the historical context: that of the colonization project. As Ehrlich succinctly put it:

> [A]ll major aspects of Israeli society have been structured by the conflict: the dependency on unilateral transfers in the economy, the political system and its divisions, the special nature of the state, relations among Jewish ethnic groups – occidental versus oriental – the evolution of fundamentalist messianic trends in Jewish religion . . . [59]

If so the colonization perspective suggested by Swirski, Ehrlich, Kimmerling and Shafir calls for further scholarly effort. Swirski offers a conceptual critique, Ehrlich a research program, Shafir a detailed study of a short period, Kimmerling a scheme of analysis, and the present writer a paradigmatic explication. The colonization perspective in Israeli sociology is an agenda just beginning to be realized.

NOTES

1 Maxime Rodinson, *Israel: a Colonial–Settler State?* NY: Monad. 1973, p. 77.
2 Ibrahim Abu-Lughod and BahaAbu-Laban, eds., *Settler Regimes in Africa and the Arab World*. Wilmette: The Medina UP International, 1974, page numbers not marked.
3 The most erudite study of the effects of colonization of the Palestinian population is offered by the Palestinian sociologist, Elia Zureik, *The Palestinians in Israel: a Study in Internal Colonialism*. London: Routledge and Kegan Paul, 1987. For Palestinian perspectives, see also G.T. Abed, ed., *The Palestinian Economy*. London: Routledge, 1988, Ibrahim Abu-Lughod, ed., *The Sociology of the Palestinians*. NY: St Martin's Press, 1980, and Edward Said, *The Question of Palestine*. NY: Vintage Books, 1979. For other Israeli colonization perspectives, see Uri Davis, A. Mack and N. Yuval-Davis, eds., *Israel and the Palestinians*. London: Ithaca Press, 1975 and Uri Davis, *Israel; an Apartheid State*. London: Zed Press, 1987.
4 A statement made by Israel Zangwill, English Jewish author and Zionist activist.
5 Tsvi Raanan, *Gush Emunim*. Tel Aviv: Sifriyat Poalim, 1980.
6 See David Schnall, *Radical Dissent in Contemporary Israeli Politics*. NY: Praeger, 1979.
7 Schnall, *Radical Dissent*, pp. 89–105; Nira Yuval-Davis, *Matzpen: the Israeli Socialist Organization*. Jerusalem: Papers in Sociology, The Hebrew University of Jerusalem and the Eliezer Kaplan School, 1977; Ari Bober, ed., *The Other Israel: the Radical Case against Zionism*. NY: Macmillan, 1972.
8 Haim Hanegbi, cited in Schnall, *Radical Dissent*, p. 95.
9 Gershon Shafir, *Land, Labor and the Origins of the Israeli–Palestinian Conflict, 1882–1914*. CUP, 1989, p. xi.
10 D.K. Fieldhouse, *Colonialism 1870–1945. An Introduction*. NY: St Martin's Press, 1981, pp. 4–5.

11 Shafir, *Land, Labor and Origins*, p. 8.
12 Avishai Ehrlich, "Israel: Conflict, War and Social Change." In C. Creighton and M. Shaw, eds., *The Sociology of War and Peace*. NY: Sheridan, 1987, pp. 121–122.
13 Baruch Kimmerling, "Boundaries and frontiers of the Israeli control system" in Kimmerling, ed., *The Israeli State and Society: Boundaries and Frontiers*. Albany: State University of New York Press, 1989, p. 270. Recently Kimmerling demonstrated how "paradigmatic decisions," especially those concerning the definition of the boundaries of Israeli society and its periodization, have shaped different trends in Israeli sociology. See Kimmerling, "Sociology, Ideology and Nation Building: the Palestinians and their Meaning in Israeli Sociology." *American Sociological Review* 57, 1992. The colonization perspective is situated in the context of Israeli sociological discourse in Uri Ram, "Civic Discourse in Israeli Sociological Thought." *International Journal of Politics, Culture and Society* 3, 1989.
14 See Dan Horowitz and Moshe Lissak, *The Origins of the Israeli Polity*. University of Chicago Press, 1978, especially chapter 2: "The Origins of Dual Society."
15 Sammy Smooha, *Israel: Pluralism and Conflict*. Berkeley: University of California Press, 1978, pp. 37–38.
16 Shlomo Swirski, "Comments on the Historical Sociology of the Yishuv Period." *Notebooks for Research and Critique* 2, 1979.
17 The journal was founded in Paris in 1975. For a collection of articles from it, see Roth Rothchild, ed., *Forbidden Agenda: Intolerance and Defiance in the Middle East*. London: Al Saqi Books, 1984.
18 A. Ehrlich, "Israel: Conflict, War and Social Change," p. 129. In addition there is little research on Arabs by Arabs in Israel. There is only a single full-time Arab faculty member in a sociological department in Israeli universities, Majad Al-Haj in Haifa University. These points were also noted by S. Smooha and O. Cibulski, *Social Research on Arabs in Israel, 1948–1976: A Bibliography*. University of Haifa, 1978.
19 Ehrlich, "Israel: Conflict, War and Social Change," p. 131.
20 First published in 1893. See Frederick Jackson Turner, "The Significance of the Frontier in American History." In G. R. Taylor, ed., *The Turner Thesis*. Boston: Heath, 1956. For the debates on Turner, see also Ray Allen Billington, *The American Frontier Thesis: Attack and Defence*. American Historical Association Pamphlet no. 101, 1971; Richard Hofstadter; *The Progressive Historians*. NY: Knopf, 1968; R. Hofstadter and S.M. Lipset, eds., *Turner and the Sociology of the Frontier*. NY: Basic Books, 1968; David W. Noble, *The End of American History*. Minneapolis: University of Minnesota Press, 1978..
21 Baruch Kimmerling, *Zionism and Territory: the Socio-Territorial Dimension of Zionist Politics*. Berkeley: Institute of International Studies, University of California, Research Series no. 51, 1983.
22 To state this argument is not to accept the "invisibility" of native people beyond the moving frontiers of the U.S.A. See below.
23 Kimmerling, *Zionism and Territory*, p. 18. The *Yishuv* refers to the pre-1948 Jewish community in Palestine.
24 Kimmerling, *Zionism and Territory*, p. 30.
25 Kimmerling, *Zionism and Territory*, pp. 19–25.
26 Cf. Kimmerling, *Zionism and Territory*, pp. 19–25.
27 Kimmerling, *Zionism and Territory*, p. 81.
28 Kimmerling, *Zionism and Territory*, tables 2.2 and 2.3.

29 Kimmerling, *Zionism and Territory*, p. 143.
30 Kimmerling, *Zionism and Territory*, pp. 183–211.
31 Kimmerling, *Zionism and Territory*, p. 8.
32 Howard Lamar and Leonard Thompson, eds., *The Frontier in History: North America and South Africa Compared*. New Haven: Yale UP, 1981, cited in Gershon Shafir, "Changing Nationalism and Israel's 'Open Frontier' on the West Bank." *Theory and Society* 13, 6, 1984, p. 805.
33 See S.N. Eisenstadt, *Israeli Society*. London: Weidenfeld and Nicolson, 1967.
34 Shafir, *Land, Labor, and Origins*, p. 3.
35 See Yonathan Shapiro, *The Formative Years of the Israeli Labor Party: The Organization of Power 1918–1930*. London: Sage, 1976.
36 Shafir, *Land, Labor, and Origins*, p. 3.
37 Shafir, *Land, Labor, and Origins*, p. 4.
38 Shafir draws here on George Frederickson, *White Supremacy: A Comparative Study of American and South African History*, Oxford University Press, 1981, and "Colonialism and Racism: The United States and South Africa in Comparative Perspective." In Frederickson, *The Arrogance of Race*. Middletown: Wesleyan University Press, 1988.
39 F. Parkin, *Marxism and Class Theory*. NY: Columbia University Press, 1979, pp. 44–48, cited in Shafir, *Land, Labour and Origins*, p. 3. And see Edna Bonacich, "The Past, Present and Future of Split Labor Market Analysis." Research in *Race and Ethnic Relations* 1, 1979.
40 Shafir, *Land, Labor, and Origins*, pp. 45–90.
41 Shafir, *Land, Labor, and Origins*, pp. 91–122.
42 Shafir, *Land, Labor, and Origins*, pp. 123–186.
43 JCA – a Paris-based body founded by the Baron Maurice de Hirsch to settle East European Jews in various countries.
44 Shafir, *Land, Labor, and Origins*, p. 188.
45 Shafir, *Land, Labor, and Origins*, p. 19.
46 Shafir, *Land, Labor, and Origins*, p. 146.
47 Shafir, *Land, Labor, and Origins*, p. 184.
48 Shafir, *Land, Labor, and Origins*, p. xii.
49 Schnall, *Radical Dissent*, pp. 89-105; Yuval-Davis, *Matzpen*; Bober, ed., *The Other Israel*, Haim Hanegbi, Moshe Machover and Akiva Orr, "The Class Nature of Israeli Society." *New Left Review* 65, 1971.
50 Shafir, *Land, Labor, and Origins*, p. xii
51 Shafir, *Land, Labor, and Origins*, pp. xii–xiv.
52 Shafir, *Land, Labor, and Origins*, p. xii.
53 Shafir, *Land, Labor, and Origins*, p. 214.
54 Shafir, *Land, Labor, and Origins*, p. 220.
55 Baruch Kimmerling, "Between the Primordial and the Civil Definition of the Collective Identity: Eretz Israel or The of Israel?" In E. Cohen, M. Lissak and U. Almagor, eds., *Comparative Social Dynamics: Essays in Honour of S.N. Eisenstadt*. Boulder: Westview Press, 1985.
56 Kimmerling, "Boundaries and Frontiers," p. 277.
57 Kimmerling, "Boundaries and Frontiers," p. 265.
58 Shafir, "Changing Nationalism," p. 824.
59 Ehrlich, "Israel: Conflict, War and Social Change," p. 140.

5

ZIONISM AND COLONIALISM

A comparative approach

Gershon Shafir

Critical Israeli academicians tend to belong to the Zionist left, an affiliation which affects considerably their historical perspective. They tend to see the year 1967 as a watershed between a pre-1967 moral, contained and basically united Israel and a post-1967 occupying, expansionist and divided Jewish state. Hence, they are willing to point to colonialist features in the Israeli conduct in the occupied territories and trace all the present social and political predicaments to the making of Greater Israel in 1967.

This dichotomy is the departure point of Gershon Shafir's analysis of early Zionism as a colonialist phenomenon. Very much in the vein of other articles in this collection, he looks for the past in order to understand the present and he interprets the past out of the present. Thus, Israeli colonialism post-1967 has its roots in pre-1948 Zionism. What Shafir claims here is that while the mode of Jewish settlement in Palestine changed throughout the years – adapting itself to the political and economic realities of the day – the character or nature of this settlement was and remained colonialist. This is another example of how Israeli historians come closer to the Palestinian narrative on the one hand, and how the historiographical research touches upon the raw nerves of Israeli society, on the other. Any reference to Zionism as colonialism is tantamount in the Israeli political discourse to treason and self-hatred.

* * *

Studies telling the story of Israeli state-building usually have two plots. One tells the story of the Zionist immigrants who constructed their institutions according to their ideals and ideologies, mostly socialist ideas imported from the Pale of Settlement, occasionally in disagreement with other non-socialist immigrants who had different blueprints for the state-to-be. The other tells the story of the interaction between Palestinian-Arabs, who were unalterably opposed to the creation of a Jewish state in Palestine, and the Jewish immigrants, who were intent on protecting their emerging commonwealth. These two plots, however, rarely intersect.

These separate plots should be twined since Israeli state- and society-building were not solely an internal Jewish affair. In fact, the distinct characteristics of the Jewish–Palestinian conflict influenced and decisively shaped the character of the Jewish state-to-be and continue to do so in myriad ways. Some of the unique features and institutions of Israeli society, the overlong period of the Labor Movement's domination, the focal place of the Histadrut, even the kibbutz, are distinct corollaries of the Israeli–Palestinian conflict.

Further, I argue that socialist ideals and other imported blueprints played a lesser role in creating the Israeli state than the circumstances in which the Jewish immigrants found themselves in Palestine. The most crucial circumstances were found in the land and the labor markets where, as will be shown, through a prolonged period of trial and error the immigrants made hard choices that determined the character of the *yishuv* and the future Israeli state and society.

Historians, political scientists, and sociologists of Israeli society holding the perspective that disassociates state-building and national conflict and, simultaneously, privileges consciousness at the expense of existence, tended to emphasize those characteristics of the Zionist settlement in Palestine that appear to distinguish it from colonial encounters. The separate development of Jewish and Palestinian societies was widely used as proof that the former could not have exploited the latter, while the universalist socialist ideologies of the most authoritative group among the young immigrants is presented as an impediment to any potential or lingering colonial characteristic in Zionist settlement.

In response to the Likud's large-scale settlement plans in the West Bank, a new critical perspective, according to which Israel had come to resemble Northern Ireland, Algeria in the 1950s and 1960s, and/or the white supremacist regime of South Africa, appeared in the public discourse.[1] The authors of this perspective routinely drew a sharp line of demarcation between pre-1948 Zionist settlement in the coastal zone and inland valleys of Palestine and the post-1977 colonization of the West Bank and the Gaza Strip. The latter was seen as a radical departure, even better, as the corruption of Zionism; the colonial Athena seemed to have sprung full-grown from the head of her non-colonial father, Zeus. But, in spite of the many differences between the two settlement drives, they also exhibited uncanny resemblances, enough indeed to make one wing of the Labor Movement proclaim continuity, and the rest of the movement wince and shuffle uneasily while complaining that its distinctiveness was being stolen. These responses, however, can also indicate that the attempt to recommence Israeli history in 1967 has been too sweeping: its proponents ignored the similarities between the two phases of Israeli colonization and, consequently, failed to seize it as a propitious context for a revision of the dominant interpretation of the past and its long debilitating legacies.

Where others see historical bastards, I find a streak of historical ancestry. I offer, therefore, a theoretical and conceptual perspective that highlights the continuous centrality of colonization in Zionism and at the same time gives appropriate weight to the changes that have taken place, under new circumstances, within the framework of settlement. European colonialism, after all, did not create just one model of overseas society, and it seems to me that we can understand the transformation of Israeli society since 1967 most fruitfully as a transition from one method of European colonization to another one.

This argument will be presented in three parts. In Section I, I will provide a typology of European overseas colonies, present the dominant Israeli colonization method, and examine it in relation to the type of European colony it most closely resembled. In the second section, I will examine the ways in which the Zionist movement adapted the European model to the conditions prevailing in Palestine for its purposes in two separate periods (1908–1920 and 1948–1967). Finally, in Section III, I will appraise the character of Israeli society in the 1970s and 1980s in light of the transition from the older to a newer model of colonization. Special attention will be paid to the impact this transition had on enhancing those characteristics Zionism shared with other colonization drives while stripping away its more idiosyncratic characteristics and, finally, I will reflect briefly on the reasons for Israeli decolonization in the West Bank and the Gaza Strip.

I Methods of colonization

D.K. Fieldhouse and George Fredrickson offer a four-way typology of colonies: the *occupation* and *mixed* colonies of Spain, the *plantation* model of Portugal, and the *pure settlement colony* of England. The *occupation colony* evolved to ensure military control of strategic locations without, however, undertaking to transform their economic order. Examples of this model abound in South East Asia and coastal Africa. The other three models were based on settlement by Europeans on a significant scale that led, on its part, to the introduction of new forms of land and labor appropriation.

In the *plantation colony*, in lack of "a docile indigenous labor force," the settlers acquired land *directly* and imported an indentured or unfree labor force to work their monocultural plantations. The best known example of this method of settlement was the South in the United States. *Mixed colonies* used coercive methods to elicit labor from the native population, but potential antagonism between the two groups was dampened through miscegenation. The mountainous regions of Latin America supply us with the obvious examples of mixed colonies. The *pure settlement colony* established "an economy based on white labor" which, together with the forcible removal or the destruction of the native population, allowed the settlers "to regain the sense of cultural and ethnic homogeneity that is identified with a European concept of nationality." Among colonial societies, the pure, or homogenous, settlement colony had the largest settler populations who, in fact, sought to become the majority in their chosen land. These colonies have also reproduced consequently, in varying degrees, the complex economies and social structures of the metropolitan societies. Australia and the North in the United States exemplify this type.[2] I need to complement Fredrickson's typology with another category: the *ethnic plantation colony* that is based on European control of land and the employment of local labor. The planters, in spite of their preference for local labor, also sought, inconsistently and ultimately unsuccessfully, massive European immigration. Algeria was an example of this hybrid type.

The dilemma facing the early Zionist immigrants in Palestine was whether to aim for an ethnic plantation or a pure settlement colony. It was the pure, or homogenous, type of colonization that won out, but it was realized less fully in Palestine than in most other colonial frontiers.

Before examining the specific character of the Zionist method of pure settlement, I will list the differences between Palestine and other frontiers of settlement, and between Zionism and other movements of colonization. I argue that while these differences gave Zionist colonization a particular cast, they have not eliminated its fundamental similarity with other pure settlement colonies.

(a) Colonization was undertaken by great powers, whereas Jews had no colonial metropole of their own and not until the onset of the British Mandate was Jewish immigration encouraged, and even then only for a limited period.

(b) While most land intended for colonization was chosen according to its economic potential, Zionists selected their target area ideologically.

(c) In the most densely populated pure settlement colonies, the native populations were nomadic, but only a small section of the Palestinian population was tribal and nomadic; and it was in the process of expanding its own area of residence and cultivation from the hilly regions to the coastal zone and the inland valleys when Zionist settlement commenced.

(d) Land was "free" in most European settlement colonies, whereas land was not easily acquired by Zionist settler-immigrants. In 1903, Ussishkin asked:

> as the ways of the world go, how does one acquire landed property? By one of the following three methods: by force – that is, by conquest in war, or in other words, by robbing land of its owner; by forceful acquisition, that is, by expropriation via governmental authority; and by purchase with the owner's consent.

He ruled out the first method as being "totally ungodly," and added "we are too weak for it." He also thought it unlikely that Jewish settlers would receive a charter to expropriate land owned by either Arab peasants or landowners. "In sum, the only method to acquire Eretz Israel, at any time and under whatever political conditions, is purchase with money."[3] The need to pay money for land created, in Kimmerling's terminology, "low frontierity" in Palestine; but, at least until the 1948/9 War of Independence, also led to a less violent process of primitive territorial accumulation than was typical of other colonies.[4]

(e) In many of the European colonies, menial labor was reserved for slaves or indentured workers while Jewish planters had to hire seasonal unskilled wage labor.

(f) The share of immigrants without independent means and refugees was larger among Jewish immigrants to Palestine than in most other movements of colonization.

The question, of course, is how did the Zionist leaders and rank and file manage to accomplish as much as they did under such adverse conditions, and within a relatively short timespan? The answer seems to be that they required a variety of external resources – both great power support and massive financial subsidies – as well as a great deal of flexibility to adjust themselves (and their imported ideologies) to the inhospitable circumstances of settlement in Palestine and to be willing to limit their territorial aspirations. Many of the unique characteristics of Zionist colonization were not rooted in the purportedly non-colonial character of Zionism but were intended to compensate the settler-immigrants for the adverse conditions prevailing in the land and labor markets of Palestine precisely in order to ensure the successful colonization of Palestine and the creation there of a pure, or homogeneous Jewish, settlement. Significantly, until recently none of the Zionist solutions disposed of the problems they were meant to resolve.

II The Labor-Zionist method of colonization

(a) The formative period (1908–1920)

It is clear from Fredrickson's typology that all European settlement colonies were not alike. In most the settler-immigrants sought direct control of land but differed in the choice of their respective labor forces. The major division lies between societies like South Africa and the South in the United States that relied heavily on cheap labor and erected color bars to separate and elevate all whites over blacks and create a plantation colony, and societies like Australia and the North in the United States that preferred to exclude non-white workers altogether and create a pure settlement type colony. The question faced by Jewish immigrants in Palestine was whether they wanted to exclude Palestinians from their society or make them into a lower economic caste.

No preconceived notions but trial and error led the Zionist institutions to develop their method of colonization. In all, I distinguish six distinct stages of Jewish activity in the land and labor markets in the thirty or so years that preceded the First World War. These six stages can further be divided into two clusters of three: the first three correspond to the period of the First Aliya (1882–1903, of about 20,000–30,000 immigrants); the latter three to the period of the Second Aliya (1904–1914, of about 35,000–40,000 immigrants). At the time, about 425,000 Palestinians lived in Palestine.

With the arrival of the earliest Zionist immigrants in 1882, the first attempt was made to create a *pure settlement colony*. This was to be based on a small holding farmer stratum that made its living mostly by copying the dry farming field-crop agriculture typical of Palestine and the Middle East. But the new immigrants soon discovered the obstacle that was to burden all rural Jewish immigration to Palestine: the income earned by dry farming could not meet the European standard of living to which even relatively poor Eastern European Jews were accustomed. The impossibility of attaining a standard of living acceptable to Jewish immigrants was tantamount to their displacement from Palestine. They begged for assistance from a member of the Rothschild family and, within less than a year after their arrival in Palestine, a tutelary administration began reorganizing most of the First Aliya's colonies.

In this second stage between 1882 and 1900, the *yishuv* in Palestine was transformed into an *ethnic plantation colony*. Baron Edmund de Rothschild reorganized the failing settlements of the First Aliya with the help of French experts who acquired their experience in Northern Africa and sought to copy the model of French agricultural colonization in Algeria and Tunisia. This was the typical pattern of monocultural colonial plantation agriculture, though on a much smaller scale, in this case mostly of vineyards, that relied on employment of a large, unskilled, and seasonal Palestinian Arab labor force mixed with a small Jewish labor force. The extensive employment of Arab workers, dictated by their lower wages, limited the potential for Jewish demographic growth in Palestine and pointed out the contradiction between market-based colonization and Jewish national aspirations.

When scholars assert that Zionism differed radically from classical European colonialism, their argument is that Zionists rejected the rigid ethnic or racial hierarchy typical of the plantation and ethnic plantation colony, though, I contend, not of all colonial models.[5] A similarly mistaken evaluation was made by the PLO, which, seeking in the late 1960s to emulate the success of the FLN in ejecting the French settlers from Algeria by ridding Palestine of its Jewish settlers, overlooked the fact that the ethnic plantation colony began to decline in its importance in Palestine already in the first decade of this century.

The third phase began with a new crisis: in 1900, Rothschild himself had enough of pouring money into the plantation system and abruptly terminated his involvement. The plantations were ruthlessly rationalized, the wages paid to the Jewish workers reduced and, not being able to subsist in the mode to which they were accustomed, many left the country and were replaced by Arab workers. Simultaneously, there was an even bigger crisis – the process of land accumulation was interrupted by Rothschild's departure, while the World Zionist Organization (WZO), established by Herzl and German and Austrian Jews in 1897, remained opposed to land purchases before receiving political guarantees for Jewish colonization. As a result of the interruption of Jewish land purchases new immigrants could not fulfil the expectation they shared with most immigrants to overseas European colonies – to become small landholders. During the Second Aliya, the focus of state formation was transferred to the labor market.

Consequently, a new wave of experimentation began. In a brief and frustrated fourth phase, propertyless immigrant Jews entered the labor market again, attempting in an idealist fashion to lower their standard of living to the level of Palestinian Arab workers. The first stages in the lives of both First and Second Aliyot, if so, were based on imitation, i.e., embracing respectively Arab agricultural methods and standards of living. These attempts were abandoned, in both cases, within months.

While the inadequacy of the First Aliya's original design enhanced the transition toward a capitalist plantation system and an ethnic plantation type of society, the frustration of the Second Aliya's initial strategy intensified the aim of pure settlement, which alone seemed capable of providing employment to masses of Jewish immigrants.

The *critical* step, in Israeli state-building and nation formation, took place with inauguration of the fifth stage. In 1905, a group of Jewish workers abandoned the aim of downward wage equalization and substituted for it a struggle for the "conquest of labor" to be undertaken by their *Hapoel Hatzair* party. Its slogan was "a necessary condition for the realization of Zionism is the conquest of all jobs in Palestine by Jews." This attempt to monopolize for Jewish workers, at first all manual labor, subsequently at least all skilled jobs, indicated a desire for the exclusion of Palestinian workers from the new society in the making.

What were the results of this strategy? The organized Jewish workers had only very limited success in convincing Jewish plantation owners that, since without workers, Jews were unlikely to ever attain a Jewish majority in Palestine, they should be favored over the cheaper and more pliant Palestinian workers. The Jewish agricultural workers of the Second Aliya did not conquer the labor market, but their struggle left an indelible mark on the course of Israeli state construction.

The struggle for the "conquest of labor" in fact transformed the Jewish workers into militant nationalists who sought to establish a homogenous Jewish society in which there would be no exploitation of Palestinians, nor would there be competition with Palestinians, because there would be no Palestinians. Starting in 1905, the aim of the Jewish laborers was nationalist exclusivism. Since the organized workers were too weak to homogenize the settler society, they needed outside help and found "their Rothschild" in the World Zionist Organization. Whereas Rothschild copied the French models of colonization, the WZO's various bodies were influenced by German internal colonization practices.

In 1909, with the beginning of the WZO's colonization work in Palestine, a sixth phase opened in the saga of Jewish settlement. Otto Warburg and Arthur Ruppin, the directors of the World Zionist Organization's Palestine Land Development Company, sought to emulate in Palestine the "internal colonization" model developed by the Prussian government in order to create a German majority in its eastern, Polish, marches. The territories were annexed to Prussia as a consequence of the division of Poland in the eighteenth century. In the second half of the nineteenth century, the Prussian government and German nationalists, including the young Max Weber, were alarmed by what they saw as the "denationalization" of these districts as a result of the crisis of German grain production and the consequent flight of German agricultural workers to the cities of Germany and to the United States and their replacement by Polish workers. Bismarck set up a colonization commission that purchased the estates of bankrupt Prussian Junkers, subdivided them into small holdings, and sold them in favorable conditions to German farmers. It was this state-initiated, non-market based colonization, motivated by nationalist considerations, which found its way into Zionism.

Already in 1901, the WZO set up its Jewish National Fund to nationalize land in Palestine. Land purchased by the JNF from Palestinian and other landowners became the perpetual and collective property of the Jewish people: it could only be sublet and, then, only to Jews. In 1908, the WZO adopted the plan of the German Jewish sociologist Franz Oppenheimer that combined three aims: internal colonization, land nationalization, and cooperation, and resolved to establish in Palestine "settlement-cooperatives." This plan inspired the PLDC's support for the organizational experiments that ultimately led to the kibbutz. Since most kibbutzim were built on nationalized land provided by the JNF, no Palestinians could be employed in them. Competition was done away with, along with exploitation, and a homogenous Jewish economic sector was created. The kibbutz became the cornerstone of a vertically and horizontally integrated network of Jewish owned and Jewish-operated economic enterprises and social institutions that were centralized in 1920 under the institutional umbrella of the Histadrut – the state-in-the-making.

The Second Aliya's revolution against the First Aliya did not originate from opposition to colonialism as such but out of frustration with the inability of the ethnic plantation colony to provide sufficient employment for Jewish workers, i.e., from opposition to the particular form of their predecessors' colonization. The Second Aliya's own method of settlement, and subsequently the dominant Zionist method, was but another type of European overseas colonization – the "pure settlement colony" also found in Australia, Northern U.S., and elsewhere. Its threefold aim was control of land, employment that ensured an European standard of living, and massive immigration.

Whereas the First Aliya established a society based on Jewish supremacy, the Second Aliya's method of colonization was separation from Palestinians. This form of pure settlement rested on two exclusivist pillars: on the WZO's Jewish National Fund and on the Jewish Labor Movements trade union – the Histadrut. The aims of the JNF and the Histadrut were the removal of land and labor from the market, respectively, thus closing them off to Palestinian Arabs.

The exclusivism of the Labor Movement, however, remained partial. Since the organized workers wished for a homogenous Jewish society, their perspective substituted the priority of demography over territory, which remained the hallmark of other strands within Zionism. Though initially Zionists, one and all, were territorial maximalists, in 1937, and again in 1948, a growing segment within the Labor Movement expressed its willingness to accept the partition of Palestine between a Jewish and a Palestinian or preferably a Transjordanian state. Partition was acceded to precisely because such a strategy was capable of reducing the obstacles posed by Palestinian demographic preponderance.[6] In order to increase the ratio of Jewish population to unit of land, the leaders of the Labor Movement recognized that the territory taken possession of by Jews would have to be limited.

Labor leaders, like other Zionists, emphasized Jewish historical rights in Palestine, but they also stated that Jewish immigrants had "to earn" these rights in the present – by gaining control of and developing the land. The Labor Movement, in short, learned to deal with the disappointment caused by the restricted Jewish demographic potential in Palestine – limited, initially by the preference of most Eastern European Jews to migrate to other destinations, and later by the tragic losses of the Holocaust – by imposing realistic self-limitations.

Instead of a "working class," the new self-designation of the Second Aliya's organized workers became the "*Labor Movement*" or, alternatively, the *laboring settlement* (*hityashvut ovedet*). Israel Kolatt, one of the prominent historians of the Second Aliya, was intrigued by the fact that "one of the distinguishing characteristics of the Eretz Israeli labor movement is its being a settlement movement,"[7] but it is doubtful whether one can call a labor movement a settlement movement at the same time. Rather, in the second decade of this century, the former was transformed into the latter and the laborer became for all practical purposes a settler.

On the explicit ideological plane, a new synthesis evolved: the employment of socialist practices with the aim of furthering Jewish colonialism! The *Poalei Zion Party* rediscovered in 1912 the writings of an unlikely ideologue: Nachman Syrkin, a territorialist, who rejoined the WZO. Syrkin shared with Borochov the quest for a synthesis of working class nationalism with a universal historical project. This he found in the cooperative movement, and his theoretical formulation signaled the beginnings of the appropriation of the kibbutz for socialist ideology (an ideological evolution fully accomplished only by the Third Aliya).[8]

(b) Consolidation (1948–1967)

This self-limiting solution, derived from Zionist weakness and the experience of debilitating labor market competition, and expressed through a non-ideological posture of "constructivism," was carried to its logical culmination after the War of Independence. In the demographic sphere, Israel saw the largest wave of Jewish immigration, coinciding with the outflux of the majority of Palestinian Arabs. In the territorial sphere, a situation of *de facto* partition was established, and for the first and only time a clear Jewish majority was secured in part of Palestine. All in all, it seemed that the aim of Jewish pure settlement had been accomplished.

The post-1948 period has recently been characterized by S.N. Eisenstadt, Dan Horowitz, and Moshe Lissak as the era of the "routinization of the Zionist revolution," or of the "institutionalization of the pioneering values," which diluted their purportedly universalist content.[9] I argue that independent Israelis experienced neither a growing inability to regulate conflicts nor the "overburdening" of the promise of universalism and consequent danger of "ungovernability."[10]

On the contrary, the period between the War of Independence and the Six Day War witnessed attempts to replace the partially exclusivist institutional structures of Zionism with the formal universalism of the Israeli state. But the continued existence within Israeli society and politics of institutions that evolved with exclusivist intent during the *yishuv* did not bode well for such attempts.

Whereas the military organizations, educational network, and labor exchanges of the Labor Movement were abolished and integrated into the state structure, the colonizing bodies of Zionism and its Labor wing continued their independent existence and carried on their exclusionary tasks. The Jewish Agency, the WZO, and its JNF did so *vis-à-vis* foreign and international law, the Histadrut *vis-à-vis* Israeli-Arabs. Hevrat Haovdim (the Histadrut's holding company of its enterprises) remained, by and large, the private sector of the Labor Movement; though its voluntary component, the kibbutzim, grew weaker, as its compulsory element, Kuppat Holim, grew stronger. Arab inhabitants received the vote, but until 1965 were separated from the Jewish sector of Israeli society by being placed under a military government. Even afterwards, their participation in the labor market remained controlled by the Histadrut's labor exchanges. Many of the *mizrachi* immigrants (i.e., from North Africa and the Middle East) were also relegated to the margins of the economy in development towns and slum neighborhoods, though, not being restricted by exclusionary institutions, partially emerged from under the umbrella of the Labor Movement in the political sphere. Overall, important inroads were made into the exclusivist institutional network, but the universal principles of citizenship were subverted both by the concentration of resources by the state, and by administering tasks, undertaken in other societies by state institutions, by enduring colonizing bodies, such as the Jewish National Fund and the Jewish Agency.

III Radicalization and decolonization

The 1967 War opened the door to the radicalization of Zionist colonization. By radicalization I mean the shedding of the particular characteristics that resulted from the weakness of Zionism and were associated with the domination of the movement by its Labor wing. After the Six Day War, Israel saw dramatic shifts in all three spheres – land, labor, and demography – wherein the peculiarities of Zionist colonization were found. Concomitantly, potent primordial forms of legitimacy gained in strength.

Post-1967 Israeli governments – from both the Labor Party and the Likud – for all practical purposes abolished the *de facto* "partition" effected by the War of Independence. The settlement strategy was extended to regulate security relations with surrounding Arab countries. The first *settlement* drive, the Alon Plan, which unofficially guided Israeli settlement policy until 1977, centered on the sparsely populated rift of the Jordan River and aimed at the incorporation of maximum territory and minimum population. Though Alon's Plan was still conceived within the framework of the Labor Movement's well-established demographic reasoning, ominously the Labor Party also agreed to incorporate unauthorized settlement in Gush Etzion and Hebron into its settlement map (it was from here that the future leaders of *Gush Emunim* came forth), and embarked on a "salami policy" of territorial expansion. The Alon Plan was extended in 1973 by the far more ambitious Galili Plan. Gradually, there was transition from Alon's *military frontier* to a combination of a *messianic frontier* and a *suburban frontier*.[11]

The purchase of land was replaced to a large extent by the other two "ungodly" means mentioned by Ussishkin in 1903: conquest in war and, subsequently, expropriation by the assumption of the right to public land. With the prevalence of these methods the earlier differences between the ungodly, i.e., explicitly colonial, powers and Israel had all but disappeared.

The traditional layout of settlements under Labor domination was also dramatically altered when the Likud came to power. Settlement in the pre-independence era and during the years 1967–1977 sought to create a compact and contiguous pattern to ensure mutual protection, the exclusion of Palestinian population from the intended Jewish area, and as a way of marking future boundaries. The 1981 Drobless Plan sought to scatter Jewish settlements among Arab towns and villages in order to ensure that no homogenous Palestinian inhabited area, the potential core of a Palestinian state, would remain. In other words, the new settlement pattern intended to undo, or rather ignored, Palestinian demography as a limiting factor.

In independent Israel, the Histadrut did away with the threat of Palestinian Arab competition in the labor market and brought about the gradual substitution of the exclusionary strategy of "Hebrew labor" with a scheme, that for all practical purposes, amounted to a caste system.[12] After 1967, this caste system was dramatically expanded when the

Histadrut acceded to the reintroduction of over one hundred thousand non-citizen Palestinians to the labor market. The classical economic separatism of the Labor Movement was no more. As a result of the economic stagnation ushered in by the Yom Kippur War and the high concentration of unemployment in development towns, there was a rebirth of the exclusionary labor market goals, advocated, among other measures of radical exclusivism, by Meir Kahane.[13] Kahane's aims, however, were not accompanied by a willingness to accept territorial self-limitation; Kahane and his followers had recognized no need for self-limitation.

Though new approaches emerged in response to the new circumstances created by the Six Day War, they could not be implemented immediately. First, the habits of the mind associated with the demographic calculus of the Labor Movement's colonization, the *de facto* partition created in its wake and willy-nilly adopted by other parties, had to be challenged. After all, a substantial part of the National Religious party, the cradle of *Gush Emunim* in 1974, supported the British Partition Plan of 1937 and the United Nations 1948 Partition Plan. In the years before the Six Day War, Herut, the Likud's predecessor, showed "little inclination" to challenge the territorial status quo and the military concept on which it was based.[14] But the conquest of 1967 allowed new groups to find their day on the colonial frontier. As a potential settlement movement, *Gush Emunim* settlers were supported by non-religious groups and individuals, for example, the activists of the Movement for Greater Israel and the Ein-Vered circle of Labor kibbutz members, precisely because they followed the traditional course of settlement that carried the seeds of legitimation in a society where pioneering was a core value and a major source of prestige and influence. Even so, *Gush Emunim*'s settlement drive began only in 1973 and the Likud's own plan to settle one hundred thousand Jews in the West Bank was adopted only by the second Begin government. And even the Likud did not annex the West Bank but preferred to employ the trusted method of land control – colonization – associated with its ideological nemesis, the Labor Movement.

The disassociation of settlement from demographic and labor market concerns was not the primary cause of the decline of Zionist universalism which was – and being a colonial project, had to be – narrow in scope. It did undermine, however, the traditional Labor Zionist self-limitation, its "constructivist" approach, that was based on an appreciation of Palestinian demographic presence. The post-1967 era in Israel was one of cultural transformation, of a far-reaching, though ultimately inconclusive, legitimational shift. This shift resulted from the efforts of the supporters of territorial expansion to find a popularly acceptable replacement for the demographic calculus that was deeply ingrained in most Israelis. The hallmark of the new ideology of colonization was a transition not from rational universalism to exclusivism, but from economically justified to primordially legitimated forms of exclusivity. The rise of the organic Likud–National Religious party coalition, and the retreat from democratic values and in certain areas from modernity itself, were part of this "cultural revolutions."[15] The latter oscillated in the 1980s between the *fully exclusivist* pure, or homogenous, settlement colony perspective of the various advocates of "transfer," above all Rabbi Kahane, that remained a relatively small but growing segment of the Israeli population, and the more powerful wing of the Likud and *Gush Emunim* that adopted a *supremacist* approach, typical of the hierarchical structure and its attendant rigid primordial (and in many cases racial) justification of the *plantation colony*.

Though religious and secular ideological factors were relied upon to justify *Gush Emunim*'s and Drobless's colonization drives, these were not sufficiently potent to alter the Palestinian–Jewish demographic ratio on the West Bank (with the exception of east Jerusalem, where the "pull" of the comforts of urban life in proximity to a large Jewish population center contributed to the "push" of the ideological factors). The vast majority of the Palestinians in the West Bank neither ran away nor were driven out in consequence of the Six Day War. Birth rates in the West Bank, like in other underdeveloped regions, remain high. Israelis, like Protestants in Quebec and in Ireland, feel threatened by the "revanche des berceaux." The casting aside of territorial self-limitation by Israel after 1977 has made Israel face in an unprecedented fashion, in spite of massive Jewish immigration from the USSR and its successor states, the problem of Palestinian demography.[16] Though advocating and implementing changes in land and labor relations, these remained constrained by the demographic calculus of the Labor Movement which aspires for a homogenous Jewish society. It is still in this respect, and in these terms, that the future of Israeli society is likely to be determined.

Peacemaking between Israelis and the PLO signals a new, late wave in the decolonization of overseas European societies. Colonization, or the founding of "new societies," as Fieldhouse and Fredrickson pointed out, was not made of one cloth. The new relationship between Israel, under the Labor government, and the PLO (as well as its parallels in South Africa and in Northern Ireland) amounts to decolonization in an instance of partially successfully established "pure settlement colony." Whereas settler-immigrants and their descendants on Europe's other "frontiers of settlement" mixed, in different measures, with the native populations, marginalized and destroyed them or were expelled, Palestinians still continue to pose a basic challenge to the resolve and the identity of Jews in Israel. Though Jewish immigration was not as extensive as the waves that went to the United States and other destinations, the colonists in Israel had no colonial metropole and became natives. (Likewise, the ANC and the South African Communist party recognized white settlement in South Africa as "colonialism of a special type.") The partial realization of the settlers' goals, who sank deep, or renewed, historical roots and established societies with distinct cultural, ethnic, and religious markers, means that the decolonization required for peacemaking in Israel, as had been recognized by the PLO in November 1988, will also be partial and will be played out in the West Bank, Gaza, and East Jerusalem.

Another aspect of this process, though one tied to it indirectly, concerns those Palestinians who have become, and in many ways act as, Israeli citizens. The dilemma of the relations between Israel's Jewish majority and the Arab minority is whether the latter will be recognized as a national minority with corresponding rights or be given the option of being integrated as individuals while, simultaneously, the institutions of Jewish "pure settlement" colonization that were retained by the State of Israel will be done away with. Some of these, such as the Histadrut, are already being downsized and losing the employment function evolved to assist Jews. Either approach would add a measure of internal decolonization to the process of decolonizing the West Bank and Gaza Strip.

My intention in this chapter was to do away with the customary frameworks that analysed Israeli society, dividing up its history between two airtightly sealed and separated periods: the pre- and post-1967 eras. To that end, I propose to use a single theoretical framework, based on the colonial dimensions of Israeli society and now on its ongoing, though still very partial, decolonization.

NOTES

Source An earlier version of this paper has been presented under the title: "Anomalies of Zionist Colonization and Their Normalization," in the Conference on "Trends in the Transformation of Israeli Society," at the Hebrew University, Jerusalem, in December 21–22, 1989.

1 See, for example, Yehoshofat Harkabi, *Israel's Fateful Decisions* (London: I.B. Tauris & Co., 1988); Emmanuel Sivan, "On the Eve of the Intifada's Third Year," *Haaretz*, December 8, 1989 (Hebrew).
2 D.K. Fieldhouse, *The Colonial Empires from the Eighteenth Century* (NY: Weidenfeld & Nicolson, 1966), pp. 11–22, 372; George Fredrickson, "Colonialism and Racism: The United States and South Africa in Comparative Perspective," in *The Arrogance of Race* (Middletown: Wesleyan University Press, 1988), pp. 218–21.
3 Menahem Ussishkin, "Our Program," in *The Ussishkin Book* (Jerusalem, Havaad Lehotzaat Hasefer, 1964), pp. 105–106 (Hebrew).
4 Baruch Kimmerling, *Zionism and Territory* (Berkeley: The Institute of International Studies, 1983), pp. 106, 145–46.
5 See a recent example of this thinking in Bernard Avishai, "Zionist Colonialism: Myth and Dilemma," in *A New Israel: Democracy in Crisis, 1973–1988* (NY: Ticknor and Fields, 1990).

6 One reason for the appeal of the Peel Commission's partition plan to Ben Gurion was that it proposed the transfer of about one hundred thousand Palestinians from among those residing in the projected Jewish state into the Palestinian state-to-be.

7 Israel Kolatt, "Ideology and the Impact of Realities Upon the Jewish Labour Movement in Palestine, 1905–1919." (Ph.D. dissertation, The Hebrew University of Jerusalem, 1964), p. 260 (Hebrew).

8 Nachman Syrkin, "*Achva*," *Haachdut*, 4, 33, June 13, 1913, and "The Jewish Question and the Jewish Socialist State," in Nachman Syrkin, *Writings*, Vol. 1 (Tel Aviv, 1939), pp. 53–59 (Hebrew).

9 See S.N. Eisenstadt, *The Transformation of Israeli Society* (London: Weidenfeld and Nicolson, 1985), pp. 351–52.

10 Dan Horowitz and Moshe Lissak, *Trouble in Utopia: The Overburdened Polity of Israel* (Albany: State University of New York Press, 1989), p. 131.

11 See Gershon Shafir, "Changing Nationalism and Israel's 'Open Frontier' on the West Bank," *Theory and Society*, 13, 6 (1984), pp. 803–27.

12 See Michael Shalev, "Jewish Organized Labor and the Palestinians: A Study of State/Society Relations in Israel," in Baruch Kimmerling, ed., *The Israeli State: Boundaries and Frontiers* (Albany: State University of New York Press, 1989).

13 See Gershon Shafir and Yoav Peled, "Thorns in Your Eyes: The Socioeconomic Basis of the Kahane Vote," in Asher Arian and Michal Shamir, eds., *The Elections in Israel – 1984* (Tel-Aviv: Ramot, 1986); and Yoav Peled, "Labor Market Segmentation and Ethnic Conflict: The Social Basis of Right Wing Politics in Israel," in Asher Arian and Michal Shamir, eds., *The Elections in Israel – 1988* (Boulder, Co.: Westview, 1990).

14 Dan Horowitz, *Israel's Concept of Defensible Borders*, Jerusalem Papers on Peace Problems, No. 16, 1975, p. 5.

15 See Ian Lustick, *For the Land and the Lord: Jewish Fundamentalism in Israel* (NY: Council on Foreign Relations Press, 1988); Baruch Kimmerling, "Between the Primordial and the Civil Definitions of the Collective Identity: Eretz Israel or the State of Israel?" in Erik Cohen, *et al.*, eds., *Comparative Social Dynamics* (Boulder, Co.: Westview, 1985), pp. 262–83; Erik Cohen, "The Changing Legitimations of the State of Israel," *Studies in Contemporary Jewry*, 5, 1989, pp. 148–65; and Harkabi, *Israel's Fateful Decisions*.

16 A good illustration of the preoccupation with demography is Dov Friedlander and Calvin Goldscheier, "Israel's Population: The Challenge of Pluralism," *Population Bulletin*, 39, 2 (1984), pp. 36–37.

Part III

THE SOCIAL HISTORY OF THE CONFLICT

6

RAILWAY WORKERS AND RELATIONAL HISTORY

Arabs and Jews in British-ruled Palestine

Zachary Lockman

In his concluding remarks Beshara Doumani pointed to the need for writing history "from below" as part of an effort to reintroduce the Palestinians back into Palestine's history. This historiographical approach is bringing back into history other "forgotten" communities: workers and peasants, women and children, on both sides of the conflict. This trend is also manifested clearly in this article by Zachary Lockman. The dominant agenda hitherto in the historiography of the conflict was elitist and purely political, as well as pro-Zionist and modernizationist. The reconstruction of the lives of workers, farmers, town dwellers as well as women and children can help balance and widen the scope of the historical research.

As Lockman shows in this analysis of the relationship between Jewish and Arab railway workers in the 1920s, we also learn something new about the mechanism of a national conflict. The political centers, in this case particularly the Zionist trade unions, were actively undermining any chance for bi-national formations and fought strongly, despite their socialist ideology, against any manifestations of class solidarity. Several other works have looked at the attempts during the mandatory period to cement class or group solidarity in the face of segregationist agendas of the political centers. If this approach continues there is a hope for an alternative view, from below, on Palestine's history providing some hope for a better future.

* * *

During the period of Ottoman rule over the Arab East, from 1516 until the end of the First World War, the term Palestine (*Filastin*) denoted a geographic region, part of what the Arabs called *al-Sham* (historic Syria), rather than a specific Ottoman province or administrative district. By contrast, from 1920 to 1948, Palestine existed as a distinct and unified political (and to a considerable extent economic) entity with well-defined boundaries. Ruled by Britain under a so-called mandate granted by the League of Nations, Palestine in that period encompassed an Arab majority and a Jewish minority.

By now a fairly substantial historical and sociological literature on Palestine during the mandate period has accumulated. Broadly speaking, several features can be said to characterize this literature.[1] For one, it gives disproportionate attention to elites and to diplomatic, political, and military history, to the disadvantage of other social groups and of the social, economic, and cultural dimensions of the development of the Arab and Jewish communities in Palestine. There is also, for a variety of reasons, a great quantitative (and to some extent qualitative) disparity between the published research on the policies and activities of the Zionist movement, its component parties and institutions in Palestine, and more broadly the development of the Yishuv, the pre-state Jewish community in Palestine, on the one hand, and the literature on the political, social, economic and cultural history of Palestine's Arab community on the other. I would also argue that many, if not most, of the historians, sociologists, and others who have contributed to this literature have worked from within (and implicitly accepted the premises of) either Zionist or Arab/Palestinian nationalist historical narratives. As a result, much of the published research, while often valuable and important in its own right, nonetheless fails to adopt a sufficiently critical stance toward the categories of historical analysis which it deploys.

These characteristics are to varying degrees related to the historiographical issue on which I would like to focus here, an issue central to the way in which the modern history of Palestine has been framed but which has only recently begun to be subjected to a serious critique. The paradigm of historical interpretation informing much of the literature has been premised on the implicit or explicit representation of the Arab and Jewish communities in Palestine as primordial, self-contained, and largely monolithic entities. The Yishuv, and to a lesser extent the Palestinian Arab community, are usually depicted as coherent and unconflicted objects which developed along entirely distinct paths in accordance with dynamics and as the result of factors largely unique and internal to each. The paradigm thus assumes that the Arab and Jewish communities in Palestine interacted only in very limited ways and only *en bloc* and certainly did not exert a formative influence on one another, as whole communities or through the interrelations of their component parts. By extension, communal identities are regarded as natural, rather than as constructed within a larger field of relations and forces that differentially affected (or even constituted) subgroups among both Arabs and Jews.

We may call this the dual society model because its posits the existence of two essentially separate societies with distinct and disconnected historical trajectories in mandatory Palestine. This model manifests itself most clearly, perhaps, in the work of leading Israeli scholars, who start from the premise that the history of the Yishuv (and later of Israel) can be adequately understood in terms of the interaction of the Yishuv's own internal social, political, economic, and cultural dynamics with those of world Jewish history. The influence of the largely Arab environment within which the Zionist project and the Yishuv developed and the matrix of Arab–Jewish relations and interactions in Palestine is defined a priori not as constitutive but as marginal and is largely excluded from consideration.

A classic example is S. N. Eisenstadt's 1967 study, *Israeli Society*, which promises to provide "a systematic analysis of the development of the Jewish community in Palestine from its beginning in the late 1880s up to the present day."[2] As Talal Asad (among others) has pointed out, Palestinian Arabs play virtually no role whatsoever in this analysis. The Yishuv seems to have developed in a vacuum, its evolution propelled by the articulation and triumph of values conducive to successful institution building.[3] Eisenstadt's students, Dan Horowitz and Moshe Lissak, embrace the dual society model even more explicitly in their influential *Origins of the Israeli Polity: Palestine under the Mandate*:

> In Mandatory Palestine two separate and parallel economic and stratification systems of different levels of modernization emerged which maintained only limited mutual relations. Our contention is that this phenomenon arose due to the influence of ideological and political pressures exerted within each of the two national communities.[4]

The dual society model also informs most work on the mandate period by Palestinian and other Arab scholars, though it is usually not explicitly theorized. No Arab historian or sociologist suggests that the Zionist project did not, in the long run, have a tremendous impact on Palestinian Arab society. But that society is usually represented as a pre-existing, pre-formed entity which was then threatened, encroached upon and, in 1947–49, largely destroyed by an aggressively expanding Yishuv. Interaction between Arabs and Jews is largely limited to the sphere of political and military conflict, rather than seen as having had a significant impact on the development of Palestinian Arab society in other spheres as well.[5] Many of the foreign scholars who have published research on the modern history of Palestine have also shared this focus on one or the other of the two communities, which are depicted as essentially separate and self-contained entities.

The dual society paradigm does of course allow for a single significant mode of interaction between Arabs and Jews in Palestine: conflict, violent or otherwise. This is one reason for the disproportionate attention in the literature to the political, diplomatic, and military dimensions of the relations between Arabs and Jews. However, the criticism which Avishai Ehrlich recently put forward with regard to Israeli sociologists can also be extended to many historians of modern Palestine. Arab-Jewish conflict, Ehrlich argues

> is not integrated analytically into the theoretical framework of the sociological discourse. . . . [It] is not perceived as a continuous formative process which shaped the institutional structure and the mentality of the Israeli social formation (as well as that of the Palestinian Arab society). At best, if at all, the Arabs and conflict are regard as an external addendum, an appendix to an internally self-explanatory structure: an appendix which erupts from time to time in a temporary inflammation.[6]

The scarcity of historians with a command of both Arabic and Hebrew has no doubt contributed to the prevalence and persistence of the dual society model, as have the insularity, self-absorption, and reluctance to challenge the prevailing consensus characteristic of (but of course not unique to) societies many of whose members perceive themselves as still engaged in a life-or-death struggle to secure their collective existence against grave threats and realize their national(ist) project. But the dominance of this paradigm also reflects (and reinforces) the way in which most scholars have implicitly or explicitly conceptualized their object of study. The result has been an historiography which has hardly questioned the representation of the two communities as self-evidently coherent entities largely uninfluenced by one another. This approach has rendered their mutually constitutive impact virtually invisible, tended to downplay intracommunal divisions and focused attention on episodes of violent conflict, implicitly assumed to be the sole normal or even possible form of interaction. It has also helped divert attention away from exploration of the processes whereby communal identities and nationalist discourses in Palestine were constructed (and contested), including the ways in which boundaries between (and within) communities were drawn and reproduced, and practices of separation, exclusion, and conflict articulated.[7]

The emergence of a relational paradigm

In recent years the utility of this paradigm has been increasingly challenged by Israeli, Palestinian, and foreign scholars who have consciously sought to problematize and transcend, or at least to render more complex, both Zionist and Palestinian nationalist historical narratives and categories. This project of critique and reconceptualization has involved a move beyond the narrowly political to explore the social, economic, and cultural histories of each community. More important, it has also reflected a new commitment to relational history, rooted in an understanding that the histories of Arabs and Jews in modern (and especially mandatory) Palestine can only be grasped by studying the ways in which both these communities were to a significant extent constituted and shaped within a complex matrix of economic, political, social, and cultural interactions. This project has also sought to explore how each was shaped by the larger processes by which both were affected, for example the specific form of capitalist development which Palestine underwent from the nineteenth century onward, markets for labor and land, Ottoman patterns of law and administration, and British colonial social and economic policies.

This turn to relational history was greatly facilitated by the new forms of interaction between Israeli and Palestinian societies that developed in the aftermath of Israel's 1967 conquest of the remainder of mandatory Palestine and the extension of Israel's rule to encompass fully one-half of the Palestinian people. The subsequent decades of occupation, conflict, and crisis have made it increasingly clear that at the core of the Arab–Israeli conflict lies the Zionist–Palestinian conflict. This has led Israeli Jewish intellectuals in particular to seek a new, demythologized understanding of their past as a way of making sense of the political, social, and cultural changes their own society has undergone as a result of this historic encounter. For their part, Palestinian intellectuals and scholars in the occupied West Bank and Gaza and elsewhere have, since 1967, acquired a much deeper and more nuanced understanding of Israeli politics, society, and culture, which has opened the way to a better understanding of Zionist and Israeli history. Foreign scholars have also contributed innovative new work in recent years.[8]

One risk in adopting a relational approach, of course, is that the specificity of the histories of Arabs and Jews in Palestine may be lost sight of. It was this – or perhaps more precisely, a concern that the history of the Palestinians would continue to be largely subsumed within a Zionist historical narrative, thereby denying them an independent identity and agency – that Palestinian political scientist Ibrahim Abu-Lughod seems to have been warning against a decade ago when he rebuked historians of Palestine for assuming that it is impossible to "study the historical development of the Palestinian Arab community at any particular point in modern times without taking immediate cognizance of the presence – effective or fictitious – of the Jewish community as represented by the Zionist movement." While admitting that it is "difficult to disentangle Palestinian history and culture from the endemic conflict between Palestinian and Zionist and Palestinian and British imperialist," Abu-Lughod insisted that "the Palestine of 1948 was a very different Palestine from that of 1917 and the difference is not solely the result of the impact of either imperialist or Zionist."[9]

Abu-Lughod is certainly right to argue that the very disproportionate attention paid to Zionism and the Yishuv, and the not unrelated neglect (and implicit marginalization) of Palestine's Arab majority, has had a distorting effect on our overall understanding of the modern history of Palestine. His assertion that "the social and cultural evolution of the Palestinians in modern times is in desperate need of study" is also entirely justified. Without question, more (and better) research on the history of the Palestinian Arab community as a distinct (though of course not homogeneous or internally unconflicted) entity is urgently needed. At the same time, however, historians cannot avoid seeking to grasp how the development of Palestine's Arab community was shaped by a complex set of economic, social, cultural, and political forces, including those generated by the Zionist project and British colonialism. The same applies, of course, to historians of Zionism and the Yishuv. We must certainly recognize, though, that there will inevitably be some tension between the effort to achieve a relational perspective and respect for the historical specificity of each community.[10]

The project of reconstructing a relational history of Palestine is still in its initial stages, and many issues remain to be examined or re-examined. In the context of the preceding discussion and in order to illustrate the utility of a shift in focus from the internal dynamics of a single community (as the dual society paradigm would prescribe) to the domain of Arab–Jewish interaction, I briefly explore here one particular case from the British mandate period: the evolving relations between Arab and Jewish railway workers, especially those employed at the railway repair and maintenance workshops on the outskirts of Haifa.

Several factors make exploration of this group particularly interesting. Unlike nearly all Arab-owned enterprises and most Jewish-owned enterprises in Palestine, the Palestine Railways (an agency of the mandatory Government of Palestine) employed both Arabs and Jews. It was, therefore, one of the few enterprises in which Arabs and Jews worked side by side, encountering similar conditions and being compelled to interact in the search for solutions to their problems. The Palestine Railways was also one of the country's largest employers, with a work force of about

2,400 in 1924, reaching a war-swollen peak of 7,800 in 1943. This work force, comprised of numerous unskilled Arab peasants hired to build and maintain roadbed and track, also included substantial numbers of skilled personnel in the running and traffic departments and at stations across the country and, in 1943, some 1,200 Arab and Jewish workers employed at the Haifa workshops.[11] Indeed, until the proliferation of British military bases during the Second World War, the Haifa workshops constituted Palestine's largest concentration of wage workers.

In addition, the railwaymen were among the first industrial workers in Palestine to organize themselves. An organization of Jewish railway workers was established as early as 1919, while Arab railway workers began to evince interest in trade unionism soon thereafter and would go on to play a key role in founding and leading the Palestinian Arab labor movement. Moreover, it was in large part the interaction of Jewish and Arab railway workers that first compelled the Zionist labor movement and the various left-Zionist political parties, as well as the largely Jewish but anti-Zionist communists, on the one hand, and various forces in the Arab community on the other, to confront, in both ideological and practical terms, the question of relations between the Jewish and Arab working classes in Palestine.

The extent, duration, and character of the interactions among Arab and Jewish railway workers were exceptional, making them an atypical group in many respects. That very atypicality, that group's location astride communal boundaries, may, however, serve to highlight some of the problematic features of the nationalist and conventional scholarly narratives of the mandate period. It may also allow us to get beyond the usual counterposing of cooperation and conflict as mutually exclusive binary opposites, a dichotomization which tends to presume the prior existence of two distinct entities between which one or the other of these states obtains, thereby obscuring the larger field within which those entities are constituted and interrelate in whole or in part. The more open-ended concept of interaction may be of greater utility in exploring the ways in which relations among the members of this group (and others) took shape within a broader (and historically specific) economic, political, and cultural matrix. At the end of this essay I will point to some of the broader implications of this approach, which I believe may contribute to a rereading of the history of the Zionist–Palestinian conflict.[12]

Hebrew labor and Arab workers

Although Palestine's first railroad line, a French-financed project linking Jaffa on the Mediterranean coast to Jerusalem high in the hill country, was opened in 1892 and the subsequent two-and-a-half decades witnessed substantial railway development, very little is known about the railway workers themselves until after the First World War. At that point the railway work force seems to have been drawn mainly from the local Arab population, along with many Egyptians conscripted for labor service with the British forces conquering Palestine from the Ottomans and a small number of Syrian, Greek, and other foreign skilled workers.[13] These workers were joined from 1919 onward by Jewish immigrants from Russia and Poland channeled into railroad jobs by agencies of the Zionist Organization and by the employment offices of the two labor-Zionist parties, the social-democratic Ahdut Ha'avoda (Unity of Labor) and its nonsocialist rival Hapo'el Hatza'ir (The Young Worker).[14] The Zionist movement was anxious to lay the basis for the large-scale immigration and settlement finally made possible by the Balfour Declaration of November 1917, in which Britain had committed itself to supporting the establishment in Palestine of a "national home" for the Jews.

For the labor-Zionist parties and, from 1920 onward, for their creation the Histadrut (the General Organization of Hebrew Workers in the Land of Israel), which soon became not only the central institution of the labor-Zionist movement but also a dominant force in the Yishuv as a whole, placing new Jewish immigrants in jobs on the railroads was not simply or even primarily a matter of securing their individual livelihoods. It was part of the broader campaign for the conquest of labor (*kibbush ha'avoda*), a campaign the goal of which was the achievement of Hebrew labor (*'avoda 'ivrit*).[15] These were central elements in the discourse and practice of the labor-Zionist movement. Though they had roots in the socialist ideology which adherents of labor Zionism brought with them from Eastern Europe, they were in large part the product of the Jewish workers' encounter with Palestinian realities in the decade before the First World War.

Those immigrants' desire to proletarianize themselves and create a Jewish working class in Palestine which would both wage its class struggle and assert itself as the vanguard of the Zionist movement as a whole foundered on the fact that the gradual, though incomplete, integration of Palestine into the capitalist world market and the transformation of agrarian relations in the countryside from the late nineteenth century onward, coupled with rapid population growth, had created a growing pool of landless Arabs available for wage labor in the new Jewish agricultural settlements, as well as in the towns and cities. The domination of the local labor market by large numbers of Arab workers willing to work for low wages and a severe shortage of employment opportunities owing to the country's underdevelopment posed a serious problem for the Zionist project. Unless employment in jobs with wages approaching European rates could be found or created, it was unlikely that Jewish immigrants would come to Palestine in significant numbers or remain there long, and the firm implantation of an ever-growing Yishuv would be very much in doubt.

Through a process of trial and error, the labor-Zionist movement gradually developed two complementary strategies to deal with this situation.[16] To create employment opportunities and develop the Yishuv's increasingly self-sufficient economic base, the Histadrut, less a conventional trade union federation than a highly centralized instrument of the Zionist project, used funds supplied largely by the Zionist Organization (which until the 1930s was dominated by bourgeois Zionists) gradually to build up its own high-wage economic sector in which only Jews would be employed, including a ramified network of industrial, transport, marketing and service enterprises and new forms of collective and cooperative agricultural settlement (the *kibbutz* and the *moshav).* At the same time, the labor-Zionist movement engaged in a sustained effort to gain for Jews a larger share of the existing and newly created jobs in other sectors by trying to induce Jewish and other private employers and the British administration to hire Jewish workers instead of less expensive and (at least initially) less demanding Arab workers. This in turn required an effort to pressure Jewish workers who sought easier ways of making a living to accept and remain at even the most difficult and poorly paid occupations. The Histadrut leadership insisted that the fate of the Zionist project in Palestine depended upon the success of this relentless campaign for the conquest of labor and the achievement of maximal Hebrew labor (that is, Jewish employment) in every sector of Palestine's economy.[17]

Joint organization among the railway workers

Achieving the conquest of labor on the Palestine Railways proved particularly difficult, however. Few Jewish immigrants channeled into railroad jobs were willing to endure for very long the low wages, long hours, harsh conditions, and abusive treatment characteristic of railway work in Palestine, so whenever better jobs were available, the Jewish immigrants quit. The leaders of the first organization of railway workers in Palestine, the exclusively Jewish Railway Workers' Association (Agudat Po'alei Harakevet, RWA), founded in 1919, and leaders of the Histadrut to which that union was affiliated thus found that labor Zionism's struggle to strengthen Hebrew labor in this economically and politically vital sector conflicted with what most Jewish workers perceived to be their own self-interest.

It soon became apparent that a significant number of Jews could be kept working as railwaymen only if wages and working conditions were significantly improved. However, the Jewish railway workers, though disproportionately represented among the skilled workers, accounted for only a small minority (ranging from 8 to 12 percent) of the railway work force as a whole. No matter how well organized, the Jewish railway workers could not hope to improve their wages and working conditions by their own efforts. This brought to the fore the issue of cooperation between the Jews and the Arab railwaymen who constituted the great majority of the work force, especially the Arab foremen and skilled workers in Haifa. The issue became especially acute when in the summer of 1921 Arab railway workers in Haifa (to which the Palestine Railways' main maintenance and repair workshops were being transferred from Lydda) approached their unionized Jewish coworkers about the possibility of cooperation; some even expressed interest in joining the Histadrut, attractive not only because of its apparent strength as a labor organization but also because it offered its members such services as health care, interest-free loans, and access to consumer cooperatives.

That the Haifa workshops were the scene of these initial contacts is not surprising. As noted earlier, before the Second World War these shops constituted the largest single concentration of industrial wage labor in Palestine, employing side by side hundreds of Arab, Jewish, and other workers, many of them skilled or semiskilled. In the 1920s, a substantial Jewish minority lived alongside an Arab majority in Haifa, which was a rapidly growing and relatively cosmopolitan city already on its way to becoming Palestine's main port and industrial center.[18] In this atmosphere it was possible for Jewish workers, especially recent arrivals from Russia who had been radicalized by the October Revolution and its aftermath, to establish contact with an emerging stratum of relatively skilled and educated Arab workers and foremen interested in trade unionism. Some of the latter were no doubt influenced by the activities of the Jewish union, but others may already have become acquainted with trade unionism in their countries of origin (for example, those from Syria or Egypt) or through contact in Palestine with non-Jewish European workers, mainly Greeks and Italians, who had their own mutual aid societies.

Thus, developments on the ground among the railway workers themselves first put the issue of relations between Jewish and Arab workers on the agenda of the Zionist labor movement and later kept it there. Well into the 1920s, the question of joint organization (*irgun meshutaf*) was extensively (and often hotly) debated within and among the contending left-Zionist parties within the Histadrut. In these debates party leaders and Histadrut officials expressed a broad range of conflicting perspectives about joint organization, ranging from enthusiasm to strenuous opposition.

On the one hand, many left-Zionists professed loyalty to the principle of class solidarity across ethnic lines. As socialists standing at the head of what they regarded as a better-organized and culturally more

advanced Jewish working class, they felt that they had a moral obliga-
tion to help their less class-conscious and largely unorganized Arab
fellow workers – a sort of proletarian *mission civilisatrice*.[19] Although
this perspective was tinged with paternalism and replete with contradictions and ultimately could not be separated from the broader issue
of the Zionist project's implications for Palestine's Arab majority, it would
nonetheless be a mistake to lose sight of the subjective moral impulse
involved and of the extent to which even the most exclusivist practices
were embedded in a discourse of socialism and proletarian internationalism.

Arguments based on morality and principle were complemented by
more pragmatic arguments. Some labor-Zionist leaders argued that the
best way to eliminate the threat that cheap unorganized Arab labor posed
to expensive organized Jewish labor and enhance job opportunities for
Jews was to help Arab workers organize themselves. Organized Arab
workers would presumably be better able to raise their wages, elimi-
nating or at least reducing the wage differential which led employers to
prefer them to Jews. It is unlikely that such a strategy could have been
effective in the labor market that existed in Palestine at that time, but it
nonetheless had its proponents, among them (in the early 1920s, at least)
David Ben-Gurion, the Histadrut's increasingly powerful secretary and
pre-eminent leader of Ahdut Ha'avoda.[20]

But labor-Zionist leaders also expressed anxiety about joint organization's possible consequences for the Zionist project. The admission of
Arabs to the Histadrut or its constituent trade unions, or even their organization into separate unions under the Histadrut's tutelage, was likely
to conflict with the long-term goal of increasing Jewish employment; and
once organized, the Arab workers might not be controllable. "From the
humanitarian standpoint, it is clear that we must organize them," said
one Histadrut official in December 1920, "but from the national standpoint, when we organize them we will be arousing them against us.
They will receive the good that is in organization and use it against
US."[21] Histadrut leaders were also well aware that in neighboring Egypt,
for example, the trade unions were under the influence of the nationalists and played a significant role in the anticolonial struggle.[22]

In the end, the most important factor prodding the Histadrut toward
action was probably the fear that if the Histadrut did not organize Arab
workers, the Palestinian Arab nationalist movement – defined in labor-
Zionist discourse not as an authentic national movement but rather as
an instrument of exploitative and reactionary Arab landlords and clerics
– might seize the initiative with potentially dangerous consequences for
the Zionist project. In January 1922 the Histadrut majority, led by Ben-
Gurion and his allies, endorsed joint organization among the railway
workers, a decision reaffirmed and extended to encompass workers in

other mixed workplaces at the Histadrut's third congress in July 1927. However, these resolutions also required that any joint union of Arabs and Jews be composed of separate and largely autonomous national sections for each, with the Jewish sections to remain affiliated to the Histadrut.[23] From the standpoint of labor Zionism, this approach had the apparent virtue of reconciling the demands of proletarian internationalism and Zionism: The Histadrut would demonstrate its commitment to helping Arab fellow workers unionize and improve their lot while at the same time preserving the exclusively Jewish character of the Histadrut and its trade union organizations, which would thus be free to carry out their national (i.e., Zionist) tasks, including immigration, settlement, economic development and the struggle for Hebrew labor.

Abortive unity

This position was not, however, acceptable to the Arab skilled workers and foremen who spoke for a substantial number of other Arabs employed in the Haifa railway workshops and elsewhere. As they became increasingly aware that the Histadrut was an integral part of the Zionist movement, the Arabs insisted that any joint union of Jews and Arabs not be divided into separate national sections and not have any links with the Histadrut. Ilyas Asad, one of the Arab workers' leaders, told his Jewish colleagues at a March 1924 meeting of the Railway Workers' Association council that

> I am striving to establish ties between the Jewish and Arab workers because I am certain that if we are connected we will help one another, without regard to religion or nationality. Many Arab workers do not wish to join nationalist organizations because they understand their purpose and do not wish to abet a lie. They saw on the membership card [of the railway workers' union] the words Federation of Jewish Workers [i.e., the Histadrut] and they cannot understand what purpose this serves. I ask all the comrades to remove the word Jewish, and I am sure that if the agree there will be a strong bond between us and all the Arabs will join. I would be the first who would not want to join a nationalist labor organization. There are many Arab nationalist organizations, and we do not want to join them, and they will say we have joined a Jewish nationalist organization.[24]

As a result of these differences, negotiations between Arab and Jewish railway workers' leaders over the formation of a joint union for all the railway workers in Palestine were for years unsuccessful. In 1924, however, adherents of Po'alei Tziyon Smol (Workers of Zion – Left), a party which occupied the extreme left end of the Zionist spectrum, won effective control of the RWA. Although committed to establishing a Jewish homeland in Palestine, this small but vigorous party simultaneously regarded itself as the authentic revolutionary vanguard of the world Jewish proletariat (and unsuccessfully sought admission to the Comintern as such); rejected participation in the Zionist Organization, which it regarded as an instrument of the Jewish bourgeoisie; and denounced the Histadrut majority's determination to build up a separate high-wage economic enclave for Jews in Palestine.[25] This party won growing support among the rank and file of the (still exclusively Jewish) railway workers' union because its call for militancy and class struggle was attractive to many disgruntled workers whose already miserable wages and working conditions were being exacerbated by layoffs and management efforts to cut costs, and who had lost patience with demands by the Ahdut Ha'avoda-dominated Histadrut for self-sacrifice in the national cause. Po'alei Tziyon Smol also advocated a position on the question of joint organization that seemed to offer a real prospect of achieving unity between Arabs and Jews, which many of the Jewish workers had come to see as an absolutely essential precondition for improving their situation. The party not only rejected the notion of separate national sections within the railway workers' union but also wanted the Histadrut itself to undergo what it termed a separation of functions: that is, to transfer its Zionist functions to a separate organization and transform itself into a Jewish–Arab trade union federation committed solely to the class struggle.

After an intensive effort, the new railway union leadership came to terms with the leaders of the Arab workers in November 1924. The Arab unionists agreed to join their Jewish colleagues in a new international union with the understanding that they would play an equal role in running the union and that the new organization would disaffiliate from the Histadrut if it refused to accept the separation of functions. By the end of November 1924, several hundred Arab workers had joined the union (now known as the Union of Railway, Postal and Telegraph workers, URPTW), transforming an organization which had since its inception as the RWA been virtually all Jewish into one whose membership was roughly half-Jewish and half-Arab and encompassed some 20 to 25 percent of the railway work force.[26]

This joint union of Arabs and Jews survived for only a few months. Most of the Arab unionists soon concluded that their Jewish colleagues were not sincerely committed to achieving unity as originally conceived nor to developing a completely independent and apolitical trade union dedicated only to the interests of all the railway workers. The Arabs also grew impatient with what they took to be dissembling, if not outright deception, on the part of their Jewish colleagues, whom they came to believe were not being straightforward with them about their commitment to the Zionist project.

Their suspicions and doubts were not without basis in reality. Even as they spoke of proletarian internationalism and Arab–Jewish solidarity, the Jewish union leaders continued to work behind the scenes with the Histadrut to increase Jewish employment by incessant lobbying of railways management, the government of Palestine, and the Colonial Office but also by pressing Jewish foremen to hire only Jewish job applicants.[27] The Histadrut's campaign for Hebrew labor on the railways, to which even the new Po'alei Tziyon Smol-influenced leadership was party, was a source of tremendous resentment among the Arab rank and file, who felt that they were being discriminated against in hiring and promotion and feared displacement by Jewish immigrants.[28]

The Arab unionists also felt that their Jewish colleagues were taking advantage of the Arabs' ignorance of Hebrew and limited understanding of Yishuv politics. That the Arab unionists did not fully grasp their Jewish colleagues' politics is suggested by the fact that, as late as November 1924, Hasanayn Fahmi, one of the Arabs co-opted onto the union's central committee, was asking his Jewish colleagues whether or not there was in fact any connection between the union he had just joined and the Zionist movement and whether or not they themselves were Zionists. In this and other instances, Po'alei Tziyon Smol activists tended to provide evasive or disingenuous responses in order to downplay their commitment to Zionism, avoid alienating the Arab unionists, and preserve the joint union. But there were also instances of deliberate deception. At a meeting of the union's council in January 1925, for example, the Jewish translator who was rendering the proceedings into Arabic for the benefit of the Arab delegates deliberately watered down the Zionist content of a speech by Ben-Gurion to make it more palatable to the Arabs.[29] These things made the Arab unionists vulnerable to criticism, from the Arab nationalist press and activists and from among the rank and file, that the Arab unionists were being duped and exploited by the Zionists. In the first months of 1925, most of the Arab trade unionists who had joined the URPTW's leadership only a few months earlier quit, taking most of the Arab rank and file with them.

The Jewish unionists and the Histadrut attributed the collapse of the joint union to sabotage by the communists, Palestine Railways management, or both. Activists of the still almost exclusively Jewish but strongly anti-Zionist Palestine Communist Party (known as the PKP, from its initials in Yiddish) had sought to alert the Arab railway workers that they were joining a union still closely affiliated with the Zionist Histadrut and led by committed Zionists; but at the beginning of 1925 the communists were in fact urging the Arab workers not to leave the joint union but rather to remain within it and struggle to reform it. Palestine Railways management had an obvious interest in keeping its work force divided and does seem to have used selective wage increases and equally selective dismissals to signal its anti-union attitude to the Arab rank and file; but the decision of most of the Arab workers to leave the union cannot be attributed solely or even mainly to management pressure. In fact, the Histadrut's attempt to pin the blame on "outside agitators" tells us less about the actual causes of the breakup in early 1925 than it does about labor Zionism's conception of its own project and of Arabs, which rendered it unable to come to terms with its own role in this failure.[30]

In the summer of 1925, a few months after the breakup of the joint union, the seceding Arab unionists joined forces with the leaders of a mutual aid society for Arab railway workers and established a new, exclusively Arab organization, the Palestinian Arab Workers' Society (PAWS).[31] Although PAWS initially consisted almost exclusively of Arab railway workers in Haifa, its new name and its program indicated its founders' ambition to make it the Arab counterpart of the Histadrut, an organization which would eventually encompass all the Arab workers in Palestine. Until the emergence of rival communist-led trade union federations in the 1940s, PAWS was indeed the largest and most important Palestinian Arab labor organization, uniting a fluctuating membership drawn from various trades and locales around a more stable core of Haifa railway workers, whose own organization would later be formally known as the Arab Union of Railway Workers (AURW).[32]

Tenuous cooperation

From 1925 until the end of the mandate period, then, two separate unions were active among the railway workers. Relations between the AURW and the older, larger and wealthier union led by Jews, soon back in the hands of supporters of Ben-Gurion and the Histadrut majority and known from 1931 as the International Union of Railway, Postal and Telegraph Employees in Palestine (IU), were often rocky, with alternating periods of cooperation and of conflict.[33] The main impetus for cooperation was the glaringly obvious fact that, confronted by a highly intransigent management backed by a miserly colonial state, neither union was sufficiently strong on its own to achieve very much for its membership: the IU had some 250 dues-paying members in 1927, and the AURW even fewer. Chronic discontent by the rank and file over low wages and poor working conditions was periodically exacerbated by what the workers perceived as arbitrary and abusive acts by management, including wage cuts, layoffs, and short hours. The resulting sense of grievance and the understanding that disunity meant weakness

113

generated demands from rank-and-file Arab and Jewish workers that their leaderships put aside their differences and work together.

Typically, pressure from below and upsurges of rank-and-file militancy led the two unions' leaders to negotiate the formation of an *ad hoc* joint committee based in Haifa. This committee, comprising representatives of both unions, would then proceed to organize protest meetings, draw up memoranda of grievances and demands, and represent the railway workers in talks with management. These joint committees tended, however, to be rather shortlived. After a few months they were increasingly undermined by conflicts between the two unions, ultimately resulting in the joint committee's dissolution and barrages of mutual recriminations as each side accused the other of selfishly sabotaging unity and the workers' interests. As a result, relations between the two unions were not infrequently clouded by bitterness and mistrust.

In large measure, this mistrust was generated by the steadfast insistence of the IU that it was the sole legitimate representative of all the railway workers in Palestine, Jewish and Arab. The Jewish-led union thus refused to regard its Arab counterpart as an equal partner that authentically represented the Arab railway workers and even launched sporadic drives to undermine it by directly recruiting Arab workers. The IU's claim to exclusivity was bolstered by its retention, until 1936, of a number of Arab members attracted by its much more effective and visible presence in the workplace and as a national organization, the perception that behind the IU stood the wealthy and powerful Histadrut, and an ability to offer its members access (via the Histadrut) to services that were totally beyond the AURW's means, including health care, loans, and legal aid.

For their part the AURW's leaders accepted the legitimacy of, and were willing to cooperate with, the IU, but only as the representative of the Jewish railway workers. The Palestinian unionists enormously resented the IU's refusal to extend reciprocal recognition, its attempts to recruit Arab workers and its continued commitment to Hebrew labor, manifested in constant lobbying to get more Jews hired. Arabs who joined the IU were denounced by AURW leaders as dupes or lackeys of the Zionists, if not outright traitors.

However, the rank and file's desire for cooperation was such that neither leadership could afford to appear to be seen as openly opposed to unity. For example, even when IU leaders concluded that the benefits of cooperation were accruing disproportionately to the AURW, broke up joint committees and initiated drives to recruit Arab workers, they sought to place the blame for the collapse of cooperation on their erstwhile Arab partners, whom they accused of inactivity or bad faith.[34] The Arab unionists displayed a similar concern for rank-and-file opinion: On several occasions in the late 1920s they went so far as to distribute leaflets in Hebrew to the Jewish railway workers to make known their version of what had led to the breakup of a joint committee and to accuse the IU leadership of acting in bad faith and undermining the workers' unity.[35] Moreover, at least until the outbreak in 1936 of a countrywide Arab revolt against British rule and Zionism, Arab railway unionists generally ignored or resisted pressure from the Palestinian nationalist movement to terminate cooperation with Jewish unionists. It is significant, too, that the dream of a single union for all of Palestine's railway workers remained very much alive among the rank and file right up to 1936, and in a more subdued way even beyond, though its realization was always blocked by the same issues that had undermined unity in 1925.

The extent to which this apparently widespread desire for cooperation at the institutional level was accompanied by the development of social relationships between Arab and Jewish workers at the personal level, within or outside the workplace, is unclear. In the early 1920s, at least, some Jewish railway workers lived in predominantly Arab neighborhoods of Haifa, and elsewhere the long shifts characteristic of railway work threw Jews and Arabs together, especially at remote locations. A report in 1928 of Arab workers attending the funeral of a Jewish coworker suggests some degree of social interaction.[36] In his memoirs, Bulus Farah, an Arab unionist (and later a communist activist) who went to work in the Haifa workshops in 1925 as a fifteen-year-old apprentice, spoke of the "mutual understanding" that had prevailed there and suggested that the Jewish workers respected their Arab coworkers for their technical abilities.[37] This is not implausible, given that most of the Jews were new to industrial work and some may have seen the Arabs as examples of the proletarian authenticity for which they were striving. Over the years, Arab and Jewish union leaders do seem to have developed personal relationships: Yehezkel Abramov, a longtime Jewish railway union leader, would in his old age remember sitting around with colleagues from the AURW on the Tel Aviv beachfront after a joint meeting with management.[38]

Yet Abramov also conveyed his frustration that most of his fellow Jews could not be bothered to learn or use the names of Arab coworkers and instead referred to specific individuals simply as "the Arab."[39] Unlike his colleagues, Abramov took the trouble to learn Arabic and made a point of sitting with Arab workers during lunch breaks at the Haifa workshops. That he regarded himself as exceptional in this regard suggests a high degree of social separation: Though Arabs and Jews may have worked side by side, apparently in their leisure time within and outside the workplace they generally kept to themselves. In the 1920s and the early 1930s the IU sponsored cultural and educational activities for its Jewish and Arab members, and the meetings which it sponsored jointly with the AURW were usually held in Arab coffee-houses. But there are no reports of Jewish workers frequenting Arab coffee-houses, the main site of leisure-time social interaction among men in urban Arab neighborhoods; and relatively few Arab workers took part in the cultural and social institutions sponsored by the Histadrut or other Jewish organizations.

In mixed cities like Haifa, some degree of interaction in public spaces was inevitable and persisted until 1948. Despite Zionist campaigns to boycott Arab in favor of Jewish produce, many Jews, (especially from the working class) continued to frequent Arab markets to take advantage of lower prices; and some Jews continued to live in Arab neighborhoods, where rents were lower. But Jews were increasingly concentrated in exclusively Jewish neighborhoods, for example the string of new workers' suburbs just north of Haifa, especially after outbreaks of violence in 1921, 1929, and especially 1936–39, made mixed neighborhoods unsafe.

Wartime resurgence and postwar militancy

In addition to exacerbating residential, social and economic segregation, the intercommunal violence and tensions which accompanied the 1936–39 revolt made cooperation between Arab and Jewish railway workers even on purely economic issues all but impossible. By contrast, the period of 1940 to 1946 witnessed unprecedented solidarity between Arab and Jewish workers, not only among the railwaymen but in many other mixed enterprises as well. This may seem ironic in retrospect, since by the end of 1947 Palestine was engulfed in a full-scale civil war. But during the Second World War and immediately after it, a short-lived conjuncture created new possibilities for militant joint action, though they were eventually eclipsed by escalating political tensions.

The Palestinian working class, Arab and Jewish, expanded very dramatically during the war. Disruption of the usual sources of supply stimulated development of the country's industrial base, as did the demand created by the enormously swollen British and Allied military presence. Military bases and related service enterprises proliferated, drawing tens of thousands of Arab peasants and townspeople into wage labor at work sites which also employed Jews. The railway sector shared in this expansion. After suffering during the 1930s because of growing competition from motor transport and then the Arab revolt, the war years witnessed the rapid extension of railroad lines, a tripling of freight tonnage carried per kilometer, and a large increase in the work force of the Palestine Railways.[40]

Labor shortages in many sectors strengthened the workers' bargaining position, while high inflation pushed them toward action. In Palestine as elsewhere in Britain's domain during this period, the British colonial authorities moderated their hostility to trade unions, created a new apparatus to monitor and mediate labor disputes, and looked more favorably on labor legislation. In these circumstances there ensued an unprecedented wave of unionization and militancy which affected Arab workers most dramatically because they had hitherto been less active and less organized. The leaderships of both the Histadrut and the PAWS regarded this development with some ambivalence. By contrast, this upsurge was encouraged by, and in turn benefited, newly reinvigorated left-wing forces in both the Arab community and the Yishuv which implicitly challenged nationalist leaderships on both sides by advocating class solidarity and political compromise between Arabs and Jews.

During the war a new Arab left emerged in Palestine, organized in the communist-led National Liberation League ('Usbat al-Taharrur al-Watani, NLL). Left-wing trade union activists, among them veterans of the AURW, won significant support in unions hitherto under the control of the more conservative PAWS leadership, as well as in newly organized unions, leading ultimately to a split in the Arab trade union movement and the establishment of a left-led Arab Workers' Congress aligned with the NLL. In the Yishuv, the initially kibbutz-based socialist-Zionist Hashomer Hatza'ir (Young Guard) movement, which advocated a bi-national Palestine and Arab–Jewish class solidarity and was trying to extend its influence among Jewish urban workers, now emerged as a serious force on the left flank of the Histadrut leadership. In a sense, Hashomer Hatza'ir can be said to have replaced the defunct Po'alei Tziyon Smol at the left end of the Zionist spectrum; and it won significant support among militant Jewish workers, including railway workers in what had become known as Red Haifa. The Jewish communist movement also resurfaced during and after the war. Largely discredited in the Yishuv because of its support for the 1936–39 Arab revolt, it now sought to gain legitimacy and support from the wartime popularity of the Soviet Union, whose Red Army the Yishuv hailed as the main force fighting the Nazis, and by trying to ride the wave of worker activism. The Jewish communists also moderated their long-standing hostility to Zionism and sought admission to the Histadrut, from which they had been purged two decades earlier.

Among the railway workers the changing circumstances were first manifested in unprecedentedly smooth relations between the IU and the AURW from 1940 onward. The IU tacitly recognized that under the prevailing circumstances, recruitment of Arab workers was unrealistic and rapprochement with the AURW therefore unavoidable, while the paralysis of the Arab nationalist movement during the war years and strong rank-and-file pressure made the AURW leadership more amenable to cooperation.[41] A series of job actions and short strikes culminated, much to the unhappiness of the Histadrut and PAWS leaderships, in a three-day occupation of the Haifa workshops in February 1944.[42] Unrest continued after the end of the war in Europe, manifested during 1945 in a number of brief wildcat strikes by railway and postal workers, now among the most militant and experienced (and of course most integrated) segments of the Palestinian working class. The NLL's newspaper, *al-Ittihad*, hailed these incidents as "clear proof of the possibility of joint action in every workplace," provided that the workers steered clear of interference by both Zionism and "Arab reaction."[43]

The Arab communists' prescription seemed to find confirmation in April 1946, when a planned strike by Jewish and Arab postal workers in Tel Aviv spontaneously expanded to encompass some 13,000 Arab and Jewish postal, telegraph, railway, port and public works department workers, along with 10,000 lower- and middle-level white-collar government employees. This general strike paralysed the British colonial administration and won the support of much of Jewish and Arab public opinion. The Arab and Jewish communists naturally saw in it a wonderful manifestation of class solidarity, "a blow against the 'divide and rule' policy of imperialism, a slap in the face of those who hold chauvinist ideologies and propagate national division," but warned the strikers against "defeatist and reactionary elements, Arab and Jewish." Conservative newspapers on both sides were less enthusiastic. The conservative nationalist newspaper, *Filastin*, for example, attacked PAWS for allegedly colluding in what it regarded as a politically motivated and Zionist-inspired movement. The right-wing Jewish daily, *Ma'ariv*, hailed the strike at first but later denounced it as detrimental to the Zionist cause.[44]

The strikers ultimately won many of their demands, and their victory gave a strong boost to the fledgling Arab labor movement. The following year witnessed the rapid growth of unions and the spread of worker activism, especially in the army camps and at the oil refinery and the Iraq Petroleum Company's pipeline terminal in Haifa. In these workplaces Arab and Jewish workers often cooperated in pursuit of higher wages and better conditions, although relations between the Histadrut and the Arab unions were never entirely free of friction.

Civil war and partition

That friction was exacerbated, and the postwar wave of activism ultimately brought to an end, by the rising political tensions which accompanied the escalation in 1947 of the three-way struggle among the Zionist movement, the Palestinian nationalist movement, and the British to determine the fate of Palestine. In 1944 the Zionists had launched a campaign to force Britain, their erstwhile protector and ally, to open Palestine to Jewish immigration and move toward Jewish statehood,

1947 UN vote [handwritten marginalia]

which in turn helped stimulate the revival of the Palestinian Arab nationalist movement. Unable to suppress opposition or achieve a negotiated solution, an exhausted and isolated Britain turned the Palestine issue over to the United Nations, whose General Assembly adopted a resolution on November 29, 1947, recommending the partition of Palestine into independent Arab and Jewish states. Partition was rejected by the leaders of Palestine's Arab community, still two-thirds of the country's population, who saw it as a violation of their right as the indigenous majority to self-determination in an undivided Palestine. Partition was accepted by most of the leaders of the Yishuv and of the Zionist movement, for whom a sovereign Jewish state, even if in only part of Palestine, was still a tremendous achievement.[45]

Violence between Arabs and Jews erupted almost immediately after the vote and quickly escalated into a cycle of terrorist violence and counter-violence directed mainly against civilians. By the end of December over 350 people had lost their lives in the civil war engulfing Palestine. The single bloodiest incident of this first month of violence was touched off on December 30, 1947, when operatives of the right-wing Zionist Irgun Z'va'i Le'umi (National Military Organization, usually referred to in Hebrew by its acronym, Etzel), commanded by Menachem Begin, threw a number of grenades into a crowd of some 100 Arabs gathered at the main gate of the British owned oil refinery on the northern outskirts of Haifa in the hope of finding work as day laborers. Six were killed and forty-two wounded in what Etzel claimed was an act of retaliation for recent attacks on Jews elsewhere in Palestine. Within minutes of the incident, an outraged mob of Arab refinery workers and outsiders turned on the Jewish refinery workers, killing forty-one and wounding forty-nine before British army and police units arrived.[46]

News of the bloodshed at the oil refinery quickly reached the nearby repair and maintenance workshops of the Palestine Railways. Tensions were already high there because of the deteriorating political and security situation in the country, and now they soared to explosive levels as some of the younger Arab workers threatened their Jewish coworkers (of whom there were fewer than a hundred at the time) and tried to shut down the machinery. The railway workshops were, however, spared the orgy of bloodletting which had engulfed the oil refinery. The veteran Arab unionists, some of whom had been among the founders of PAWS, quickly intervened, faced down the hot-heads, and kept the peace until buses could be brought to transport the Jewish workers home safely. The workshops were then shut for ten days, until relative calm had been restored in Haifa and security arrangements put in place.[47]

In the following months, Palestine descended into full-scale civil war, but the railway workshops continued to function as normally as external circumstances allowed. The existence of Arab and Jewish union cadres with extensive experience of cooperation and a tradition of mutual respect allowed these workers to avoid, for a time at least, being drawn into the maelstrom of intercommunal violence. After April 1948, however, the question of relations between Arabs and Jews at the Haifa workshops became moot. The work force there was left almost exclusively Jewish when most of the city's Arab population fled as Jewish military forces besieged their neighborhoods. The same transformation took place throughout the country. Though the work force of the Palestine Railways had been mostly Arab, the flight or expulsion from their homes of half of Palestine's Arab population during 1947 to 1949 left the work force of the new Israel Railways almost entirely Jewish.[48] Nearly four decades of interaction among Arab and Jewish railway workers thus came to an abrupt end.

Rethinking Palestinian history

There are students of the Zionist–Palestinian conflict who have pointed to instances of cooperation between Jews and Arabs in mandatory Palestine, especially cooperation among workers, as evidence that the conflict need not have taken the course it did, that a peaceful solution which met the basic needs of both Arabs and Jews might have been found had the voices of reason, compromise, and working-class solidarity on both sides prevailed. The history of the mandate period thus becomes a story of missed opportunities, or a morality tale in which the so-called bad guys on both sides triumph over the peacemakers, whose weakness and ineffectuality is somehow never really accounted for.[49]

I am not making that argument here. On the contrary, the Zionist and Palestinian nationalist movements clearly sought irreconcilable objectives and were on a collision course from the very start. Moreover, although during the mandate period Arab and Jewish railway workers were involved in persistent efforts to cooperate and developed a sense of solidarity that at times transcended (or at least moderated) national divisions, relations among them were profoundly affected by the dynamics of the broader Zionist–Palestinian conflict, as the *dénouement* of their interaction in 1948 conclusively demonstrated. In addition, as I noted earlier, the railway workers were in many respects an atypical group.

In the history recounted here, one can find instances of both conflict and cooperation between Jews and Arabs. Instead of trying to locate the sole or essential meaning of relations among Arab and Jewish railway workers in either term, however, it may make more sense to shift our focus to the ways in which intercommunal as well as intracommunal identities, boundaries, and projects were constructed and reproduced, and place in the foreground the contestation which always characterized those processes. Thus among the Arab railway workers some unionists who certainly regarded themselves as nationalists strongly opposed to what they saw as Zionist encroachment on their homeland nonetheless defied the official nationalist line by embracing a discourse of worker solidarity across ethnic boundaries that promoted cooperation with Zionist Jews. Similarly, contending political forces among the Jewish railway workers put forward conflicting definitions of what it meant to be a Jew and a worker in Palestine and widely differing notions of how to relate to the Arab majority of the railway work force. More broadly, the existence of a more or less unified market for unskilled and semiskilled labor in Palestine, especially in the government sector, and the circumstances and exigencies which employment by the colonial administration generated, helped shape perceptions, strategies, and relationships among all members of the Palestine Railways work force. In this sense, the Arab and Jewish railway workers not only "made themselves" (to borrow E. P. Thompson's imagery) but also "made" each other within a broader matrix of relations and forces.

It is not only with respect to the railway workers that a relational approach which focuses on the mutually constitutive interactions between Arabs and Jews in Palestine may prove useful, however. For example, I suggested earlier that the urgent need to exit (at least partially) a labor market dominated by abundant low-wage Arab labor prompted the labor-Zionist movement to strive to construct a relatively self-sufficient, high-wage economic enclave for Jews in Palestine. This imperative also propelled the unrelenting struggle for Hebrew labor and other practices couched in the language of worker solidarity and class struggle but aimed largely at excluding or displacing Arab workers. These practices exacerbated intercommunal tensions but also facilitated labor Zionism's drive for hegemony over rival social and political forces *within* the Yishuv. By the mid-1930s this strategy, implemented mainly by the Histadrut (whose membership encompassed more than a quarter of the Yishuv's population in 1936) and its affiliated economic, social, cultural, and military institutions, had helped the Zionist labor camp become the dominant force within the Yishuv and the international Zionist movement. In this sense, many of the institutions and practices which for an entire historical period, from the 1930s into the 1970s, were considered among the most distinctive features of the Yishuv and of Israeli society (e.g., the kibbutz, the powerful public and Histadrut sectors of the economy, the cult of pioneering, the role of the military) can be understood as directly or indirectly the product of the Zionist project's interaction with Arabs and Arab society on the ground in Palestine.

Similarly, while Israeli sociologists have conventionally explained the subordinate social location and status of Israel's Oriental Jews – the majority of the country's Jewish population, which derives from Arab countries or from elsewhere in Asia or Africa, as opposed to Eastern

Europe – in terms of the failure of these culturally traditional people to adapt successfully to a modern society, recent critical scholarship has stressed their relegation to the bottom ranks of the labor market (where they displaced or replaced Palestinian Arabs) and official denigration of their culture, defined by the dominant groups in Israel as backward (Arab).[50] Before the First World War some Zionist leaders had already envisioned Yemeni Jews as replacements for Palestinian Arab agricultural workers and actually sponsored Yemeni Jewish immigration to Palestine. After 1948, it was largely Jewish immigrants from Arab countries who filled the social vacuum created by the flight or expulsion of the vast majority of the Arabs who had lived within the borders of the new state of Israel. From this perspective, then, it can be argued that the matrix of Jewish–Arab interactions in Palestine played a central role in shaping ethnic relations within Jewish society in Palestine (and later Israel).

Arab society in Palestine was, in turn, profoundly influenced by the Zionist project in a variety of ways. There was, of course, the catastrophic displacement of 1947–49, but in the preceding decades Jewish immigration, settlement, investment, and state building had already had an important impact on Arab society. That impact can be seen in the direct and indirect effects of Jewish land purchases, settlement and agricultural practices on Arab agrarian relations, the complex effects on the Arab economy of the large-scale influx of capital that accompanied Jewish immigration and development, and the effects of the economic and social policies implemented by a British administration committed to fostering a Jewish national home in Palestine but also concerned about alienating the country's Arab majority.

Most of the scholars who have so far deployed a relational approach have tended to emphasize the structural economic relationships between Arabs and Jews in Palestine, especially markets for land and labor. This emphasis has been extremely useful as a corrective to the conventional historiography, but it can marginalize questions of meaning and conduce to an economistic reductionism. Yet neither the evolution nor the content of a distinctly Palestinian Arab culture, identity, and national movement can be adequately understood except in relation to the specific character of the Palestinians' confrontation with Zionism. Nor can one make sense of the labor-Zionist project without taking into account not only labor market strategies but also the ways in which the Arab worker and the Arab working class in Palestine were represented and the roles they were made to play in labor-Zionist discourse. At a crucial stage, it was to a significant extent in relation to those (always contested) representations of Arab workers that labor Zionism articulated its own identity, its sense of mission, and its strategy to achieve hegemony within the Yishuv and realize its version of Zionism.[51] The modes of interaction between the Arab and Jewish communities in Palestine and their mutually constitutive impact on one another must therefore be seen as discursive as well as material.[52]

As historians and others explore the history of modern Palestine in new ways, as the object of inquiry is reconceived, and as a different set of concepts and categories is deployed, it will become increasingly clear that the two communities were neither natural nor essentially mono-lithic entities; nor were they hermetically sealed off from one another, as the conventional historiography assumes. Rather, the two communi-ties interacted in complex ways and had a mutually formative effect on one another, both as communities and through relationships which crossed communal boundaries to shape the identities and practices of various subgroups. These complex and contested processes operated at many levels and in many spheres, including markets for labor, land, agricultural produce and consumer goods, business ventures, residen-tial patterns, manufacturing and services, municipal government, and various aspects of social and cultural life. These interactions also had an important but little-explored spatial dimension manifested in shifts and reorientations in demographic, economic, political and cultural relations and flows among and within different settlements, villages, urban neigh-borhoods, towns, cities, and regions of Palestine.

A number of recently published works already manifest new approa-ches to the histories of Arabs and Jews in Palestine. These approaches challenge conventional categories, across hitherto unquestioned bound-aries, and treat Palestine not as *sui generis* but as suitable for comparative study. This process will be furthered as more scholars frame and explore new and different kinds of problems while drawing on both Arabic and Hebrew source materials. In the long run, I would hope, it will be possible to put the pieces together and move toward a new relational synthesis of the history of mandatory Palestine and, more broadly, of Palestinian history over the past two centuries. Such a synthesis will need to inter-rogate and transcend nationalist narratives on both sides, respecting what is specific to the histories of Arabs and Jews in Palestine even as it explores the ways in which those histories were (and remain) inextri-cably and fatefully intertwined.

NOTES

My thanks to Joel Beinin, Beshara Douniani, Joel Migdal, and the editors of *Comparative Studies in Society and History* for their helpful comments on earlier versions of this essay. This version was completed while I was a Visiting Fellow at Princeton University's Shelby Cullom Davis Center for Historical Studies, for whose financial support and intellectual stimulation I am grateful.

1 Much of what follows also applies to the literature on Palestine in the late Ottoman period and to Israel and the Palestinians inside and outside what had been Palestine after 1948 as well. But it is especially relevant to the four

decades during which Palestine existed as an administratively unified entity, before partition, war, Palestinian displacement, and massive Jewish immigration radically altered the terms of the interaction between Arabs and Jews in Palestine. For surveys of the field, see Kenneth W. Stein, "A Historiographic Review of Literature on the Origins of the Arab–Israeli Conflict," *The American Historical Review*, 96:5 (December 1991), 1450–65; Tarif Khalidi, "Palestinian Historiography: 1900–1948," *Journal of Palestine Studies*, 10:3 (Spring 1981), 59–76; and Beshara B. Doumani's important essay, "Rediscovering Ottoman Palestine: Writing Palestinians into History," *Journal of Palestine Studies*, 21:2 (Winter 1992), 5–28 (Chapter 2 of this book).

2 (New York: Basic Books, 1967). 1.

3 Talal Asad, "Anthropological Texts and Ideological Problems: An Analysis of Cohen on Arab Villages in Israel," *Review of Middle East Studies*, 1 (1975), 14 n. 11 (also excerpted in *MERIP Reports*, 53 [December 1976]). See also Gershon Shafir, *Land, Labor and the Origins of the Israeli–Palestinian Conflict 1882–1914* (Cambridge: Cambridge University Press, 1989), 1–7.

4 (Chicago: University of Chicago Press), 1978, 13: first published in Hebrew as *Miyishuv limedina: yehudei eretz yisra'el bitequfat hamandat keqehila politit* (Tel Aviv: 'Am 'Oved, 1977).

5 For example: 'Abd al-Wahhab at-Kayyali, *Ta'rikh filastin al-hadith* (Beirut: Al-Mu'assasa al-'arabiyya lil-dirasat wa'l-nashr, 1970), or Muhammad Nakhlah, *Tatawwur al-mujtami' fi filastin* (Kuwait: Mu'assasat Dhat al-Salasil, 1983).

6 "Israel: Conflict, War and Social Change," in Colin Creighton and Martin Shaw, eds., *The Sociology of War and Peace* (Houndmills, Hampshire: The Macmillan Press, 1987), 131.

7 For example, research on the gendered character of those identities, discourses and practices has gotten underway only recently.

8 The Israeli scholars who have pioneered what might be called the revisionist tendency of Israeli historiography include Baruch Kimmerling, Gershon Shafir, Michael Shalev, Lev Luis Grinberg, Tamar Gozanski, Shlomo Swirski, Ella Shohat, and the contributors to the now-defunct journal *Mahbarot limehkar velebikoret*. For a discussion of some of the revisionist works on the events of 1947–49 and of the political conjuncture out of which they emerge, see Zachary Lockman, "Original Sin," in Zachary Lockman and Joel Beinin, eds., *Intifada: the Palestinian Uprising Against Israeli Occupation* (Boston: South End Press, 1989); see also Laurence J. Silberstein, ed., *New Perspectives on Israeli History: the Early Years of the Stale* (New York: New York University Press, 1991).

Given the dispersion, statelessness, and subordination that characterize Palestinian life, the continuing centrality of the struggle for national self-determination and the limited resources at the disposal of most Palestinian scholars, explicit revisionism has perhaps not surprisingly been less in evidence among Palestinians. Nonetheless, a number of studies manifest what I call a relational approach, most notably Elia Zureik's *The Palestinians in Israel: A Study in Internal Colonialism* (London: Routledge and Kegan Paul, 1979). A number of other Palestinian scholars have produced studies which depart from conventional narratives in approach and choice of subject, including Salim Tamari, Musa al-Budayri, Mahir al-Sharif, 'Abd al-Qadir Yasin, Philip Mattar, and Muhammad Muslih. Various Palestinian research centers and institutions of higher education have in recent years also published important work in Arabic on aspects of Palestinian social and cultural history.

Among works produced by scholars who are neither Israeli nor Palestinian, pride of place belongs to Roger Owen's edited volume, *Studies in the Economic and Social History of Palestine in the Nineteenth and Twentieth Centuries* (Carbondale, Ill.: Southern Illinois University Press, 1982), and especially to his introduction, which explicitly discusses various conceptualizations of Palestinian history. Innovative work has also been produced by Talal Asad, Theodore Swedenburg, Rachelle Taqqu, and Joel Beinin. This survey is of course by no means exhaustive.

9 "The Perils of Palestiniology," *Arab Studies Quarterly*, 3:4 (Fall 1981), 403–11. The subsumption of Palestinian identity, agency, and history is obviously related to the longstanding disparity in the relative power and status of Israeli Jews and Palestinians. While the former are citizens of an established nation-state, most of the latter live under alien (and often repressive) rule, whether within or outside their historic homeland, and as a people are still denied national self-determination in any part of Palestine.

10 The catastrophic disruption of Palestinian Arab society in 1947–49 and the consequent destruction of many of the source materials from which Palestinian social and cultural history might have been reconstructed, combined with the relative abundance of material on the Jewish side, make it very difficult to avoid privileging the history and perspectives of the Yishuv – a skewing which my own research presented here does not, I admit, entirely escape.

11 Palestine Railways, *Report of the General Manager, passim*.

12 This discussion of the railway workers is drawn from a larger research project which explores interactions among Jewish and Arab workers, trade unions, labor movements, and leftist political parties during the mandate period.

13 The Syrians were not, of course, actually considered foreign until Britain and France divided up geographic Syria into the four new political entities of Syria, Lebanon, Palestine, and Transjordan. On the railway workers in the early postwar period, see Bulus Farah, *Min al-'uthmaniyya ila al-dawla al-'ibriyya* (Nazareth: al-Sawt, 1985), 40–46.

14 See the transcripts of interviews with Yehezkiel Abrarnov (April 9, 1972) and Efrayyim Shvartzman (March 20, 1972), Center for Oral Documentation, Archive of Labor and Pioneering, at the Lavon Institute for the Study of the Labor Movement, Tel Aviv [hereafter cited as AL].

15 From its inception at the turn of the century and with diminishing consistency up to 1948, the labor-Zionist movement tended to use Hebrew ('*ivri*) instead of Jewish (*yehudi*) to refer to itself and its project. This was an expression of labor Zionist denigration and rejection of Diaspora Judaism, which it associated with statelessness, powerlessness, and passivity, and its exaltation of the (suitably mythologized) ancient Hebrews as a socially normal and politically sovereign nation living in its homeland and working its soil. By conceiving of themselves as Hebrews, a new and different type of Jew living in the Land of Israel and free of the defects allegedly produced by two thousand years of exile, these Zionists meant to emphasize their authenticity and their rootedness in Palestine.

16 Gershon Shafir has analysed most effectively how labor-Zionist ideology, and the practices and institutions associated with it, were strongly shaped by the markets for labor and land in which the immigrants of the second Aliya (wave of Jewish immigration) found themselves when they arrived in Palestine between 1903 and 1914 (see his *Land, Labor and the Origins of the Israeli–Palestinian Conflict*).

17 For a classic statement of the doctrine of Hebrew labor, see David Ben-Gurion, 'Avoda 'Ivrit (Tel Aviv: Histadrut, 1932), translated into English and published in London as Jewish Labour at about the same time. Ben-Gurion went so far as to accuse Jewish private employers (mainly citrus farmers) who preferred Arab to Jewish workers of "economic antisemitism." On the campaigns to impose Hebrew labor on Jewish farmers, see Anita Shapira, Hama'avak hanikhzav: 'avoda 'ivrit, 1929–1939 (Tel Aviv: Hakibbutz Hame'uhad, 1977).

18 Haifa's population rose from some 18,000 in 1918 to nearly 100,000 by 1936. On the city's development in this period see May Seikaly, "The Arab Community of Haifa, 1918–1936: A Study in Transformation" (Ph.D. disser., Somerville College, Oxford University, 1983), and Joseph Vashitz's uneven but useful study, "Jewish–Arab Relations at Haifa under the British Mandate" (unpublished manuscript, kindly provided by the author).

19 Some went so far as to depict the Jewish proletariat in Palestine as the vanguard of a mighty movement which would liberate the oppressed workers of the entire Arab East, though this theme, not unpopular early in the decade, faded away thereafter. See for example Ben-Gurion's August 1921 theses for the Ahdut Ha'avoda party congress, first published in issue 91 of the party organ, Kuntres, and later republished in Anahnu veshcheineinu (Davar: Tel Aviv, 1931), a collection of his essays and speeches on the Arab question, 61–62.

20 See for example his speech published in Kuntres, 106 (January 1922).

21 AL, protocols of meeting of the executive committee of the Histadrut [hereafter EC/H], December 20, 1920.

22 On the Egyptian labor and nationalist movements in this period, see Joel Beinin and Zachary Lockman, Workers on the Nile: Nationalism, Communism, Islam, and the Egyptian Working Class, 1882–1954 (Princeton, NJ: Princeton University Press, 1987), chs. 4–5.

23 Din veheshbon lave' ida hashlishit shel hahistadrut (Tel Aviv, 1927), 155.

24 Kuntres, 165 (March 4, 1924).

25 The only serious study of this party is Elqana Margalit, Anatomia shel smot: Po'alei Tziyon be'eretz yisra'el (1919–1946) (Y. L. Peretz: Jerusalem, 1976).

26 The available figures are not entirely consistent or reliable, but at the end of 1924 the union was apparently comprised of some 529 Jewish and Arab railway workers, out of a work force of almost 2,400. Almost all the Jews, but only 10 to 15 percent of the Arabs, employed on the railroad belonged to the union; most if not all of the Arab union members seem to have been skilled or semiskilled workshop workers, foremen, and other more or less permanent personnel from the running and traffic departments. On the size and composition of the union membership, see AL 104/25a, memorandum of the URPTW to the general manager, Palestine Railways; AL 208/14a, Central Committee of the URPTW to EC/H, November 30, 1924; AL 237/1; and also the figures given in Din veheshbon, 64. None of these figures include the unionized postal and telegraph workers, whose numbers were in any case much smaller.

27 On these ongoing efforts, see for example EC/H, October 10, November 7, 1922; secretariat of the Histadrut executive committee [hereafter abbreviated as S/FC/H], October 25, 1925; Central Zionist Archives, S9/1424a, NURPTW to the Zionist Executive, November 1929; Meirowitz to the Labor Department of the Jewish Agency, March 29, April 27, 1930,

28 On shop-floor sentiments, see Farah, Min al-'uthmaniyya, 42–43.

29 AL 208/14a, CC/URPTW to EC/H, November 30, 1924, and *Haifa,* 6 (January 1, 1925, 43–44; interview with Avraham Khalfon, January 29, 1976, AL, Center for Oral Documentation.

30 I discuss this question more fully in "We Opened Up the Arabs' minds: Labor-Zionist Discourse and the Railway Workers of Palestine, 1919–1929," *Review of Middle East Studies,* 5 (1992).

31 On the emergence of the PAWS, see *Haifa,* 15 (April 30, 1925), 117–18; *Filastin,* March 6, 1925; *al-Yarmuk,* October 22, 1925; al-Budayri, *Tatawwur;* and Yasin, *Ta'rikh.*

32 Though it may sometimes be anachronistic, for the sake of clarity and consistency I will use AURW throughout to denote the Arab railway workers organized within PAWS.

33 Though the Jewish-led union was known between 1927 and 1931 as the National Union of Railway, Postal and Telegraph Workers, for the sake of clarity I will henceforth refer to it as the IU.

34 See for example AL 237/24, Grobman to Ben-Tzvi, May 1928; AL 208/815a, Dana to S/EC/H, January 6, 1935.

35 See for example AL 490/3.

36 In a Hebrew-language leaflet issued by PAWS, AL 237/21, September 29, 1928.

37 Farah, *Min al-'uthmaniyya,* 41.

38 Oral interview, May 14, 1987.

39 In our interview Abramov used the Yiddish term *der Araber,* reflecting the widespread use of that language among new immigrants from Eastern Europe. By contrast, Abramov noted, the Arabs were more respectful of Jewish coworkers and referred to them by name.

40 Paul Cotterell, *The Railways of Palestine and Israel* (Abingdon, Oxfordshire: Tourret Publishing, 1984), ch. 5.

41 AL 237/26b, Berman to EC/H, May 3, 1940; AL 237/16, IU, central committee meeting of November 9, 1940.

42 Hashorner Hatza'ir archives, Aharon Cohen papers, 6 (5), "'Al hashvita bevatei hamal'aha shel harakevet"; AL 208/3660, "Hashvita bevatei hamal'aha behaifa"; *Filastin,* February 5, 1944; *Mishmar,* February 6, 1944; *Haqiqat al-Amr,* February 8, 1944; *Palestine Post,* February 6, 1944.

43 June 17, 1945.

44 See the Palestinian press for April 1946; AL 425/33, joint leaflet of the PKP and NLL, April 18, 1946; AL, EC/H, April 24, 1946; Israel State Archives, 65/779, Arab Workers' Congress, *Bayan,* April 25, 1946.

45 This is not to say that the Zionist leadership actually desired or expected the establishment of a Palestinian Arab state. The Jewish Agency, the *de facto* leadership of the Yishuv, had in fact secretly reached an informal understanding with King Abdullah of Transjordan whereby the king would occupy and annex much of the territory assigned to the Arab state. See Avi Shlaim, *Collusion Across the Jordan: King Abdullah, the Zionist Movement, and the Partition of Palestine* (New York: Columbia University Press, 1988).

46 See the report of the committee of inquiry appointed by Haifa's Jewish community, AL 250/40–3–9, and contemporary press accounts. Although the Jewish Agency promptly denounced the Etzel attack outside the Haifa refinery as an "act of madness," it also authorized its own military force, the Hagana, to retaliate for the massacre of Jews at the refinery by attacking and killing Arab civilians in the outlying village of Balad al-Shaykh on December 31.

47 Oral interview with Efrayim Krisher, a former leader of the Jewish railway workers' union, May 13, 1987.
48 The best work on the causes of Palestinian displacement is Benny Morris, *The Birth of the Palestinian Refugee Problem, 1947–1949* (Cambridge: Cambridge University Press, 1987); on Haifa in particular, see pages 73–93.
49 Aharon Cohen's *Israel and the Arab World* (London: W. H. Allen, 1970) is a classic of this genre, as it contains much useful information.
50 See Shlomo Swirski, *Israel: the Oriental Majority* (London: Zed Press, 1989), and Ella Shohat, "Sephardim in Israel: Zionism from the Standpoint of its Jewish Victims," in *Social Text*, 19/20 (Fall 1988), 1–35.
51 I explore this question in "Exclusion and Solidarity: Labor Zionism and Arab Workers in Palestine," in Gyan Prakash, ed., *After Colonialism: Imperialism and the Colonial Aftermath* (Princeton: Princeton University Press, forthcoming).
52 Itamar Even-Zohar's work on the evolution of Hebrew culture in Palestine suggests one path along which a relational approach to Palestinian culture might be developed. See "The Emergence of a Native Hebrew Culture in Palestine, 1882–1948," *Poetics Today*, 11: 1 (Spring 1990), 175–91, and his other articles in that same issue.

7

THE ROLE OF THE
PALESTINIAN PEASANTRY IN
THE GREAT REVOLT (1936–9)

Ted Swedenburg

Ted Swedenburg was one of the first historians in the West who dissociated himself from the common discourse of modernization which had been applied to studies on Palestine's history. His work combined two of the main features of recent orientations in the conflict's historiography. On the one hand, he brings to the fore marginalized groups, in this case the rebelling peasants of Palestine in the 1930s; on the other, he chose to analyse their history as part of an anti-colonialist movement. By adopting this approach, his work forms a major component in the new historiography which focuses on history from below, and adopts a colonialist perspective towards Zionism, as did the critical Israeli sociologists on the other.

The article shows that when the Palestinian peasant revolt of the 1930s is viewed from these two new angles, it can be seen as an active uprising by an alliance of non-elite groups within the society, forcing the traditional notable elite to take a firmer and more committed stance for the sake of the society as a whole. It is no wonder that such a description seemed to other researchers as fitting equally well the making of the 1987 Intifada. The history of peasants in Palestine, for a long while comprising about 70 per cent of the population, has already been tackled by leading Palestinian sociologists, but one feels that more history is going to be produced in the coming years about Palestine's nature and future, if only because of the contemporary debates within Palestinian society.

* * *

Between 1936 and 1939, a major anti-colonial rebellion known among Arabs as the Great Revolt shook the mandate territory of Palestine. The struggle pitted a poorly armed peasant movement against the might of the world's pre-eminent colonial power, Great Britain. Despite the militancy and duration of the revolt, scholarly work on this period tends to emphasize the shortcomings of the insurgent movement and, in particular, to discount the role of the peasantry. Dominant accounts generally define the fellahin as "traditional, backward, and conservative," as "activated by tribal and religious loyalties,"[1] and as "too isolated, ignorant and poor" to play a significant role in the national movement.[2] Because they consider the peasants to be completely dominated by the local ruling class, these scholars view them as incapable of political initiative. Moreover, they attribute the disintegration of the revolt to the traditional clannish, factional, and regional divisions among fellahin that prevented them from maintaining a unified movement. The rebellion's demise is thus seen as due to the peasantry's accession to leadership in the vacuum left by the urban elites. A parallel argument, which imposes a model derived from industrial capitalism upon an agrarian society, attributes the uprising's defeat to its failure to develop a strong leadership. Since only a revolutionary party could have provided the command structure and social program necessary for victory, the peasantry as a class is considered incapable of providing guidance. Such analyses not only dismiss the crucial role of the peasants, who made up 75 per cent of the population of Palestine,[3] but also ignore their legitimate social and political demands.

I propose, as an alternative, to read existing historical accounts "against the grain" so as to bring the marginalized Palestinian peasantry to the center of my analysis.[4] I will argue that the peasantry's relation to the ruling notables was never simply one of complete subservience. As Gramsci notes, a dominant class's hegemony is never "total or exclusive"; it is, rather, a process, a relation of dominance that has, as Raymond Williams says, "continually to be renewed, recreated, defended and modified. It is also continually resisted, limited, altered, challenged by pressures not all its own." The Palestinian peasantry, therefore, while subordinated to the rule of the notables, nonetheless possessed a long tradition of opposition to their hegemony. It also possessed a history of challenging capitalist penetration and state formation. Such traditions of resistance were kept alive in popular memory and could be drawn upon as powerful tools of mobilization in moments of rupture. These "folk" traditions were not isolated, however, from other influences. They did not exist in a state of pristine purity, but were affected and transformed both by the dominant ideologies of the notables, who led the nationalist movement, and by alternative discourses emanating from more radical factions of the educated middle class. Also the fellahin's "common sense" notions[6] and their forms of political mobilization were jolted by the rapidly changing material conditions of the British mandate period. The Palestine peasantry, in short, was not simply an unchanging, backward social category.

During the course of the revolt, the rebels, who represented a broad alliance of peasants, workers, and radical elements of the middle class, developed an effective military force and began to implement social and political programs that challenged a'yan (notable) leadership of the nationalist movement and threatened the bases of mercantile–landlord dominance. The threat of a counter-hegemonic peasant leadership with a class-based program caused large numbers of wealthy urban Palestinians to flee the country. The movement also posed a serious threat to British strategy in the region and forced them to expend considerable military energies to crush the rebellion, which they succeeded in doing only after more than three years of struggle.

In order to recuperate and to assess the Palestinian peasants' achievements and traditions of resistance, I will trace the historical evolution of Palestinian society and its prevailing ideologies prior to the rebellion, going back to the period before capitalism was imposed as the mode of production in Palestine. This will lay the foundation for understanding of the pivotal role of the struggles of the Palestinian against the expansion of the Ottoman state, Zionist colonization, and British occupation that culminated in the Great Revolt.[7]

Palestine in the precapitalist era

In the period immediately prior to its occupation by Egypt's ruler Muhammad 'Ali in 1831, Palestine was only loosely controlled and integrated into the Ottoman empire.[8] At best, Ottoman sway extended to Palestine's towns and their immediate environs. But even the towns, dominated by notables whose authority was based on religious or genealogically claimed "noble" status, enjoyed substantial autonomy and frequently rebelled against Ottoman authority.[9] Towns along the coast had suffered a decline in the late eighteenth century due to the demise of the cotton trade with France and the ravages inflicted by the successive invasions of coastal Palestine by Egypt's 'Ali Bey (1770–71) and France's Napoleon Bonaparte (1799).[10] By the early nineteenth century the center of gravity had shifted to the towns of the interior highlands. While these urban centers in no way rivaled the great commercial emporia and textile-producing cities of northern Syria (Damascus, Homs, Hama), they were important centers of local and regional trade and artisanal production (particularly the olive oil of Nablus). In an era of weak imperial authority, these towns were generally dominated by the countryside. The population of the rural areas was concentrated in the central highlands of the Galilee, Jabal Nablus (Samaria), and Jabal al-Khalil (Judea). Here, clan-based coalitions organized along highly fluid "tribal" lines (Qays and Yemen) competed over local resources and political power. A rudimentary class structure separated the shaykhs of the leading patrilineages (*hamulas*) and the district tax collectors (*shuyukb al-nawabi*) from the mass of peasant producers.[11] The shaykhs' obligations to the Ottoman state were to maintain security and to collect taxes, a portion of which they retained. In practice they only sporadically remitted taxes to the state; more frequently they defended their autonomy by raising rural confederations to fend off tax-foraging expeditions sent out by the Ottoman governors of Damascus and Sidon.[12] Local class antagonisms were thus somewhat mitigated by the benefits that the peasantry gained in supporting their local chieftains against direct Ottoman rule.

The lowlands of Palestine – the plains of the coast and the Jordan and Esdraelon valleys – functioned as a hinterland for the highlands. But they were not merely an empty zone. The plains were cultivated but sparsely populated. Villagers who resided permanently in the more secure and salubrious hills and foothills went down to the lowlands to work the nearby plains on a seasonal basis. In contrast to the highlands, where individual ownership (*mulk*) by the head of the extended family predominated and where orchard and vine cultivation was typical, the peasants of the plains participated in *musba* or "communal" tenure and practiced extensive grain cultivation.

Unlike the highlands, in the lowlands agricultural practices interpenetrated with pastoralism, for both villagers and nomads used marginal and fallow lands to pasture their herds. The relation between peasants and nomads, usually represented as implacably hostile, was actually one of complexity and fluidity, characterized by moments both of cooperation and of struggle. Commentators who have described conditions on the plain as "anarchic" and have singled out the Bedouin as the chief cause of desolation merely reproduce the viewpoint of the Ottoman state. In fact the lowlands were simply a zone where peasants, nomads, bandits (both of peasant and of nomadic stock), and the forces of the state vied for control, with no group able to take decisive command. Bedouin chiefs commonly ruled over certain areas and "protected" peasants against the forces of the state (and against thieves and other nomadic tribes), in return for protection fees paid as a form of rent.

Precapitalist ideologies

Although the peasants of Palestine recognized the Ottoman sultans as successors to the Prophet and thus as legitimate rulers, in practice they exercised a great deal of independence from the state; Ottoman authority may have been legitimate but it scarcely intervened in everyday life. The local shaykhs served as mediators between the peasants and the state, but, given the balance of forces, they enjoyed virtual autonomy. Their own authority rested upon their imputed "noble" descent. As is typical in precapitalist societies,[13] relations between the "noble" shaykhs and their inferiors appeared highly personalized and intimate. This appearance in fact served to refract the underlying relations of exploitation, recasting them in terms consonant with the constitution of amicable interpersonal relations. Class antagonisms were also softened by the shared interests of shaykhs and peasants in defending highland villages from state intervention and in struggling against competing rural confederations. In addition, peasants were positioned in their productive relations through idioms of kinship,[14] while other relations based on village, regional, and "tribal" ties also served to divide peasants internally.[15] These vertical cleavages were not insuperable, for the various confederations (including Bedouin) were able to unite under the leadership of the shaykhs to resist foreign invaders, as in the broad-based 1834 rebellion against Egyptian occupation.[16] The principles of these dynamics of division and unity are expressed in the famous proverb, "I and my brother [unite to fight] against my cousin, but I and my cousin [unite to fight] against the stranger."[17]

Lack of state control over rural areas was also reflected in the distinctly "folk" character of peasant Islam. Mosques were virtually unknown in the villages, for rural religious practice centered instead on the worship of saints (*walis*) whose shrines (*maqams*) dotted the countryside. Nearly every village possessed at least one *maqam* where peasants went to plead for the *wali*'s intercession on their behalf.[18] A proliferation of shrines underlined the localized, particularistic nature of Palestinian folk Islam. However, other aspects of popular religion point equally to its socially unifying effects. For one thing, it was not *strictly* Islamic, for Muslim peasants visited many Christian churches and respected them as holy shrines.[19] Feasts (*mawsim*) celebrated in honor of various prophets also enhanced popular unity. For example, the *mawsim* of Nabi Rubin (Reuben), held south of Jaffa, attracted pilgrims from all the nearby towns and villages and lasted for a full lunar month.[20] The *mawsim* of Nabi Musa (Moses), celebrated near Jericho, was an even bigger event, attended by peasants, city-dwellers, and Bedouin from all over southern Palestine and Jabal Nablus.[21] Such feasts, joining peasants from a wide area together with town-dwellers, were important rituals of popular solidarity.

Despite localized folk practices, the peasants of Palestine remained part of the wider Ottoman Islamic community which owed its loyalty to the sultan in Istanbul. In theory at least, their broader sense of belonging involved diffuse notions of duties and obligations to the Ottoman state, including the duty to pay taxes. Although the prevailing balance of forces in practice diminished the effects of such sentiments of loyalty to imperial authority, they held the potential to override localized interests. As the Ottoman authorities increased their hold over the provinces, they could draw on such sentiments to impose their hegemony.

Palestine's integration into the world market

During the course of the nineteenth century, Palestine, like most of the non-Western world, was integrated into the capitalist world market, which dramatically transformed its social structure. These changes were not a "natural" evolutionary process, but required the sharp intervention of the Ottoman state under pressure from the European powers. Such developments began with the Egyptian invasion of Palestine and the rest of Syria, and Ibrahim Pasha's vigorous efforts to secure order there between 1831 and 1840. After the Egyptian exodus, the transformation proceeded more slowly as the Ottomans gradually subdued the towns and pacified the countryside, making the atmosphere safe for export agriculture and commerce.

The process involved a major shift in the local balance of forces. Ottoman authorities broke the power of the rural confederations and shifted control over local administration and tax collection from the independent-minded rural shaykhs to an emerging class of urban a'yan or notables, the Porte's local partners in its project of "reform." Their local power eroded, many rural shaykhs subsequently shifted their base of operations to the towns and merged with the urban notable class.

The a'yan took command over much of agricultural production, besides seizing political control over rural areas. Notable families and an emerging commercial bourgeoisie acquired vast properties in the wake of a series of new land laws beginning with the Ottoman Land Code of 1858. These new laws required individual registration of title to what was considered state or miri land and facilitated a massive land grab. The a'yan, who controlled the state apparatus administering the laws, were best positioned to profit from the situation. Many peasants failed to register their properties, some to avoid paying the registration fee, others to keep their names off government rolls and so escape conscription into the Ottoman army. Still others, rather than simply lose their lands in this fashion, registered their properties (sometimes a whole village) in the name of a powerful notable, who then served as their "patron" in their relations with the state. Other forms of alienation occurred when the Ottoman government decreed that specific tracts of land, especially in the northern plains, were "not permanently cultivated" or when it confiscated particular domains for "security" reasons. Such properties were put up for sale, and the largest of them were often purchased by absentee owners residing in Beirut. Peasants who had customarily farmed these lands were transformed into sharecroppers working for large landowners; a similar change occurred among those who "voluntarily" registered their lands in the names of notables. As cash gained in importance in the regional economy and as the Ottomans began to demand taxes in cash, numbers of fellahin fell into debt to usurers, either notables or commercial bourgeois members of the local ruling bloc. Many peasants foreclosed on their loans, lost title to their lands, and became share-croppers. Others, who remained "independent" small or middle peasants, often became deeply dependent on their creditors.

The effects of these transformations were uneven. Land alienation was concentrated in the central and northern plains of the coast and the Esdraelon valley, where Ottoman authorities were most concerned to establish permanent settlements and where the most profitable crops for export to Europe could be grown. The highlands, however, generally remained a stronghold of small holdings but even there many peasants were forced to take out loans and thereby became dependent on money-lending notable "patrons."

The subordination of the local economy to the needs of the capitalist world economy paralleled the subjugation of the peasantry. Pacification of the countryside and the onset of landlord-merchant control over agrarian production created a dramatic rise in agricultural exports. As a cash economy gradually developed, peasants were increasingly forced to sell part of their product on the market. Already by the 1870s, Palestine exported significant amounts of wheat, barley, sesame, olive oil, and citrus to Europe and to regional markets.[22]

Such transformations were not motivated simply by external factors but were integrally linked to the rise of leading classes composed of two sectors: first, the notables, predominantly Muslim, who owned large tracts of land, engaged in moneylending, and dominated the increasingly centralized government and religious apparatuses; and, second, the commercial bourgeoisie, composed chiefly of Palestinian and Lebanese Christians, Jews, Europeans, and European protégés, who were representatives of banking and merchant capital but who also owned large tracts of land.[23] Muslim notables, allied with Christian merchants, constituted the dominant sector, whose hegemony was organized under the form of what social scientists have termed "patron–client" relations, or pyramid-shaped networks of notables and their peasant client-clans.

Ideologies of notable dominance: patrons and clients

Notable patrons used their power and influence to assist their peasant clients in dealing both with the state and with other groups (such as peasants belonging to other patronage networks and Bedouin). In return, peasants supported their patrons in political struggles. The notables also provided sharecroppers with their subsistence needs during the year and made regular advances to them on holidays. In addition, they carried over the sharecroppers' debts in case of a series of poor harvests.[24] Similar favors were accorded to their smallholdings "clients" as well as to farm laborers who worked for landlords on a seasonal basis. The hierarchical relation between notable and peasant appeared to involve a high degree of mutuality and reciprocity. On the basis of an empirical description of this system many observers have concluded that it is wrong to conceive of Palestinian society during this era in terms of social classes.[25]

What most observers have done is to accept, at face value, native conceptions (with a notable bias) about how politics and economics "worked." In fact, the patron–client system was simply the form that class relations assumed as Palestine was integrated into the capitalist world market as a dependency of the industrialized European powers. During this period landlords and usurers seized control over the countryside and manipulated existing precapitalist means of domination for their own interests.[26] The form that the relations between the fundamental classes took – "paternalism" in the sphere of production (cash advances by patrons to peasants) and "patronage" in the socio-political sphere (an "exchange" of favors) – tended to refract the fundamentally exploitative relations between landlord-usurers and peasants.[27] Politicoeconomic relations between them were represented as "exchanges" between individuals unequal in status – notables whose superior birth and noble lineage qualified them to rule and to manage property, and peasants who had internalized their position of inferiority and who behaved deferentially toward their superiors. On the other hand, "politics" in the larger sense of the "affairs of state" appeared as a struggle among the notables themselves, in which peasant clients played only a supporting role. The notables acted as "their" peasants' representatives to the government, a role acquired not through democratic elections but by ascribed superior status. The literature that characterizes political struggle in this period as "factionalism" in fact disguises a high degree of class unity at the upper level. But on the lower levels, patron–client ideology largely reinforced and rigidified pre-existing vertical cleavages based on idioms of clan, village, and regional distinctions. The patron–client system did not assume the form of exchanges between "free" individuals, as under full-blown capitalism. Instead, the system of exploitation required an extra-economic element, the force of status hierarchy, to justify the "exchange" between persons of unequal position. Economic relations between patron and client were always expressed in such terms as "honor," gift-giving, kinship. Although paternalism and patronage provided the ideological basis for rule by the notables, their hegemony did not go unchallenged by the fellahin. There was room for struggle even on the basis of such an ideology. From the peasants' point of view, the system was designed to guarantee them the rights to a "fair" and "just" exchange. A notable could not charge too much rent without appearing to break his end of the bargain, without seeming to fail in his duty to uphold a standard of *noblesse oblige*. This meant that a landlord-usurer who charged peasants high interest on loans was simultaneously forced to advance them additional credit to maintain his labor force. In addition, the patron had to provide his client with the culturally regulated minimum of subsistence in order to neutralize potential class antagonisms. This level of subsistence was determined through similar struggles of a distinctly class character, for the peasant was able to use the notable's dependence on his labor as a wedge to demand adherence to the notion of "fair" exchange. In the political realm, peasants (primarily the smallholder) could shift their allegiance if they received insufficient benefits from their patron. The patron–client alliances were thus far more fluid in composition than the model of a solid pyramidal structure purveyed by social scientists would suggest.[28]

Subordination of the political economy of Palestine to nineteenth-century Western industrial capitalism entailed, paradoxically, the reinforcement of precapitalist or "feudal" ideologies. While peasants increasingly worked for capital, they did so under transformed precapitalist forms of productive relations and ideologies. In order to make these transformations, the notables had to "work on" precapitalist ideologies of hierarchy, so as to reinforce the peasants' attitude of deference and to reproduce their sensibility of mutuality and exchange. The conditions of peripheral capitalism required a much more active ruling-class hegemony than had been needed in the precapitalist era. Ruling-class ideologies now had to penetrate deeply the cultural life of the peasantry,[29] including their religious "common sense." As a consequence folk practices were substantially transformed by notables in this period.

The organization of the feast of Nabi Musa exemplifies this process. In the latter half of the century, the Ottomans appointed the Husaynis – a rising notable clan from Jerusalem – as hosts of the Nabi Musa feast and custodians of the shrine.[30] Festivities were now launched at Jerusalem with a procession in which the banner of Nabi Musa was brought from the Husayni-owned Dar al-Kabira where it was housed. Notables led the procession followed by crowds from the city and the villages. At the site of the feast itself (near Jericho), the Husaynis and the Yunises, another Jerusalem notable family, served two public meals a day to all visitors.[31] Such rituals demonstrated notable generosity and claims to supremacy in powerful ways.

At the same time as unifying folk practices were subsumed under notable control, saint worship came under increasing attack by religious reformers, particularly from the Salafiya movement. Mosques, where state-backed Islamic orthodoxy was preached, replaced the *maqams* as

[margin note: Notable-hosted feasts]

village centers of worship. The chief reason for the suppression of saint worship was the localism it expressed.[32] Though such folk practices were not immediately wiped out, they were forced into regression as more and more peasants were "educated" and came to regard such activities as "un-Islamic."

The emergence of organized opposition

The piecemeal implementation of notable domination confined resistance against land transfers and growing state control to a localized, sporadic, and manageable level. No large-scale eruptions or even jacqueries occurred. However, opposition was still significant. For instance, many peasants demonstrated their opposition to the changing state of affairs by leaving their villages to settle as farmers in Transjordan or by migrating overseas. Others chose to join gangs of bandits, which continued to operate in the hills despite increasing pressure from security forces. Young men sought refuge with Bedouin tribes or even resorted to self-mutilation to avoid conscription into the army. Perhaps the major form of resistance in this period took place at the point of production. Palestinian peasants, particularly in the plains where sharecropping predominated, were often described at the time as "lazy, thriftless and sullen."[33] As James Scott has observed, "foot-dragging and dissimulation" are a common form of resistance under unequal power relations.[34] While such resistance may not have posed a grave danger to the new system, it at least slowed the process of accumulation.

Peasant opposition to the colonization of Palestine by foreigners in fact presented the greatest threat to the hegemony of local notables. In 1878, Jewish settlers from Europe, with the backing of powerful capitalist financial interests, began to take advantage of the general land-grab in Palestine by acquiring lands and establishing agricultural colonies in the fertile coastal plains and the Esdraelon valley. By 1914, 12,000 Jews lived in such colonies, which produced valuable citrus and wine exports and encompassed over 162,500 acres of land concentrated in the richest agricultural regions. Most estates were purchased from absentee landowners in Beirut who had only recently acquired them. As new colonies were set up, large numbers of peasant sharecroppers were forcibly removed from the lands they considered their birthright, although they may never have formally "owned" them. Jewish settlers who established colonies even on "marginal" lands were able to improve them due to their access to capital and advanced scientific techniques, and so denied nomads and peasants their customary-use rights to these common lands for grazing and gathering.

Palestinian notables were not at this stage implicated in any great degree in land sales to Jewish settlers. They protested Jewish immigration and land purchases as early as 1891, but their efforts were largely "sporadic and nonsystematic" and limited to sending formal petitions of protest to Istanbul.[35] The advances made by urban Jews in commerce and industry were perceived as a greater threat to the interests of the Arab upper classes, particularly the commercial bourgeois sector, than were their purchases of agricultural properties.

In contrast, peasants whose livelihoods were directly threatened by Jewish colonies – especially those who cultivated and who pastured their herds in the northern and central plains – reacted in militant fashion. By 1883, displaced peasants and Bedouin were already attacking, raiding, robbing, and generally harassing the new Jewish settlements. Although spontaneous and fragmented, this violent opposition meant that the government was routinely forced to call out troops to drive fellahin off lands purchased by Jewish colonists. These activities eventually prompted the notables to protest the Zionist influx, albeit feebly.

The a'yan's ineffectiveness in confronting the external threat began to undermine their own legitimacy (and that of the Ottoman state in general) in the eyes of many Palestinians. The disastrous experiences that befell dispossessed peasant sharecroppers in particular prompted them to question the usefulness of the patron–client system. Arab nationalism, emerging at the same moment, was able to tap these sentiments. As a nascent movement that advocated in its different versions either complete Arab independence from the Ottoman empire or greater autonomy, it became a significant social force in the wake of the ferment aroused by the Young Turk revolution (1908). Although the nationalist movement was less important in Southern Syria (Palestine) than in Lebanon and Northern Syria, and though it was dominated by notables and the commercial bourgeoisie, nonetheless there arose within it a radical wing composed of elements of the educated middle class. Opposition to Zionism was one of the Palestinian radical nationalists' chief themes, which they advanced through a new means of communication that had sprung up in this era of enhanced political freedom, namely newspapers. Although the early Arab nationalist movement is usually characterized as a strictly urban phenomenon, beginning in 1909 the political activities of its militant wing included helping to organize peasant attacks on Jewish settlements.[36] These raids increased in tempo in the years immediately preceding World War I, but this militant sector of the developing Arab national movement and its peasant connections assumed real prominence only during the years following the war.

notables not helping peasants

The British occupation of Palestine and the mandate, 1918–29

Expectations for national independence rose sharply in Greater Syria as World War I and the privations it caused came to a close. These hopes intensified in 1918 with the establishment of an Arab government at Damascus under Prince Faysal. Many young Palestinian radicals from the educated middle class held prominent positions in the new Sharifian government. At the same time, their influence in Palestine began to outstrip that of the more moderate notables. Through organizations such as al-Nadi al-'Arabi (the Arab Club) and al-Muntada al-Adabi (the Literary Club), the radicals pushed for a program of complete independence of Palestine from Britain and for its political unity with the rest of Syria. By contrast, the Palestinian notables who had organized Muslim–Christian Associations in all the towns favored a separate political autonomy for Palestine under British protection. The euphoria that followed the end of the war was dampened by the Balfour Declaration, which announced Britain's intention of establishing a "national home for the Jewish people" in Palestine. This tarnished Britain's local reputation and helped win broad popular support for the militant nationalist program. Popular radicalism in turn pressured the notable *zu'ama* or "chiefs" to adopt more combative positions themselves. The militants capitalized on the moment by pushing through a resolution advocating Palestine's political unity with Syria at the notable-dominated First Palestine Arab Congress.[37]

In this period the radicals not only organized effectively in the public arena but also secretly purchased arms and prepared for armed revolt favor of Faysal.[38] So effective was the radicals' work among the peasantry that in December 1919, British Naval Intelligence reported with concern that fellahin were listening with keen interest to both Damascus and local newspapers advocating pan-Arabism and discussed the possibility of anti-Zionist actions.[39] Despite widespread illiteracy, "advanced" pan-Arab and anti-Zionist ideas circulated among the peasantry and helped to mobilize them. At least one organized act of violence against the British occurred. In April 1920, Palestinian radicals (connected to the Arab government at Damascus) organized over 2,000 armed Bedouin from the Hawran (Syria) and the Baysan valley of Palestine in an attack on British military forces.[40] The countrywide anti-British upsurge that the radicals expected to ensue did not, however, come to fruition.

In the same month, soon after Faysal was crowned as king of Syria, radicals intervened in the Nabi Musa procession at Jerusalem. In 1919 the practice of delaying the procession for speeches had been introduced;[41] this year Musa Kazim al-Husayni, Jerusalem's mayor and a leading notable, praised Faysal in his speech, while young activists made "inflammatory" declamations from the balcony of the Arab Club. The crowds, including peasants from the surrounding villages, responded by roaming the streets of the Old City, attacking Jewish residents.[42] This event transformed the *mawsim* of Nabi Musa from a folk festival into an annual nationalist demonstration.[43]

In May 1921, clashes between Arabs and Jews at Jaffa led to generalized fighting and attacks on Jewish settlements throughout the country. The British military quickly and violently restored order. Two months later King Faysal's troops at Damascus were defeated by the French, who dismantled the Arab government. The moment of crisis had ended. Great Britain, which now held a mandate to govern Palestine under the auspices of the League of Nations, strengthened its control. The threat of pan-Arab militants to *a'yan* hegemony and their ability to mobilize the peasantry subsided. The notables, who favored a policy of peaceful negotiations with the British authorities rather than mass mobilization as the means of achieving the nationalist goals, re-emerged as the dominant force within the national movement.

During the 1920s, the notables reasserted their hegemony over the Arab population of Palestine through a consolidation of their role as "natural" leaders of the national movement. British authorities in turn absorbed members of notable families into important administrative positions in the mandate government.[44] As chief agents of state rule in the late Ottoman and mandate periods, they expected to emerge as the country's rulers once Great Britain granted Palestine its independence. Their principal means of organization, the Muslim–Christian Associations, were not mass-membership bodies but were composed of religious leaders, property owners, those who held positions in the Ottoman administration, and "noble" families of rural origin – in short, the *a'yan* class. These associations periodically met in Palestine Arab Congresses and in 1920 set up an Arab Executive, chaired by Musa Kazim al-Husayni, to tend to the daily affairs of the national movement. At the same time, mandate authorities co-opted a young militant from a prominent notable family, Hajj Amin al-Husayni, making him first Grand Mufti (1921) and then president of the Supreme Muslim Council (SMC) in 1922. As "Head of Islam in Palestine," Hajj Amin gradually consolidated all Islamic affairs under his administration and began to compete with the more cautious Arab Executive for leadership of the nationalist movement.[45]

The notables continued to lead the Arab population of Palestine in the mandate period under the ideology of patronage. *A'yan* served as mediator between the people and the British authorities. Politics was strictly reserved for organizations (the Muslim–Christian Associations, the SMC) "qualified" to lead. Once the radical pan-Arab threat had passed and Palestine was established as a territorial unit, notables were able to co-opt the growing popular self-awareness of "Palestinian Arabness" that arose in response to the Zionist threat and to alien rule.[46] Furthermore, the British bolstered the *a'yan* position by ruling through their agency and by upholding their control over rural areas.[47]

In spite of the fact that the legitimacy of notable leadership was constructed on "national-popular" sentiments, the notables themselves were caught in a fundamentally contradictory position, for while the *a'yan* posed as leaders of nationalist aspirations, they served as officials in the British mandate administration. Rifaat Abou-el-Haj sums up the predicament of Palestinian notables (characteristic of all Mashriq elites):

> [As the nationalist elite] actually began to collaborate with the new ruling powers, the [elite] cadre managed to portray itself in the "vanguard" of resistance against outside domination – in some instances even taking a revolutionary posture. The other role it adopted for itself was that of realist-pragmatist mediator with which it defended its compatriots against the direct and therefore presumed odious rule of the foreigners.[48]

The British in Palestine depended in particular on erstwhile "radical" Amin al-Husayni to act as such a mediator. The Mufti worked hard to prevent outbursts and to pacify the Muslim community, channeling nationalist energies (including those of his former comrades) into legal activities.[49]

The contradictory position of the Palestinian notables – at once servants of the British mandate and leaders of "the nation" – was rendered even more unstable than that of Arab elites elsewhere, due to the competition of the Zionist movement. Since Zionists opposed the establishment of any legislative body in Palestine that would relegate the Jews to a minority position, they effectively blocked the development of national Palestinian institutions of self-rule. Had not the threat of Jewish immigration appeared somewhat limited due to internal problems of the Zionist movement, conditions might have been more unstable in the 1920s. But meanwhile, the Zionists were quietly building an infrastructure that served as the basis for expansion of the Jewish community in the 1930s and made the Yishuv virtually self-governing.[50]

The lack of progress in the creation of Palestinian institutions of self-rule began to undermine even the notables' own liberal self-image. Steeped in Western liberal ideas,[51] the *a'yan* expected the British to behave toward them according to the standards of justice that Great Britain preached. As it gradually became clear that the British authorities did not adhere in practice to the standards that the two groups supposedly shared, Palestinian liberal notables became disillusioned. Both notables and liberal intellectuals developed an ambivalent attitude toward the

West and, in particular, Britain.[52] Although the notables never entirely abandoned their affection for Britain since service in the mandate administration was still profitable, disaffection for British policies slowly undermined their confidence in diplomatic discussions between "gentlemen" as the best means of resolving the national question.

Rapidly changing agrarian conditions during the 1920s were potentially more unsettling to a'yan hegemony. Land purchases by the Zionists continued apace, resulting in the dispossession of increasing numbers of peasants. The notables' appeals that the government halt the process were ineffectual. Moreover, by 1928, land sales to the Zionists by Palestinian landowners had eclipsed those by non-Palestinians.[53] A section of the notable class was thus enriching itself through land sales to Zionists and contributing directly to peasant landlessness, especially in the northern and central plains. This portion of the a'yan, clustered around the leadership of the Nashashibi clan, which opposed the Husayni dominance in the national movement, generally comprised its wealthier and commercial elements, who used their profits for urban construction and expansion of citrus production.

Small but growing numbers of peasant holders also sold their lands to Zionist developers, usually not for profit but to pay off debts. Peasant indebtedness to usurers who charged high rates of interest was exacerbated by the mandate government's rationalization of rural property taxes, now set at a fixed percentage based on the net productivity of the soil (that is, minus the cost of production). This meant that the capital-intensive Jewish agricultural enterprises paid lower rates because of higher "labor costs." Regressive indirect taxes added to the peasants' financial burden. The weight of taxation therefore fell disproportionately on poor Palestinian fellahin, whose contributions helped to finance industrial and agricultural development in the Jewish sector and to pay Britain's expenses in defending the Jewish "national home."[54] The British administration also ensured that taxes were more efficiently collected by enlisting the services of the village mukhtars (headmen) to maintain rural security and to pass on taxes and information to the government.[55]

As a consequence of such pressures, by 1930 some 30 per cent of all Palestinian villagers were totally landless, while as many as 75 to 80 per cent held insufficient land to meet their subsistence needs.[56] Some peasants made up this imbalance by renting additional farmlands, but most now depended on outside sources of income for survival. During peak periods of economic activity in the mandate, about one-half of the male fellahin workforce (over 100,000 persons) engaged in seasonal wage employment outside the village (on road or construction projects, in citrus harvesting and packing, and so forth). Often the entire male population of a village was recruited to work as a team on short-term construction projects.[57] Thus Palestinian rural villagers no longer filled a purely "peasant" position in the economic structure; increasingly they assumed a dual economic role as peasants and as casual laborers. So while notable landowners and moneylenders maintained economic dominance over the villages, particularly through client networks, the new experiences of peasants in the wider labor market altered their "traditional" fellahin subjectivities and provided alternative sources of income.

Indebtedness and expropriation at the hands of Zionist colonies forced a significant sector of the peasantry to emigrate permanently to the rapidly growing metropolises of Haifa, Jaffa, and Jerusalem. There they worked mainly as casual laborers and as a "scuffling petty bourgeoisie" in petty trading and services, a class situation typical of urban centers in underdeveloped colonial social formations.[58] Permanent wage work was difficult to come by in the face of competition from Jewish workers who monopolized positions in the more advanced Jewish economic sector. The work that Arab workers did obtain was extremely low-paying, due to an abundant labor supply and the difficulties inherent in organizing casual workers. As a consequence, the costs of Arab labor were never fully met by wages but were subsidized by the workers' access to subsistence agriculture and support networks at home in the village.[59]

These rural-to-urban migrants did not remain passive in the face of such conditions. On the contrary, they set up various associations based on village of origin which ignored the *hamula* distinctions that were so divisive at home.[60] They also joined semi-political organizations headed by artisans, enlisted in trade unions whenever possible, and came in contact with militant religious reformers like Shaykh 'Izz al-Din al-Qassam. Their entry into the urban wage workforce helped to weaken clan, village, and regional divisions; these new experiences also had an impact on the home villages, with which migrants maintained close contact. Thus the old cleavages that buttressed patron–client networks were slowly breaking down under the impact of capitalist development. The nationalist leadership tried to reverse the process by making frequent appeals to the British on behalf of the impoverished peasantry, but this had little effect on British policies or on economic conditions.[61] Furthermore, the fellahin were increasingly skeptical of the *a'yan*'s sincerity. By 1927, according to a British official, the notables were apprehensive that the peasantry "show[ed] a growing tendency to distinguish between national and Effendi [notable] class interest."[62]

The brewing crisis in agriculture, closely tied to steady Zionist progress in the 1920s (between 1919 and 1929 the Jewish population of Palestine had doubled, reaching 156,000 persons[63]), was a major factor igniting the violence that erupted over expanded Zionist claims to the Wailing Wall at Jerusalem (known by Arabs as the Buraq, the western wall of the Haram al-Sarif, third holiest shrine in Islam). The Mufti as usual tried to settle the problem through the good offices of the British, at the same time attempting to allay the anger of the populace, who saw in Zionist "religious" expansionism a condensed form of the general danger Zionism posed to Palestinian Arab sovereignty.[64] A series of provocative demonstrations at the wall by Zionist extremists took place during 1929. Finally, on 23 August, peasant villagers, influenced by the propaganda work of nationalist militants, arrived in Jerusalem for Friday prayers armed with knives and clubs. Hajj Amin made every effort to calm the crowds, but radical religious shaykhs made speeches inciting them to action.[65] Violence broke out against Jews in Jerusalem and quickly spread throughout the country; British forces restored order in brutal fashion.

The widespread nature of the violence demonstrated that the mass of the population was ready to take direct action against the Zionist threat, independently of the cautious notable leadership. Unfortunately they could also be incited to ugly sectarian violence, which assumed the dimensions of a pogrom at Hebron and Safad. One of the most important forms of organization to emerge from this outbreak was the guerrilla band known as the Green Hand Gang established by Ahmad Tafish in the Galilee hills in October 1929. Composed of men associated with radical circles who had taken part in the August uprising, the band launched several attacks on Zionist colonies and British forces in the north.[66] The band's organization probably resembled that of the gangs of peasant bandits who traditionally operated in the Palestine hills and who were a growing security problem in the 1920s.[67] But unlike them, Ahmad Tafish's band had an overt political purpose. Although quickly subdued, the Green Hand Gang aroused considerable sympathy among the peasantry who, the Shaw Commission concluded in 1930, were "probably more politically minded than many of the people of Europe."[68] This atmosphere of popular agitation provided new opportunities for alternative political forces within the national movement to challenge notable hegemony.

Harbingers of revolt, 1930–35

The early 1930s were characterized by extremely unstable conditions, which the Palestinian zu'ama were incapable of controlling. Contradictions piled one on top of another, ushering in a series of crises that, by fits and starts, led to the explosion of 1936.

One major destabilizing factor was the global depression. Due chiefly to forces released by the worldwide economic downturn, Jewish immigration to Palestine jumped sharply in the early 1930s. Between 1931 and 1935 the Jewish community grew from 175,000 to 400,000 persons, or from 17 to 31 per cent of the total population of Palestine. The advance of anti-Semitism in Poland, the tightening of the US quota system in 1929, and the triumph of Nazism in Germany all contributed to the floodtide of immigration to Palestine.[69]

The effects of Jewish immigration upon Palestinian Arab society were uneven. Between the late 1920s and 1932, the country suffered a recession and a steep rise in Arab unemployment. But with the refugee influx, the economy expanded in the 1933–36 period, while the rest of the world (except the Soviet Union) languished in deep depression. As a result of an agreement, known as the Ha'avara, between the World Zionist Organization and the Nazis, Jews leaving Germany were able to import large amounts of capital into Palestine. Nearly 60 per cent of all capital invested in Palestine between August 1933 and September 1939 entered by means of the Ha'avara.[70] This capital inflow permitted wealthy Jews greatly to increase their investments in industry, building, and citriculture. In addition, rapid British development of Haifa as a strategic eastern Mediterranean port meant the construction of a new harbor, an oil pipeline (which began pumping oil from Iraq in 1935), refineries, and a railroad during the same period.[71] As a consequence, job opportunities for Arab workers expanded. The greatest share of jobs, however, went to Jewish workers, as Zionist leaders and especially the Histadrut (the Zionist labor federation) made sure that the burgeoning Jewish economic sector provided for the new Jewish immigrants. This caused resentment among Arab workers and led to clashes with Jews over access to jobs.[72] The economy suffered another recession from 1936 to 1939, which affected semi-proletarianized Arab workers much more deeply than largely unionized Jewish labor.

The capital influx accompanying Jewish immigration increased the pace of land purchases as well. Zionist acquisitions from large Palestinian owners and small peasants now assumed greater importance than in the 1920s.[73] An increasingly desperate economic situation constrained peasants to sell their lands, for by 1936 the average debt of a peasant family – 25 to 35 pounds per year – equaled or surpassed their average annual income of 27 pounds.[74] The money peasants earned from land sales usually did little more than release them from debt and propel them toward the urban slums. Due to inflated real-estate prices, large Palestinian landowners, on the other hand, could make huge profits by selling their estates to the Zionists. Some owners arbitrarily raised rents to force their tenants off the land prior to concluding such a sale, in order to avoid paying compensation to the peasants.[75] A law, decreed in 1933, extending greater rights to tenants contributed to a noticeable increase in disputes between landlords and peasants over tenancy rights. Militant nationalists were involved in encouraging such conflicts.[76] By the mid-1930s the government was routinely forced to call out large numbers of police in order to evict sharecroppers from sold properties as, more and more frequently, peasants resisted dispossession through violent means.[77]

The bankruptcy of the notables' policies was therefore increasingly apparent: they had made no progress toward achieving national independence and were incapable of stemming the Zionist tide of increasing population, land settlement, and economic development. The *a'yan*'s inability to achieve successes threatened their hold over the national movement and made it difficult for them to claim the discourses of nationalism or even Islam as their exclusive property. Moreover, the notable front had splintered over disagreements on national strategy. Opposition to Husayni leadership crystallized around the Nashashibi clan, which represented the richest landowners, citrus growers, and entrepreneurs. More heavily involved than other notables in land sales to the Zionists, and the greatest beneficiaries of citrus exports to England, the Nashashibi-led groups of the notable-mercantile class opposed pan-Arab unity and were ready to accept less than total independence from Britain.[78] This group, which established the National Defense Party in 1934, had a certain base of support through its patron–client networks.[79]

The radical nationalists took advantage of the openings provided by the series of crises and by the swelling of their ranks with a new contingent of young men educated in mandate institutions. As Göran Therborn notes, the training of an intellectual stratum in colonial situations often generates revolutionary ideologies, due to the disparity between the nature of the training they receive, suitable for an advanced capitalist society, and the colonial form of subjection.[80] The mandate educational system in Palestine produced young men whose qualifications were not commensurate with the holy roles assigned to them, and so their discontent generated new and critical forms of subjectivity.

The 1930s witnessed an upsurge in Palestine of independent political organizing by the educated middle class, just as in the rest of the Arab world, where a new generation of radical nationalists were raising slogans of socioeconomic justice and Arab unity and developing novel forms of political organization.[81] Palestinian radicals set up a variety of bodies such as the Young Men's Muslim Association, the Arab Youth Conferences, and the Arab Boy Scouts (independent of the international Baden-Powell movement). The most important organization was the Istiqlal (Independence) Party, established in 1932, whose roots lay in the old Istiqlal movement associated with the Sharifian government at Damascus.[82] Led by elements of the educated middle class and the disaffected offspring of notable families, it appealed to educated professionals and salaried officials: lawyers, doctors, teachers, government employees.[83] Unlike other Palestinian parties founded in the 1930s, it was organized not on the basis of family or clan loyalties but around a political program, and thus it was the first (excluding the Communist) to appeal to and construct a new and modern form of subjectivity. It also distinguished itself by centering its political actions on opposition to the British mandate government rather than aiming them at the Jewish community alone.

The Istiqlal took a "populist" political stance representative of an aspiring national bourgeoisie.[84] Its adherents criticized the chronic unemployment besetting Arab workers, and the high taxes, rising prices, and unjust government treatment that the peasants suffered under. The Istiqlal advocated the establishment of a nationalist parliament and the abolition of "feudal" titles, such as *pasha, bey,* and *effendi,* that were common among the notables. In 1933, Istiqlalists began to attack the notable leadership, asserting that, because it had remained abject in the face of Zionism and imperialism, Palestinian nationalism was not the cause of the *zu'ama* but, rather, that of the poor.[85] The Istiqlalists therefore attempted to mobilize the popular classes along the faultlines of class antagonisms by constructing a popular-democratic discourse that took advantage of fellahin disaffection from the notables and used it for "national" purposes.[86]

In 1934, however, only a year and a half after its founding, the Istiqlal Party ceased to function effectively. Aided by the party's division into pro-Hashemite and pro-Saudi factions, Hajj Amin al-Husayni was able to sabotage it. Many Istiqlalists subsequently joined the Mufti's Palestine Arab Party, which, paradoxically, made it into something more than simply a clan-based grouping.[87] In addition, their entry pushed Hajj Amin to take a more militant stance. But even after their party's demise, Istiqlalists continued to be active as individuals, while other independent groupings stepped up their organizing efforts. The Arab Youth Congress attempted to prevent illegal Jewish immigration by organizing units to patrol the coasts.[88] Arab labor garrisons were set up at Jerusalem, Haifa, and Jaffa to defend Arab workers against attacks by Jewish workers trying to prevent Jewish capitalists from hiring Arabs.[89]

Efforts to mobilize the peasantry were even more consequential. Educated young men from the villages, who returned home to serve as teachers, spread radical nationalist notions among the fellahin, particularly in the northern foothills of Jabal Nablus (the region known as the Triangle, comprising the environs of Nablus, Janin, and Tulkarm) where villages had lost land to Zionist colonies on the coastal and Esdraelon plains.[90] Poetry was an especially significant vehicle for this dissemination of nationalist ideas and sentiments in the countryside. Written in simple language and style, nationalist poetry frequently criticized the notable leadership.[91] According to Ghassan Kanafani, it often took the form of "almost direct political preaching."[92] Poems and songs by artists like Ibrahim Tuqan, 'Abd al-Karim al-Karmi, and 'Abd al-Rahim

Mahmud were well known in the countryside and recited at festive and public occasions. Peasants had access to newspapers (which began to appear daily after the 1929 riots) and magazines that printed nationalist poetry; the anthropologist Hilma Granqvist reports that fellahin from the village of Artas who went to Bethlehem for market heard newspapers read aloud in the coffee shops there.[93] Probably most villages had similar access to the printed word. Al-Baquri claims that the poetry of the nationalist bards "rang out on the lips of the fighters and popular masses" during the 1936–39 revolt.[94]

The Palestine Communist Party should be mentioned in this context, even though its impact on events was minimal. Founded in 1922, the PCP remained primarily a Jewish organization until 1929, when the Comintern ordered it to undergo "Arabization."[95] At its Seventh Congress in 1930, it began to orient itself programmatically toward the peasantry. Asserting that in an agricultural country like Palestine it was "the peasant revolution" that was "the most significant," it called for the confiscation of estates held by big Arab landowners, religious institutions, and Jewish colonies, and for their distribution to landless and land-poor peasants. The PCP urged peasants to refuse to pay taxes and debts and advocated armed rebellion. It also proposed conducting propaganda at the mosques on Fridays and at popular festivals like Nabi Musa, for "it is during such mass celebrations that the fighting capacity of the fellahin is appreciably aroused."[96] In addition, the PCP campaigned vigorously on behalf of Bedouin and peasants dispossessed by Zionist colonization.[97] But due to its paucity of Arab members, the fact that no cadre lived in villages, and widespread perceptions that it was chiefly a Jewish organization, the party's influence in the Palestinian Arab community remained circumscribed. In any case, after the onset of the Comintern's Popular Front strategy, the PCP dropped its call for agrarian revolution (typical of the world Communist movement's ultra-left "Third Period") and began trying to build closer ties with middle-class nationalists. 'Abd al-Qadir Yasin asserts that the party's social demands were influential among workers and peasants by the mid-1930s,[98] but such claims are difficult to verify, since the PCP's ideas were not backed up by practices. At best, Communist notions may have influenced radical nationalist individuals with whom the party maintained contact.

A wave of renewed violence in 1933 further demonstrated the notables' tenuous hold over the nationalist movement. Violence rapidly spread through the urban centers (and some villages) of the country after an anti-British demonstration at Jaffa in October led to clashes with police. Unlike the situation in 1929, this violence was aimed specifically at the British mandate administration, which represented a significant shift in the movement's strategy and political awareness. The British leaned harder than ever on the Mufti to keep these disturbances from getting out of hand. In return for preventing the fellahin from following the "extremists" and for restraining demonstrations, the British granted the Supreme Muslim Council complete control over *waqf* (religious endowment) finances.[99] But as tensions mounted, Hajj Amin's position as mediator became more precarious. He moved in two directions at once, trying both to maintain good relations with the British by reining in the national movement and to retain credibility with the populace by adopting a militant posture.

Hajj Amin's primary activities concerned land sales, a significant issue of public concern. The Palestinian Arab press frequently editorialized against land traffic with the Zionists, and in the early 1930s the Muslim–Christian Associations and the Arab Executive had sent agents out to the villages, urging peasants not to sell their land.[100] In the fall of 1934 the Mufti and the SMC initiated a more vigorous campaign, mobilizing the ideology and institutions of Islam to fight land sales (and to maintain Hajj Amin's influence with the peasantry). The Mufti toured areas where transactions were occurring, to explain the dangers they posed to the nation and condemn them as acts of sin and high treason.[101] In January 1935, he issued a *fatwa* (legal opinion) on the matter that forbade traffic in land with the Zionists and branded *simsars* (real estate brokers) as heretics (*mariq*).[102] But religious propaganda alone could not reverse the economic forces that led the peasants into indebtedness and forced them off the land. The dire agrarian situation was exacerbated by a series of crop failures between 1929 and 1936 and by competition from cheap agricultural imports, their prices depressed by the global economic downturn.[103] The Mufti recognized, in theory, the need for structural changes, and he called for (1) measures to protect peasants from big landowners; (2) the establishment of national industries; (3) aid to small farmers; and (4) a campaign of purchasing national products.[104] But the SMC's only concrete action was to put some tracts of land under *waqf* (mortmain) protection.

By the mid-1930s the political impasse in Palestine forced even the Mufti to realize that more drastic measures might be called for. Accordingly, in late 1933 a young associate of Hajj Amin's, 'Abd al-Qadir al-Husayni, organized a secret military group known as Munazzamat al-Jihad al-Muqaddas (Organization for Holy Struggle).[105] At the same time, various groupings of radicals were also preparing for military struggle. And in 1934, according to Palestine Communist Party propaganda, a popular bandit known as Abu Jilda was carrying out significant armed activity in the countryside. Abu Jilda's "partisan detachments," the Communists claimed, were pulling the country toward disorder and toward armed revolt against the colonial authorities.[106]

The revolt of al-Qassam

The spark that ignited the explosion came from an independent organization intimately connected to the peasantry and semi-proletariat created by the agrarian crisis. That organization was founded by radical Islamic reformer Shaykh 'Izz al-Din al-Qassam. A native of Jabla, Syria, and a key figure in the 1921 revolt against the French, al-Qassam took refuge in Haifa after fleeing Syria under sentence of death. A man of great religious learning who had studied at Cairo's al-Azhar, al-Qassam was associated with the Islamic reform (Salafiya) movement,[107] as well as with certain Sufi *turuq*.[108] He quickly achieved prominence in Haifa as a preacher and teacher. Unlike other political activists in Palestine, al-Qassam concentrated his efforts exclusively on the lower classes with whom he lived.[109] He set up a night school to combat illiteracy among the casual laborers (recent migrants from rural areas) of Haifa shantytowns and was a prominent member of the Young Men's Muslim Association. In 1929 al-Qassam was appointed marriage registrar of Haifa's Shari'a court. The duties of this office, which required that he tour northern villages, permitted him to extend his efforts to the peasantry, whom he encouraged to set up growing and distribution cooperatives[110]

Using his religious position, al-Qassam began to recruit followers from among the fellahin and the laborers of Haifa, organizing them into clandestine cells of not more than five persons. By 1935 he had enlisted 200, perhaps even 800, men.[111] Many received military training, carried out after dark; all were imbued with al-Qassam's message of strict piety, of struggle and sacrifice, of patriotism, the necessity for unity, and the need to emulate early Islamic heroes.[112] In the 1920s, al-Qassam made a name for himself by attacking as un-Islamic certain folk religious practices still common in the Haifa area.[113] Such censure accorded with al-Qassam's Salafiya leanings and recalled the actions of 'Abd al-Karim, leader of the 1924–27 anti-Spanish rebellion in the Moroccan Rif. A Salafiya advocate like al-Qassam, 'Abd al-Karim had banned a number of traditional folk religious practices in the interests of promoting unity among the Rif rebels.[114] Al-Qassam's political activities also paralleled those of Hasan al-Banna, founder of the Muslim Brothers (al-Ikhwan al-Muslimin) in Egypt. Just as al-Banna recruited his first followers in the new towns of the Canal Zone, so al-Qassam recruited in the newly developing city of Haifa. But while al-Banna attracted the new Egyptian petty bourgeoisie, al-Qassam focused on the recently dispossessed peasants working as casual laborers in the slums.[115]

Al-Qassam's appeal to religious values was not simply a return to tradition or a retreat into the past, but instead represented a real transformation of traditional forms for revolutionary use in the present.[116] He seized on popular memories of the Assassins and the wars against the Crusaders by invoking the tradition of the *fida'iyin*, the notion of struggle that involved sacrifice. His clandestine organization resembled that of a Sufi order: his followers grew their beards "wild" and called themselves shaykhs.[117] This was not as incongruous as it might seem, for, as Thomas Hodgkin argues, the Islamic worldview contains elements that can be articulated together to constitute a revolutionary tradition.[118] Al-Qassam's efforts represent such an articulation and condensation of nationalist, religious "revivalist" and class-conscious components in a movement of anti-colonial struggle.

Although his followers may have begun carrying out small armed attacks on Zionist settlements as early as 1931,[119] it was not until November 1935 that al-Qassam decided the moment was ripe for launching a full-scale revolt. Accompanied by a small detachment of followers, he set out from Haifa with the aim of raising the peasantry in rebellion. An accidental encounter with the police led to a premature battle with the British military, however, and al-Qassam died before his rebellion could get off the ground.

Nonetheless, his example electrified the country. Independent radical organizations eulogized al-Qassam and gained new inspiration from his revolutionary project. Al-Qassam rapidly achieved the status of a popular hero, and his gravesite became a place of pilgrimage.[120] His legacy also included the many Qassamites still at large and prepared for action, as well as militant nationalists who set up fresh political groupings in the towns and organized armed bands on the Qassam model. Urban radicals also redoubled their organizing in the villages in preparation for a new anti-British outbreak.[121] In such a highly charged atmosphere, only a small event was needed to trigger an explosion.

The Great Revolt (al-Thawra al-Kubra)

That incident occurred on 13 April 1936, when two Jews were murdered in the Nablus Mountains, perhaps by Qassamites. Following a wave of brutal reprisals and counter-reprisals, the government declared a state of emergency. In response, "national committees" led by various militant organizations sprang up in the towns and declared a general strike. The notables followed along, trying to retake control of the unruly movement. On 25 April all the Palestinian parties (including the Nashashibi's National Defense Party) met with the national committees and set up a coordinating body known as the Higher Arab Committee (HAC), with Amin al-Husayni as its president. Although the HAC grew out of the notables' move to regain their dominant position, nonetheless, as a merging of the independent radical groupings with the traditional

[handwritten margin note: Higher Arab Committee]

leadership it was more representative than the old Arab Executive had been.[122] The HAC quickly declared that the general strike would continue until the British government put an end to Jewish immigration to Palestine, and it restated the other basic national demands – the banning of land sales and the establishment of an independent national government.

Though it initially sprang up in the towns, the revolt's focus rapidly shifted to the countryside. A conference of rural national committees convened in May and elaborated a specific peasant agenda, including a call for nonpayment of taxes and the denunciation of the establishment of police stations in villages at fellahin expense.[123] In addition, Istiqlalists (still active as individuals) toured the countryside of the Triangle to mobilize support for the general strike, while both Qassamites and SMC preachers spread propaganda and attempted to organize among peasants.[124]

In mid-May, armed peasant bands in which Qassamites featured prominently appeared in the highlands. They were assisted by armed commandos in the towns and by peasant auxiliaries who fought part-time. Though connected to the urban national committees, in general these bands operated independently of the Mufti and the HAC.[125] From mountain hideouts they harassed British communications, attacked Zionist settlements, and even sabotaged the Iraq Petroleum Company oil pipelines to Haifa. This last activity posed a particular threat to British global hegemony, for in the 1930s Great Britain still controlled the bulk of Middle East oil, and the Haifa pipeline was crucial to imperial naval strategy in the Mediterranean.

The towns, in a state of semi-insurrection, were finally brought under control by the British in July, which left the countryside as the undisputed center of revolt.[126] In the following month Fawzi al-Qawuqji, hero of the Syrian Druze rebellion of 1925, resigned his commission in the Iraqi army and entered Palestine with an armed detachment of pan-Arab volunteers, declaring himself commander-in-chief of the revolt.[127] Although the military effectiveness of the rebel movement was improved and al-Qawuqji was hailed as a popular hero throughout the country, he never managed to unite all the diverse bands under his command.

While popular forces fought the British in the countryside, the notables of the HAC – only one of whom had been arrested – were negotiating with the enemy for a compromise to end the conflict. British authorities increased the pressure in late September by launching tough counter-measures – boosting their military force to 20,000, declaring martial law, and going on a new defensive. The HAC was also constrained by the onset of the agricultural season: peasants wanted to resume work, but, more important, harvest season started in September on the plantations of wealthy citrus-growers.[128] The HAC, preferring negotiations to mass mobilization, which threatened notable leadership, called off the six-month-old general strike on 10 October, with the understanding that the Arab rulers (of Iraq, Transjordan, and Saudi Arabia) would intercede with the British government on the Palestinians' behalf and that the government would act in good faith to work out new solutions. A long interim period ensued. While notables pinned their hopes on a Royal Commission of Inquiry, activists and rebel band leaders toured the villages and purchased weapons in preparation for a new round of fighting.

In July 1937, the British Peel Commission published its recommendations for the partition of Palestine into Arab and Jewish states. Arab reaction was universally hostile; even the Nashashibi faction which had defected from the HAC condemned the partition proposal. Feelings ran especially high in the Galilee, a highland region with few Jewish residents, which the plan of partition included in the proposed Jewish state.[129] In September, following the assassination of the British district commissioner for Galilee (possibly by Qassamites), the second phase of the revolt erupted. British authorities responded by banning the HAC and deporting or arresting hundreds of activists. The Mufti managed to evade arrest by escaping to Lebanon in October. Shortly thereafter, fierce fighting broke out. With the notable leadership in exile or imprisoned, command now shifted decisively to the partisans in the countryside.

Rebel bands were most active in the Nablus and Galilee highlands, the areas of greatest popular resistance. The Jerusalem-Hebron region, where the Munazzamat al-Jihad al-Muqaddas operated, was also an important center. In these districts the various bands set up their own court system, administrative offices, and intelligence networks. While peasants and ex-peasant migrants to the towns composed the vast majority of band leaders and fighters, young urban militants played important roles as commanders, advisers, arms transporters, instructors, and judges.[130] Qassamites were particularly well represented at the leadership level. By taxing the peasantry, levying volunteers, and acquiring arms through the agency of experienced smugglers,[131] the bands were able to operate autonomously from the rebel headquarters-in-exile set up by the notable leadership at Damascus. A network of militants in the towns, particularly from among the semi-proletariat, collected contributions, gathered intelligence, and carried out acts of terror against the British, the Zionists, and Arab *simsars* and collaborators.[132]

In the summer and fall of 1938 the rebellion reached its peak. Some 10,000 persons had the insurgent bands, now sufficiently well organized for a handbook of instructions to be issued for their members.[133] Commanders of the largest bands established a Higher Council of Command to enhance military coordination. Most of the Palestinian highlands were in rebel hands, and by September government control over the urban areas had virtually ceased.

Once rebels gained the upper hand in the towns, the peasant character of the revolt expressed itself even more clearly. Rebel commanders ordered all townsmen to take off the urban headgear, the fez, and to don the peasant headcloth, the *kafiya;* urban women were commanded to veil. This action was both practical, in that it protected rebels from arrest by the British when they entered the towns, and symbolic, in that it signified the countryside's hegemony over the city. Insurgents also instructed urban residents not to use electric power, which was produced by an Anglo-Jewish company. Few dared disobey these orders. Large sums of money were extracted from wealthy city-dwellers as contributions to the revolt, and particularly large "contributions" were demanded from the big orange-growers and merchants at Jaffa who supported the Nashashibi opposition.[134]

On 1 September, the joint rebel command issued a declaration that directly challenged the leading classes' dominance over the countryside. Although limited in scope, the declaration represented a social program which went beyond the merely "national" goals of the *a'yan*. In it the commanders declared a moratorium on all debts (which had so impoverished the peasantry and by means of which notables controlled agricultural production) and warned both debt collectors and land agents not to visit the villages. Arab contractors, who hired work teams for the construction of police posts in the villages and roads to facilitate access to rebel strongholds, were also ordered to cease operations. In addition, the statement declared the cancellation of rents on urban apartments, which had risen to scandalously high levels. This item was particularly significant in that, by linking the needs of peasants and urban workers, it revealed the new class alliance underpinning the revolt.[135]

The rebels' interference with landlord-usurer control over the countryside and their demands for contributions from the wealthy constituted a "revenge of the countryside," which prompted thousands of wealthy Palestinians to abandon their homes for other Arab countries. Well-off Palestinians tended to view the rebels as little better than bandits. In part this charge was justified, for there were serious discipline problems within the rebel camp, despite the considerable advances the bands achieved in coordination and unity of purpose. For instance, clan or family loyalties occasionally interfered with the class or national interests of certain rebel commanders, who carried out petty blood-feuds under cover of nationalist activity.[136] Some peasants were alienated by the coercive manner employed by particular leaders to collect taxes and by their favoritism toward certain clans. Moreover, although class divisions among the peasants were not well developed, villagers were by no means homogeneous in their class interests. The assassination of a *mukhtar* who collaborated with the British, for example, was likely to alienate those members of his *hamula* who benefited from the *mukhtar's* ties to outside forces.

Most accounts of the revolt stress the internal problems faced by the rebels. Although such criticisms are exaggerated and detract from the rebels' positive accomplishments, they cannot simply be dismissed. The British and the Nashashibis were able to exploit the contradictions within the rebel movement through such means as the formation of "peace bands" in late 1938 to do battle with the rebels. Although representative primarily of the interests of landlords and rural notables, the "peace bands" were manned by disaffected peasants.[137]

More important for British strategy than the "peace bands" was the signing of the Munich Agreement on 30 September 1938. This allowed Britain to free one more army division for service in Palestine and to launch a military counteroffensive. Is it possible that British Prime Minister Chamberlain signed the Munich Agreement not merely to appease Hitler momentarily but also to protect Britain's oil supply in the Mediterranean from "backward" but dangerous bands of peasants? It would be difficult to chart a clear cause–effect relation, but it is evident at least that, for the British chiefs of staff, Palestine was a crucial strategic buffer between the Suez Canal and potential enemies to the north (Germany, Soviet Union) and was an indispensable link in land communications. With war looming on the horizon in Europe, Britain was seeking desperately to end the disturbances in Palestine.[138]

In any event, the Munich Agreement had disastrous consequences not just for Czechoslovakia but for the rebellion in Palestine as well. By 1939 the rebels were fighting a British military force of 20,000 men as well as the RAF. In addition, Orde Wingate, a British officer, organized a counter-insurgency force of Jewish fighters known as the Special Night Squads to terrorize villagers and to guard the oil pipeline.[139] The British counter-offensive increased pressure on the rebels and prompted further internal problems, such as abuses in collecting taxes and contributions and an upsurge in political assassinations.

However, the intensified military offensive was still not enough to finish off the rebellion, so the British launched a diplomatic one as well. In March 1939 the government issued a White Paper declaring that it was opposed to Palestine becoming a Jewish state, that Jewish immigration would be limited to 75,000 over the next five years, that land sales would be strictly regulated, and that an independent Palestinian state would be set up in ten years with self-governing institutions to be established in the interim. Although both the notables and the rebels rejected the White Paper, the Palestinian populace responded to it more favorably.[140] Clearly, while it did not satisfy the maximum national demands, the White Paper represented a concession wrung from the British by armed resistance. Zionist reaction against the White Paper, by contrast, was much more virulent.

The revolt was gradually crushed by extreme external pressures and the resultant internal fracturing of the movement. After over three years of fighting, the intervention of substantial British military forces aided by the Zionists, and nearly 20,000 Arab casualties (5,032 dead, 14,760 wounded[141]), the rebellion was finally subdued. In July the last major rebel commander was captured; once the war with Germany began in September 1939, fighting ended altogether. An entirely new set of circumstances on the international scene were to determine subsequent events in Palestine.

Conclusion

I have tried to propose an alternative to the prevailing analyses of the Great Revolt in Palestine, which represent Palestinian society as so fractured by vertical cleavages that neither the class nor national unity necessary for success in the anti-colonial, anti-Zionist struggle could emerge. Given the prevailing social structure, so the argument goes, once the Palestinian peasantry took leadership of the revolt it could only act true to its inherently "backward" character. Arnon-Ohanna's assessment is typical: "The absence of cooperation and mutual responsibility, the deep-seated divisiveness of a society based on patriarchal lines and *hamulas*, the ancient inter-village and inter-*hamulas* wrangles over stretches of land and water sources, over blood feuds, family honor and marital problems – these were simply transferred to the [guerrilla] bands movement."[142] According to many of those who make such an argument, only one force could have ensured victory: a modern, revolutionary party.[143]

I have argued that the model of vertical cleavages was essentially ideological, in that it was the form through which the Palestinian ruling class maintained its political and economic hegemony. As an ideology of rule, it worked by refracting the underlying class structure of the society, making relations of exploitation appear as amicable "exchanges" between persons of unequal status. In an effort to show that class antagonisms overdetermined this relation, I argue that peasants manipulated the dominant ideology in their struggle for a better life. Although peasants lived in a state of subordination, landlord–notable domination was never total but was resisted on the basis of the very *terms* of the dominant ideology, that is, the struggle for a "just" exchange.

What is more, peasants possessed traditions of resistance, which they could call on in moments of crisis to forge a movement of opposition. I have charted a genealogy of these traditions of resistance prior to 1936. Despite its weak and often broken lines of descent, its vague and hidden traces, there are strong indications of such a tradition: a semi-autonomous existence prior to 1831, banditry and unorthodox religious practices, resistance to the expansion of the Ottoman state and to land registration in the late nineteenth century, and spontaneous struggles against new colonies of European Jews. Buried deeper within popular consciousness, moreover, were memories of earlier struggles, such as that of Salah al-Din (Saladin) against those earlier European invaders, the Crusaders. Such traditions do not necessarily imply practices of a conservative or retrograde nature, for, as Raymond Williams has argued, the "residual" can be an important source for progressive political practices even in advanced industrial societies.[144]

I have stressed too that the fellahin's folk heritage was not a pure, unblemished one. Their "common sense" was penetrated and altered over time by dominant ideologies of the state during the resurgence of Ottoman power in the second half of the nineteenth century, and by the nationalist idioms of the notables in the mandate period. Peasant consciousness was influenced as well by radical ideas emanating from militants of the middle class. Older traditional notions came to be articulated with the newer discourses of the nation, democracy and reformist Islam. In some cases, as with al-Qassam's attack on folk Islamic practices, popular traditions were modified in order to enhance the unity of the popular movement. In other instances, traditional practices such as banditry were transformed into powerful modern vehicles of struggle.

My aim has also been to demonstrate that the Palestinian peasantry was not an unchanging "backward" component of Palestinian society, but that it underwent constant change in the period under study. During the nineteenth century it was transformed from a class of relatively independent producers to one dominated by landowners and usurers, producing to a growing extent for the capitalist world market. A substantial number of peasants were displaced by Zionist colonization and indebtedness, forced out of agriculture altogether, and made into casual laborers. The fellahin were transformed further in the twentieth century, assuming a dual character as peasants and as casual workers. The partial integration of peasants into the wage circuit of "free" labor socialized peasant-workers in new ways and contributed to the dissolution of the precapitalist institutions in the village. Although the notables and the British tried mightily to uphold the hierarchies of patron–client networks, the grounds on which they were established were destabilized by the advances of Zionism and the notables' own failure to achieve "national" goals. Peasants totally abandoned by the system – dispossessed of their lands by Zionist colonies and driven into the towns as a subproletariat – eagerly embraced new ideas and practices that challenged notable dominance.

All these forces came into play during the Great Revolt. The peasant-led movement represented a congealing of nationalism, religious revivalism, and clan consciousness, no element of which can be neatly disentangled from the others. Here I have underscored the emergence within the rebel movement of specific demands and practices of the peasantry as a class, in part because in other accounts this aspect is so underplayed. The refusal to pay taxes, the moratorium on debts, the heavy contributions levied against the wealthy: all these rebel practices aimed at addressing the needs of the peasants. In addition, the declared moratorium on rental payments for apartments indicates the movement's close linkage with the urban semi-proletariat. The campaign of terror launched against collaborators, land agents, *mukhtars,* and Arab police officers represented a serious attempt to deal with traitors whose activities had hurt peasants, even though by all accounts it was carried to unnecessary extremes. While such demands and actions on the part of the rebels did not, strictly speaking, constitute "revolutionary" practice, they nonetheless posed a considerable threat to the political and economic hegemony of the notables. They also show that to claim that the rebels had *no* discernible, coherent social or political program is to oversimplify the issue considerably.[145]

We have seen how the rebels were able partially to overcome "traditional" modal divisions based on region and clan. The establishment of a council of command by the leading commanders was an important political step in this direction, as were the efforts of Qassamites who organized on the basis of an Islamic discourse colored by the interests of the popular classes. Such factors made crucial contributions to the remarkable degree of coherence that the rebellion was able to achieve.

Much has been made, in accounts of the rebellion, of the internal problems besetting the rebel forces. Indeed, misguided practice – such as regional, familial, and lineage loyalties which overrode fidelity to the movement, and the resort to assassination, brutality, and heavy-handed methods in extracting "contributions" from peasants – posed real problems for the movement and undermined its ability to sustain broad popular support. It is difficult here to achieve a "correct" analytical balance. But we should remember that throughout the world, unsavory practices have been common during moments of social upheaval. We should not therefore focus on them exclusively in order to discount an entire movement. Such problems would not necessarily have magically been transcended under the guidance of a "revolutionary" party and leadership, for a party is no guarantee of a successful outcome for social struggle. To focus attention on the absence of a party, as many have done, is to belittle the militant, honest leadership and forms of organization that the peasantry and semi-proletariat were able to muster. While some commanders were given to self-aggrandizement and petty feuding, many others (most of whom remain anonymous) deserve to be remembered. Qassamites, who played a key leadership role, were particularly noted for their devoutness and honesty, and 'Abd al-Rahim al-Hajj Muhammad, the most respected commander, was renowned for his nationalist convictions, for his opposition to political assassination, and for his tirelessness as a fighter.[146]

If anything, it was the formidable strength of the enemy that was more crucial to the peasant rebels' defeat than their purported "backwardness." The British, determined to maintain control over this area of major strategic importance (particularly the harbor at Haifa, the oil pipeline, and communication routes to India), mustered a substantial military force to fight the rebels. In addition, the powerful Jewish community was enlisted to assist the British efforts. Jews were enrolled in the police and the constabulary; Jewish fighters were organized into special counterinsurgency squads by Orde Wingate. Zionist revisionists, without British approval, launched terrorist attacks against the Arab community. Moreover, the rebellion gave the Zionists the opportunity to build up their military capabilities. While by the end of the revolt the Arab community was substantially disarmed, the Zionists in the meantime had put 14,500 men, with advanced training and weaponry, under arms.[147] This military imbalance between the two communities, enhanced during World War II, was an extremely important factor in the disaster that befell the Palestinian Arabs in 1948.

I have tried, then, to develop a counterargument to the dominant analysis of the Great Revolt. The "master narrative" of the rebellion tends to proceed by defining (and thereby diminishing) the peasants and casual laborers as "traditional," "backward," "fanatical," or even "terrorists." By presenting the peasantry as essentially unchanging, this approach also permits scholars to ignore the very real history of peasant resistance which preceded the rebellion. Other writers sympathetic to the revolt often disparage it for lacking a revolutionary party at its helm. Such arguments allow analysis to trivialize or ignore the accomplishments of the revolt and to concentrate on other questions, such as the role of the middle class, the treachery of the notables, or the Palestine Communist Party (which in fact was largely irrelevant to this affair[148]). What is at stake in such a dismissal is that the legitimate social and political desires of subaltern popular social movements have gone unheeded by the "progressive" as well as the dominant commentaries. Scholarly work that would constitute a social history of the revolt, including an investigation of the cultural life of the peasantry, the economic organization of the countryside, traditions of resistance, and ideologies of domination and opposition, has therefore scarcely begun.[149]

For this reason, I have stressed in polemical fashion the positive accomplishments of the peasantry in the course of the Great Revolt – achievements which have so often been minimized. This should be seen, then, only as a tentative step toward the development of a complete analysis, which requires the investigation of both structures of dominance and movements of opposition in their complex historical relation.

NOTES

Source This article is reprinted from Edmund Burke III and Ira M. Lapidus (eds), *Islam, Politics, and Social Movements* (Berkeley, 1988), pp. 169–203. Copyright © 1988 The Regents of the University of California. Reprinted by permission of the University of California Press.

1 Musa Budeiri, *The Palestine Communist Party, 1919–1948: Arab and Jew in the Struggle for Internationalism* (London: Ithaca Press, 1979), pp. 46–47.
2 Ann Mosely Lesch, *Arab Politics in Palestine, 1917–1939: The Frustration of a Nationalist Movement* (Ithaca: Cornell University Press, 1979), p. 17.
3 Ibrahim Abu-Lughod, "The Pitfalls of Palestiniology: A Review Essay," *Arab Studies Quarterly* 3 (1981): 403–11.
4 Methodologically this requires a strategy of reading from the margins of existing works on the history of Palestine. This chapter does not pretend to be an exhaustive survey but is meant to suggest further avenues of research. A major problem is that the role of peasant women cannot be recovered through such a reading strategy; other means are required to develop an analysis of this important question.
5 Gramsci's notion of hegemony is summarized by Raymond Williams, *Marxism and Literature* (Oxford: Oxford University Press, 1977), pp. 112–13.
6 Antonio Gramsci, *Selections from the Prison Notebooks*, ed. and trans. Quintin Hoare and Geoffrey Nowell Smith (New York: International Publishers, 1971), pp. 323–26, 419–25.
7 The conclusions of the following four sections are based in part of my M.A. thesis: Theodore Swedenburg, "The Development of Capitalism in Greater Syria, 1830–1914: An Historico–Geographical Approach," University of Texas at Austin, 1980.
8 Palestine was only united as an administrative entity under the British mandate. In the Ottoman period, it was ruled from various cities such as Damascus, Sidon, Beirut, and Jerusalem. I am treating it here as a geographical unit.
9 Aref el-Aref, "The Closing Phase of Ottoman Rule in Jerusalem," Moshe Ma'oz, ed., *Studies on Palestine during the Ottoman Period* (Jerusalem: Magnes Press, 1975).
10 Constantin F. Volney, *Travels throughout Syria and Egypt in the Years 1783, 1784, and 1785*, vol. 2 (England: Gregg International Publishers, 1973).
11 This class structure is comparable to what Rey terms a "hierarchical society": Pierre-Philippe Rey, "Les formes de la décomposition des sociétés précapitalistes au Nord-Togo et le mécanisme des migrations vers les zones de capitalisme agraire," in Emile le Bris et al., eds, *Capitalisme négrier* (Paris: Maspero, 1976), pp. 195–209.
12 Volney, *Travels*, pp. 252–53. A similar relationship among peasants, their overlords, and the state characterized conditions in Southeast Asia during the same period: Michael Adas, "From Avoidance to Confrontation: Peasant Protest in Precolonial and Colonial Southeast Asia," *Comparative Studies in Society and History* 23 (1981): 217–47.

13 Karl Marx, *Grundrisse*, trans. Martin Nicolaus (New York: Vintage Books, 1973).

14 Maurice Godelier, "Infrastructures, Societies and History," *Current Anthropology* 19 (1978): 63–68. Empires based on a tributary mode of production typically left economic systems based on kinship intact, only modifying them to ensure that tribute was rendered. See also Samir Amin, *The Arab Nation* (London: Zed Press, 1978), pp. 87–102.

15 The situation in Palestine resembled that of the Kabyle Mountains of Algeria, where during the same era "league feuds channeled or drained off the energies of the peasants and diverted them from the social struggle. . . . Even though the leagues and alliances . . . veiled social tensions and disjunctures, these were nonetheless manifest": René Gallissot, "Pre-Colonial Algeria" *Economy and Society* 4 (1975): 424–25.

16 Mordechai Abir, "Local Leadership and Early Reforms in Palestine, 1800–1834," in Ma'oz, ed., *Studies on Palestine*, pp. 284–310.

17 Taufik Canaan, *Mohammedan Saints and Sanctuaries in Palestine* (London: Luzac, 1927), p. 251. Such proverbs are typical of mountain peasants of the Arab world and of "segmentary" Bedouin societies. (For Morocco, see David M. Hart, *The Aith Waryaghar of the Moroccan Rif* [Tucson: University of Arizona Press, 1976].) My own reading of this proverb diverges from the usual interpretation given by anthropologists, who see it exclusively in terms of kinship and alliance. I suggest a broader political interpretation.

18 Canaan, *Mohammedan Saints*.

19 Ibid., p. 98.

20 Ibid., pp. 215–16.

21 Ibid., p. 193.

22 Alexander Schölch, "The Economic Development of Palestine, 1856–1882," *Journal of Palestine Studies* 39 (1981): 35–58.

23 Alexander Schölch, "European Penetration and the Economic Development of Palestine, 1956–85," in Roger Owen, ed., *Studies in the Economic and Social History of Palestine in the Nineteenth and Twentieth Centuries* (Carbondale: Southern Illinois Press, 1982), pp. 10–87.

24 Ya'akov Firestone, "Crop-sharing Economics in Mandatory Palestine," *Middle Eastern Studies* 11 (1975): 10.

25 Lesch, *Arab Politics*, p. 89.

26 For criticisms by anthropologists of the patron–client model as applied to Mediterranean societies, see Michael Gilsenan, "Against Patron–Client Relations," in Ernest Gellner and John Waterbury, eds, *Patrons and Clients* (London: Duckworth, 1977), pp. 167–83; Luciano Li Causi, "Anthropology and Ideology: The Case of 'Patronage,'" *Critique of Anthropology* 4/5 (1975): 90–109; and Paul Littlewood, "Patronage, Ideology and Reproduction," *Critique of Anthropology* 15 (1980): 29–45.

27 Littlewood, "Patronage," pp. 37–38.

28 See David Seddon, *Moroccan Peasants* (Folkestone, Ky.: Dawson, 1981), p. 92, and Göran Therborn, *The Ideology of Power and the Power of Ideology* (London: New Left Books, 1980), pp. 56–57, 61–62, for discussions which support this line of argument.

29 Gramsci, *Selections*, p. 54.

30 J.C. Hurewitz, *The Struggle for Palestine* (New York: W.W. Norton, 1950), p. 54.

31 Canaan, *Mohammedan Saints*, pp. 197, 204–5.

32 Gilsenan, "Against Patron–Client Relations," pp. 53, 151–52; see also Albert Hourani, *Arabic Thought in the Liberal Age, 1799–1939* (London: Oxford University Press, 1962), p. 150.

33 Claude Regnier Conder, *Tent Work in Palestine* (New York: D. Appleton, 1878), p. 267.
34 James Scott, "Hegemony and the Peasantry," *Politics and Society* 7 (1977): 284.
35 Yehoshuah Porath, *The Emergence of the Palestinian-Arab National Movement, 1918–1929* (London: Frank Cass, 1974); Neville Mandel, *The Arabs and Zionism before World War I* (Berkeley and Los Angeles: University of California Press, 1975), pp. 70, 214–22.
36 Mandel, *Arabs and Zionism*, pp. 70, 214–22.
37 Porath, *Emergence*, pp. 7–8.
38 Abdul-Wahhab Kayyali, *Palestine: A Modern History* (London: Croom Helm, 1978), pp. 71–72; Porath, *Emergence*, pp. 129–30.
39 Kayyali, *Palestine*, p. 73.
40 Nathan Weinstock, *Le Sionisme contre Israel* (Paris: Maspero, 1969), p. 169.
41 Kayyali, *Palestine*, p. 75.
42 Lesch, *Arab Politics*, p. 89.
43 Hurewitz, *Struggle*, p. 54.
44 Ylana M. Miller, *Government and Society in Rural Palestine 1920–1948* (Austin: University of Texas Press, 1985), pp. 16–18.
45 Hurewitz, *Struggle*, pp. 52–53.
46 Miller, *Government*, pp. 27, 54–62.
47 Ibid.
48 Rifaat Abou-el-Haj, "The Social Uses of the Past: Recent Arab Historiography of Ottoman Rule," *IJMES* 14 (1982): 187.
49 Porath, *Emergence*, pp. 200–202.
50 Miller, *Government*, pp. 24–25, 47.
51 Hourani, *Arabic Thought*, passim. For an example of a liberal Palestinian mode of argument, see George Antonius, *The Arab Awakening* (London: Hamish Hamilton, 1938).
52 Walid Khalidi, ed., *From Haven to Conquest* (Beirut: Institute for Palestine Studies, 1961), p. 72.
53 Yehoshuah Porath, *The Palestinian Arab National Movement: From Riots to Rebellion, 1929–1939* (London: Frank Cass, 1977), pp. 83–84.
54 Talal Asad, "Anthropological Texts and Ideological Problems: An Analysis of Cohen on Arab Villages in Israel," *Review of Middle East Studies* I (1975): 1–40.
55 Gabriel Baer, "The Office and Functions of the Village Mukhtar," in J.S. Migdal, ed., *Palestinian Society and Politics* (Princeton: Princeton University Press, 1980), pp. 103–23.
56 Shulamit Carmi and Henry Rosenfeld, "The Origins of the Process of Proletarianization and Urbanization of Arab Peasants in Palestine," *Annals of the New York Academy of Sciences* 220 (1974): 470.
57 Ibid., pp. 481–82.
58 Ken Post, *Arise Ye Starvelings: The Jamaican Labour Rebellion of 1938 and Its Aftermath* (The Hague: Martinus Nijhoff, 1978), pp. 133–36.
59 Sarah Graham-Brown, *Palestinians and Their Society, 1880–1946: A Photographic Essay* (London: Quartet Books, 1980), p. 150. For a theoretical analysis of this phenomenon in South Africa see Harold Wolpe, "The Theory of Internal Colonialism: The South African Case," in Ivar Oxall et al., eds, *Beyond the Sociology of Development* (London: Routledge and Kegan Paul, 1975), pp. 229–52.
60 Rachel Taqqu, "Peasants into Workmen: Internal Labor Migration and the Arab Village Community under the Mandate," in Migdal, *Palestinian Society*, p. 271.

61 Miller, *Government*, pp. 79–89.
62 Nels Johnson, *Islam and the Politics of Meaning in Palestinian Nationalism* (London: Routledge and Kegan Paul, 1982), p. 37.
63 David Hirst, *The Gun and the Olive Branch* (New York: D. Appleton, 1977), vol. 2, p. 63.
64 Philip Mattar, "The Role of the Mufti of Jerusalem in the Political Struggle over the Western Wall, 1928–29," *Middle Eastern Studies* 19 (1983): 104–18.
65 Ibid., p. 114; Lesch, *Arab Politics*, pp. 210–11.
66 Kayyali, *Palestine*, p. 156; Shai Lachman, "Arab Rebellion and Terrorism in Palestine 1929–1939: The Case of Sheikh Izz al-Din al-Qassam and His Movement," in Elie Kedourie and Sylvia G. Haim, eds, *Zionism and Arabism in Palestine and Israel* (London: Frank Cass, 1982), p. 56.
67 Ivan Spector, *The Soviet Union and the Muslim World, 1917–1956* (Seattle: University of Washington Press, 1956), p. 100.
68 Ibid., p. 156. The Shaw Commission's statement reflects an ethnocentric and classist bias that assumes that the non-Western peasantry was inherently apolitical. In fact, movements of peasants have posed the greatest threat to imperialist rule in the underdeveloped world.
69 Porath, *Palestinian Arab*, p. 40.
70 Lenni Brenner, *Zionism in the Age of Dictators* (Highland Park, N.J: Lawrence Hill, 1983), p. 65; Weinstock, *Sionisme*, pp. 135–36.
71 Carmi and Rosenfeld,"Origins," p. 476.
72 Porath, *Palestinian Arab*, pp. 129–30.
73 Ibid., pp. 182–84.
74 Weinstock, *Sionisme*, p. 64.
75 Porath, *Palestinian Arab*, pp. 103, 105.
76 Kenneth Stein, "Legal Protection and Circumvention of Rights for Cultivators in Mandatory Palestine," in Migdal, ed., *Palestinian Society*, pp. 250–54.
77 Kayyali, *Palestine*, p. 179.
78 Porath, *Palestinian Arab*, p. 67.
79 Lesch, *Arab Politics*, pp. 110–11.
80 Therborn, *Ideology*, pp. 17, 46.
81 Philip S. Khoury, "Islamic Revivalism and the Crisis of the Secular State in the Arab World: An Historical Reappraisal," in I. Ibrahim, ed., *Arab Resources: The Transformations of a Society* (London: Croom Helm, 1983), pp. 219–20. Women's organizations emerged in Palestine as a new form of mobilization in this period, but those discussed in the literature were led by the wives of the notable leaders (Mrs Matiel E.T. Mogannam, *The Arab Woman and the Palestine Problem* [London: Herbert Joseph, 1937]) and were similar in form to the Muslim–Christian Associations. It is possible that their example inspired mobilization by women of the educated middle classes, but for now we can only conjecture.
82 Kayyali, *Palestine*, pp. 167–68.
83 'Abd al-Qadir Yasin, *Kifah al-Sha'b al-Fisastini qabl al-'am 1948* (Beirut: PLO Research Center, 1975), pp. 125–26; Flurewitz, *Struggle*, p. 63.
84 Yasin, *Kifah al-Sha'b*, pp. 125–26. This national bourgeoisie existed, however, in embryo only.
85 Ibid., pp. 125–26; Kayyali, *Palestine*, pp. 167–68, 172.
86 For a discussion of populism see Ernesto Laclau, *Politics and Ideology in Marxist Theory* (London: New Left Books, 1977), especially p. 109.
87 Kayyali, *Palestine*, p. 187; Porath, *Palestinian Arab*, pp. 16–17.
88 Zvi Elpeleg, "The 1936–39 Disturbances: Riot or Rebellion?" *Wiener Library Bulletin* 29 (1976): 41.

89 Kayyali, *Palestine*, p. 177.
90 Porath, *Palestinian Arab*, p. 181.
91 Adnan Abu-Ghazaleh, "Arab Cultural Nationalism in Palestine during the British Mandate," *Journal of Palestine Studies* 3 (1972): 48–49.
92 Ghassan Kanafani, *The 1936–39 Revolt in Palestine* (Committee for a Democratic Palestine, n.d.), p. 17.
93 Abu-Ghazaleh, "Arab Cultural Nationalism," p. 87; Hilma Granqvist, *Marriage Conditions in a Palestinian Village* (Helsingfors: Societas Scientarium Fennica, 1931), p. 99.
94 Abd al-'Al, al-Baquri, 'Al-thawra bayn barakat al-jamahir wa tadahun al-qiyadat," *Tali'ah* 7, no. 4, p. 95.
95 Joel Beinin, "The Palestine Communist Party, 1919-1948," *MERIP Reports* 55 (1977): 8–9.
96 The resolutions of the Seventh Congress are reproduced in Spector, *Soviet Union*, pp. 91–104.
97 Beinin, "Palestine Communist Party," p. 12; Budeiri, *Palestine Communist Party*.
98 Yasin, *Kifah al-Shab*, p. 143.
99 Kayyali, *Palestine*, p. 175.
100 Porath, *Palestinian Arab*, pp. 92–93.
101 Ibid., pp. 96–97.
102 Yasin, *Kifah al-Shab*, pp. 147–48.
103 Firestone, "Crop-sharing," pp. 17–18.
104 Yasin, *Kifah al-Shab*, pp. 146–48.
105 Kayyali, *Palestine*, pp. 179–80.
106 Budeiri, *Palestine Communist Party*, p. 77.
107 It has been claimed that al-Qassam was a student of Muhammad 'Abduh's, but S. 'Abdullah Schleifer, in "The Life and Thought of 'Izz-al-Din al-Qassam," *Islamic Quarterly* 23 (1979): 61–81, asserts that 'Abduh's influence on al-Qassam was very limited.
108 Al-Qassam's grandfather and granduncle were prominent shaykhs of the Qadari order in his hometown of Jabla, and al-Qassam taught for a time in a school maintained by that *tariqa*. Al-Qassam is said to have belonged to the Tijaniyya and Naqshbandi *turuq*, the latter of which was involved in anti-colonial struggles in Syria during the nineteenth century: Schleifer, "Life and Thought," pp. 62–63, 69.
109 Lachman, "Arab Rebellion," p. 77.
110 Porath, *Palestinian Arab*, pp. 133–34; Kayyali, *Palestine*, p. 180; Schleifer, "Life and Thought," p. 47.
111 Kayyali, *Palestine*, p.180; Porath, *Palestinian Arab*, p.137.
112 Hirst, *Gun and Olive Branch*, p. 76.
113 Schleifer, "Life and Thought," p. 68; Lachman, "Arab Rebellion," p. 62.
114 Hart, *Aith Waryaghar*, pp. 170ff., 377ff.
115 Gilsenan, "Against Patron–Client Relations," pp. 217–28.
116 Laclau, *Politics and Ideology*, p. 157. Al-Qassam's practices recall Walter Benjamin's notion of the "dialectical image," a reconstellation of materials from the past in the revolutionary present: Susan Buck-Morss, "Walter Benjamin – Revolutionary Writer (1)," *New Left Review* 128 (1981): 50–75. See also Williams's category of the "residual": *Marxism*, pp. 121–27.
117 Lachman, "Arab Rebellion," p. 64.
118 Thomas Hodgkin, "The Revolutionary Tradition in Islam," *History Workshop* 10 (1980): 148–49.
119 Lachman, "Arab Rebellion," p. 65; Yasin, *Kifah al-Shab*, p. 154, maintains that armed action began only in 1933.

120 Lachman, "Arab Rebellion," p. 72.

121 Ibid., p. 74; Kayyali, *Palestine*, pp. 182–83.

122 James J. Zogby, "The Palestinian Revolt of the 1930's," in I. Abu-Lughod and B. Abu-Laban, eds, *Settler Regimes in Africa and the Arab World* (Wilmette, Ill.: Medina University Press, 1974), pp. 182–83.

123 Kayyali, *Palestine*, p. 192.

124 Lachman, "Arab Rebellion," p. 78; Porath, *Palestinian Arab*, pp. 179–82.

125 Porath, *Palestinian Arab*, pp. 192–93.

126 Ibid., pp. 179–82.

127 The Palestinians had shown solidarity with the rebellion of 1925, when the Mufti had headed an emergency committee to aid the Druze: Michael Assaf, *The Arab Movement in Palestine* (New York: Masada Youth Organization of America, 1937), p. 39.

128 Porath, *Palestinian Arab*, pp. 211–21; Kayyali, Palestine, p. 201.

129 Lesch, *Arab Politics*, p. 122.

130 Porath, *Palestinian Arab*, p. 261.

131 Tom Bowden, *The Breakdown of Public Security: The Case of Ireland 1916–1921 and Palestine 1936–1939* (Beverly Hills: Sage, 1977). Among the usual items the smugglers trafficked in was hashish.

132 Kayyali, *Palestine*, p. 212; Porath, *Palestinian Arab*, pp. 249–50; Lachman, "Arab Rebellion," p. 80.

133 Porath, *Palestinian Arab*, p. 247; Yuval Arnon-Ohanna, "The Bands in the Palestinian Arab Revolt, 1936–39: Structure and Organization," *Asian and African Studies* (Jerusalem) 15 (1981): 232. According to Arnon-Ohanna (p. 233), band membership was between 6,000 and 15,000.

134 Porath, *Palestinian Arab*, pp. 267–69.

135 Ibid., pp. 267–68; Kayyali, *Palestine*, p. 214.

136 Porath, *Palestinian Arab*, p. 269.

137 Ibid., pp. 251, 262, 269.

138 Gabriel Sheffer, "Appeasement and the Problem of Palestine," *IJMES* (1980): 377–99.

139 Christopher Sykes, *Cross Roads to Israel* (London: New English Library, 1967), p. 193.

140 Porath, *Palestinian Arab*, p. 293.

141 Walid Khalidi, ed., *From Haven to Conquest* (Beirut: Institute for Palestine Studies, 1971), pp. 848–49.

142 Arnon-Ohanna, "Bands," p. 247.

143 Those who advance the "solution" of the revolutionary party are of various political persuasions and include Porath, *Palestinian Arab*, p. 269; Yasin, *Kifah al-Shab*, pp. 195–96; Budeiri, *Palestine Communist Party*, p. 107; Weinstock, *Sionisme*, p. 178; Tom Bowden, "The Politics of Rebellion in Palestine, 1936–39," *Middle Eastern Studies* II (1975): 147–74; Kayyali, *Palestine*, p. 231.

144 Williams, *Marxism*, pp. 121–27.

145 This claim is made by, for instance, Graham-Brown, *Palestinians*, p. 171.

146 Porath, *Palestinian Arab*, p. 183; Elpeleg, "1936–39, Disturbances," pp. 48–49; Lesch, *Arab Politics*, p. 223.

147 Hirst, *Gun and Olive Branch*, p. 104.

148 For instance, Samih Samara, *Al-'amal al-shuyu'i fi filastin: al-tabaqa wa-al-sha'b fi mawajaba al-kuluniyaliya* (Beirut: Dar al-Farabi, 1979). Budeiri, *Palestine Communist Party*; Alain Greilsammer, *Les communistes israéliens* (Paris: Presses de la Fondation Nationale des Sciences Politiques, 1978). For a review of this growing body of literature, see Alexander Flores, "The Palestine Communist Party during the Mandatory Period: An Account of Sources and

Research," *Peuples méditerranéens* II (1987): 3–23, 175–94. Such studies touch only lightly on the 1936–39 rebellion and contain little socioeconomic analysis of the Palestinian social formation.

149 The work of Sarah Graham-Brown is a noteworthy exception. On this point, see Ibrahim Abu-Lughod, "The Pitfalls of Palestiniology: A Review Essay," *Arab Studies Quarterly* 3 (1981) 403–11.

Part IV

THE NEW HISTORY OF
THE 1948 WAR

8

THE DEBATE ABOUT 1948

Avi Shlaim

In the late 1980s, a series of books written by mostly Israeli scholars challenged the common Israeli historiographical interpretation of the 1948 war. The works of historians such as Benny Morris, Avi Shlaim and Ilan Pappé triggered a public debate in Israel; one which intensified in 1998 during Israel's jubilee celebrations. The revisionist historians became known in Israel and outside the country as the 'new historians' – a term which is synonymous with a critical non-Zionist evaluation of past and present realities in the land of Israel and Palestine.

In this article, Avi Shlaim charts the conventional Zionist interpretation of the war and compares its main components to the works by the revisionist historians. As he shows, several of Israel's foundational myths and hence their relevance to present contemplation of the past and future in the Jewish state have been irrevocably undermined by these professional researchers.

* * *

"Conquerors, my son, consider as true history only what they them-selves have fabricated."[1] Thus remarked the old Arab headmaster to young Saeed on his return to Haifa in the summer of 1948 in Emile Habiby's tragicomic novel *The Secret Life of Sa'id, the Ill-Fated Pessoptimist.* The headmaster spoke about the Israelis more in sorrow than in anger: "It is true they did demolish those villages . . . and did evict their inhabi-tants. But, my son, they are far more merciful than the conquerors our forefathers had years before."[2]

Most Israelis would be outraged by the suggestion that they are conquerors, yet this is how they are perceived by the Palestinians. But the point of the quote is that there can be no agreement on what actu-ally happened in 1948; each side subscribes to a different version of events. The Palestinians regard Israelis as the conquerors and themselves as the true victims of the first Arab–Israeli war, which they call *al-Nakba* or the disaster. Palestinian historiography reflects these perceptions. The Israelis, whether or not they were conquerors, were the indisputable victors in the 1948 war, which they call the War of Independence. Because they were the victors, among other reasons, they were able to propagate more effectively than their opponents their version of this fateful war. History, in a sense, is the propaganda of the victors.

The conventional Zionist account of the 1948 war goes roughly as follows. The conflict between Jews and Arabs in Palestine came to a head following the passage, on 29 November 1947, of the United Nations partition resolution that called for the establishment of two states, one Jewish and one Arab. The Jews accepted the U.N. plan despite the painful sacrifices it entailed, but the Palestinians, the neighboring Arab states, and the Arab League rejected it. Great Britain did everything in its power toward the end of the Palestine Mandate to frustrate the establishment of the Jewish state envisaged in the U.N. plan. With the expiry of the Mandate and the proclamation of the State of Israel, seven Arab states sent their armies into Palestine with the firm intention of strangling the Jewish state at birth. The subsequent struggle was an unequal one between a Jewish David and an Arab Goliath. The infant Jewish state fought a desperate, heroic, and ultimately successful battle for survival against overwhelming odds. During the war, hundreds of thousands of Palestinians fled to the neighboring Arab states, mainly in response to orders from their leaders and despite Jewish pleas to stay and demon-strate that peaceful coexistence was possible. After the war, the story continues, Israeli leaders sought peace with all their heart and all their might but there was no one to talk to on the other side. Arab intransi-gence was alone responsible for the political deadlock, which was not broken until President Anwar Sadat's visit to Jerusalem thirty years later.

This conventional Zionist account or old history of the 1948 war displays a number of features. In the first place, it is not history in the proper sense of the word. Most of the voluminous literature on the war was written not by professional historians but by participants, by politicians, soldiers, official historians, and a large host of sympathetic chroniclers, journalists, biographers, and hagiographers. Second, this literature is very short on political analysis of the war and long on chronicles of the military operations, especially the heroic feats of the Israeli fighters. Third, this literature maintains that Israel's conduct during the war was governed by higher moral standards than that of her enemies. Of particular relevance here is the precept of *tohar haneshek* or the purity of arms, which posits that weapons remain pure provided they are employed only in self-defense and provided they are not used against innocent civilians and defenseless people. This popular heroic–moralistic version of the 1948 war is the one that is taught in Israeli schools and used extensively in the quest for legitimacy abroad. It is a prime example of the use of a nationalist version of history in the process of nation building.

Until recently this standard Zionist version of the events surrounding the birth of the State of Israel remained largely unchallenged outside the Arab world. The fortieth anniversary of the birth of the state, however, witnessed the publication of a number of books that challenged various aspects of the standard Zionist version. First in the field, most polemical in its tone, and most comprehensive in its scope, was Simha Flapan's, *The Birth of Israel: Myths and Realities*. A former director of the Arab Affairs Department of the left-wing Mapam Party and editor of the Middle East monthly, *New Outlook*, Flapan wrote his book with an explicit political rather than academic aim in mind: to expose the myths that he claimed served as the basis of Israeli propaganda and Israeli policy. "The myths that Israel forged during the formation of the state," writes Flapan, "have hardened into this impenetrable and dangerous ideological shield."[3] After listing seven myths, to each of which a chapter in the book is devoted, Flapan frankly admits the political purpose of the whole exercise. "It is the purpose of this book to debunk these myths, not as an academic exercise but as a contribution to a better understanding of the Palestinian problem and to a more constructive approach to its solution."[4]

Other books that were critical in their treatment of the Zionist rendition of events, though without an explicit political agenda, included Benny Morris, *The Birth of the Palestinian Refugee Problem, 1947–1949*,[5] Ilan Pappé, *Britain and the Arab–Israeli Conflict, 1948–51*,[6] and my own *Collusion across the Jordan: King Abdullah, the Zionist Movement and the Partition of Palestine*.[7] Collectively we came to be called the Israeli revisionists or the new historians. Neither term is entirely satisfactory. The term "revisionists" in the Zionist lexicon refers to the right-wing followers of Ze'ev Jabotinsky who broke away from mainstream Zionism in 1925, whereas

173

the new historians are located on the political map somewhere to the left of the mainstream. The term "new historians" is rather self-congratulatory and by implication dismissive of everything written before the new historians appeared on the scene as old and worthless. Professor Yehoshua Porath of the Hebrew University of Jerusalem has suggested as alternative terms prehistory and history. But this is only slightly less offensive toward the first category of historians. So, for lack of a better word, I shall use the label "old" to refer to the proponents of the standard Zionist version of the 1948 war and the label "new" to the recent left-wing critics of this version, including myself.

The first thing to note about the new historiography is that much of it is not new. Many of the arguments that are central to the new historiography were advanced long ago by Israeli writers, not to mention Palestinian, Arab, and Western writers. To list all these Israeli writers is beyond the scope of this article, but a few examples might be appropriate. One common thread that runs through the new historiography is a critical stance toward David Ben-Gurion, the founder of the State of Israel and its first prime minister. Whereas the old historians tend to view Ben-Gurion as representative of the consensus among the civilians and military elites, the new historians tend to portray him as the driving force behind Israel's policy in 1948, and particularly the policy of expelling the Palestinians. Many of the recent criticisms of Ben-Gurion, however, are foreshadowed in a book written by the former official historian of the Israel Defense Forces (IDF), Lieutenant-Colonel Israel Baer, while he was in prison after being convicted of spying for the Soviet Union.[8]

A significant start in revising the conventional Zionist view of British policy toward the end of the Palestine Mandate was made by Gavriel Cohen in a volume with a characteristically old-fashioned title – *Hayinu Keholmim*, "we were as dreamers."[9] Yaacov Shimoni, deputy-director of the Middle East Department in the Foreign Ministry in 1948, published a highly perceptive article on the hesitations, doubts, reservations, and differences of opinion that attended the Arab decision to intervene in Palestine in May 1948.[10] This article, which is at odds with the dominant Zionist narrative, is all the more noteworthy for having been written by an insider. Meir Pail wrote another corrective to the notion of a monolithic Arab world, focusing in particular on the conflict between King Abdullah of Jordan and the Palestinians.[11] The Zionist version of the causes of the Palestinian refugee problem was called into question by a number of Israeli writers and most convincingly by Rony Gabbay.[12] Finally, the argument that Israel's commitment to peace with the Arabs did not match the official rhetoric can be traced to a book published under a pseudonym by two members of the Israeli Communist Party.[13]

Although many of the arguments of the new historiography are not new, there is a qualitative difference between this historiography and the bulk of the earlier studies, whether they accepted or contradicted the official Zionist line. The difference, in a nutshell, is that the new historiography is written with access to the official Israeli and Western documents, whereas the earlier writers had no access, or only partial access, to the official documents. This is not a hard and fast rule; there are many exceptions and there are also degrees of access. Nevertheless, it is generally true to say that the new historians, with the exception of the late Simha Flapan, have carried out extensive archival research in Israel, Britain, and America and that their arguments are backed by hard documentary evidence and by a Western-style scholarly apparatus.

Indeed, the upsurge of new histories would not have been possible without the declassification of the official government documents. Israel adopted the British thirty-year rule for the review and declassification of foreign-policy documents. If this rule is not applied by Israel as systematically as it is in Britain, it is applied rather more liberally. Both Britain and Israel have also started to follow the American example of publishing volumes of documents that have been professionally selected and edited. The first four volumes in the series of *Documents on the Foreign Policy of Israel* are an invaluable and indispensable aid to research on the 1948 war and the armistice negotiations that ended it.[14]

On the Arab side, there is no equivalent of the thirty-year rule. In the relevant Arab archives little access to materials on the 1948 war is allowed, and this restriction does pose a serious problem to the researcher. It is sometimes argued that no definitive account of the 1948 war, least of all an account of what happened behind the scenes on the Arab side, is possible without proper access to the Arab state archives. But difficulty should not be construed as impossibility. In the first place, some official Arab documents are available. A prime example is the report of the Iraqi parliamentary committee of inquiry into the Palestine question, which is packed with high-level documents.[15] Another example is the collection of official, semi-official, and private papers gathered by the Institute for Palestine Studies.[16] In addition, there is a far from negligible literature in Arabic that consists of first-hand accounts of the disaster, including the diaries and memoirs of prominent politicians and soldiers.[17] But even if none of these Arabic sources existed, the other available sources would provide a basis for an informed analysis of the 1948 war. A military historian of the Middle Ages would be green with envy at the sight of the sources available to his contemporary Middle Eastern counterpart. Historians of the 1948 war would do much better to explore in depth the manifold sources that are available to them than to lament the denial of access to the Arab state archives.

If the release of rich new sources of information was one important reason behind the advent of historical revisionism, a change in the general political climate was another.[18] For many Israelis, especially liberal-minded ones, the Likud's ill-conceived and ill-fated invasion of Lebanon in 1982 marked a watershed. Until then, Zionist leaders had been careful to cultivate the image of peace lovers who would stand up and fight only if war was forced upon them. Until then, the notion of *ein breira*, of no alternative, was central to the explanation of why Israel went to war and a means of legitimizing her involvement in wars. But while the fierce debate between supporters and opponents of the Lebanon War was still raging, Prime Minister Menachem Begin gave a lecture to the IDF Staff Academy on wars of choice and wars of no choice. He argued that the Lebanon War, like the Sinai War of 1956, was a war of choice designed to achieve national objectives. With this admission, unprecedented in the history of the Zionist movement, the national consensus round the notion of *ein breira* began to crumble, creating political space for a critical reexamination of the country's earlier history.[19]

The appearance of the new books on the 1948 war excited a great deal of interest and controversy in Israeli academic and political circles. A two-day conference on the end of the War of Independence, organized by the Dayan Centre and the Institute for Zionist Research at Tel Aviv University in April 1989, turned into a confrontation between the old Zionist version represented by historians, journalists, and veterans of that war and the new version represented by Benny Morris and myself. Several of the speakers argued, with good reason, that the new historians did not develop a new school or new methodology of historical writing but used conventional historical methods to advance new interpretations of the events of 1948. On the merits of the new interpretations, opinions were sharply divided. Members of the old guard, especially the Mapai old guard, bristled with hostility and roundly condemned the new interpretations. The response of the Israeli academic community, both at the conference and in subsequent reviews and discussions, was more measured. Some of the findings of the new historiography, and especially the findings reported in Benny Morris's book, became widely accepted in the Israeli academic community and found their way into university reading lists and high school textbooks.

Among the critics of the new historians, the most strident and vitriolic was Shabtai Teveth, Ben-Gurion's biographer. Teveth's attack entitled "The New Historians" appeared in four successive full-page installments in the Israeli daily *Ha'aretz* on 7, 14, and 21 April and 19 May 1989. Teveth subsequently published an abridged and revised version of this series in an article entitled "Charging Israel with Original Sin" in the American–Jewish monthly, *Commentary*. In this article, Teveth describes the new history as a "farrago of distortions, omissions, tendentious readings, and outright falsifications."[20] Teveth pursues two lines of attack. One line of attack is that the new historiography "rests in part on defective evidence, and is characterized by serious professional flaws."[21] The other line of attack is that the new historiography is politically motivated, pro-Palestinian, and aimed at delegitimizing Zionism and the State of Israel.

In support of this claim, Teveth quotes a passage from Benny Morris's article on "The New Historiography," a passage that states that "how one perceives 1948 bears heavily on how one perceives the whole Zionist/Israeli experience. . . . If Israel was born tarnished, besmirched by original sin then it was no more deserving of that [Western] grace and assistance than were its neighbours." Teveth goes on to say that the original sin with which Shlaim charges Israel consists of "the denial to the Palestinian Arabs of a country," while Morris charges Israel with "creating the refugee problem" and both charges "are false."[22]

Teveth must have gone through the two books in question with a fine-tooth comb to discover evidence of the political motive that he attributes to their authors, but he came up with nothing. This is why he was reduced to quoting from the *Tikkun* article, which he builds up, in a farrago of distortions of his own, into the political manifesto of what he calls "the new historical club." But even the quote from the article does not demonstrate any political purpose; all it does is to point out that Western attitudes toward Israel are influenced by perceptions of how Israel came into the world. This is surely undeniable. Benny Morris replied in *Ha'aretz* and in a second article in *Tikkun* that, as far as he is concerned, the new historiography has no political purposes whatsoever. The task and function of the historian, in his view, is to illuminate the past.[23] My own view is that the historian's most fundamental task is not to chronicle but to evaluate. The historian's task is to subject the claims of all the protagonists to rigorous scrutiny and to reject all those claims, however deeply cherished, that do not stand up to such scrutiny. In my view many of the claims advanced by the old historians do not stand up to serious scrutiny. But that does not mean that everything they say is untrue or that Israel is the sole villain of the piece. In fact, neither Benny Morris nor I have charged Israel with original sin. It is Shabtai Teveth who, in face of all the evidence to the contrary, continues to cling to the doctrine of Israel's immaculate conception.[24]

It is Teveth's counterattack that is politically motivated. Like so many other members of the Mapai old guard, he is unable to distinguish between history and propaganda. Any attempt to revise the conventional wisdom with the help of new evidence that has come to light is therefore immediately suspect as unpatriotic and calculated to harm the reputation of the leader and the party who led the struggle for independence. For Teveth and other members of the Mapai old guard, the

177

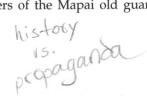
history vs. propaganda

events in question do not yet fully belong to history but represent their party's and their country's finest hour. They are too wedded, personally and politically, to the heroic version of the creation of the State of Israel to be able to treat the new historiography with an open mind.

Interestingly, individuals on the political right in Israel, whether scholars or not, respond to the findings of the new historiography with far greater equanimity. They readily admit, for example, that Israel did expel Palestinians and even express regret that she did not expel more Palestinians since it was they who launched the war against her. Right-wingers tend to treat the 1948 war from a realpolitik point of view rather than a moralistic one. They are therefore spared the anguish of trying to reconcile the practices of Zionism with the precepts of liberalism. It is perhaps for this reason that they are generally less self-righteous and more receptive to new evidence and new analyses of the 1948 war than members of the Mapai old guard. The latter put so much store by Israel's claim to moral rectitude that they cannot face up to the evidence of cynical Israeli double-dealings or brutal expulsion and dispossession of the Palestinians. It is an axiom of their narrative that Israel is the innocent victim. And it is their concern with the political consequences of rewriting history that largely accounts for the ferocity of their attacks on the new historiography.

Although politics and history have gotten mixed up in the debate about 1948, and although this debate often resembles a dialogue of the deaf, the very fact that a debate is taking place is a welcome change from the stifling conformity of the past. A. J. P. Taylor once remarked that history does not repeat itself, it is historians who repeat one another. The old historiography on the emergence of Israel is a striking example of this general phenomenon. As for the new historiography, whatever its faults, it at least has the merit of stimulating a reexamination of time-hallowed conventions.

Six major bones of contention can be identified in the ongoing debate between the new and the old historians: Britain's policy at the end of the Palestine Mandate, the Arab–Israeli military balance in 1948, the origins of the Palestinian refugee problem, the nature of Israeli–Jordanian relations during the war, Arab war aims, and the reasons for the continuing political deadlock after the guns fell silent. Let me now review briefly the main arguments and counterarguments on these six key issues in the debate, bearing in mind that I am not a detached or neutral observer but one of the protagonists in the debate.

British policy

The first bone of contention concerns British policy in Palestine between 29 November 1947 and 14 May 1948. Zionist historiography, reflecting the suspicions of Zionist leaders at that time, is laden with charges of hostile plots that are alleged to have been hatched against the Yishuv during the twilight of British rule in Palestine. The central charge is that Britain armed and secretly encouraged her Arab allies, and especially her client, King Abdullah of Jordan, to invade Palestine upon expiry of the British Mandate and do battle with the Jewish state as soon as it came into the world. For Ernest Bevin, the foreign secretary in the Labour government headed by Clement Attlee, is reserved the role of chief villain in this alleged conspiracy.

Ilan Pappé, using English, Arabic, and Hebrew sources, has driven a coach and horses through the traditional Zionist rendition of British policy toward the end of the Mandate, and I tried to follow along the trail that he has blazed.[25] The key to British policy during this period is summed up by Pappé in two words: Greater Transjordan. Bevin felt that if Palestine had to be partitioned, the Arab area could not be left to stand on its own but should be united with Transjordan. A Greater Transjordan would compensate Britain for the loss of bases in Palestine. Hostility to Hajj Amin al-Husayni, who had cast his lot with the Nazis during World War II, and hostility to a Palestinian state, which in British eyes was always equated with a Mufti state, were important and constant features of British policy after the war. By February 1948, Bevin and his Foreign Office advisers were pragmatically reconciled to the inevitable emergence of the Jewish state. What they were not reconciled to was the emergence of a Palestinian state.

The policy of Greater Transjordan implied discreet support for a bid by Abdullah – nicknamed "Mr. Bevin's little king" by the officials at the Foreign Office – to enlarge his kingdom by taking over the West Bank. At a secret meeting in London on 7 February 1948, Bevin gave Tawfiq Abul Huda, Jordan's prime minister, the green light to send the Arab Legion into Palestine immediately following the departure of the British forces. But Bevin also warned Jordan not to invade the area allocated by the UN to the Jews. An attack on Jewish state territory, he said, would compel Britain to withdraw her subsidy and officers from the Arab Legion. Far from being driven by blind anti-Semitic prejudice to unleash the Arab Legion against the Jews, Bevin in fact urged restraint on the Arabs in general and on Jordan in particular. Whatever sins were committed by the British foreign secretary as the British Mandate in Palestine approached its inglorious end, inciting King Abdullah to use force to prevent the emergence of a Jewish state was not one of them.

If Bevin was guilty of conspiring to unleash the Arab Legion, his target was not the Jews but the Palestinians. The prospect of a Palestinian state was pretty remote in any case because the Palestinians themselves had done so little to build it. But by supporting Abdullah's bid to capture the Arab part of Palestine adjacent to his kingdom, Bevin indirectly helped to ensure that the Palestinian state envisaged in the UN partition plan would be stillborn. In short, if there is a case to be made against Bevin, it is not that he tried to abort the birth of the Jewish state but that he endorsed the understanding between King Abdullah and the Jewish Agency to partition Palestine between themselves and leave the Palestinians out in the cold.

The Zionist charge that Bevin deliberately instigated hostilities in Palestine and gave encouragement and arms to the Arabs to crush the infant Jewish state thus represents almost the exact opposite of the historical truth as it emerges from the British, Arab, and Israeli documents. The charge is without substance and may be safely discarded as the first in the series of myths that have come to surround the founding of the State of Israel.

The military balance

A second myth, fostered by official and semi-official accounts of the 1948 war, is that the Israeli victory was achieved in the face of insurmountable military odds. Israel is pictured in these accounts as a little Jewish David confronting a giant Arab Goliath. The war is portrayed as a desperate, costly, and heroic struggle for survival with plucky little Israel fighting off marauding armies from seven Arab states. Israel's ultimate victory in this war is treated as nothing short of a miracle.

The heroism of the Jewish fighters is not in question, nor is there any doubt about the heavy price that the Yishuv paid for its victory. Altogether there were 6,000 dead, 4,000 soldiers and 2,000 civilians, or about 1 percent of the entire population. Nevertheless, the Yishuv was not as hopelessly outnumbered and outgunned as the official history would have us believe. It is true that the Yishuv numbered merely 650,000 souls, compared with 1.2 million Palestinian Arabs and nearly 40 million Arabs in the surrounding states. It is true that the senior military advisers told the political leadership on 12 May 1948 that the Haganah had only a "fifty-fifty" chance of withstanding the imminent Arab attack. It is true that the sense of weakness and vulnerability in the Jewish population was as acute as it was pervasive and that some segments of this population were gripped by a feeling of gloom and doom. And it is true that during three critical weeks, from the invasion of Palestine by the regular armies of the Arab states on 15 May until the start of the first truce on 11 June, this community had to struggle for its very survival.

But the Yishuv also enjoyed a number of advantages that are commonly down-played by the old historians. The Yishuv was better prepared, better mobilized, and better organized when the struggle for Palestine reached its crucial stage than its local opponents. The Haganah, which was renamed the Israel Defense Forces on 31 May, could draw on a large

reserve of Western-trained and homegrown officers with military experience. It had an effective centralized system of command and control.
And, in contrast to the armies of the Arab states, especially those of Iraq
and Egypt, it had short, internal lines of communication that enabled it
to operate with greater speed and mobility.

During the unofficial phase of the war, from December 1947 until
14 May 1948, the Yishuv gradually gained the upper hand in the struggle against its Palestinian opponents. Its armed forces were larger, better
trained, and more technologically advanced. Despite some initial setbacks, these advantages enabled it to win and win decisively the battle
against the Palestinian Arabs. Even when the Arab states committed their
regular armies, marking the beginning of the official phase of the war,
the Yishuv retained its numerical superiority. In mid-May the total
number of Arab troops, both regular and irregular, operating in Palestine
was between 20,000 and 25,000. The IDF fielded 35,000 troops, not
counting the second-line troops in the settlements. By mid-July the IDF
fully mobilized 65,000 men under arms, by September the number rose
to 90,000, and by December it reached a peak of 96,441. The Arab states
also reinforced their armies, but they could not match this rate of increase.
Thus, at each stage of the war, the IDF significantly outnumbered all the
Arab forces ranged against it, and by the final stage of the war its superiority ratio was nearly two to one.[26]

The IDFs gravest weakness during the first round of fighting in May–
June was in firepower. The Arab armies were much better equipped,
especially with heavy arms. But during the first truce, in violation of
the UN arms embargo, Israel imported from all over Europe (especially
from Czechoslovakia) rifles, machine guns, armored cars, field guns,
tanks, airplanes, and all kinds of ammunition in large quantities. These
illicit arms acquisitions enabled the IDF to tip the scales decisively in its
own favor. In the second round of fighting the IDF moved on to the offensive, and in the third round it picked off the Arab armies and defeated
them one by one. The final outcome of the war was thus not a miracle
but a faithful reflection of the underlying Arab–Israeli military balance.
In this war, as in most wars, the stronger side ultimately prevailed.

The origins of the Palestinian refugee problem

A third bone of contention between the old and the new historians
concerns the origins of the Palestinian refugee problem. The question is:
Did they leave or were they pushed out? Ever since 1948 Israeli
spokesmen have maintained that the Palestinians left the country on
orders from their own leaders and with the expectation of a triumphant
return. Accounts written by old historians echo the official line. Arab
spokesmen have with equal consistency maintained that Israel forcibly

expelled some 750,000 Palestinians from their homes and that Israel, therefore, bears the full responsibility for the creation of the Palestinian refugee problem. The question of origin is thus directly related to the question of responsibility for solving the Palestinian refugee problem. Arab claims that the notion of forcible "transfer" is inherent in Zionism, and that in 1948 the Zionists simply seized the opportunity to displace and dispossess the Arab inhabitants of the country, rendered this controversy all the more acrimonious.

Benny Morris in his book *The Birth of the Palestinian Refugee Problem* investigated this subject as carefully, dispassionately, and objectively as it is ever likely to be investigated. Morris found no evidence of Arab leaders issuing calls to Palestine's Arabs to leave their homes and villages or any trace of a radio or press campaign urging them to flee. On the Israeli side, he found no blanket orders handed down from above for the systematic expulsion of the Palestinians. He therefore rejected both the Arab order and the Jewish robber-state explanations. His much quoted conclusion is that "The Palestinian refugee problem was born of war, not by design, Jewish or Arab. It was largely a by-product of Arab and Jewish fears and of the protracted, bitter fighting that characterized the first Arab–Israeli war; in smaller part, it was the deliberate creation of Jewish and Arab military commanders and politicians."[27] Benny Morris has already replied in detail to Teveth's criticisms, and it would serve no useful purpose for me to give a blow-by-blow account of the battle between them.[28] But it seems to me that Teveth's position on the origins of the Palestinian refugee problem is about as sophisticated as the old saying, *haya ness vehem nassu* – there was a miracle and they ran away. Anyone who believes that will believe anything.

Another category of critics of Benny Morris's book consists of Israeli Orientalists. Some Orientalists, like Yehoshua Porath, have been highly supportive. Others, like Asher Susser, Emmanuel Sivan, and Avraham Sela, have written in a more critical vein while giving credit where credit is due. The recurrent criticism from this professional quarter is that Morris has made very little use in his book of Arabic sources. In response to this criticism, Morris posed a question: would the consulting of the Arabic materials mentioned by the critics have resulted in a fundamental revision of the analysis of the Palestinian exodus or added significantly to the description of this exodus given in his book?[29] Avraham Sela concedes that the use of the Arabic sources would probably not have changed the main conclusions of Morris's study on the causes of the Palestinian exodus. But he goes on to argue that neglect of the available Arabic sources and heavy reliance on the Israeli documents is liable to produce an unbalanced picture.[30]

While a number of Israeli Orientalists hold that Morris attached too much weight to Israeli actions, compared with other factors, in the creation of the Palestinian refugee problem, many other reviewers felt that in his conclusion Morris lets Israel off rather lightly. An observation that is frequently made, by Western as well as Palestinian reviewers, is that the evidence presented in the body of the book suggests a far higher degree of Israeli responsibility than that implied by Morris in his conclusion.[31] But despite the shortcomings of Morris's conclusion, his book remains an outstandingly original, scholarly, and important contribution to the study of a problem that lies at the heart of the Arab–Israeli conflict.

Israeli–Jordanian relations

A fourth issue that gave rise to a lively controversy in Israel is the nature of Israeli–Jordanian relations and, more specifically, the contention that there was collusion or tacit understanding between King Abdullah and the Jewish Agency in 1947–49. That there was traffic between these two parties has been widely known for some time and the two meetings between Golda Meir and King Abdullah in November 1947, and May 1948 have even been featured in popular films. Nor is the charge of collusion a new one. It was made in a book published by Colonel Abdullah al-Tall who had served as a messenger between King Abdullah and the Jews, following Tall's abortive coup and defection to Egypt.[32] A similar charge was leveled against Ben-Gurion by Lieutenant-Colonel Israel Baer in the book he wrote in his prison cell following his conviction of spying for the Soviet Union.[33] Tall condemned King Abdullah for betraying his fellow Arabs and selling the Palestinians down the river. Baer condemned Ben-Gurion for forming an unholy alliance with Arab reaction and British imperialism. A number of books and articles on Zionist–Hashemite relations have also been written by Israeli scholars, the most recent of which are by Dan Schueftan and Uri Bar-Joseph.[34] But out of the recent crop of books on this rather unusual bilateral relationship, it is my own book *Collusion across the Jordan* that achieved real notoriety on both sides of the Jordan and has been singled out for attack by the old historians.

The central thesis advanced in my book is that in November 1947 an unwritten agreement was reached between King Abdullah and the Jewish Agency to divide Palestine between themselves following the termination of the British Mandate and that this agreement laid the foundation for mutual restraint during the first Arab–Israeli war and for continuing collaboration in the aftermath of this war. A subsidiary thesis is that Britain knew and approved of this secret Hashemite–Zionist agreement to divide up Palestine between themselves, not along the lines of the U.N. partition plan.

This thesis challenges the conventional view of the Arab–Israeli conflict as a simple bipolar affair in which a monolithic and implacably hostile

Arab world is pitted against the Jews. It suggests that the Arab rulers were deeply divided among themselves on how to deal with the Zionist challenge and that one of these rulers favored accommodation rather than confrontation and had indeed cut a deal with the Jewish Agency to partition Palestine at the expense of the Palestinians. The thesis also detracts from the heroic version that pictures Israel as ringed by an unbroken circle of Arab hostility and having to repel a concerted all-out attack on all fronts. Not surprisingly, the official history of the War of Independence fails to even mention the unwritten agreement with King Abdullah.[35] Even when this agreement is acknowledged, the official line is that Abdullah went back on it at the critical moment and that it consequently had no influence, or only a marginal influence, on the conduct of the war.[36]

Regurgitating the official line, Shabtai Teveth hotly denies that the Jewish leaders were involved in collusion or had an ally on the Arab side. He coyly admits that "Israel and Jordan did maintain a dialogue" but goes on to argue that "at most theirs was an understanding of convenience. . . . There was nothing in such an understanding to suggest collusion designed to deceive a third party, in this case the Palestinian Arabs."[37] Again, anyone who believes this will believe anything. If all that transpired between Israel and Jordan was a dialogue, then it was a rather curious kind of a dialogue because it lasted thirty years, because it was clandestine, because it was directed against a common rival, and because money changed hands. That the dialogue broke down between May and August 1948 is not in doubt. But surely, if one takes a long-term view of this relationship, "strategic partnership" if not "unholy alliance" would be a more appropriate term than a dialogue.

Teveth is evidently so wedded to the doctrine of Israel's immaculate conception that he is totally impervious to any evidence that contradicts it. He has made up his mind, and he does not want to be confused by the facts. His article provides a fine example of the absurd lengths to which the old historians are capable of going to suppress unpalatable truths about the way in which Israel came into the world. Judged by the rough standards of the game of nations, the dalliance between the Zionists and the Hashemite king was neither extraordinary nor particularly reprehensible. Both sides acted in a pragmatic fashion to advance their own interest. A problem arises only as a result of the claim that Israel's conduct was based on morality rather than self-interest.

The relations between Jordan and Israel in the 1948 war were reviewed recently by Avraham Sela in a 66-page article in *Middle Eastern Studies*. Sela's use of archival sources and his comprehensive examination of the literature on this subject, especially in Arabic, make this a valuable contribution to the historiography of the 1948 war. It does not lead me, however, to revise any of the arguments I advanced in *Collusion across the Jordan*. Sela's thesis is that "the conditions and basic assumptions that had constituted the foundations of the unwritten agreement between Abdullah and the Jewish Agency regarding the partition of Palestine as early as the summer of 1946 were altered so substantively during the unofficial war (December 1947–May 1948) as to render that agreement antiquated and impracticable."[38]

I believe that despite all the changes, the earlier accord and the long history of cooperation – going back to the foundation of the Amirate of Transjordan in 1921 – continued to exert some influence over the conduct of the two sides during the war. Sela maintains that in the early part of the war, the two sides, and especially the Israeli side, behaved according to the old adage *à la guerre comme à la guerre*. Even if this is a valid conclusion regarding Israel, it is emphatically not valid, in my view, in relation to Jordan. Although the accord was no longer binding and contact was severed, each side – and especially Jordan – continued to pursue limited objectives and acted with restraint toward the other until the war ended. Although they became enemies at the height of the war, they remained in Uri Bar-Joseph's apt phrase, "the best of enemies."

In conclusion, Sela tells us that war is a complex and intricate phenomenon. This is indisputable. One reason for this complexity is that war involves both politics and the use of force. The old historiography deals mostly with the military side of the war. I tried to redress the balance by looking at the political side of the war and more particularly at the interplay between politics and strategy. Sela goes on to state that "The collusion myth implicitly assumes the possibility for both Zionist and Palestinian acceptance of the partition plan and its peaceful implementation."[39] I assume nothing of the kind. On the contrary, precisely because the Palestinians rejected partition, I consider collaboration between Abdullah and the Jewish Agency to have been a reasonable and realistic strategy for both sides. In other words, I accept that in the period 1947–49 Israel had no Palestinian option or any other Arab option, save the Jordanian option. King Abdullah was the only Arab head of state who was willing to accept the principle of partition and to coexist peacefully with a Jewish state after the dust had settled. From March to April 1948 this understanding was subjected to severe strain as the Jews went on the offensive. In the period May–July 1948, the two sides came to blows. From Abdullah's postwar vantage point, this was merely a *fitna*, a family quarrel, and the Jews had started it. And after the initial outburst of violence, both sides began to pull their punches, as one does in a family quarrel.

There remains the question of whether the term "collusion" is appropriate for describing the relations between Abdullah and the Jewish

Agency and later the State of Israel. Some of the criticisms of the book were directed at its title rather than its substance. It was for this reason that for the abridged and revised paperback version of the book I opted for the more neutral title, *The Politics of Partition*.[40] In the preface to the new edition I explained that although I had dropped the offensive word from the title, I was still of the opinion that the Israel–Jordan linkup involved at least some of the elements associated with collusion: "it was held behind a thick veil of secrecy; its existence was hotly denied by the participants; it was directed against a third party; it involved more than a modicum of underhand scheming and plotting; and it was consciously and deliberately intended to frustrate the will of the international community, as expressed through the United Nations General Assembly, in favour of creating an independent Arab state in part of Palestine."[41] On reflection, I rather regret that I changed the title of my book. The original title was an apt one. Collusion is as good a word as any to describe the traffic between the Hashemite king and the Zionist movement during the period 1921–51, despite the violent interlude in the hot summer of 1948.

Arab war aims

Closely related to Israeli–Jordanian relations is the question of Arab war aims in 1948, a fifth bone of contention between the old and the new historians. The question is: Why did the Arab states invade Palestine with their regular armies on the day that the British Mandate expired and the State of Israel was proclaimed? The conventional Zionist answer is that the motive behind the invasion was to destroy the newly born Jewish state and to throw the Jews into the sea. The reality was more complex.

It is true that all the Arab states, with the exception of Jordan, rejected the UN partition plan. It is true that seven Arab armies invaded Palestine the morning after the State of Israel was proclaimed. It is true that the invasion was accompanied by blood-curdling rhetoric and threats to throw the Jews into the sea. It is true that in addition to the regular Arab armies and the Mufti's Holy War army, various groups of volunteers arrived in Palestine, the most important of which was the Arab Liberation Army, sponsored by the Arab League and led by the Syrian adventurer Fawzi al-Qawuqji. More importantly, it is true that the military experts of the Arab League had worked out a unified plan for the invasion and that this plan was all the more dangerous for having had more limited and realistic objectives than those implied by the wild Pan-Arab rhetoric.

But King Abdullah, who was given nominal command over all the Arab forces in Palestine, wrecked this plan by making last-minute changes. His objective in sending his army into Palestine was not to prevent the establishment of a Jewish state, but to make himself master of the Arab part of Palestine, which meant preventing the establishment of an independent Palestinian state. Since the Palestinians had done next to nothing to create an independent state, the Arab part of Palestine would have probably gone to Abdullah without all the scheming and plotting, but that is another matter. What is clear is that, under the command of Glubb Pasha, the Arab Legion made every effort to avert a head-on collision and, with the exception of one or two minor incidents, made no attempt to encroach on the territory allocated to the Jewish state by the UN cartographers.

There was no love lost between Abdullah and the other Arab rulers, who suspected him of being in cahoots with the enemy. Abdullah had always been something of a pariah in the rest of the Arab world, not least because of his friendship with the Jews. Syria and Lebanon felt threatened by his long-standing ambition to make himself master of Greater Syria. Egypt, the leader of the anti-Hashemite bloc within the Arab League, also felt threatened by Abdullah's plans for territorial aggrandizement in Palestine. King Farouk made his decision to intervene in Palestine at the last moment, and against the advice of his civilian and military experts, at least in part in order to check the growth of his rival's power. There were, thus, rather mixed motives behind the invasion of Palestine. And there was no single Arab plan of action during the 1948 war. On the contrary, it was the inability of the Arabs to coordinate their diplomatic and military plans that was in large measure responsible for the disaster that overwhelmed them. The one purpose that the Arab invasion did not serve was the ostensible one of coming to the rescue of the embattled Palestinians. Nowhere was the disparity between pan-Arab rhetoric and the reality greater than in relation to the Palestinian Arabs.[42] The reality was one of national selfishness, with each Arab state looking after its own interests. What was supposed to be a holy war against the Jews, quickly turned into a general land grab. Division and discord within the ranks of the ramshackle Arab coalition deepened with every successive defeat. Israel's leaders knew about these divisions and exploited them to the fullest. Thus, they launched an offensive against the Egyptian army in October and again in December 1948 in the confident expectation that their old friend in Amman would keep out. The old historians, by concentrating almost exclusively on the military operations of 1948, ended up with the familiar picture of an Arab–Israeli war in which all the Arabs were united by a single purpose, all were bent on the defeat and destruction of Israel. In retrospect, however, the political lineup on the Arab side in 1948 appears much more complicated and the motives behind the invasion of Palestine much more mixed.

187

The elusive peace

Last but not least of the contentious questions in the debate between the old and the new historians is the question of why peace proved unattainable in the aftermath of the first Arab–Israeli war. At the core of the old version lies the notion of Arab intransigence. According to this version, Israel strove indefatigably toward a peaceful settlement of the conflict but all her efforts foundered on the rocks of Arab intransigence. The new historians believe that postwar Israel was more intransigent than the Arab states and that she consequently bears a larger share of the responsibility for the political deadlock that followed the formal ending of hostilities.[43]

Evidence to back the new interpretation comes mainly from the files of the Israeli Foreign Ministry. These files burst at the seams with evidence of Arab peace feelers and Arab readiness to negotiate with Israel from September 1948 onward. The two key issues in dispute were refugees and borders. Each of the neighboring Arab states was prepared to negotiate with Israel directly and prepared to bargain about both refugees and borders.

King Abdullah proposed an overall political settlement with Israel in return for certain territorial concessions, particularly a land corridor to link Jordan with the Mediterranean, which would have enabled him to counter Arab criticisms of a separate peace with Israel. Colonel Husni Zaim, who captured power in Syria in March 1949 and was overthrown four months later, offered Israel full peace with an exchange of ambassadors, normal economic relations, and the resettlement of 300,000 Palestinian refugees in Syria in return for an adjustment of the boundary between the two countries through the middle of Lake Tiberias.[44] King Farouk of Egypt demanded the cession of Gaza and a substantial strip of desert bordering on Sinai as his price for a *de facto* recognition of Israel. All three Arab rulers displayed remarkable pragmatism in their approach to negotiations with the Jewish state. They were even anxious to preempt one another because they assumed that whoever settled up with Israel first would also get the best terms. Zaim openly declared his ambition to be the first Arab leader to make peace with Israel.

In each case, though for slightly different reasons, David Ben-Gurion considered the price being asked for peace as too high. He was ready to conclude peace on the basis of the status quo; he was unwilling to proceed to a peace that involved more than minuscule Israeli concessions on refugees or on borders. Ben-Gurion, as his diary reveals, considered that the armistice agreements with the neighboring Arab states met Israel's essential needs for recognition, security, and stability.[45] He knew that for formal peace agreements Israel would have to pay by yielding substantial tracts of territory and by permitting the return of a

188

substantial number of Palestinian refugees, and he did not consider this a price worth paying. Whether Ben-Gurion made the right choice is a matter of opinion. That he had a choice is now undeniable.

The controversy surrounding the elusive peace is examined in a book by Itamar Rabinovich, former Rector of Tel Aviv University and one of Israel's leading experts on modern Arab politics. The title of the book, inspired by a poem by Robert Frost, is *The Road Not Taken: Early Arab-Israeli Negotiations*. This title implies that the failure of these talks was not inevitable, that there was another road leading to peace – the road not taken. But the book does not advance any thesis nor does it engage directly in the debate between the old and the new historians. Rabinovich prefers to remain above the battle. So reluctant is he to assign blame, that his book ends without an explicit conclusion. All he would say is that "the choices of 1948–49 were made by Arabs, Israelis, Americans and others. The credit and responsibility for them belong to all."[46] Rabinovich's implicit conclusion, however, is that because of the instability of the Arab regimes, Ben-Gurion was justified in his refusal to assume any political risks for the sake of peace. Yet in every crucial respect Rabinovich's account undermines the claim of the old historians that Israel encountered total Arab intransigence and confirms the revisionist argument that Israeli intransigence was the much more serious obstacle on the road to peace.[47]

Conclusion

This article is concerned with the old Zionist version of the first Arab–Israeli war and with the challenge to this version posed by the new historiography. My conclusion is that the traditional version is deeply flawed and needs to be radically revised in the light of the new information that is now available. To put it bluntly, this version is little more than the propaganda of the victors. The debate between the old and the new historiography, moreover, is not of merely historical interest. It cuts to the very core of Israel's image of herself. It is for this reason that the battle of the historians has excited such intense popular interest and stirred such strong political passions.

The debate about 1948 between the old and the new historians resembles the American debate on the origins of the cold war. That debate evolved in stages. During the 1950s, the so-called traditionalist view held sway. According to this view, Soviet expansionism was responsible for the outbreak of the cold war, while American policy was essentially reactive and defensive. Then, in the context of the Vietnam war and the crisis of American self-confidence that accompanied it, a new school of thought emerged, a revisionist school of mostly younger, left-wing scholars. According to this school, the cold war was the result of the onward march of American capitalism, and it was the Soviet Union that reacted defensively. Following the opening up of the archives, a third school of thought emerged, the postrevisionist school. A reexamination of the assumptions and arguments of both traditionalists and revisionists in the light of new evidence gradually yielded a postrevisionist synthesis. The hallmark of postrevisionism is not to allocate blame to this party or the other but to try to understand the dynamics of the conflict that we call the cold war.

The debate about the origins of the Arab–Israeli conflict seems to be following a similar pattern. A traditionalist school, consisting of participants and propagandists as well as historians close to the political establishment, laid the entire blame for the 1948 war and its consequences at the door of the Arabs. Then, following the opening of the archives, a new school of mostly left-wing historians began to reinterpret many of the events surrounding the creation of the State of Israel. These historians take a much more critical view of Israel's conduct in the years 1947–49 and place on her a larger share of the blame for the creation of the Palestinian refugee problem and for the continuing political impasse in the Middle East. The debate between the old and the new historians is bitter and acrimonious, and it is conducted in a highly charged political atmosphere. It is melancholy to have to add that there is no sign yet of the emergence of a postrevisionist synthesis. Battles between historians, like real battles, evidently have to run their course.

NOTES

Avi Shlaim is the Alastair Buchan Reader in International Relations at the University of Oxford and a Fellow of St. Antony's College, Oxford, U.K.

1 Emile Habiby, *Al-Waqā' i' al-Gharība fi Ikhtifā' Sa'īd Abīal-Naḥs al-Mutashā' il* (The Secret Life of Sa'id, the Ill-Fated Pessoptimist) (Beirut: Dār Ibn Khaldūn, 1974), 37.
2 Ibid., 35.
3 Simha Flapan, *The Birth of Israel: Myths and Realities* (New York: Pantheon, 1987), 8.
4 Ibid., 10.
5 Benny Morris, *The Birth of the Palestinian Refugee Problem, 1947–1949* (Cambridge: Cambridge University Press, 1988).
6 Ilan Pappé, *Britain and the Arab–Israeli Conflict, 1948–51* (London: Macmillan, 1988).
7 Avi Shlaim, *Collusion across the Jordan: King Abdullah, the Zionist Movement and the Partition of Palestine* (Oxford: Clarendon Press, 1988).
8 Israel Baer, *Bitahon Israel: Etmol, Hayom, Mahar* (Israel's Security: Yesterday, Today, Tomorrow) (Tel Aviv: Amikam, 1966).
9 Gavriel Cohen, "Hamediniyut Habritit Erev Milhemet Ha'atzma'ut," in *Hayinu Keholmim* (We Were as Dreamers), ed. Yehuda Wallach (Givatayim: Massada, 1985).

10 Yaacov Shimoni, "Ha'aravim Likrat Milhemet Israel-'Arav, 1945–1948" (The Arabs and the Approaching War with Israel, 1945–1948), *Hamizrah Hehadash* 47, 3, (1962).

11 Meir Pail, "Hafqa'at Haribonut Hamedinit shel Filastin miyedei Hafalestinim" (The Expropriation of the Political Sovereignty over Palestine from the Palestinians), *Ziyonut* 3 (1973).

12 Rony E. Gabbay, *A Political Study of the Arab–Jewish Conflict: The Arab Refugee Problem* (Geneva: Librairie E. Droz, 1959).

13 A. Yisra'eli (Moshe Machover and Akiva Orr), *Shalom, Shalom – ve'ein Shalom: Yisra'el-Arav, 1948–61* (Peace, Peace – and There is No Peace: Israel and the Arabs, 1948–61) (Jerusalem, 1961).

14 Israel State Archives and Central Zionist Archives, *Political and Diplomatic Documents, December 1947–May 1948*, ed. Gedalia Yogev (Jerusalem: Israel Government Press, 1980); Israel State Archives, *Documents on the Foreign Policy of Israel, May–September 1948*, vol. 1, ed. Yehoshua Freundlich (Jerusalem: Israel Government Press, 1981); *Documents on the Foreign Policy of Israel: October 1948–April 1949*, vol. 2, ed. Yehoshua Freundlich (Jerusalem: Israel Government Press, 1984); and *Documents on the Foreign Policy of Israel: Armistice Negotiations with the Arab States, December 1948–July 1949*, vol. 3, ed. Yemima Rosenthal (Jerusalem: Israel Government Press, 1986).

15 Iraqi Government, *Taqrīr Lajnat al-Taḥqīq al-Niyābiyya fī Qaḍiyyat Filastīn* (Baghdad, 1949).

16 See the references in Walid Khalidi, "The Arab Perspective," in *The End of the Palestine Mandate*, ed. William Roger Louis and Robert W. Stookey (London: I. B. Tauris, 1986).

17 For a review of this literature, see Avraham Sela, "Arab Historiography of the 1948 War: The Quest for Legitimacy," in *New Perspectives on Israeli History: The Early Years of the State*, ed. Lawrence J. Silberstein (New York: New York University Press, 1991).

18 Benny Morris, "The New Historiography: Israel Confronts Its Past," *Tikkun* 3, 6 (November–December 1988). This much discussed article is reprinted in Benny Morris, *1948 and After: Israel and the Palestinians* (Oxford: Clarendon Press, 1990).

19 One historian of Zionism, Anita Shapira, was prompted by Menachem Begin's claim to embark upon a reexamination of the defensive ethos of Zionism throughout the pre-state period. Tom Segev, "The Anguish of Poor Samson," *Ha'aretz*, 16 October 1992. Anita Shapira, *Land and Power: The Zionist Resort to Force, 1881–1948* (New York: Oxford University Press, 1992), vii.

20 Shabtai Teveth, "Charging Israel with Original Sin," *Commentary*, September 1989, 33.

21 Ibid., 25.

22 Ibid.

23 Morris, *Ha'aretz*, 9 May 1989; idem, "The Eel and History: A Reply to Shabtai Teveth," *Tikkun* 5, 1 (January–February 1990); idem, *1948 and After*, 27–29.

24 See my letters to the Editor, *Commentary*, February and July 1990.

25 Pappé, *Britain and the Arab–Israeli Conflict*; Shlaim, *Collusion across the Jordan*; idem, "Britain and the Arab–Israeli War of 1948," *Journal of Palestine Studies* 16, 4 (Summer 1987). On the theory that the British wanted to reduce the Jewish part of Palestine to a "rump state," see William Roger Louis, *The British Empire in the Middle East, 1945–1951: Arab Nationalism, the United States, and Postwar Imperialism* (Oxford: Clarendon Press, 1984), 372–79.

191

26 Flapan, *The Birth of Israel*, Myth Six, especially the table with three different estimates of troop numbers on p. 196; Morris, *1948 and After*, 13–16. A study based on privileged access to IDF sources supports the revisionist line by showing that the United Nations arms embargo hurt the Arabs much more than it hurt IDF: Amitzur Ilan, *The Origins of the Arab–Israeli Arms Race* (forthcoming).

27 Morris, *The Birth of the Palestinian Refugee Problem*, 286

28 In addition to the articles in *Ha'aretz* and *Commentary*, Teveth published "The Palestine Arab Refugee Problem and Its Origins," *Middle Eastern Studies* 26, 2 (April 1990).

29 Morris, *Ha'aretz*, 23 April and 1 May 1992.

30 Sela, *Ha'aretz*, 4 and 11 October 1991.

31 See, for example, Michael Palumbo, "What Happened to Palestine? The Revisionists Revisited," *The Link* 23, 4 (September–October 1990); Rashid Khalidi, "Revisionist Views of the Modern History of Palestine: 1948," *Arab Studies Quarterly* 10, 4 (Autumn 1988); Ibrahim Abu-Lughod, "The War of 1948: Disputed Perspectives and Outcomes," *Journal of Palestine Studies* 18, 2 (Winter 1989); Nur Masalha, *Expulsion of the Palestinians: The Concept of "Transfer" in Zionist Political Thought, 1882–1948* (Washington, D.C.: Institute for Palestine Studies, 1992).

32 'Abdullah al-Tall, *Kārithat Filastīn: Mudhakkirāt 'Abdullāh at-Tall, Qā'id Ma'rakat al-Quds* (The Palestine Catastrophe: The Memoirs of Abdullah al-Tall, Leader of the Battle for Jerusalem) (Cairo: Dar al-Qalam, 1959).

33 Baer, *Bitahon Israel*.

34 Dan Schueftan, *Optzya Yardenit: Israel, Yarden Vehapalestinim* (Jordanian Option: Israel, Jordan and the Palestinians) (Yad Tabenkin: Hakkibutz Hame'uhad, 1986); Uri Bar-Joseph, *The Best of Enemies: Israel and Transjordan in the War of 1948* (London: Frank Cass, 1987).

35 Israel Defense Forces, *Toldot Milhemet Hakomemiyut* (History of the War of Independence) (Tel Aviv: Ma'aracbot, 1959).

36 See, for example, the author's interview with Yigael Yadin, acting chief of staff in 1948, in Shlaim, *Collusion across the Jordan*, 236.

37 Teveth, "Charging Israel with Original Sin," 28.

38 Avraham Sela, "Transjordan, Israel and the 1948 War: Myth, Historiography and Reality," *Middle Eastern Studies* 28, 4 (October 1992): 627.

39 Ibid., 680.

40 Avi Shlaim, *The Politics of Partition: King Abdullah, the Zionists and Palestine, 1921–1951* (Oxford: Oxford University Press, 1990).

41 Ibid., viii.

42 See, for example, Avi Shlaim, "The Rise and Fall of the All-Palestine Government in Gaza," *Journal of Palestine Studies* 20, 1 (Autumn 1990).

43 Flapan, *The Birth of Israel*, Myth Seven; Shlaim, *Collusion across the Jordan*; Morris, *1948 and After*, 22–27; and Ilan Pappé, *The Making of the Arab-Israeli Conflict, 1947–1951* (London: 1. B. Tauris, 1992), chaps. 8–10.

44 Avi Shlaim, "Husni Zaim and the Plan to Resettle Palestinian Refugees in Syria," *Journal of Palestine Studies* 15, 4 (Summer 1986).

45 David Ben-Gurion, *Yoman Hamilhama* (War Diary), ed. Gershon Rivlin and Elhanan Orren (Tel Aviv: Ministry of Defense, 1982), 3: 993.

46 Itamar Rabinovich, *The Road Not Taken: Early Arab–Israeli Negotiations* (New York: Oxford University Press, 1991), viii.

47 For a detailed critique of Rabinovich see Benny Morris, "A Second Look at the 'Missed Opportunity,' or Smoothing Out History: A Review Essay," *Journal of Palestine Studies* 24, 1 (Autumn 1994).

9

THE CAUSES AND CHARACTER OF THE ARAB EXODUS FROM PALESTINE

The Israeli defense forces intelligence service analysis of June 1948

Benny Morris

The most explosive revisionist Israeli work on the 1948 war is Benny Morris's analysis of the making of the Palestinian refugee problem. The conventional Israeli claim was that the Palestinians left after being ordered to do so by their own leaders, as well as by leaders of neighboring Arab states. In his book, Morris shows that there was no such call and that at least in part the Palestinian historiographical claim of expulsion and uprooting was justified. This revelation not only undermines the Israeli myth of Palestinian voluntary flight, it questions the Israeli moral dictum of "purity of arms". It transpires from Morris's account that in some cases the expulsion was accompanied by massacres and brutal conduct. This account has left an uneasy impression on the more conscientious Jewish readers and led to a fierce debate in the Israeli press on the morality of Zionism.

I chose here the third article from Morris's second book on the war, 1948 and After, which shows his empirical methodology in unearthing the causes for the Palestinian exodus in 1948. He wishes mainly to convey a complicated and multi-causal explanation for the flight, trying to put forward a version which on the one hand rejects the Israeli claim of voluntary flight and on the other, the Palestinian narrative of mass expulsion. As we shall see, this position is rejected by several Palestinian historians as well as by my own work. So, while the "new history" of Israel comes close to the Palestinian historical narrative, fundamental gaps still remain.

* * *

Since 1948, two contradictory explanations have dominated the historical debate about the causes of the Palestinian Arab exodus. The "traditional" Arab explanation was that the Yishuv had mounted a preplanned, systematic campaign of expulsion already unleashed in the first months of the first Israel–Arab war. The official Jewish explanation was that the exodus had been part of a "plot" in which the Arab leaders, inside and outside Palestine, had asked or ordered the Palestinian masses to flee their homes in Jewish-controlled territory in order to embarrass the emergent Jewish state, to justify the subsequent Arab invasion of 15 May, and to clear the ground physically, as it were, for the advance of the invading Arab armies.

The events in Palestine in 1948–9, which resulted in the Arab mass exodus, were far more complex and confused than either coherent explanation indicates. A great deal of fresh light is shed on the multiple and variegated causation of the Arab exodus in a document which has recently surfaced, entitled "The Emigration of the Arabs of Palestine in the Period 1/12/1947–1/6/1948 (*t'nu'at ha'hagira shel arvi'yei eretz yisrael ba't'kufa 1/12/1947–1/6/1948*)".[1] Dated 30 June 1948, it was produced by the Israel Defence Forces Intelligence Service during the first weeks of the First Truce (11 June–9 July) of the 1948 war. The document consists of two parts, typewritten in stencil foolscap pages: a nine-page text and a fifteen-page appendix. The text analyses the number of refugees, the stages of the exodus, its causes, the destinations of the refugee communities, and the problem of their initial absorption in the host areas. The appendix, proceeding district by district, traces – village by village – the dates, causes, and destinations of the emigration, and the numbers involved. The details in the appendix serve in large measure as the basis for the statistical breakdown in the text. The report does not state who ordered the Intelligence Service to produce the analysis and why. It is possible that the analysis was produced at the behest of Defence Minister and Prime Minister David Ben-Gurion or acting IDF chief of staff and OC Operations, General Yigael Yadin. These men, like other members of the newly formed IDF General Staff, no doubt wanted to understand the Palestinian exodus, which had at first surprised, indeed astonished, the Yishuv leaders.[2]

The weeks of the First Truce gave the Intelligence Service officers their first prolonged respite in more than six months from the demands of daily, battle-geared operations. The major waves of Palestinian emigration (before June 1948) had occurred in the preceding weeks, during the second half of April and in May, making an analysis of the phenomenon topical and relevant. Added urgency was perhaps provided by the political context. Internally, elements in the left-wing Mapam Party (The United Workers Party), a mainstay of the Israeli coalition government, began during May and June to berate Ben-Gurion and his dominant

Mapai Party (Land of Israel Labour Party) openly for waging a "war of expulsion" against the Palestinians. In the international arena, the Palestinian refugee problem moved in June to centre stage. Instrumental in pushing the refugee problem to the fore was the newly appointed UN Mediator for Palestine, Count Folke Bernadotte, who that month began his peace shuttles around the Middle East.

But, to judge from its conclusions, the Intelligence Service analysis of the exodus was hardly produced with an eye to easing the situation of the Israeli negotiators in their dealings with the Mediator, the UN in general, or the US. Rather than suggesting Israeli blamelessness in the creation of the refugee problem, the Intelligence Service assessment is written in blunt factual and analytical terms and, if anything, contains more than a hint of "advice" as to how to precipitate further Palestinian flight by indirect methods, without having recourse to direct politically and morally embarrassing expulsion orders. "The factor of surprise, prolonged [artillery] barrages making loud explosive sounds, [use of] loudspeakers in Arabic [to spread frightening 'black propaganda' messages], proved their great efficacy when used properly (as in Haifa particularly)", states the report. And, under the heading of "general comments", the report adds: "Incidentally, no attempt was made to attach fearful-sounding sirens to the wings of aircraft bombing enemy points – their effect could be great." The comment is included in a discussion of means which might precipitate civilian flight.

This detour into advice is the only departure in the documents from straightforward analysis, whose aims, as explained in the "general introduction", are "to measure the dimensions of the emigration and its various stages of development, to elucidate the various factors which directly bore upon [caused] the movement of population and to indicate the destinations of the exodus."

The Intelligence Service then gives an assessment of the number of refugees involved, allowing for a 10–15 per cent margin of error regarding the refugee population from areas inside the Jewish state as defined by the 1947 UN Partition Plan Resolution. A greater measure of inaccuracy, states the report, must be allowed for in its estimates of refugee numbers from areas lying outside the 1947 Jewish state boundaries. The facts and figures cited below, it must be emphasized, are for the period up to 1 June 1948 (except for the Jenin area, also included in the analysis, whose population fled in the last week of May and during the first week of June).

On the eve of the UN Partition Plan Resolution of 29 November 1947, according to the report, there were 219 Arab villages and four Arab, or partly Arab, towns in the areas earmarked for Jewish statehood – with a total Arab population of 342,000. By 1 June, 180 of these villages and towns had been evacuated, with 239,000 Arabs fleeing the areas of the

Jewish state. A further 152,000 Arabs, from 70 villages and three towns (Jaffa, Jenin, and Acre), had fled their homes in the areas earmarked for Palestinian Arab statehood in the Partition Resolution, and from the Jerusalem area. By 1 June, therefore, according to the report, the refugee total was 391,000, give or take about 10–15 per cent. Another 103,000 Arabs (60,000 of them Negev beduin and 5,000 Haifa residents) had remained in their homes in the areas originally earmarked for Jewish statehood. (This figure excludes the Arabs who stayed on in Jaffa and Acre, towns occupied by Jewish forces but lying outside the 1947 partition boundaries of the Jewish state.)

The Intelligence Service identified four stages in the Palestinian exodus up to 1 June. Stage one, December 1947–February 1948, affected only a small number of places and involved a relatively small number of refugees, mainly from the coastal plain. The reference in the report is to the flight of much of the Arab middle class from the towns of Haifa and Jaffa.

Stage two, covering March, involved only a small number of emigrants. Emigration in general that month was in decline, but the report registers an increase in the exodus from the Jaffa and the Sea of Galilee areas.

In stage three, during April 1948, there was a "moderate increase" on almost all fronts in the rate of emigration, according to the report. The Intelligence Service ascribes the increase to the Arab evacuation of Tiberias (18–19 April), Haifa (22 April–1 May) and the Tel-Hai (Galilee Panhandle) districts, which were a result of major Haganah offensives in those areas in the second half of April.

Stage four, in May 1948, is defined as "the main and decisive stage in the emigration movement of the Arabs of Palestine. A psychosis of emigration began to develop, a crisis of confidence in Arab strength." As a result, says the Intelligence Service, there was a great increase in the rate of emigration from the Tel-Hai, Gilboa, Jaffa, and Western Galilee districts, and evacuation began of the Arab villages in the Negev. May was the "record month"of the Arab exodus, according to the report. In the predominantly Jewish coastal plain, May marked "the final chapter", meaning that all the area's Arab inhabitants fled, except for only a few villages. It was "the end of the job (siyum hamelacha)".

Two comments are perhaps worth making about the report's analysis of the stages of the Arab exodus: (a) The Intelligence Service does not provide any statistical breakdown of the numbers involved in each stage, and (b) the description of the rate of emigration in April as "moderate" appears questionable, in the light of the large numbers of refugees caused by the Haganah conquest of Haifa, and the major Haganah offensives in the Galilee and along the approaches to Jerusalem.

Looking to the causes of the Palestinian exodus, the core of the report, the Intelligence Service first clears the ground by dismissing the relevance of a number of factors. The report states:

> One can assume that this emigration did not come as a result of economic factors – be it a serious lack of employment, food or any other economic hardship. The Arab economy [during the period up to June 1948], so long as the inhabitants stayed in their places, was not damaged in a manner which destroyed the population's capacity to subsist. The economic factor was a motive force [for emigration] only in the very earliest stages of the exodus, when the rich Arabs sought to safeguard their property and firms by getting out quickly.

According to the report, there were "fluctuations" in the state of the Palestine–Arab economy in the cities, "which was a factor accelerating emigration for some social strata". But, taking the broad view, the economic factor was not "a serious factor when speaking of the mass emigration of the Arabs of Palestine".

The report then goes on to dismiss as precipitants of the exodus what it defines as "pure political factors". Political decisions and developments, in the narrow sense of the word, had "no effect on the exodus", states the report. The Intelligence Service went on to reject specifically any linkage between the major political developments of May – the British withdrawal, the establishment of the state of Israel, the Arab declarations of intent to destroy the Jewish state and to go to war – and the mass emigration of that month. "It must be noted here that if there were places where the political factor was a motive force in the exodus, then it was limited to the cities and, there, to a very limited social class."

What the Intelligence Service is saying here is that Arabs did not leave the areas of the Jewish state because of opposition to the establishment of the state or political opposition to the prospect of life under Jewish rule. According to the detailed survey in the appendix, only one Arab village or community, Arab Jallad (?), in the coastal plain, fled on 15 May, because of "the influence of the declaration of establishment of the Jewish state".

The report then outlines what the IDF Intelligence Service regards, in June 1948, as the factors which precipitated the exodus, citing them "in order of importance":

1. Direct, hostile Jewish [Haganah/IDF] operations against Arab settlements.
2. The effect of our [Haganah/IDF] hostile operations on nearby [Arab] settlements ... (... especially – the fall of large neighbouring centres).

3. Operations of the [Jewish] dissidents [the Irgun Z'va'i Leumi and Lohamei Herut Israel].
4. Orders and decrees by Arab institutions and gangs [irregulars].
5. Jewish whispering operations [psychological warfare], aimed at frightening away Arab inhabitants.
6. Ultimative expulsion orders [by Jewish forces].
7. Fear of Jewish [retaliatory] response [following] major Arab attack on Jews.
8. The appearance of gangs [irregular Arab forces] and non-local fighters in the vicinity of a village.
9. Fear of Arab invasion and its consequences [mainly near the borders].
10. Isolated Arab villages in purely [predominantly] Jewish areas.
11. Various local factors and general fear of the future.

The Intelligence Service then gives a detailed breakdown and explanation of these factors, stressing that "without doubt, hostile [Haganah/IDF] operations were the main cause of the movement of population".

The wave of emigration in each district, explains the report, followed hard upon "the increase and expansion of our [Haganah/IDF] operations in that district". May brought a major increase in large-scale Jewish operations; so it also witnessed the widespread mass emigration of Arabs. "The departure of the British ... of course helped the [Arab] evacuation, but it appears that the British withdrawal freed our hands for action more than it influenced the [Arab] emigration directly."

The Intelligence Service notes that it was not always the dimensions of a Jewish attack which counted: it was "mainly the psychological" factors which affected the rate of emigration. The report cites "surprise", protracted mortar barrages, and use of loudspeakers broadcasting threatening messages as factors which had a strong influence in precipitating flight.

An attack on one village or town often affected its neighbours. "The evacuation of a certain village because of an attack by us prompted in its wake many neighbouring villages [to flee]", states the report. This was especially true of the fall of large villages or towns. "The fall of Tiberias, Safad, Samakh, Jaffa, Haifa and Acre engendered in their wake many waves of emigrants." The psychological motive force in operation here was *"im ba'arazim nafla shalhevet"* ("If the cedars caught fire ... ", a paraphrase of 1 Kings 5: 13).

The report concludes: "It is possible to say that at least 55 per cent of the total of the exodus was caused by our [Haganah/IDF] operations and by their influence". To this the Intelligence Service adds the effects of the operations of the dissident Jewish organizations, "who directly [caused] some 15 per cent ... of the emigration". The Intelligence Service notes that the activities of the dissidents were of especial importance in the Jaffa–Tel Aviv area, in the coastal plain to the north, and around Jerusalem. "Elsewhere, they had no direct effect on the [Arab] evacuation."

The Intelligence Service cites the "special effect" of the dissident operation in Deir Yassin and of the "abduction [at the end of March, 1948] of the five [Arab] notables at Sheikh Muwannis [north of Tel Aviv]".

The action at Deir Yassin, especially, greatly affected the thinking of the Arab; not a little of the immediate flight during our [Haganah/IDF] attacks, especially in the central and southern areas ... was due to this factor, which can be described as a decisive accelerating factor (*gorem mezarez mach'ri'a*).

Regarding the coastal plain, "many of the villagers ... began fleeing following the abduction of the notables of Sheikh Muwannis. The Arab learned that it was not enough to reach an agreement with the Haganah and that there were 'other Jews' of whom to beware, and possibly to beware of more than of the Haganah, which had no control over them [that is, over the dissidents]". The dissident organizations also played a decisive role in the evacuation of Jaffa and the villages around it, states the report. Altogether, the report states, Jewish – meaning Haganah / IDF, IZL, and LHI – military operations (comprising categories 1, 2, and 3) accounted for 70 per cent of the Arab exodus from Palestine.

Category 4: orders and commands by local Arab commanders and leaders, the Arab Higher Committee, and the Transjordan government – accounted for some "5 per cent of the villages" evacuated, according to the Intelligence Service. These orders to evacuate were given for "strategic reasons ... out of a desire to turn the village into a base for attack on the Jews or out of an awareness that there was no possibility of defending the village or out of a fear that the village could turn into an [anti-Arab] Fifth Column, especially if it reached an agreement with the Jews". The latter cause was especially important in the Gilboa area (threats by the Arabs to leave directed at the Zu'abiya beduin), in the Sea of Galilee area ("Circassian villages"), in the Tel-Hai district along the Syrian border, and "in the Jerusalem area (Arab Legion orders to evacuate a string of villages to set up bases in northern Jerusalem, and the order of the Arab Higher Committee to Issawiya [to evacuate])".

Category 5: Jewish "whispering" (psychological warfare) operations, usually involving "friendly advice" by Jewish liaison officers to Arabs to quit their villages – according to the IDF Intelligence Service (which ran the liaison officers), accounted for only some 2 per cent of the exodus nation-wide. But in a number of regions, states the report, "whispering" campaigns were of considerable importance. In the Tel-Hai district, for instance, such a campaign in April–May accounted for 18 per cent of the Arab exodus, and in the coastal plain villages, for 6 per cent. In the coastal plain and in the district, whispering operations were disorganized and unsystematic. But in the Tel-Hai district "the operation was carried out with predetermination, with relatively wide scope and organization" – and so led to greater results. The operation itself was carried out, explains the report, in the form of "friendly advice" by Jews to their neighbouring Arab friends.

Category 6: orders of expulsion by Jewish forces to Arab villages – accounted (up to the start of June 1948) for some 2 per cent of the total of villages evacuated, said the report. Such orders were especially "prominent" in the coastal plain, less common in the Gilboa district, and still less in the Negev. "Of course, the effect of [such an] ultimatum, like the effect of 'friendly advice', came after a certain laying of the groundwork through hostile [Jewish] operations in the area. Therefore, such [expulsion] orders are more [in the nature of] a final motivation and propellent, than a decisive factor."

Another 1 per cent of the emigration was caused, according to the report, by category 7 – Arab fear of Jewish retaliation after an Arab attack on Jews. This occurred in the Western Galilee (following the Arab attack on the Yehiam convoy), and after the attacks in April on Kibbutz Mishmar Ha'emek (western Jezreel Valley), and Kibbutz Gesher (Jordan Valley). According to the report, less than 2 per cent of the exodus was caused by categories 8, 9, and 10 combined. The arrival of Arab irregular forces in a village, villagers' fears that the impending Arab invasion would turn their homes into a battleground, and the fact of being an isolated village in a predominantly Jewish area all had little effect on the villagers.

The report names two further direct causes of flight: "general fear" and "local factors". General fear, which "had a great influence and role in the exodus", accounted for some 10 per cent of the refugees. In this context the report mentions the initial waves of emigration at the start of the hostilities, caused "at first glance, by no special reason". These were rooted in a "general fear" resulting primarily from "the crisis in confidence in Arab strength".

The Intelligence Service thus places this "crisis of confidence" in the Arab power to fight and withstand or defeat Jewish arms as "the third most important factor, after our own [i.e., Haganah/IDF] operations and those of the dissidents", in the Arab exodus. The report states that 8–9 per cent of the exodus was caused by "local factors", such as the breakdown in specific localities of Arab–Jewish peace negotiations and the Arabs' "inability to adjust to certain real situations".

Following this statistical breakdown, the report offers some "general comments" identifying some direct and indirect contributory factors which hastened, precipitated, or increased waves of emigration in various areas at different times. First and foremost, the report refers to a "psychosis of evacuation" which gripped some Arab communities during the hostilities, "increasing the rate of evacuation". It appeared, stated the report, "like a contagious disease". As an example, the Intelligence Service cites the case of Acre, which fell to Haganah forces on 17 May. There "it is possible to assume . . . that the massive arrival on the scene [a fortnight before] of the refugees from Haifa, who planted in the hearts of Acre's inhabitants a psychosis of evacuation . . . had a decisive influence". Thus, "light attacks" and "nudges" by the Jewish forces around Haifa had the effect of precipitating flight in a population already affected by "evacuation psychosis". The appearance of typhus also prompted flight. "More than the disease itself", states the report, "the panic created by the rumours of the spread of the epidemic was a factor prompting evacuation." The report points out that where there was a "strong Arab military force" the villagers did not evacuate "readily", and "only a direct and serious operation [by the Jewish forces] brought about the destruction of this [military] force, bringing flight [of the civilian population] in its wake".

At the start of the evacuation "the Arab institutions attempted to struggle against the phenomenon of flight and evacuation, and to curb the waves of emigration". The Arab Higher Committee decided to impose restrictions, and issued threats, punishments, and propaganda in the radio and press to curb emigration. The committee also tried to mobilize the governments in the neighbouring Arab states to assist in this; there was a coincidence of interests. "Especially, they tried to prevent the exodus of youngsters of military age", states the report. "But all these actions completely failed because no positive action was taken which could have curbed the factors pushing towards emigration." The sole upshot of these efforts was corruption and bribery, whereby officials began selling permits to would-be emigrants wishing to leave Palestine or to enter other countries. But this arrangement, states the report, broke down once emigration turned into a mass movement.

The penultimate section of the report deals with the destinations of the refugee communities. The authors note certain patterns. For instance, city-dwellers of rural origin often returned to their ancestral villages, as did Jaffa residents who had originated in Faluja, for example. Similarly, according to the Intelligence Service, city-dwellers who had come, or whose fathers had come, from neighbouring countries tended during the hostilities to return to those countries. Thus many Haifa residents fled directly to Lebanon and Syria. In general, the report points out, urban dwellers, including the rich, had fled directly to their final destinations whereas rural refugees tended to "hop" through a number of way-stations before reaching their final point of rest.

Often, villagers fled at first from isolated rural sites to neighbouring Arab towns or cities. Then, when the town fell to Jewish forces, they moved on. The report cites the case of the inhabitants of Beit Sussin, in the south, who first fled to Mughar, then Yibna, and then Isdud, before coming to rest in Gaza. By and large, the refugees from the villages in the first instance moved only to nearby sites. This, according to the report, caused the Haganah problems; the Jewish units, which did not have sufficient troops to garrison every captured village, faced the prospect that the villagers might attempt to return to their homes. "More than once," states the report, "[Haganah/IDF units were forced] to expel inhabitants [after they had returned to their homes]."

Without giving a numerical breakdown, the report states that the wealthier Arabs mainly emigrated directly to Arab states (meaning, primarily, to Beirut and Cairo); the poorer Arabs of the northern border areas fled to Syria and Lebanon: and the inhabitants of the south and Jaffa, and some Jerusalemites and Haifa residents, moved to Egyptian-held territory (meaning mainly the Gaza strip). Most of the emigrants to Transjordanian-held territory came from the Sea of Galilee area, the Jezreel valley, the Gilboa area, Acre, Jaffa, and the Jerusalem area.

The report ends with a look at the manner in which the refugees (by June 1948) had been absorbed in the host countries or areas. The wealthier Arabs, by and large, had no absorption problems. But most of the emigrants were poor, most had left without the bulk of their belongings, and this had led to "severe absorption problems", says the report. This had prompted the governments of the host countries to try to persuade the refugees to go back and to put pressure, especially on able-bodied males, "to return to the front". Transjordanian radio from Jerusalem, for example, in May broadcast lectures to the Palestinians to go back and lend a hand in the war effort, maintaining that "there was no danger to the lives of those returning".

Some Israelis feared that the embittered refugees might be turned into soldiers who would return to fight against Israel. The Intelligence Service analysis dismissed this danger: "The Arab emigrant did not turn into a fighter, his only interest now is in collecting money [philanthropy]. He has resigned himself to the lowest form of life, preferring it to mobilizing for battle." In conclusion, the report states that the refugees were a burden which would continue to grow and weigh upon the Arab states, especially as "no serious and comprehensive organized step was being taken by the Arab states in order to solve the problem".

How accurate is the information conveyed in this document? How sound is its analysis of the causes of the Palestinian exodus up to June 1948? What is its significance in relation to the traditional perceptions of the character and causes of that exodus?

In theory at least, the IDF Intelligence Service – Israel's main intelligence service in June 1948 – was very well placed to collect and analyse data about the Palestinian exodus. The officer or officers who produced this report had access to the reports of Israeli agents and Arab informants in the various Arab localities, to the signals and reports of the Haganah/IDF unit intelligence officers (one at least was attached to every battalion and brigade) and, probably, to signal traffic and reports of the various unit commanders and front commanders around the country.

It is also possible that the authors of the report were supplied, at their request, with special reports by units' intelligence officers and perhaps unit commanders as well detailing each unit's history of conquest and treatment of Arab settlements. The respite provided by the first weeks of the First Truce would have made possible the writing of such reports. An indirect indication that such reports were indeed produced and, at least in part, served as the basis of this analysis is afforded by the absence of one of the two appendices which, according to the table of contents printed on the covering page of the document, were to have accompanied the text – "appendix 1" giving "regional surveys analysing the problems of emigration in each and every district". Presumably, these surveys were to have been written by unit, front (*hazit*), or district (*nafa*) intelligence officers. Either some of them were not delivered or those delivered were regarded as inadequate for reproduction along with the text and the originally entitled "appendix 2", which details the exodus from each village, by district, around the country. (Appendix 2, in fact, was included, retitled "appendix 1".)

In the end, the authors apparently decided that the analysis, buttressed by the village-by-village appendix, was sufficient, and the regional analyses at first contemplated were left out (though sallies into regional analysis are to be found interspersed unsystematically throughout the text).

Real-time signal traffic and post-operational reporting by and large were accurate in the Haganah/IDF in 1948. But until mid-May – covering almost the whole period dealt with in the report – the Haganah was an underground force, and did not produce or store the kind of comprehensive documentation about its operations that a good regular army would have done. Much of the reporting up the chain of command and orders handed down the chain of command in the first months of 1948 were necessarily oral, and much of the signal traffic was never recorded or was subsequently lost. Hence, in producing this analysis of the exodus, the Intelligence Service perforce had to rely to some extent on the memories of commanders and local intelligence officers rather than on contemporaneous chronicling.

Moreover, the dissident organizations – the IZL and LHI, to whose operations the report attributes some 15 per cent of the exodus – produced even less written material than the Haganah and, if it existed in June, this was never made available to the Haganah and IDF. (The Haganah regarded the IZL and LHI as hostile organizations; June, indeed, marked the high point of the conflict between the groups, with the IDF killing a number of IZL combatants and sinking off Tel Aviv a ship bearing arms for the dissident force.)

Lastly, a number of operations by local Haganah units and by Jewish settlements against neighbouring Arab communities were carried out with Haganah National Staff command, authorization, or approval, and were never accurately reported upon to the National Staff *ex post facto*.

The reservations about sourcing aside, there is no reason to cast doubt on the integrity of the IDF Intelligence Service in the production of this analysis. The analysis was produced almost certainly only for internal, IDF top brass consumption. (No copy of it has surfaced in any collection of private papers of the 1948 Israeli Cabinet ministers; nor, save for the copy used in this paper, in any civilian archives. Nor was its existence or content ever referred to in any recorded political party debate.)[3] The authors of the report would have certainly been conscious of their "consumer public", and aware that many of the consumers were highly familiar with parts of the subject matter of the analysis. On the other hand, the authors will not always have been familiar enough with given incidents to catch all errors or distortions in the reports of local commanders and intelligence officers. So, while the details of the report and its analysis by and large conform with the facts as recorded in other sources from the period, a degree of analytical inaccuracy and factual imprecision and error is none the less evident. This point is worth elucidating before going on to weigh up the significance of the document.

The village-by-village survey in the appendix lists 14 villages evacuated as a result of Haganah or IDF orders or ultimatums.[4] In peacetime these villages together had a population of some 20,000. Yet in the analysis of the causes of the exodus, the report speaks of only 2 per cent "of the villages" (out of a total of 250 evacuated) as leaving because of Haganah/IDF expulsion orders. Fourteen out of 250 represents more like 5 per cent.

Moreover, the report leaves a large, poorly demarcated grey area between outright expulsion by Jewish order and evacuation of Arab villages in the course of Haganah/IDF "military operations" (which are said to account for 55 per cent of the exodus).

Some of the villages said to have been evacuated because of "military operations" (and presumably included in that 55 per cent), are seen in the detailed breakdown in the appendix to have been depopulated in a somewhat less straightforward manner. For example, the 710-strong population of Khirbet Lid (al-Awadim), near Afula, in the Jezreel Valley, is said in the appendix to have left because of "the influence of [the nearby battle of] Mishmar Ha'emek" in April 1948. But in the subsequent "comment", the appendix states: "They tried to return. And were expelled." Khirbet Lid was presumably not included under the expulsion category.

Nor was Fajja, a large village next to Petah Tikva. Part of the population left after the IZL attack on 17 March. The final evacuation on 15 May took place, according to the appendix, because of "pressure by us [and] a whispering [that is, psychological warfare] campaign". Presumably Fajja was listed among the 2 per cent of evacuations caused by psychological warfare; but, given the reference to "pressure" by the Haganah, it could also have been included perhaps in the expulsion category (which it presumably was not).

Nor was Al Khalisa, the site of present-day Kiryat Shmona, in the Galilee Panhandle. The village, with a population of 1,840, is said to have been evacuated on 11 May because of "the fall of Safad", a major Arab centre to the south. But according to the appendix, that was not all. "They wanted [to reach] an agreement with us. They were turned down. [So] they fled", states the report. Presumably, Khalisa was included under the "local factors" category rather than under the expulsion category. As in Al Khalisa, so in As Salihiya, a village of 1,520 a few kilometres to the south. "They wanted to negotiate – we did not show up", states the report. The villagers fled Palestine on 25 May.

In general, the situation on the ground made it impossible in many cases to draw a clear distinction between a Haganah/IDF or IZL "military operation" which ended in villagers fleeing their homes and "expulsion orders", which had the same effect. In some "military operations", such as the Haganah conquest of the Arab parts of Haifa, the Jewish troops by and large had no clear intention of provoking an Arab exodus and their military strategy was not calculated to produce such an outcome. In other military operations, such as the IZL attack on Jaffa, and probably the Haganah offensive in Western Galilee in May 1948, the flight of the Arab inhabitants was clearly desired and deliberately provoked by the attacking troops. The IZL/LHI attack on Deir Yassin near Jerusalem on 9 April ended not only in a massacre but also in the expulsion by the conquering unit of the surviving Arab villagers. (The Intelligence Service report catagorizes the flight of the Deir Yassin inhabitants as a result of a dissident operation rather than under the heading of expulsion.)

While the report was not produced with any propagandizing intention in mind, its authors seem to have exhibited a perhaps understandable tendency to minimize the role direct expulsion orders played in bringing about part of the Palestinian exodus. The proportion of villages expelled is computed incorrectly and a large grey area of "semi-expulsions" is included under the category of flight due to "military operations" or some other "non-expulsion" category.

Moreover, the report also includes a number of factual errors and omissions in this context; presumably these were the result of misinformation in the reports by local unit commanders and field intelligence officers. For instance, part of the population of the Arab town of Beisan (Beit Shean) is said to have fled on 1 May because of "fear and the influence of [the fall of Arab] Haifa". The remainder of the population, according to the appendix, is said to have left on 12 May as a result of the Haganah "conquest [of the town]. Fear. The influence of Haifa." But this is not completely accurate. Hundreds of the town's residents stayed on after the conquest, and were expelled only days later – some to Nazareth, others across the Jordan River – at Haganah command.[5]

The small village of 140 tenant farmers of Qira wa Qamun near Yoqne'am, on the western edge of the Jezreel Valley, was evacuated in March by its inhabitants after they received "friendly advice" from the local Haganah intelligence officer at Yoqne'am, Yehuda Burstein.[6] But the report gives the reason for the Qira evacuation as "fear and the influence of the attacks in the area" – not really the same thing.

More inexplicable is the omission altogether from the appendix of the fate of a string of Western Galilee villages – Az Zib, Manshiya, As Sumeiriya, Al Bassa and others – all evacuated during or before the Haganah's Operation Ben-Ami in mid-May. It is quite possible that the Haganah commander in Western Galilee or the relevant intelligence officers simply failed to submit to the Intelligence Service a report on the Arab exodus from their area.

The report's treatment of villages evacuated as a result of edicts or orders by Arab authorities, political or military, is also worth examining. Altogether, 21 villages out of the 250 are listed in the appendix as having been evacuated or partially evacuated as a result of Arab command, be it by the Arab Legion, the Arab Higher Committee, or other Arab bodies.[7] The figure is higher than the "5 per cent" cited in the report's analysis as having fled because of Arab commands. Here too the report omitted or ignored material instancing Arab advice or orders to communities to partially or completely evacuate their settlements. For example, the "defence and security section" of the (Arab) National Committee in Jerusalem, basing itself on instructions from the Arab Higher Committee issued on 8 March, in mid-April ordered the national committees in the Sheikh Jarrah, Wadi Joz, Sa'ad wa Sa'id, Musrara, and Katamon quarters of Jerusalem to order the women, children, and the old in their areas to leave their homes and move to areas "far away from the dangers. Any opposition to this order . . . is an obstacle to the holy war . . . and will hamper the operations of the fighters in these districts."[8]

In early May, units of the Arab Legion entered the town of Beisan and reportedly ordered the evacuation of all women and children.[9] At about the same time, the Arab Liberation Army was reported to have ordered the villagers in Fureidis, south of Haifa, to "evacuate the women and children from the village and to make ready to evacuate the village completely."[10] In general, the IDF Intelligence Service report fails to stress the importance in the Arab exodus of the early departure in many cases from the villages of the women and children. This tended to sap the morale of the menfolk who were left behind to guard the homes and fields, contributing to the final evacuation of villages. Such two-tier evacuations – women and children first, the men following weeks later – occurred in Qumiya in the Jezreel Valley, among the Ghawarina beduin in Haifa Bay, and in various other places.

What then is the significance of the IDF Intelligence Service report in understanding the Palestinian exodus of 1948? To begin with, it thoroughly undermines the traditional official Israeli "explanation" of a mass flight ordered or "invited" by the Arab leadership for political–strategic reasons. Quite clearly, according to the report, Arab orders to evacuate villages were restricted to a number of areas, were guided by local strategic considerations, and affected no more than 10 per cent of the Palestinian refugee population. (About half of the villages evacuated because of Arab command, those in the Jerusalem and lower Galilee areas, were in fact subsequently repopulated by their original inhabitants once circumstances had changed.)

The report makes no mention of any blanket order issued over Arab radio stations or through other means, to the Palestinians to evacuate their homes and villages. Had such an order been issued, it would without doubt have been mentioned or cited in this document; the Haganah Intelligence Service and its successor, the IDF Intelligence Service closely monitored Arab radio transmissions and the Arabic press.

Indeed, the Intelligence Service report in its main thrust seems to go still further in undermining the official Israeli historiography. For not only is the "Arab orders" explanation seen to be limited in the numbers it affected and extremely restricted geographically; but the report goes out of its way to stress that the exodus was contrary to the political–strategic desires of both the Arab Higher Committee and the governments of the neighbouring Arab states. These, according to the report, struggled against the exodus – threatening, cajoling, imposing punishments, all to no avail. There was no stemming the panic-borne tide. (To this, a caveat must be attached. The report does not record or analyse the *dates* of the official Arab efforts to stem the exodus. The dates may be significant. Whereas there is evidence of a large number of Arab attempts to stop the exodus during December 1947 and during the first months of 1948 and in early May 1948, there is far less material of this sort relating to April and mid- and late May 1948, when the flight reached its peak.) But neither does the Intelligence Service report uphold the traditional Arab explanation of the exodus – that the Jews with pre-meditation, in centralized fashion, and systematically had waged a campaign aimed at the wholesale expulsion of the native Palestinian population.

The exodus was certainly viewed favourably by the bulk of the Yishuv's leadership; it had solved the embryonic Jewish state's chief and agonizing political–strategic problem, the existence in it of a very large actively or potentially hostile Arab minority. A tone of satisfaction with the exodus does indeed pervade the report; but from it emerges a very definite impression that the depopulation of the villages and towns was an unexpected outcome of operations the purpose of which was wholly or primarily the conquest of military positions and strategic sites in the course of a life-and-death struggle. Jewish military operations indeed accounted for 70 per cent of the Arab exodus; but the depopu-lation of the villages in most cases was an incidental, if favourably regarded, side-effect of these operations, not their aim. Had the popu-lation of the villages and towns remained *in situ* during and after the Jewish attack and conquest, the Haganah/IDF and IZL would have been faced at each site with the successive dilemma: to expel or not to expel. As it was, the population, by taking to its heels at the first whiff of grapeshot, usually solved this possible problem. The report's estimate of the proportion of villages depopulated by calculated, direct Jewish expulsion orders is none the less somewhat low. For the period up to 1 June 1948, something around 5 per cent seems closer to the mark than the 2 per cent cited. Even after adding to this the villagers "nudged" into flight by deliberate military pressures and psychological assault, one is still left with only a small proportion of the exodus accounted for in this manner.

One must again emphasize that the report and its significance pertain only up to 1 June 1948, by which time some 300,000–400,000 Palestinians had left their homes. A similar number was to leave the Jewish-held areas in the remaining months of the war. The circumstances of the second half of the exodus – during the IDF conquest of Lydda and Ramle, and the central Galilee in July, the northern Negev in October–November, and the northern Galilee in October – are a different story. But for an understanding of the Palestinian exodus until 1 June, one must, according to IDF Intelligence, reach mainly for the vast middle ground between pre-planned, outright IDF expulsion and Arab-engineered, Machiavellian flight. There, amid the frightening, threatening boom of guns, the loss of confidence in Arab might, the flight of relatives and friends, the abandonment of nearby towns, and a general, vast fear of the uncharted future, one will find the bulk of the pre-June Palestinian refugees.

NOTES

I would like to thank the warm and efficient archivists at the Hashomer Hatza'ir Archive for helping me find material and for giving me access to the Aharon Cohen Papers before they had been finally organized and made generally available.

1 The document is to be found in the newly organized and released private papers of Aharon Cohen, the long-standing director of the Mapam (United Workers Party) Arab Department and a leading Middle East affairs expert, in the Hashomer Hatza'ir Archive (Givat Haviva, Israel), 10.95.13 (1). A notation in Cohen's hand on the cover page of the document says: "Sent – 8/7/48 – Received 11/7/48". Apparently it was sent to him by a contact in the IDF Intelligence Service or in the General Staff.

   All quotations in this article are from the Intelligence Service report unless otherwise stated.

   Using the term "IDF Intelligence Service" in this context is something of a misnomer. The Haganah's Intelligence Service (the Shai), founded in the mid-1930s, continued to function as the Yishuv's main intelligence service down to the summer of 1948. At the end of May 1948 the Haganah itself became the Israel Defence Forces, the army of the new State of Israel. But the underground army's Intelligence Service, for bureaucratic reasons, in fact continued to exist through June, and was only reorganized and renamed the IDF Intelligence Service at the beginning of July. But the fact that officially the Haganah ceased to exist by the start of June makes it incongruous to speak of a report produced by the Haganah Intelligence Service at the end of June. (The IDF Intelligence Service, incidentally, in 1949, after a shake-up involving the dismissal of its head, Lieutenant-Colonel Isser Be'eri, and its merger with the already-existing IDF Operations/Intelligence Department, was renamed the IDF Intelligence Department which, in turn, became IDF Intelligence Branch – its current name – in 1953.)

2 For the Yishuv's astonishment at the exodus, see, for example, the memorandum by Israeli Foreign Minister-designate Moshe Shertok (Sharett) on his meeting in Washington with US Secretary of State George Marshall, Dean Rusk, and other State Department officials on 8 May 1948, in Gedalia Yogev (ed.), *Documents on the Foreign Policy of the State of Israel, May–September 1948*, I (ISA, Government Press, 1981), 758, 760. At the meeting, Shertok referred to "the astounding phenomenon" of the Palestinian exodus, and said "something quite unprecedented and unforeseen was going on".

3 The report was received by Cohen, a member of the Mapam Centre and of the party's Political Committee, on 11 July 1948. These party institutions, through the summer, very frankly and thoroughly debated the Yishuv's policy towards the Palestinian Arabs, covering such subjects as expulsions, the possibility of a refugee return, etc. Yet neither Cohen nor anyone else ever referred in these recorded debates to the IDF Intelligence Service analysis. One possible explanation is that the report, being contemporary and on a sensitive subject, was regarded by Cohen as something too "hot" to use or refer to openly. Mapam, Cohen, and his contact might have been in deep trouble. Ironically, only a few years later Cohen landed in prison after being convicted of unauthorized contacts with Soviet agents.

4 The villages named are Ad Dumeira (population 620 – evacuated 10 Apr. 1948); Miska (population 650 – evacuated 15 Apr. 1948); Khirbet as Sarkas

(evacuated 15 Apr. 1948); Arab an Nufei'at (population 910 – evacuated 10 Apr. 1948); Khirbet Azzun (population 994 – evacuated 3 Apr. 1948); and Arab al Foqara (population 340 – evacuated 10 Apr. 1948), all in the coastal plain; Dana (population 400 – evacuated 28 May 1948), in the Gilboa district; and Zarnuga (population 2,600 – evacuated 27 May 1948); Yibna (population 5,920 – evacuated 4 June 1948); Huj (population 800 – evacuated 28 May 1948); Arab Rubin (population 1,550 – evacuated 1 June 1948); Kaukaba (population 1,870 – evacuated 17 May 1948); Sumsum (population 1,200 – evacuated 12 May 1948); and Najd (population 600 – evacuated 12 May 1948), all in the south. It is worth noting that the expulsions detailed in the appendix are almost all part of two "series" – one in the northern coastal plain on 10–15 April 1948 and the other in the northern Negev approaches on 27–8 May 1948.

5 See Binyamin Etzioni (ed.), *Ilan Va'shelah*, an account of the Golani Brigade's operations in 1948 produced by the unit's soldiers (IDF Publications (Ma'arachot), Tel Aviv, 1950?), 146. See also Central Zionist Archives S53 – 437 (the Eliezer Granovsky Papers), Yosef Weitz to Eliezer Granovsky, 25 May 1948; and Yosef Weitz, *Diaries* (Massada, Tel Aviv, 1965) iii. 301–2, entry for 13 June 1948.

6 Interview with Eliezer Be'eri (Bauer), Kibbutz Hazore'a, April 1984.

7 The report lists the following villages as evacuated, or partly evacuated, at higher Arab command; Shu'fat, Beit Hanina, Al Jib, Judeira, Beit Nabala, and Rafat (total population 4,000–5,000 – all on Arab Legion orders) all on 13 May 1948; Issawiya (population 780 – evacuated at Arab Higher Committee command on 30 Mar. 1948); Ar Ruweis, on 24 Apr. 1948; Ad Dahi, Nein, Tamra, Kafr Misr, At Tira, Taiyiba, and Na'ura, all in the Gilboa district and evacuated on 20 May 1948, after threats from Arab irregulars; and, in the Sea of Galilee area, Adasiya (evacuated on 15 May 1948 at Transjordanian command); and Sirin, Ulam, Hadatha, and Ma'adhar (all in the Galilee, evacuated at the command of the Arab Higher Committee on 6 Apr. 1948). Within months, the populations of Shu'fat, Beit Hanina, Al Jib, Judeira, Issawiya, and Tamra had returned to their homes.

8 ISA, FM 2570/11, announcement by the National Committee of Jerusalem, 22 Apr. 1948.

9 CZA, A246–13 (the manuscript of the Weitz Diaries), entry for 4 May 1948.

10 Private information.

10

A CRITIQUE ON
BENNY MORRIS

Nur Masalha

The rewriting of the 1948 events by revisionist Israeli historians has been received with mixed feelings among Palestinian historians. On the one hand, it was a relief to find out that after years of being branded as mere propaganda, major Palestinian claims were proved to be acceptable on the basis of professional historical research. On the other hand, there was something disturbing and annoying in these claims becoming valid only after Israeli Jews made them, as if Palestinian historians were suspect of non-professionalism.

More important than all this is the fact that there is still a wide gap between historians of both sides. This is demonstrated here by the work of Nur Masalha, a Palestinian historian living and working in Britain. Masalha takes issue with Benny Morris's claim that expulsion in 1948 was not the consequence of either Zionist ideology or the implementation of a master plan. Representing here also the position of the distinguished Palestinian historian, Walid Khalidi, Masalha claims that Zionist transfer plans from as early as 1882 were translated into an expulsion plan in 1948. This is an important debate, not only about the causes of the exodus, but about the essence of Zionism. If this Palestinian historical perspective is valid then 1948 can repeat itself and Israeli historians will have to adopt an even more severe and critical approach to their society and its moral conduct in the past and in the present.

* * *

Since the publication in 1988 of *The Birth of the Palestinian Refugee Problem*, Benny Morris has come to be seen as the ultimate authority on the Palestinian exodus of 1948. And indeed, his work has contributed to demolishing some of the long-held (at least in Israel and in the West) misconceptions surrounding Israel's birth. His newly published collection of essays, *1948 and After: Israel and the Palestinians*, revisits the ground covered in *Birth*, bringing to light new material he discovered or which became available only after completion of the first book.

Morris's work belongs to what he calls the "New Historiography." He does not like the term "revisionist" historiography, in part because it "conjures up" images of the Revisionist Movement in Zionism, and thus causes "confusion." He further eschews the term because "Israel's old historians, by and large, were not really historians, and did not produce real history. In reality they were chroniclers, and often apologetic" (*1948*, p. 6). Morris examines this "old" – orthodox and official – historiography in the opening essay of his new volume, referring to the historians who produced it over three decades since 1948 as "less candid," "deceitful," and "misleading" (p. 2). As examples, he cites the accounts provided by Lieutenant-Colonel (ret.) Elhanan Orren, a former officer at the Israel Defense Force (IDF) History Branch, in his *Baderckh el Ha'ir* (On the Road to the City), a detailed account of Operation Dani, published by the IDF Press in 1976, and *Toldot Milhemet Hakomemiyut* (History of the War of Independence), produced by the General Staff/History Branch, as well as Ben-Gurion's own "histories" *Mideinat Yisrael Hamehudeshet* and *Behilahem Yisrael* (pp. 2–5). The "new" histories, on the other hand, include the works of Avi Shlaim, Ilan Pappé, Simha Flapan, Uri Milstein, Michael Cohen, Anita Shapira, Uri Bar-Joseph, and others (p. 8). Clearly those histories thoroughly demolished a variety of assumptions which formed the core of the "old" history. And although those who argue the case of "revisionism" are a fringe group in Israel, they are an important one.

Two remarks are in order in this regard; first, having myself examined many of the "old" and official Hebrew chronicles, it is quite clear that Morris does not always live up to his claim of using this material in a critical manner and as a result this casts doubts on his conclusions. For instance, in *Birth*, Morris quotes uncritically the "major political conclusion" Ben-Gurion drew from the Arab departure from Haifa and makes little effort to reconcile the "deceitfulness" of such a chronicle with uncritical reliance on it. And, generally speaking, having based himself predominantly, and frequently uncritically, on official Israeli archival and non-archival material, Morris's description and analysis of such a controversial subject as the Palestinian exodus have serious shortcomings. Second, Morris's description of the works by the "new" Israeli historians – while ignoring the recent works by non-Zionist scholars on 1948 – gives rise to the impression that these discourses are basically the outcome of a debate among Zionists which unfortunately has little to do with the Palestinians themselves.

Morris's central thesis, as first expounded in *Birth*, is summed up in following passage from his new collection:

> What occurred in 1948 lies somewhere in between the Jewish "robber state" [i.e., a state which had "systematically and forcibly expelled the Arab population"] and the "Arab order" explanations. While from the mid-1930s most of the Yishuv's leaders, including Ben-Gurion, wanted to establish a Jewish state without an Arab minority, or with as small an Arab minority as possible, and supported a "transfer solution" to this minority problem, the Yishuv did not enter the 1948 War with a master plan for expelling the Arabs, nor did its political or military leaders ever adopt such a master plan. What happened was largely haphazard and a result of the War. There were Haganah/IDF expulsions of Arab communities, some of them at the initiative or with the *post facto* approval of the cabinet or the defense minister, and most with General Staff sanctions. . . . But there was no grand design, no blanket policy of expulsion. (p. 17)

In other words, only in "smaller part" were Haganah/IDF expulsions carried out and these were impromptu, *ad hoc* measures dictated by the military circumstances, a conclusion that deflects serious responsibility for the 1948 exodus from the Zionist leadership. But can his claim that there was no transfer design and expulsion policy in 1948 be sustained? Does the fact that there was no "master plan" for expelling the Palestinians absolve the Zionist leadership of responsibility, given, *inter alia*, its campaign of psychological warfare (documented by Morris) designed to precipitate Arab evacuation? How can Morris be so categorical that there was no Israeli expulsion policy when his own work rests on carefully released partial documentation and when much of the Israeli files and documents relating to the subject are still classified and remain closed to researchers? Is it inconceivable that such a "transfer" policy was based on an understanding between Ben-Gurion and his lieutenants rather than on a blueprint? Morris himself writes in an article in *Ha'Aretz* (entitled "The New History and the Old Propagandists," 9 May 1989) in which he discusses the transfer notion and Ben-Gurion's role in 1948: "One of the hallmarks of Ben Gurion's greatness was that the man knew what to say and what not to say in certain circumstances; what is allowed to be recorded on paper and what is preferable to convey orally or in hint." Ben-Gurion's admiring biographer Michael Bar-Zohar states: "In internal discussions, in instructions to his men [in 1948] the

Old Man [Ben-Gurion] demonstrated a clear position: It would be better that as few a number as possible of Arabs should remain in the territory of the [Jewish] state." (Bar-Zohar, *Ben-Gurion* [in Hebrew], vol. 2, p. 703).

Morris claims (*1948*, p. 16) that it "was the Arab contention . . . that the Yishuv had always intended forcible 'transfer'." Is this merely an "Arab contention," or perhaps, a figment of Arab imagination? Yet the evidence Morris adduces points to a completely different picture. In his 9 May 1989 article in *Ha'Aretz*, Morris traces "the growth of the transfer idea in Ben-Gurion's thinking" from the second half of the 1930s. "There is no doubt," Morris writes,

> that from the moment [the Peel proposal was submitted] . . . the problem of the Arab minority, supposed to reside in that [prospective Jewish] state, began to preoccupy the Yishuv's leadership obsessively. They were justified in seeing the future minority as a great danger to the prospective Jewish state – a fifth political, or even military, column. The transfer idea . . . was viewed by the majority of the Yishuv leaders in those days as the best solution to the problem.

In *Birth* (p. 25) Morris shows that Ben-Gurion advocated "compulsory" transfer in 1937. In his *Ha'Aretz* article he writes of "the growth of the transfer idea in Ben-Gurion's thinking" and that in November 1947, a few days before the UN General Assembly's partition resolution, a consensus emerged at the meeting of the Jewish Agency Executive in favor of giving as many Arabs in the Jewish state as possible citizenship of the prospective Arab state rather than of the Jewish state where they would be living. According to Morris, Ben-Gurion explained the rationale in the following terms:

> If a war breaks out between the Jewish state and the Palestine Arab state, the Arab minority in the Jewish state would be a "Fifth Column"; hence, it was preferable that they be citizens of the Palestine Arab state so that, if the War breaks out and, if hostile, they "would be expelled" to the Arab state. And if they were citizens of the Jewish state "it would (only) be possible to imprison them."

Does not this show that the Yishuv's leaders entered the 1948 war at least with a transfer desire or mindset?

Morris argues that a new approach emerged in 1948 among the ruling Mapai Party leaders, presided over by Ben-Gurion, in support of a transfer "solution" to the "Arab demographic problem."

> Ben-Gurion ... understood that war changed everything; a different set of "rules" had come to apply. Land could and would be conquered and retained; there would be demographic changes. This approach emerged explicitly in Ben Gurion's address at the meeting of the Mapai Council on 7 February: Western Jerusalem's Arab districts had been evacuated and a similar permanent demographic change would be expected in much of the country as the war spread. (*1948*, pp. 39–40)

Other prominent Mapai leaders such as Eliahu Lulu (Hacarmeli), a Jerusalem branch leader, and Shlomo Lavi, an influential Kibbutz movement leader, echoed the same approach. In an internal debate at the Mapai Centre on 24 July 1948, held against the background of the expulsion of Lydda and Ramle, Shlomo Lavi stated that "the ... transfer of Arabs out of the country in my eyes is one of the most just, moral and correct things that can be done. I have thought this ... for many years" (*1948*, p. 43). Lavi's views were backed by another prominent Mapai leader, Avraharn Katznelson: There is nothing "more moral, from the viewpoint of universal human ethics, than the emptying of the Jewish State of the Arabs and their transfer elsewhere. ... This requires the use of force" (*1948*, p. 44). Contrary to what Morris claims, there was nothing new about this approach of "forcible transfer," nor did it emerge out of the blue merely as a result of the outbreak of hostilities in 1948.

The Yishuv's leaders "obsessively" pursued transfer schemes from the mid-1930s onwards. Transfer Committees were set up by the Jewish Agency between 1937 and 1942 and a number of Zionist transfer schemes were formulated in secret. (A thorough discussion of these schemes will be found in my forthcoming book on the transfer concept.) Shortly after the publication of the Peel Commission report, which endorsed the transfer idea, Ben-Gurion wrote in his diary (12 July 1937): "The compulsory transfer of the Arabs from the valleys of the proposed Jewish state could give us something which we never had ... a Galilee free of Arab population" (Ben-Gurion, *Zichronot* vol. 4, 12 July 1937, pp. 297–99). Already in 1937, he believed that the Zionists could rid themselves of "old habits" and put pressure on the Mandatory authorities to carry out forced removal. "We have to stick to this conclusion," Ben-Gurion wrote,

> in the same way we grabbed the Balfour Declaration, more than that, in the same way we grabbed Zionism itself. We have to insist upon this conclusion [and push it] with our full determination, power and conviction. ... We must uproot from our hearts the assumption that the thing is not possible. It can be done.

Ben-Gurion went on to note: "We must prepare ourselves to carry out" the transfer (ibid., p. 299). Ben-Gurion was also convinced that few, if any, of the Palestinians would be willing to transfer themselves "voluntarily," in which case the "compulsory" provisions would eventually have to be put into effect. In an important letter to his 16-year-old son Amos, dated 5 October 1937, Ben-Gurion wrote: "We must expel Arabs and take their places ... and if we have to use force – not to dispossess the Arabs of the Negev and Transjordan, but to guarantee our own right to settle those places – when we have force at our disposal" (Shabtai Teveth, *Ben-Gurion and the Palestinian Arabs*, Oxford, 1985, p. 189). It is explicit in the letter of 5 October that the transfer had become clearly associated with expulsion in Ben-Gurion's thinking. In reflecting on such expulsion and the eventual enlargement and breaking through of the Peel partition borders, Ben-Gurion used the language of force, increasingly counting on Zionist armed strength. He also predicted a decisive war in which the Palestinian Arabs aided by neighboring Arab states would be defeated by the Haganah (ibid.). From the mid-1930s onwards he repeatedly stated his advocacy of transfer.

The debates of the World Convention of Ihud Po'alei Tzion – the highest political forum of the dominant Zionist world labor movement – and the Zurich 20th Congress in August 1937 revealed a Zionist consensus in support of transfer. Eliahu Lulu, for instance, had this to say at the debate of the Ihud Po'alei Tzion convention:

> This transfer, even if it were to be carried out through compulsion – all moral enterprises are carried out through compulsion – will be justified in all senses. And if we negate all right to transfer, we would need to negate everything we have done until now: the transfer from Emek Hefer [Wadi al-Hawarith] to Beit Shean, from the Sharon [coastal plain] to Ephraem Mountains, etc. ... the transfer ... is a just, logical, moral, and humane programme in all senses.[1]

During the same debate, Shlomo Lavi expressed a similar view: "The demand that the Arabs should move and evacuate the place for us, because they have sufficient place to move to ... in itself is very just and very moral ...."[2] There were, of course, Zionist leaders who supported "voluntary" transfer, but to suggest as Morris does that the notion of "forcible transfer" is merely an "Arab contention" or that it was only in 1948 that Mapai leaders such as Ben-Gurion adopted the radical new approach of using force to transform Palestine's demographic reality is a misrepresentation of the facts, of which Morris must be aware.

Is Morris's conclusion that a Zionist transfer/expulsion policy was never formulated borne out by the evidence he adduces in *Birth* and in *1948*? In *Birth*, Morris describes how the Yishuv military establishment, presided over by Ben-Gurion, formulated in early March 1948 and began implementing in early April Plan Dalet in anticipation of Arab military operations. According to Morris, the essence of Plan Dalet "was the clearing of hostile and potentially hostile forces out of the interior of the prospective territory of the Jewish State. ... As the Arab irregulars were based and quartered in the villages and as the militias of many villages were participating in the anti-Yishuv hostilities, the Haganah regarded most of the villages as actively or potentially hostile" (*Birth*, p. 62). Morris goes on to explain that Plan Dalet "constituted a strategic–ideological anchor and basis for expulsions by front, district, brigade and battalion commanders ... and it gave commanders, *post facto*, a formal, persuasive covering note to explain their actions" (*Birth*, p. 63). In *1948* (p. 21), Morris states:

> In conformity with Tochnit Dalet (Plan D), the Haganah's master plan. ... The Haganah cleared various areas completely of Arab villages – the Jerusalem corridor, the area around Mishmar Haemek, and the coastal plain. But in most cases, expulsion orders were unnecessary; the inhabitants had already fled, out of fear or as a result of Jewish attack. In several areas, Israeli commanders successfully used psychological warfare ploys to obtain Arab evacuation (as in the Hula Valley, in Upper Galilee, in May).

He further notes: "if the denial of the right to return ... was a form of 'expulsion', then a great many villagers – who had waited near their villages for the battle to die down before trying to return home – can be considered 'expellees'" (*Birth*, p. 343, note 7). Even if we do accept that Plan Dalet was not a political blueprint or a "master plan" for a blanket expulsion of the Arab population, and even if the plan "was governed by military considerations," how can Morris square his own explanations with his conclusion that there existed no Haganah/IDF "plan" or policy decision to expel Arabs from the prospective Jewish state?

Furthermore, in the context of "decision-making" and "transfer" policy, Morris shows in his essay "Yosef Weitz and the Transfer Committees, 1948–49," how Weitz, the Jewish National Fund executive in charge of land acquisition and its distribution among Jewish settlements and an ardent advocate of mass Arab transfer since the 1930s – he was on the Jewish Agency's Transfer Committees between 1937 and 1942 – "was well placed [in 1948] to shape and influence decision-making regarding the Arab population on the national level and to oversee the implementation of policy on the local level" (*1948*, p. 91). From early 1948,

Weitz began to exploit the conditions of war to expel Arab villagers and tenant-farmers, some of whom cultivated lands owned by Jewish institutions. He personally supervised many local evictions during the early months of war, frequently with the assistance of local Haganah commanders (*1948*, pp. 92–98). Moreover, Morris explains:

> Everyone, at every level of military and political decision-making, understood that a Jewish state without a large Arab minority would be stronger and more viable both militarily and politically. The tendency of local military commanders to "nudge" Palestinians into flight increased as the war went on. Jewish atrocities ... (massacres of Arabs at Ad Dawayima, Eilaboun, Jish, Safsaf, Majd al Kurum, Hule (in Lebanon) Saliha, and Sasa, besides Dayr Yasin and Lydda and other places) – also contributed significantly to the exodus. (*1948*, p. 22)

I cannot see how the above explanation regarding "decision-making" can be reconciled with Morris's denial of a transfer policy. And does it matter in the end whether such a policy was actually formulated, or whether it was just *de facto* and clearly understood at every level of military and political decision-making?

On the basis of the revelations, documentation, and factual findings brought to light by Morris (and other "new" historians), the traditional Palestinian contention that there was a Zionist consensus on the question of finding a "solution" to the "Arab demographic problem" – the Arabs, even in 1948, still constituted two-thirds of the population of Palestine – through "transfer" of Arabs to areas outside the prospective Jewish state and barring their return to their villages and towns, is corroborated. Zionist parties of all shades of opinion – with the exception of muted, internal criticism from a few members of the Mapam and Mapai parties – were in basic agreement about the need and desirability of utilizing the 1948 War to establish an enlarged Jewish state with as small an Arab population as possible. Yosef Sprinzak, the relatively liberal secretary general of the Histadrut, a critic of the forcible transfer policy, had this to say at the 24 July 1948 meeting at the Mapai Centre, some ten days after the Lydda–Ramle expulsion:

> There is a feeling that *faits accomplis* are being created ... the question is not whether the Arabs will return or not return. The question is whether the Arabs are [being or have been] expelled or not. ... This is important to our moral future. ... I want to know who is creating the facts? And the facts are being created on orders. ... [There appears to be] a line of action ... of expropriation and of emptying the land of Arabs by force. (*1948*, pp. 42–43)

It is difficult, using Morris's own evidence, not to see on the part of the leaders of mainstream labor Zionism a *de facto*, forcible transfer policy in 1948.

Morris's analysis of the events of 1948 is also flawed by his treatment of the Arab exodus largely in an historical and political vacuum, without any intrinsic connection with Zionism. Although he does refer to the Zionist consensus emerging from the mid-1930s in support of transferring the Arab population, he sees no connection between this and the expulsions of 1948. This brings us to the explanatory framework underlying Morris's work: the Zionist leadership's ideological–political disposition for transferring/expelling Arabs resulted from the "security" threat (the "fifth column") the Arab population posed to the Jewish state. The facts presented earlier, on the other hand, show that the "voluntary/compulsory" transfer of the indigenous Arabs was prefigured in the Zionist ideology a long time before the 1948 war broke out and advocated "obsessively" by the Zionist leadership from the mid-1930s onwards. Consequently, the resistance of the indigenous Arab population to Zionism before and in 1948 emanated from precisely the Zionist goal of establishing a Jewish state that would, at best, marginalize the Palestinians as a small, dependent minority in their own homeland, and, at worst, eradicate and "transfer" them. The "security" threat posed by the "transferred" inhabitants of the Palestinian towns and villages resulted from the Zionist movement's ideological premise and political agenda, namely the establishment of an exclusivist state.

From the perspective of Morris's "new" historiography, there was no inherent link between the "transfer" of the Arabs and the acquisition of their lands on the one hand and Zionism's long-advocated imperative of accommodating millions of Jewish immigrants in the Jewish state on the other. The nearest thing he says which provides a hint regarding such a connection is the following:

> The war afforded the Yishuv a historic opportunity to enlarge the Jewish state's borders and, as things turned out, to create a state without a very large Arab minority. The war would solve the Yishuv's problem of lack of land, which was necessary to properly absorb and settle the expected influx of Jewish immigrants. (*1948*, pp. 39–40)

Would Zionism have succeeded in fulfilling its imperative of absorbing the huge influx of Jewish immigrants while allowing the indigenous population to remain *in situ*? If not, could the Zionist objective of "transferring" the Arabs from Palestine have been carried out "voluntarily" and peacefully, without Arab resistance or the destruction of their society in 1948? Morris's findings constitute a landmark and are a remarkable contribution to our knowledge because they show that the evacuation of hundreds of thousands of Palestinians was a result of direct attacks, fear of attacks, intimidation, psychological warfare (e.g., the whispering campaign), and sometimes outright expulsions ordered by the Haganah/IDF leadership. Yet a wider explanatory and theoretical framework within which the exodus can be properly understood must be sought elsewhere.

NOTES

Nur Masalha, who holds an M.A. from the Hebrew University in Jerusalem and a Ph.D. in political science from the University of London, is the author of the forthcoming book *Expulsion of the Palestinians: The Concept of "Transfer" in Zionist Political Thought, 1882–1948* (Institute for Palestine Studies, Autumn 1991).
  Source: Journal of Palestine Studies XXI, no. 1 (Autumn 1991), pp. 90-97.

1. Al Darchei Mediniyotenu: Mo'atzah 'Olamit Shel Ihud Po'alei Tzion (c.s.), Din Vehisbon Male 21 July–7 August (1937) [A Full Report about the World Convention of Ihud Po'alei Tzion]. Tel Aviv, 1938, p. 122.
2. Ibid., p. 100.

Part V

PALESTINIANS
IN ISRAEL

11

THE DEMOCRATIZATION OF A TRADITIONAL MINORITY IN AN ETHNIC DEMOCRACY

The Palestinians in Israel

Nadim Rouhana and As'ad Ghanem

As noted repeatedly in this collection, present realities determine to a large extent the historiographical agenda of both Israeli and Palestinian research. This, together with a growing cooperation between historians and social scientists, has enabled us to widen the scope of the historical enterprise and include groups and communities hitherto marginalized or totally forgotten in the historical narrative. One such group is the Palestinian citizens of Israel. They were a subject for research before, but only within the Israeli context and not, as they should be, as part of the conflict's history. For political reasons, Israel claimed, and many historians capitulated, that the issue of Arabs in Israel was an internal Israeli affair.

Two Palestinian Israelis, one living in and one out of the country, have joined here to provide us with historical research on the chronicles of the Palestinian minority in Israel and its struggle for democracy and national identity. It is a rare case where an indigenous minority has to accept a majoritarian immigrant society imposed on it. As'ad Ghanem and Nadim Rouhana conclude that this unique reality strengthened the process of democratization within the Palestinian community in Israel, a process that, none the less, did not dim the national commitment of this particular Palestinian group. At a time when the fate of democracy both in Israel and in Palestine seemed doubtful and obscure, this historical account illuminates the one group which constantly adhered to democratic principles and outlook within a violent and nationalist environment.

* * *

This chapter uses the concepts and tools of political socialization to examine the ongoing process of democratization of a traditional community living in an ethnic democracy: the Palestinian community in Israel. Unlike other Third World people living in Western societies, the Palestinian citizens in Israel did not immigrate to the new system; rather, the system was imposed upon them. This distinction is important for three main reasons: *First*, immigrants who willingly choose to leave their homeland and move to a new country might do so because they believe in and wish to be governed by the values of the new system, including democratic values. The Palestinians in Israel made no such choice; in 1948, a new state was forced upon them in their homeland, involuntarily making them citizens of the newly established state of Israel. *Second*, unlike immigrants who leave their communities behind and assimilate into their new society, this community remained together *in toto*. Though truncated from the larger Palestinian society, the community maintained characteristics of a coherent group, living in more than a hundred Arab towns and villages (and in Arab quarters in cities with Jewish majorities). All the traditional links and structures – the extended family and the patriarchal relations therein, forms of subsistence, community networks, religious traditions – remained virtually intact in the new, Western-oriented, modern Israeli system. *Third*, the new system was established to serve the goals of a national group – the Jewish people – to the exclusion of this community, thereby introducing the potential for ongoing conflict.

Understanding the democratization process, the tensions emanating from the social differences between the new majority and the indigenous minority, and the contradictions of the political framework in which democratization is occurring will shed light on the paradoxes that characterize democratization in the Third World – the Arab world in particular – and in conflict situations. Such an understanding will also help us develop hypotheses on the implications of the democratization of this community for future Israeli–Palestinian interactions. The Arabs in Israel, who constitute a significant segment of the Palestinian people, are loyal to larger Palestinian goals and aspirations and at the same time are Israeli citizens with many democratic tools available to them. While they are keeping a low profile in the ongoing process of negotiations between Israelis and Palestinians, they might also have the potential to change the shape of future political arrangements between the two groups if they choose to articulate and express their political objectives democratically.

This chapter is divided into three main parts. In the first part we examine the factors that influence the democratization process of the Palestinians in Israel – both local and systemic factors, and the interaction between the two. In the second part, we examine paradoxes of the democratization process, some of which emanate from the contact between a Third World community and a modern setting, some from the conflict situation, and some from unique characteristics of the case under study. The third part examines the implications of a peaceful settlement for the democratization of other groups in the area and for future Israeli–Palestinian interaction.

Factors influencing the democratization process

As indicated by Rothstein, democracy is a contested concept; there are "no perfect democracies in the developed or the developing world."[1] While certain ideal democratic characteristics have been posited in the context of the developed world,[2] the definition of such characteristics in a Third World context is more complex. In both cases, however, the discussion of democracy focuses on the systemic level of the type of government and political regime and its relevance to democratic transformation.

In this chapter, the emphasis is placed on individuals and their interaction with the governing system – how individuals are affected by the system and how the system is modified in response to individual change. Democratization, therefore, is defined here as the individual's embracement of democratic values based on rational/legal sources of the legitimization of authority, as defined by Weber,[3] and the endorsement of democratic procedures in the interaction between authorities and citizens based on that legitimacy. Democratization is thus part and parcel of the collective political socialization determined by the interaction between the polity and the system. Accordingly, democratization of the Arabs in Israel is determined by the interaction between Israeli policy toward the Arabs and internal developments within this community. The first part of this chapter will discuss in brief the Israeli policy toward the Arabs, internal developments within this group, and the interaction between the two.[4]

The framework of Israel's policy toward its Arab citizens

Israel's policy toward its Arab population was formatively shaped by three overriding ideas:[5] that Israel was established as the state of the Jewish people; that it is a Western democracy; and that Israel has special security concerns about its Arab population that will prevail as long as the conflict with all Arabs is not resolved.

According to the first idea, Israel was established to construct a Jewish society. Its responsibility expands beyond its borders to include the Jews all over the world; therefore, "in-gathering the exiles" is given the highest priority. The meaning of a Jewish state is reflected not only in the national, official, cultural, and political symbols and means of expression of the state but also in the perception that Israel as a homeland belongs exclusively to the Jewish people rather than to its Jewish and Arab population. Most national priorities, projects, and institutions are exclusively Jewish, arguably harnessing Arab resources to serve Jewish goals.

According to the second idea, Israel was established as a democratic state applying the principles of liberal democracy. Indeed, as far as its Jewish population is concerned, Israel enjoys democratic standards similar to those of well-established Western democracies. As far as the Arab population is concerned, the vast majority of Arabs were granted citizenship after the establishment of the state. The Arabs enjoy complete freedom of worship and formal equality before the law, with the significant exception of the law of return and nationality. To what extent Arabs in Israel actually enjoy the fruits of Israeli democracy is debatable. But most researchers agree that Arabs, while benefitting from democracy, don't enjoy full equality.[6]

Finally, Israel's national security needs markedly influenced its policy toward its Arab citizens. After all, Israel was imposed on its Arab citizens against their will and immediately became embroiled in a zero-sum conflict with the Palestinians and other Arab states. It was frequently argued that an Arab population feeling nationally and culturally connected to Palestinians or to the Arab nation could be a security burden. Israel, therefore, took steps to abort and prevent any security offenses that Arabs might want to commit individually or collectively.

This triangular foundation underlying Israel's policy toward its Arab population is fraught with contradictions. The second and third principles are in conflict: While tension between security requirements of democratic states and the practice of the rule of the law increases during wartime, Israel took this tension to an extreme.[7] The way Israel defined its security needs necessitated curtailing the Arabs' democratic rights. Pinkas,[8] for example, argues that security in Israel has institutional expressions far beyond any comparable democratic state: "The Israeli public and body politic comfortably assume that if certain democratic rights are suspended or civil rights infringed it is permissible if it is in the name of security."[9]

Similarly, the first and second principles are fundamentally at odds: A state that is defined as belonging only to one people when its population is composed of two cannot offer equal opportunity and an equal voice to all its citizens. But it was, in part, this tension between the three principles that enabled Israel to enact discriminatory policies toward the Arab population. These contradictions are becoming increasingly apparent to the Arab population.

The main contradiction in this triangle, between being a democracy and being a Jewish state, has profound implications not only for the democratization of the Arab population but also for the future of democracy in Israel.[10] It is not at all clear, for example, that most Israelis consider being a democracy of greater importance than being a Jewish state and that, if forced to choose, they would opt for democracy. Although Israeli society has thus far been spared the torment of such a choice simply because the conflict was successfully buried under the excuse of "security considerations," developments in the relationship between the two societies are bringing this conflict to the surface.

The triangular foundation described above does not imply that the three ideas contributed equally to Israel's policy toward its Arab citizens or to the democratization process. The principle that Israel is the state of the Jewish people is the driving force behind most of Israel's policies toward its Arab population. Although this principle's importance overrides the importance of democracy, the idea of a democratic state nonetheless has deeply affected the democratization process.

Internal developments

Internal changes within the Arab community have provided the social and political grounds for democratization. Among the most important of these factors are demographic growth, the social transformation of the traditional Arab family, and political involvement in the Israeli system.

Demographic growth The demographic growth of the Arab population and the physical expansion of Arab towns and villages is the most conspicuous change in the Arab community since the creation of Israel. By the end of 1990, the nation had 713,400 Arab citizens (not including the 146,300 Arab residents of Jerusalem who are not Israeli citizens and 15,300 Arabs in the Golan Heights).[11] This total represents 15.3 percent of Israel's citizenry. According to figures worked out from the most conservative estimates of the Israeli Bureau of Statistics, the Arab population will number 922,990 citizens in the year 2000 (East Jerusalem's Arab community will grow to 191,700). The percentage of Arabs would depend on the future of Jewish immigration.

The increase in the Arab population created large towns. Of the 112 towns in Israel with more than 5,000 residents, 41 are Arab; 15 of those have more than 10,000 residents. Although territorial expansion has failed to match population growth, it is unmistakably visible. Physical continuation between towns is developing, laying the groundwork for Arab metropolitan areas in parts of the Galilee and in the Triangle region. In addition, Arabs live in six mixed cities: Haifa, Ramle, Lydda, Jaffa, Acre, and Upper Nazareth, which was established as a Jewish city. Recently, Arabs have been moving into Carmiel, Rehovot, Hadera, Nahariya, Eilat, and Beersheba.[12]

The increase in their number and the expansion of their physical habitat have created self-confidence and a heightened sense of community among the Arabs. Demographic growth has also opened up the possibility of developing distinct and vibrant forms of cultural life, massive political organizations, and diverse economic enterprises. It made possible dynamic political activity through the establishment of independent political parties or participation within the Jewish parties, and the gradual development of groups with distinctly different political orientations. The interaction between these groups produced political pluralism within the community.

Social and economic changes

Social and economic changes in Arab society have expedited the process of political change and contributed to the democratization of this community. While Israeli authorities encouraged the existing traditional and segmented structure of the Arab population because it facilitated the state's strategy of control,[13] they often unwittingly accelerated democratization with some of their policies.

Massive expropriation of Arab land inadvertently created a background against which deep changes in the socioeconomic structure and social values could occur.[14] While Arab rural society was transformed in the early years of the state into an unskilled proletariat,[15] the last fifteen years have witnessed the emergence of a skilled, industrialized proletariat. Similarly, a burgeoning middle class made up of professionals, small contractors, and businessmen is also emerging, but there are no signs of a middle class based on the productive industrial sector because industrialization is virtually nonexistent in the Arab community.

To cope with the new reality, Arabs had to change their social values and attitudes toward modernity. One direct outcome of land expropriation was the drastic decrease in farming, which had been the main source of income for the vast majority of Palestinians. Land was farmed by whole families with the father, the sole landowner, as the central figure of authority. The loss of land meant young workers went to work outside the family property – in workshops, farms, and businesses outside their own villages, usually in Jewish urban areas. This type of employment gave them an unprecedented degree of economic independence.

Working in the cities has had other ramifications as well. While most workers commute on a daily basis, many stay in the Jewish settlements for a week or longer at a time. It is in the work setting that most social interaction between Arabs and Jews takes place. When they have pursued these relations beyond the workplace, Arabs have been exposed to an alternative set of social relations within the family (including child rearing), between families, and between the sexes. Working in modern surroundings also has necessitated changes in work-related values, such as respect for manual work, efficacy, and so forth. The relatively democratic interactions in the workplace and the way unions operate also changed Arab workers' values.[16]

The loss of land and the associated changes revolutionized relations within the family. The economic basis for patriarchal control over the children eroded, and the father's authority declined. Perhaps the greatest blow to parental authority in general came from a reversal of dependency: Parents became reliant on their children because the younger generations were more educated and consequently more versed in the political and social language of the new system. Within the context of this more egalitarian relationship, children began to oppose authority and take part in decision making. That change became most apparent in their gaining the power to choose their own professions, marriage partners, living arrangements after marriage, child-rearing methods, and future plans.[17] The new patterns of interaction among family members were reflected in patterns of social relations in the society. Traditional respect for the elderly, a direct derivative of paternal authority, came under question, and extended-family affiliation lost its functional justification (though new functions might have arisen, as we will argue later). The weakening of extended-family ties eroded the status of the extended-family leadership, which epitomized traditional legitimacy.

A third factor that accelerated the democratization process was education. Israeli authorities took complete control over the Arab educational system. The curriculum was emptied of any content that referred to national consciousness, patriotism, national pride, historic roots, and the like.[18] Learning was completely overhauled to emphasize Zionist points of view, Hebrew literature, and some biblical studies. Perhaps most detrimental to the Arab educational system was the authorities' tight control of teacher appointments. Until the 1960s many teachers were appointed not on merit but out of "security considerations," with security broadly defined to include political activity, party affiliation, and national consciousness. This practice was meticulously followed in elementary schools, which were and still are under the complete command of the Ministry of Education and Culture. Since jobs for educated Arabs were scarce, teacher appointments became a key means of control and a form of reward for cooperating with family chiefs, traditional leaders, and sometimes directly with the authorities. Until now, teachers' colleges have to clear Arab applicants with security agencies before accepting them.

In addition to damaging education itself, this process led to a freefall in the traditional prestige that teachers enjoyed, disrespect for the curriculum, and a deep mistrust in a system that required teaching the Bible but not the Muslim Quran, Zionist nationalism but not

Palestinian nationalism, and nationalistic Hebrew literature but not Palestinian literature. The whole educational message was received with suspicion and sarcasm, which ultimately resulted in its psychological rejection. The end result was the delegitimization of the educational system as a source of political socialization. Indeed, Arab youth looked for their political education in outside agencies such as political parties, media, peer groups, unofficial activities, and so on.[19] The students often became the political educators of their teachers.

It was not until the mid-1970s that the grip of the Ministry of Education was loosened because of the increase in the number of Arab towns whose local governments controlled hiring and firing in high schools. Around the same time, sweeping change in local governments began. Governments associated with the governing Labor Party were replaced by governments under the control of the Democratic Front for Peace and Equality (centered around the Israeli Communist Party) or independent mayors. High schools became staffed with university graduates who brought to the system the new methods, values, and democratic practices they had learned in the Israeli university system. The traditional student–teacher relationship based on awe, obedience, and unquestioning acceptance was gradually giving way to more democratic relations, intellectual openness, and the right to question authority.

Educational developments facilitated the process of social and political democratization. Indeed, educational changes in the Arab community over the last four decades are most visible. For example, in the 1990–1991 academic year,[20] there were 235,557 Arab pupils in the Israeli educational system.[21] Of those, 40,271 were in secondary schools (compared to a few dozen in 1948); this figure had quintupled in twenty years.[22] Between 1948 and 1971, the total number of Arab university graduates (i.e., those who hold a B.A. degree or higher) was estimated to be 600. A survey found that a total of 328 Arabs had graduated from Israeli universities during the whole period between 1961 and 1971. In 1961 there were six graduates; in 1971 there were 82 graduates.[23] Now the number is estimated to be more than 1,000 per year. According to the latest figures,[24] non-Jewish students (mainly Arabs) constituted 6.7 percent of the Israeli undergraduate body (or 3,146 students) in the 1989–1990 academic year, 3.5 percent of M.A. students (563 students), and 3.5 percent of Ph.D. candidates (137 candidates). The number of Arabs with academic degrees is estimated to be 15,100, which represents 3 percent of Arabs aged fifteen and over. Those with thirteen to fifteen years of education number 30,700, constituting 6.1 percent of the same population group.[25]

A fourth factor that expedited democratization was the entry of women into the labor force. An economic crisis in the late 1970s and early 1980s and the increase in the standard of living made Arab society more accepting of women's entry into the labor market. The changing patterns of interaction within the nuclear family, described above, facilitated this acceptance. Though incremental, change occurred rapidly. By now the majority accepts women's work as natural. Many Arab women work in local branches of Israeli textile companies, which opened factories in Arab villages to hire women who preferred not to leave the village. Although accused of exploiting women as cheap laborers, they nonetheless have given many women the economic bases for increased independence and control over their own lives and reduced their subjection to the authority and control of the family, particularly their father and brothers.

The rise in educational levels has included Arab women, too. Girls comprise 48.3 percent of Arab high school students and 47.3 percent of intermediate school students.[26] There has been a dramatic increase in the number of women with university and professional degrees: lawyers, physicians, engineers, and others. Some are also in journalism, sports, and theater. Some university graduates tried to popularize and adapt principles of women's liberation to Arab culture. Lately, Arab women have established a number of independent organizations to defend the status of women and their rights.[27] The Arab-dominated political parties also have active women's organizations.

Independence from the family, once unthinkable for women, is now gaining acceptance. Some women leave home to live in the mixed cities for work or study. There they can liberate themselves from family limits and the influence of brothers, fathers, and other men in the family. Once they marry, the pattern of relations within their own families – husband and wife, children and parents, etc. – approximates a Western one more than it does a traditional Arab one.

These new lifestyles do not mean that all Arab women are changing their values. Because of the rapid change that occurred in a limited period, Arab society has a full spectrum of women, from the most traditional to the most liberated. Yet the overall change in women's status is unmistakable. It has added yet another dimension to the deepening evolution in social values and to the acceptance of democratic principles of interaction within the family.

In sum, Israeli policies and the ensuing changes in Arab society destabilized agencies that are essential for inculcating authoritarian and traditional attitudes: the family and the school. The family authority structure was severely disrupted as fathers lost their means of control over their children – land ownership and cultivation. And, paradoxically, the authorities' tight control over the educational system weakened the status of the authority figures within it and increased students' relative power.

Political experience and involvement in the Israeli system

The factor that had the greatest influence on the process of democratization is Arab involvement in the Israeli political system. Unlike Palestinians in the West Bank and Gaza, who have watched Israeli democracy from afar while suffering the brunt of Israeli military occupation, the Palestinians in Israel have learned about Israeli democracy through observation and participation. As mentioned earlier, Israeli democracy is constrained for Arab citizens by other state considerations, yet there is no doubt that participation in a democratic system has gone a long way toward instilling democratic values and introducing democratic practices. The Israeli system has influenced the Arabs' democratization in the following ways.

Close observation   Dependency upon the system has made most of the new generation bilingual and bicultural. Hebrew is mandatory in Arab schools from the second grade. Having lost trust in the state-run Arabic media, Arabs turned to the Hebrew media as a source of news.[28] Many educated Arabs became comfortable with both Arab and Jewish cultural works.

Politicization, the ongoing Palestinian–Israeli conflict, and near-total dependency has made many Arabs highly aware of the Israeli political system, the way it works, its values, the ideologies of the various parties, and the function of various institutions such as the Supreme Court and the state comptroller. Generally speaking, Arabs are versed in Israeli politics; educated Arabs might be more aware than their Jewish counterparts of the ideological positions of various parties and of Israeli policy *vis-à-vis* the Arab minority or the Palestinians.

Participation in parliamentary elections   Arabs have voted in every Israeli parliamentary election. In a state that relies on the parliamentary system and in which the parliament places checks and balances on the executive branch, controlled groups or protest groups often choose to affect policy in the Knesset. Participating in elections and winning a number of representatives might give the group influence over allocation of resources and distribution of power. In Israel, the government is not only subordinated to the checks and balances of the Knesset but also receives its confirmation by a simple majority of 61 Knesset members. In a multiparty system in which no one party controls the majority, a coalition between the two major parties or between one of the two major parties and smaller parties is required to achieve parliamentary majority. In exchange for coalitional support, a party might grant government participation, but it might also pay back the support by other means, such as increasing budgets, improving services, and/or granting consultation in decisionmaking. While the extent to which Arabs can influence the system is debatable, surveys show that most Arabs believe it is possible to improve their situation through parliamentary politics; only a small minority does not share this view.[29]

Indeed, from the first to the sixth Knesset, despite a slight decrease in the percentage of Arab voters, their percentage exceeded the percentage of Jewish voters. For the second Knesset (1951) the percentage of Arab valid votes (to total of potential Arab votes) reached 86 percent, and for the third (in 1955) it peaked at 90 percent.[30] These numbers do not necessarily demonstrate belief in the utility of parliamentary elections or commitment to the democratic process; at that time, it was more a reflection of the mechanism of external state control, or of internal *hamula* (extended-family) control. Since the third Knesset elections in 1955, the percentage of valid votes has dropped, reaching 68 percent, 72 percent, and 70 percent in the last three Knesset elections. During this period, the pattern of voting changed and support began shifting from Zionist parties and their Arab surrogates to Arab-dominated parties.[31] By 1988 Arab-dominated parties received about 60 percent of the Arab vote. The experience of organizing parties, campaigning for them, voting for them, and running them has added tremendously to Arab democratization.

Of the many groups, parties, and organizations that are active in the Arab sector, all but Abna' al-Balad and a branch of the Islamic movement want to be part of parliamentary elections. Abna' al-Balad (active in some villages in Galilee and the Triangle and among university students) rejects participation in elections and parliamentary politics on principle. The movement disavows the present regional arrangement and calls for the establishment of a secular state in all of historic Palestine. It does not participate in Israeli parliamentary politics because, in its view, participation represents recognition and acceptance of the present arrangement, which it does not wish to grant. A branch of the Islamic movement, particularly that under the influence of Sheikh Kamel Khatib of Kofr Kanna, also adheres to nonparticipation.[32]

Organizing and leading opposition parties In opposition parties, Arabs have learned about the democratic system's advantages and limitations through practice. The contribution of this experience to democratization might be even greater than that of involvement within the governing parties. In this regard, the influence of the Israeli Communist Party should be examined, because until the early 1980s it was the dominant force in Arab political life. Both its ideology and its methods affected the democratization process, albeit in contradictory directions.

On the one hand, the party encouraged and enhanced democratic practice *vis-à-vis* the authorities. The party perceived itself as a genuine part of the Israeli system. Its criticisms of Israeli policies were and are rooted in genuine, even patriotic, concerns for Israel and its future in the region and deep concern for the Arab population and the Palestinian people. The Communist Party used the democratic means provided by the system without hesitation. The protests the party organized and led, the new modes of political expression it introduced (such as the harsh criticism of authority), and its challenge to the system through parliamentary and extraparliamentary activities, all carried out meticulously within the framework of Israeli law, left deep impressions on the Arab population. On the social level, the party relentlessly attacked traditional sources of loyalty, such as family and religious affiliation, and encouraged new sources, such as national affiliation, political and class consciousness, and ideological commitment. It also advocated equal rights for women, educated against anti-Semitism, and promoted genuine forms of Arab–Jewish relations in the country within its own ranks. In the absence of a trustworthy and capable agent of political socialization, the party provided the main source of ideological, political, and social education for many Arabs, particularly the younger generations. All of this activity contributed to the political and social democratization of the Arab population *vis-à-vis* the system and the authorities.

On the other hand, the party might have hindered the internal democratization of the Arab community insofar as freedom of expression and opinion went. For a long time, until 1989, the party employed the equivalent of "intellectual terror" in its debates when it encountered any political views that did not fit the party line. It considered its views the absolute balance, the outcome of a *chef d'oeuvre*, and behaved as if any deviation in either direction would harm the collective interests of the community and the larger national interests.

The Communist Party came very close to claiming sole representation of the Arabs in Israel, particularly after the establishment of the Democratic Front for Peace and Equality in 1977. It tried to prevent the rise of other forces that emerged to claim representation, using severe criticism, ridicule, and even public skepticism of these forces' national loyalties and political motives. But with the emergence of new political forces, the internal weakening of the party, and the collapse of the Soviet bloc, the party changed course and gave up its "soleness" of representation. It accepted the new Arab parties as legitimate and began calling for mutual respect, cooperation, and coordination.

The party's "intellectual terror" has been abruptly replaced by an approach toward the other parties that is laying the foundation for a national democratic politics in which the multiparty system can genuinely represent the different orientations of the Arab public. In the 1989 Histadrut elections, the party coalesced with the other two Arab-dominated parties (the Progressive List for Peace and the Arab

Democratic Party) to run in one unified list. This strategy was drastically different from the 1988 national elections, in which the party harshly attacked the two parties' legitimacy and refused even to negotiate an agreement with either of them on excess votes,[33] wasting thousands of votes given to all three parties.[34]

Organizing legal extraparliamentary protest Given the rise in Arab demands and the failure of parliamentary methods to bring about significant achievements, extraparliamentary protest has been steadily increasing. It is now a popular form of protest that Arabs use regularly. Activities include general and local strikes, demonstrations, distribution of leaflets, and writing in Hebrew newspapers and magazines to influence the Jewish majority and the decisionmakers. Surveys show that Arabs in Israel are highly committed to this method in order to enhance their status and achieve their goals.[35] Unlike parliamentary struggle, extraparliamentary tactics are accepted by all political parties and factions and supported by political and social organizations.

Arab citizens also use this method to protest Israeli policies toward Palestinians in the Occupied Territories. During the uprising, the number of organized protests against Israeli policies in the territories increased sharply.[36] This rise demonstrates the Arabs' deeper understanding of the democratic system and increased ability to maneuver within it.

The process of decisionmaking about using extraparliamentary protest provides the strongest indicator of the depth of the democratization process among the Arab political elite. Decisions about national strikes and regional demonstrations are discussed in the Monitoring Committee on the Affairs of Arab Citizens (FCAAC, or *Lajnat Mutaba'at Shu'un Al Muwatineen Al Arab*) which is composed of Arab mayors, Arab Knesset members (including those with Zionist parties), representatives of political movements and social organizations, and representatives of student unions. Decisions are passed by simple majority. Without exception, the minority has abided by majority rule despite frequent deep disagreements with these decisions.

Paradoxes of democratization

Underlying the democratization of the Arab society in Israel, as noted, is the gradual transformation of patterns of interaction with authority from traditional bases to legal/rational bases, as broadly defined by Weber.[37] When examining this transformation, we uncover a number of paradoxes that reflect the contradictions of Israeli policies and the complexities of the rapid internal changes in this community. Five main paradoxes are described below:

1. *Increasingly active political participation in the national system versus constantly limited civic competence.* Civic competence is used to define the extent of an individual's or group's political influence over governmental decisions, or the degree to which government officials act to benefit a group or an individual because the officials believe they will risk some deprivation if they do not act.[38] The limited civic competence of the Arab minority as a whole has not increased with their participation in national elections.

While the percentage of Arabs who participate in national elections has not changed drastically since the first Knesset elections, the nature of the process has been transformed. In the first few elections, Arab slates that claimed to be independent but were actually initiated, organized, and completely controlled by Zionist parties competed for the Arab vote.[39] These slates, represented by co-opted leaders and based on extended family and religious affiliation, addressed in the Arab voter parochial loyalties of religion and extended family and were assisted by the Israeli system of control. But these slates gradually lost their base of support and were replaced by three Arab-dominated parties that responded to the increase in political and national consciousness and the rise in demands for equal distribution of resources. Yet this change did not by itself bring about any improvement in the Arabs' condition. The parties have very limited influence on governmental decisions regarding the Arab minority and on the decisionmaking process in general. Despite their number (six Arab and Jewish Knesset members in the three Arab-dominated parties), their coalitional weight, and therefore potential influence, is limited – because Arab parties are viewed by Zionist parties as illegitimate partners in any governmental coalition.

Whatever gains the Arabs achieved in promoting their interests as a national community were mainly secured through extraparliamentary protest. In 1976, after a national strike and many demonstrations, they were able to achieve a government freeze on most land expropriations. Likewise, they extracted promises from government officials to increase the budgets of their local governments only after mayors held a number of sit-in strikes in front of the prime minister's office. (Unlike national interests, local interests of individual towns were also served by the particular relationship of the local town government with the authorities.)

2. *Increasing support for achieving equality integratively within the state as an essential element of consensus versus increase in differential national organizations.* Calling for full equality within the state had become an element of the national Arab consensus by the mid-1980s. This demand has become a cornerstone in their collective bargaining with the state to improve their status. It is gaining more importance and

vigor in light of regional developments. Of major importance were the Palestinian uprising in the Occupied Territories and the ensuing two-state solution espoused by the Palestine National Council (PNC) in 1988. After these developments, it became clear to the Arab citizens of Israel that if a negotiated settlement were achieved, their final collective political future would be within the state of Israel.

But hand in hand with the growing insistence on full equality within the system, Arabs were establishing national organizations all over the country. The effort was pioneered by student associations in the early 1970s and followed by many others: high school students, heads of local governments, academics, the Committee for the Defense of Land, physicians, social workers, writers, artists, etc. This effort culminated in the aborted effort to hold "the congress of Arab masses" in 1980, which was to have representatives of the groups mentioned above and include the whole political spectrum. The congress was outlawed by an order from the defense minister, Menachem Begin.[40] In 1982 the FCAAC was established. Some observers consider this effort to represent the preparation of national infrastructure prior to demanding autonomy.

While we doubt that the effort was directly motivated by such considerations, it is not unlikely that if they are frustrated by the impossibility of achieving equality within the Israeli system, Arabs will consider alternative arrangements with Israel, including autonomy. Indeed, when two professors in a West Bank university advocated institutional autonomy in a local paper,[41] their article stirred a lot of debate and gained substantial attention in the community.

3. *Despite the recent increase in "security violations," a consensus was solidified that political struggle should be conducted solely within the framework of Israeli law.* Since the Arabs organized a national strike on December 21, 1987, to protest Israeli policies toward the uprising, the Israeli media and security establishment have given increasing attention to a rise in the number of "security violations" by Arab citizens.[42] Although there was an increase in acts of solidarity with the uprising, the extent of increase in security violations depends on how one defines "security violation [e.g., slogans in support of the uprising, raising a Palestinian flag, etc.]." The reaction of the Israeli public, media, and establishment was to express profound concern about any attempt by Arabs to act outside the laws of the country. In reaction, the whole Arab political spectrum asserted a collective desire to keep acts of protest within the framework of Israeli law.[43] So despite the increase of extraparliamentary protest since the beginning of the uprising, there was a meticulous effort exerted by Arab leadership to keep all acts legal and all expressions within the law. This attitude was shown to have support by consensus in in-depth

interviews we conducted with representatives of all political groups in the Arab community.[44] This respect for legal boundaries is also supported by the Arab public, as demonstrated in attitude surveys.[45]

4. *Despite the impossibility of electing a national leadership, the FCAAC is a de facto leadership for the Arabs in Israel.* It is inconceivable at the present time that the Arabs in Israel would be allowed to elect national leaders. They have not called for such elections because of the profound political implications of such a move. Instead, they have established their own parties to run in Israeli national elections and have elected their own local governments. Yet it seems that *de facto* national leadership has emerged without national elections in the form of the FCAAC.

The center of the FCAAC is a smaller committee of the Arab mayors. However, members of the FCAAC are locally elected (except for the Knesset members, who are nationally elected). As local elections are influenced by parochial loyalties, this national leadership does not necessarily represent the real aspirations and interests of the Arabs in Israel as a whole. Furthermore, even the Arab Knesset members are elected as representatives to the Israeli legislature, not as national leaders. Yet the FCAAC – which represents all the political groups in the community including Abna' al-Balad, the Islamic movement, and Arab members of Zionist parties – is considered by many in the Arab public and the establishment to be the *de facto* Arab national leadership.

5. *The increasing appeal to broader loyalties for national elections (national, political, ideological, identity) versus almost stable recourse to traditional loyalties in local elections.* The changes in the social and economic structure and values of the community made it impossible for the parochial loyalties of extended-family affiliation, religious belief, and region of residence to attract large numbers of Arab voters. By 1984 the Arab slates associated with Zionist parties disappeared from the political map, making way for parties that call upon broader loyalties such as political goals, national identity, and collective concerns. Even the Arab Knesset members in Zionist parties adhere to the political consensus that has been shaped by these new parties and address their constituencies using the elements of the consensus.

This transformation in the nature of participation in national elections does not mean, however, that parochial loyalties have disappeared. All of them are at work to some extent, at least in mobilizing some constituencies and motivating some voters. Even some of those who voted for the Communist Party did so at times out of parochial loyalty. Yet it is reasonably safe to state that whatever parochial loyalties persist among Arab voters, it would be impossible to successfully mobilize a national party based on any or all of them.[46] However, loyalty to the extended family might still be the main mobilizer in local elections, and religious affiliation might still play a significant role in religiously mixed towns.

To explore the extent of importance of the *hamula*-based vote in local elections, we examined the three most recent local elections (in 1978, 1983, and 1989) in all fifty-three Arab cities and towns that have local governments. We focused on the effect of *hamula* and religious affiliation on the election of municipal council members and mayors, who since 1978 have been directly elected by voters. The data were collected from the publications of the National Supervisor on Elections in the Department of the Interior. When data were missing, we conducted personal interviews with mayors and secretaries of local councils.

Our findings show that in all three elections in all fifty-three localities, there were only two cases in which a national political party won the office of the mayor independently of *hamula* or religious group support: Nazareth, where the Democratic Front for Peace and Equality (centered around the Israeli Communist Party) has won all elections since 1975, and Kofr Yassif, where the same party has won all elections since 1978. In either case, no *hamula* or religious politics were involved in the election process. In the remaining fifty-one localities, however, not one mayor was elected solely on an ideological or partisan basis. Winning was determined by *hamula* or religious group support, though in many cases the mayor was supported both by the *hamula* and by a party. All mayors in these cases were members of the largest *hamula* or religious group (or both) or affiliated with a coalition of *hamula*s in the town. The extent of *hamula* support varied from place to place. In some cases, for example, *hamula* lists existed on their own, while in other places they were supported by national political parties. Except for Abna' al-Balad and the Islamic movement in some cases, all political factions supported *hamula*-based elections.

Not only did mayors rely on *hamula* support, they also occasionally used various means that Zionist parties had used in the past, such as personal benefits, co-optation, and sometimes even bribes, to gain the support of family chiefs.

Hamula-based voting might be becoming even stronger instead of weaker. One indication is the difference in voting percentages for the Knesset and for local governments. For the last three Knesset elections (1981, 1984, and 1988), the percentages of Arab valid votes were 68 percent, 72 percent, and 70 percent, respectively. But for the local elections they were 87.9 percent, 88.9 percent, and 90.4 percent, respectively, consistently higher than for the Knesset elections and showing a slight increase. So it seems that *hamula*-based voting is resisting change in local elections but not in the Knesset elections. This differential change requires some explanation.

While it might be the case that many voters believe in family loyalty and that their support for a *hamula*-based list emanates from that loyalty, many others use family as a political tool. For example, an increasing number of young educated mayors who are familiar with democratic values and practices from their involvement in national politics are nonetheless elected to head local governments by *hamula*-based lists. They seem to be using the *hamula* support as a political tool to attain broader goals. *Hamula* support in local elections was also legitimized by the Democratic Front for Peace and Equality, which realized that to win some of the local elections it had to cooperate with *hamula* leaders. For a long time it advocated anti-*hamula* democratic education, as well as the slow but thorough process of change that such education would have entailed. But when this change came too slowly, the desire to control the local authorities overcame the trend against *hamula* policies.

Local elections themselves might have reinforced the *hamula*-based voting trend. After all, the local town councils control many resources and benefits that matter to town residents, including municipal hirings, zoning of development areas, budgets, and the education department. *Hamula* support for a candidate will affect distribution of jobs and local development to *hamula* members. A *hamula*, for example, can pressure the mayor to appoint a teacher, principal, town supervisor, etc., in exchange for votes. The teacher himself becomes tied to the family in return for its commitment and help. This way, the local government and the resources it controls became a tool in the hands of family chiefs to control family members, especially some of the young and educated who needed employment. *Hamula* voting is thus re-entrenched.

Although it would seem important for the extended family to vote only for family-based or family-supported lists in the local elections, such is not necessarily the case in Knesset elections. It is often in the family's interest to diversify its votes in national elections to increase its negotiating power *vis-à-vis* its main party of support. Although this diversification might begin as *hamula* interest-based behavior, over time it can change the basis for voting decisions by introducing diversity of views, legitimizing voting for different parties, and enriching political discussion.

For whatever reasons, it seems that among Arabs the political culture of local elections is distinctly different from the political culture of national elections. On the surface local Arab politics may appear to be conducted democratically, but the underlying values and means of gaining support are actually impeding democratization.

We conclude that while Arab society in Israel is not completely demo-cratized, it is undergoing a rapid and advanced process of democrati-zation. As in any process of collective social change, it is not unusual for conflicting values and practices to coexist. After all, sociopolitical change does not imply the instant replacement of one value system by another, but rather the gradual, sometimes haphazard introduction of new elements, their practice and internalization.

Facilitating this process of change is the fact that democratization at the national systemic level serves Arab national interests. Compared to the Jewish majority, Arabs as a group suffer from structural discrimina-tion and enjoy few of the country's resources and little state power. It is thus in their interest to have a completely democratic and egalitarian system. Democratic arguments therefore serve the instrumental needs of the Arab minority. Once values are advocated – even if only superfi-cially or out of pragmatic considerations – the way to their internalization opens, and people gradually make democratic values an integral part of their value system. The instrumental worth of the democratic value becomes secondary to its worth as a prized expression of belief and ideology.

While our study of local elections raises profound questions about the extent of democratization among Arabs in Israel, their political behavior on the national level shows an advanced stage of democratization. They practice democratic partisanship[47] as expressed by the acceptance of the rules, laws, and customs of political competition, and they express their political feelings openly *vis-à-vis* other groups and parties in their community. Political pluralism is reflected in the legitimacy granted to the representation of various parties – Rakah, the Progressive List for Peace (PLP), the Democratic Arab Party (DAP), and sometimes even to some Zionist parties. As mentioned earlier, this pluralism was recently apparent in the political cooperation between the PLP, Rakah, and the DAP, which joined forces in one unified list in a 1989 Histadrut election, as mentioned above.

Democratization and peaceful settlement of the Palestinian–Israeli conflict

Democratization and shared democratic values are not panaceas for resolving conflicts. When conflicting groups share the values of democ-racy, they are perhaps more likely to peacefully resolve disputes and avoid the eruption of violence. But there are no indications that this shared value can override the national, religious, and ethnic identities that might still be in conflict between two democratic collectives. In some cases, democratic expressions can increase conflict rather than decrease it, at least in the short run. Notice, for example, how democratization in Jordan gave voice to public opposition to the US intervention in the Gulf and made conflict between Israel and Jordan more likely, while the nondemocratic regime in Syria suppressed public feelings and reduced the likelihood of open conflict with Israel.

In our case, some observations are in order about the implications of democratization for a peaceful settlement of the Israeli–Palestinian conflict and the likely effect of a peaceful settlement on the process itself:

1. *It is highly likely that Arabs in Israel will continue to use only democratic and legal means to resolve their conflict with the state and to change their status within it.* It is extremely unlikely that Arabs will resort to violence either to promote their own equality or to support Palestinians in the Occupied Territories. This preference is becoming even clearer after five years of the uprising in the Occupied Territories. A distinction should be made between support for the uprising, which was and is taking place, and participation in the uprising, which is unlikely.[48]

    This distinction by itself is very important because the issues of dispute between Arab citizens and the state are vital and sometimes emotional for both groups. The extent of democratization that Arabs achieved has defused the potential for violence. Arabs' consensus on struggle within the law lessens the likelihood of violence on the Arab side, and the cooperation of some police departments with Arab leaders before Land Day demonstrations and strikes in light of the experience of 1976[49] decreases the likelihood of violence on the authorities' side.

2. *The combustive issue of the Arabs' status in a future settlement of the conflict will remain suppressed for the time being.* Although some Arab political factions think now is the time to raise it, the majority still do not. The democratic political pluralism that Arabs have achieved excludes the possibility of one faction imposing its view on the whole public. In effect, it guarantees that unless and until a majority of Arabs agree that the issue should be openly raised, it will remain in the background. Raising the issue at this time would ostensibly complicate the peace process; by not raising it, the Arabs are in fact contributing to the likelihood of that process's success.

3. *Arabs will decide democratically about the form of their relationship with Israel and a Palestinian state.* Democratic pluralism allows for and requires public debate on any changes in the status quo. If the question of autonomy, for example, is to be raised as a possible political arrangement, it will go through intensive democratic examination by the various parties and factions. Once a political idea has gained support, it is unlikely to lose it, given the process by which support is gained in this political atmosphere. Hence, the three elements of

consensus – equality for the Arabs in Israel, statehood for Palestinians in the Occupied Territories, and struggle within the framework of Israeli law – are of cardinal importance to the Arab minority as a whole.

4. *A peaceful settlement of the Israeli–Palestinian conflict might also influence the democratization process.* Paradoxically, we believe, a settlement might strain Israel's democratic nature, at least in the short run. A settlement will inevitably prompt the state and large segments of the Jewish public to emphasize the Jewish nature of Israel and the fact that it is the exclusive possession of the Jewish people. At this level of political consciousness, Arabs will point out that such an attitude contradicts democratic values and equality. While democracy is highly valued by many Jewish Israeli citizens, the Jewishness of the state, particularly after painful withdrawals from the Occupied Territories, might be more precious, and securing it could lead to suppression of Arab demands for openness, equality, democratization, and inclusion. This might be one of the serious setbacks of Israeli democracy within the 1967 borders.

5. *Democratic interactions between Israel and its Arab citizens will probably have a positive impact on Israeli–Palestinian interaction.* But it is only after Israel resolves the conflict between being a state of the Jewish people and being a democracy that the Arabs will be able to become genuine partners with the state. Indeed, the old adage that Arabs could be a bridge for genuine peace and reconciliation between Israel and the Palestinians requires that both sides follow democratic rules.

6. *The possible setback of democracy after a settlement with the Palestinian people will bring about strategic alliances between some Israeli political forces and some Arab political groups or parties.* Although some cooperation was once imposed by the Israeli Communist Party under strict conditions, the road will become more open for broader cooperation across national lines in conditions of peace. The submergence of security concerns should enable Israel to serve as a democracy for all its citizens. Cooperation and future strategic alliances between Arab and Jewish citizens based on voluntary democratic bases can open the road for the development of new shared identities and values that supersede separate national identities if these two groups are to coexist equally in the same land.

NOTES

1 See Robert Rothstein, Chapter 2 in this volume [not reprinted here].
2 See Rothstein's review, Chapter 2 in this volume [not reprinted here].
3 M. Weber, "The Three Types of Legitimate Rule," in A. Etzioni, ed., *A Sociological Reader on Complex Organizations*, 2nd edition (New York: Holt,

1969), pp. 6–15. According to Weber, legitimacy of authority rests on enactment. He argues that "the basic idea is that laws can be enacted and changed at pleasure by formally correct procedures."

4 For a more detailed discussion, see N. Rouhana, "The Political Transformation of the Palestinians in Israel: From Acquiescence to Challenge," *Journal of Palestine Studies*, Vol. 18, No. 3 (1989), pp. 38–59.

5 For more details on the conceptual framework for analysing Israel's policy toward its Arab population, see Rouhana, "Political Transformation," pp. 39–40.

6 For example, see I. Lustick, *Arabs in the Jewish State* (Austin: University of Texas Press, 1980), Chapter 5; D. Kietzmer, *The Legal Status of the Arab in Israel* (Boulder: Westview Press, 1990), Chapter 6; and Elia Zureik, *The Palestinians in Israel* (London: Routledge and Kegan Paul, 1979).

7 See Alon Pinkas, "Garrison Democracy," Chapter 4 in this volume [not printed here].

8 *Ibid.*

9 *Ibid.*

10 We disagree with Pinkas, who argues that the tension between the two is increasing in the Occupied Territories and decreasing in Israel proper. We think the tension is also increasing in Israel as the Arab population becomes more aware of the inherent contradictions described above. See Rouhana, "Political Transformation," for elaboration on the growing awareness of this contradiction.

11 Figures in this section are quoted or worked out from *The Statistical Abstract of Israel* (Jerusalem: Central Bureau of Statistics, 1991). In this source, the total figure of Arabs in Israel includes the Arab residents of East Jerusalem; the number of Arabs in Jerusalem should be subtracted from the CBS figure in order to arrive at the number of Arab citizens of Israel within the 1967 borders. (Some Arabs in Jerusalem are Israeli citizens, but their number is negligible for this calculation).

12 See Arnon Sofer, "The Arabs of Israel – From Village to Metropolis, What Next?" *Hamizrah Hehadash*, Vol. 2, pp. 97–105, in Hebrew; and A. Sofer, "Geography and Demography in Eretz Yisrael in the Year 2000," in Alouph Hareven, ed., *Another War or Towards Peace?* (Jerusalem: The Van Leer Institute, 1980), in Hebrew.

13 For a detailed discussion of how Israel's policies were designed to preserve and strengthen segmentation of the Arab community see Lustick, *Arabs*, Chapter 4.

14 E. T. Zureik, "Transformation of Class Structure Among Arabs in Israel: From Peasantry to Proletariat," *Journal of Palestine Studies* 6 (1976), pp. 39–66.

15 N. Makhoul, "Changes in the Employment Structure of Arabs in Israel," *Journal of Palestine Studies* 10 (1981), pp. 77–102.

16 Some of the value change is described in S. Smooha, *The Orientation and Politicization of the Arab Minority in Israel* (Haifa: Haifa University Press, 1980).

17 For a discussion of land loss and its impact on relations within the family see H. Rosenfeld, "The Class Situation of the Arab National Minority in Israel," *Comparative Studies in Society and History* 20 (1978), pp. 374–407; and H. Rosenfeld, "The Class Situation of the Arab National Minority in Israel," *Mahbarot Limihkar Olibikoret* 3 (1979), pp. 5–40, in Hebrew.

18 For early discussions of education, curricula, and national identity, see Y. Peres, A. Ehrlich, and N. Yuval-Davis, "National Education for Arab Youth in Israel," *The Jewish Journal of Sociology* 12 (1970), pp. 147–164; and S. Mar'i, *Arab Education in Israel* (Syracuse: Syracuse University Press, 1978).

19 For an extended discussion, see R. Lazarowitz, N. Rouhana, J. E. Hofman, and B. Beit-Hallahmi, "Impact of Curricula on Shaping the Identity of Jewish and Arab Students in Israel," *Studies in Education*, No. 19 (1978), pp. 153–168, in Hebrew.

20 Figures in this section are obtained from *The Statistical Abstract of Israel*, 1991.

21 Figures on the educational system, as provided in *The Statistical Abstract of Israel*, 1991, include students in East Jerusalem and the Golan Heights.

22 For elaboration on reasons for the increase in the number of Arab students in all levels of education, see M. Al-Haj, *Education and Social Change among Arabs in Israel* (Tel Aviv: International Center for Peace in the Middle East, 1991), pp. 71–83.

23 The figures provided in the text are based on Eli Rekhess, *A Survey of Israeli Arab Graduates From Institutions of Higher Learning in Israel – 1961–1967*, mimeograph, The Shiloah Center, Tel Aviv University, 1974.

24 *The Statistical Abstract of Israel*, 1991.

25 These figures fail to come close to comparable percentages of the Jewish population, which stand at 12.2 percent for the first and 16 percent for the second. Yet they represent a multifold increase in comparison to figures in the Arab population from previous years. For more details, see Table 22.1 in *The Statistical Abstract of Israel*, 1991.

26 For more details, see Table 22.16 in *The Statistical Abstract of Israel*, 1991.

27 Three main organizations were established in the Galilee, the Triangle, and Haifa. Some became visible when they demonstrated against incidents in which women were killed for "violating the honor of the family," a term that means having a sexual relationship before or outside marriage.

28 See the results of a survey conducted in 1976 and published in S. Smooha, *Arabs and Jews in Israel* (Boulder. Westview Press, 1989), p. 46.

29 Smooha (*Arabs and Jews*, p. 126) reports that his surveys show this minority to be 17.6 percent.

30 For a discussion of Arab voting patterns until 1984, see N. Rouhana, "Collective Identity and Arab Voting Patterns," in A. Arian and M. Shamir, eds., *Elections in Israel – 1984* (New Brunswick, NJ.: Transaction Books, 1986).

31 For an elaborate discussion of the change in Arab voting patterns, see *ibid.*

32 Khatib confirmed this in an interview on October 5, 1990. He used explanations similar to those of Abna'al-Balad.

33 According to surplus vote agreements, one of the two parties becomes eligible for the surplus votes of the other, depending among other things on the size of the surplus votes of each and the number of candidates each party wins.

34 None of the Zionist parties agreed to have an excess vote agreement with any of the three Arab-dominated parties.

35 Smooha, *Arabs and Jews*.

36 See a discussion of change in mass political activity after the uprising in N. Rouhana, "Palestinians in Israel: Responses to the Uprising," in R. Brynen, ed., *Echoes of the Intifada: Regional Repercussions of the Palestinian–Israeli Conflict* (Boulder: Westview Press, 199 1), pp. 97–115.

37 Weber, "Three Types."

38 This definition is based on Almond and Verba's discussion of citizen competence and subject competence. See G. Almond and S. Verba, *The Civic Culture: Political Attitudes and Democracy in Five Nations* (Boston: Little, Brown and Company, 1965), Chapters 6 and 7.

39 Lustick, *Arabs*; Rouhana, "Collective Identity."

40 For details, see *The Prohibited Conference* (Haifa: Al-Ittihad Press, 1981),

published by the committee for rescinding the decision to prohibit the conference of Arab masses.

41 The article was published by A. Bishara and S. Zeidani in *Al-Arabi,* December 29, 1989, in Arabic.

42 See Rouhana, "Palestinians in Israel."

43 *Ibid.*

44 This was discussed extensively in a paper delivered by N. Rouhana in 1991. The paper, entitled "Palestinianization Among the Arabs in Israel: The Accentuated Identity," was presented at the Moshe Dayan Center for Middle Eastern Studies at Tel Aviv University in a conference on The Arab Minority in Israel: Dilemmas of Political Orientation and Social Change.

45 Smooha, *Arabs and Jews.*

46 It seems the Islamic movements in Israel can mobilize broad support, but so far they haven't shown any intention of establishing a national party and running for elections to the Knesset. In the 1989 local elections, they made remarkable gains, winning five local governments. However, a party led by the Islamic movement, if established, should not be seen as relying on parochial religious affiliation but rather on a developed social and political ideology arguably anchored in Islam.

47 This definition is based on Almond and Verba, *Civic Culture,* Chapter 5.

48 Rouhana, "Palestinians in Israel."

49 On March 30, 1976, the Arab community declared a strike to protest the expropriation of Arab land by the authorities. In response, police and army units entered Arab towns, and clashes resulted in the killing of six Arab citizens. Since then, Arabs have commemorated that day as Land Day.

Part VI

THE INTIFADA IN HISTORICAL PERSPECTIVE

12

FROM SALONS TO THE POPULAR COMMITTEES

Palestinian women, 1919–89

Islah Jad

Several works have appeared in the last twenty years on women's history in Palestine. I have chosen Islah Jad's article for several reasons. First, it was written under the influence of contemporary development, namely the intifada. *This trend of trying to explain the present by referring to the past is a major feature in the new historiography on the conflict and is a recurring theme in women's history. After all, it is the relative improvement in women's position that brought to the fore women historians and with them women's history. So as the article closing this collection it again combines the salvaging of hitherto silenced voices from the past with research touching upon contemporary agendas affecting them and being affected by them.*

While quite a lot is known about the spontaneous way women organized themselves during the uprising in 1987, less is known about women's participation since the emergence of the modern Palestinian national movement. The historiographical perspective enables Jad to examine openly the role of women in the Palestinian society. Such a critical examination is one of the main features of the new Palestinian sociology and historiography. As she points out, the position of women always depended on their share within the national movement itself and was inhibited by the attitude of political Islamic movements. Hence, although the intifada *marks a new period in the role of Palestinian women in political action, it still does not signal a fundamental change in their position within the society.*

* * *

One of the distinguishing features of the uprising is the spontaneous but organized role of Palestinian women, which has commanded admiration nationally and internationally. Women are in the forefront of popular demonstrations; they confront soldiers, save the men, rescue the injured, and inform merchants of strike days. The pictures of women and girls in the media, though representing only a small part of the intense role of women, have invited many questions.

Is this role new to Palestinian women? What precise part are they playing in the *intifada*? How do men and the United National Leadership of the Uprising (UNLU) regard women's roles? Does the participation of women reflect a new stage in the history of the women's movement? Are the political role and the sacrifices of women in the uprising going to improve women's social status and their political role in the future?

This chapter attempts to answer these questions, first placing women's activities in historical context. It is based on various sources, including published studies; interviews with old and young female leaders; publications of women's groups and associations containing their political and practical programs; women's yearly reports, magazines, and irregular publications (sometimes special issues); and their publications on national occasions and International Women's Day. Findings are also based on the author's personal witness to specific events. Unfortunately, both the negligence regarding women's roles and problems on the part of society at large, and Israeli repressive policies since 1967 in the area of research and publication, have led to a dearth of serious writings on Palestinian women.

The emergence of the Palestinian national movement and women's work

Women's activities in Palestine are relatively recent, since social conditions at the beginning of this century restricted their autonomous development. In farming communities, they were responsible for ploughing and planting the field, but also bore full responsibility for the children, kitchen, and laundry. There is a consensus in our sources that women worked more than men. The economic role of rural women gave them the experience of mixing with men and liberated them from wearing the veil, unlike city women. Yet women's important economic role did not improve their social status, since the attitudes, values, and traditions of Palestinian society at the turn of the century were condescending to them. In the presence of a patriarchal and reactionary society based on religion and its laws, women were prevented from inheriting the land, and their role was considered a part of housework. In the cities, women's status was much worse. Women had to stay home at age sixteen to be prepared for a husband who often had other wives. This resulted in the segregation of men and women in the cities, with the latter usually hiding behind a complete facial veil.[1] Nonetheless, interaction with the West, which intensified during the late nineteenth century, and the spread of governmental and Western missionary schools, brought women in cities and small villages into contact with the outside world. Christian families in the cities were the main beneficiaries, while women in rural areas rarely got an education. It is therefore small wonder that Christian middle- and upper-class women formed the nucleus of the first women's associations in Palestine, beginning in 1903. The associations were limited to charitable services. They did not have a program or a center but held their meetings in private homes, schoolrooms, and churches.

After World War I, a new stage of women's activity developed. With the dissolution of the Ottoman empire, Palestine came under a British mandate whose first goal was to secure a national homeland for Jews. This sparked the Palestinian national movement to come into existence, and it in turn gave birth to the Palestinian women's movement.

Under the British mandate, two major factors influenced the forms, development, aims, and limitations of women's work:

1. The focus on ending the occupation, a common trait of women's movements under occupation, unlike those in independent countries, where the struggle is for freedom within the society.
2. The leaders and members of the women's associations and the national movement under the mandate consisted of upper-class people in the cities.[2] The class nature of the Palestinian movement's vanguard at that time dictated the type of activities carried out, which were charitable and humanitarian in nature. During that period some women in the cities participated in demonstrations on national occasions, such as the demonstrations of February 1920 and March 1921.[3]

Women protested alongside men against land sales to Zionists, the expulsion of peasants from their lands, and increasing Jewish immigration to Palestine. In August 1929, out of 120 Arabs killed by the British as they put down nationalist protests, 9 were women.

The first women's conference was held in Jerusalem in 1929; it was chaired by the wife of the Arab executive committee head, Musa Kazim al-Husayni.[4] More than 200 women attended, most of them wives and relatives of political leaders or notables, or rich women. The resolutions of the conference were similar to those of the Arab executive committee and included the rejection of the Balfour declaration and Jewish immigration. After the conference, the women drove out and demonstrated in their cars, roamed the streets of Jerusalem, passed by the foreign consulates, and stopped at the British governor's home. A delegation of women took off their veils, saying, "To serve our homeland we shall take off our veil!" and presented a memorandum with their demands.[5]

Although the creation of the Arab Women's Committee in 1929 marked a milestone of sorts, as it provided a framework for women's activities and contributed to developing the general awareness of its members, women were still not involved in the existing political parties due to sex segregation. Women went out in demonstrations surrounded by scouts for protection or in a single group marching behind men. Women's conferences and demonstrations increased after 1933, and notably during the 1936–39 revolt, but in general participation remained limited to upper-class women or students.[6] Women in the countryside helped in transporting weapons and food, and donated their jewelry to buy arms. Women hardly took part in the actual fighting, nor did they work as nurses, except in a few cases.[7] In 1948 the Jewish state was established in Palestine. Palestinians were expelled from 20 cities and 400 villages. At least 10,000 Palestinians were killed, while triple that number were wounded. Sixty percent of the Palestinians became homeless.

The wholesale destruction of a society led to a new phenomenon in 1949, that of refugee camps relying on donations for survival. One million people were involved. Three out of four Palestinians found themselves living in a state of poverty.[8] The majority at first lived on relief. Men tended to leave the camps in Palestine (the West Bank, including Jerusalem, and Gaza Strip) seeking work. Refugee camps thus became havens for women, children, and the elderly.[9] In that part of Palestine which remained outside the Jewish state, six charitable associations were established to meet the needs of an expelled and destroyed nation. Educating girls was a high priority, for it meant getting a degree and a better job than serving and sewing, the only jobs available for camp women. UNRWA also offered some services in teaching and opened training centers.

With the annexation of the West Bank by Jordan in 1950, Palestinian men and women formed the national movement in Jordan, and women became members in underground political groups such as the Jordanian Communist party, the Ba'th party, and the Arab Nationalist Movement. Nevertheless, these parties did not give enough attention to issues of women's freedom and emancipation. Out of fear of the prevailing traditional values, women members were asked not to challenge society. Women members had their own party cells, an extension of sex segregation in society. Women's activities were restricted to secretarial work, typing services, signing petitions, and delivering messages and communiqués.[10] Women members were either students, educated women, or relatives of male members. But the lasting consequence of women's work in political parties was the gradual emergence of experienced female cadres, who were to play a significant role in confronting the Israeli occupation as of 1967.[11]

Women's status in the Gaza Strip during the 1949–67 period was similar to that of women under Jordanian rule in terms of their bad economic situation and men's emigration. The area was at that time under Egyptian military rule, nondemocratic, though nationalist, in nature. Here too, then, women were the backbone of refugee camp life.

Some women participated in political parties in Gaza, whether the Palestinian Communist party (for example, Samira Saba and Mahba' al-Barbari, women communist leaders arrested in August 1952),[12] the Ba'th party (which as of 1954 included a women's section headed by May Sayegh), or the Arab National Movement. Some charitable associations provided services in refugee camps by opening nurseries, mother and child centers, and literacy centers, or by teaching simple skills such as sewing, weaving, and embroidery. By 1967 there were sixty-eight associations in Nablus, Jerusalem, Hebron, and Gaza. Most of them, however, were apolitical.[13]

The General Union of Palestinian Women (GUPW) was formed in 1965 as a consequence of the Palestinian conference in Jerusalem in 1964, which established the PLO. The GUPW was created as a mass organization to participate in liberating the homeland.[14] Due to the way it was formed and its membership, it continued the strategy of the charitable associations by "giving services to women."[15] It did not deal with social questions, since its leadership consisted of privileged, socially liberated women. Furthermore, until 1967 the PLO itself was not popular in nature. Although it was associated with some progressive Arab regimes, it lacked a clear program for resistance.

The 1967 defeat and its effects on the Palestinian women's movement

The 1967 defeat led to the occupation of what remained of Palestine, the West Bank and Gaza Strip. From the beginning Israel acted to destructure Palestinian society, with a view to integrating it into and subjugating it to the Israeli economic system. This policy resulted in socioeconomic changes that affected the family and, in turn, Palestinian women.

Women under occupation thus entered the labor market. They took up unskilled jobs at low wages in relation to those of Arab men, which were, in turn, lower than those of Israeli workers. Women also worked in the absence of any attempt to apportion housework between the sexes, which caused them psychological stress, in addition to the stress-provoking nature of the work they tended to find, which was temporary and dependent on the fluctuations of the Israeli market. Working women's oppression under Israeli rule was therefore threefold: as Palestinians, as workers, as women.

Women and the PLO

The 1967 defeat transformed the PLO into a mass representative organization, which it has remained to the present time. Its program called for reliance on "the people in arms" rather than "Arab armies" for the task of liberation. Although such slogans lacked clarity, they helped focus on the need to organize various social categories, including women. But the Palestinian resistance organizations failed to establish an agenda for women as part of the overall agenda of the revolution. Certain slogans were formulated in lieu of such an agenda, for example, "Women will be liberated when society is" or "Men and women – side by side in the battle."[16]

In the Occupied Territories, women confronted the occupation through the channels of the charitable organizations and the General Union of Palestinian Women, both of which were linked to the Palestinian leadership embodied in the National Guidance Committee (established in 1967; disbanded in 1969). In the early days of the occupation Israel ignored women, since only a handful were actually imprisoned. However, by 1968 women prisoners totalled 100, mainly accused of contacting fedayeen, concealing weapons, incitement, or membership in armed organizations.

The National Front followed the National Guidance Committee in leading the Palestinian people in the Occupied Territories, in the wake of the defeat of the Palestinian armed resistance in Jordan in 1970–71. It consisted of active personalities and leaders, including one woman whose role was to coordinate the mobilization of women in resistance to occupation.[17] The Palestinian National Front (PNF) encouraged voluntary work projects in various areas. For the first time, young men and women worked together and discussed their problems. Women participated in armed struggle and airplane hijacking; they were tortured and imprisoned, thus changing the concept that women are weak creatures and undermining the concept of "women's honor."[18] The number of women enrolled and organized in political and military organizations in the West Bank and Gaza in turn led to an increase in the number of women prisoners, which had by 1979 reached 3,000.[19]

In 1975 and 1976 student organizations were created to organize men and women, such as the Palestine Student Union, the Committee of Secondary Students (in 1975), and the Union of Secondary Students (in 1976). The creation of these organizations led to more demonstrations and increased participation by women.[20]

The charitable organizations likewise organized women to demonstrate, sending them into the streets. But all these activities were sporadic and somewhat improvised, based as they were on national issues and slogans. Women's issues were looked down on as not worth considering. This may have been due partly to the *de facto* restriction of membership to middle-class women from the major cities, which limited their influence with the camp and rural women. The only relationship between activist women and the masses was in giving them assistance in cash and in kind. This was notably the case for the In'ash Al Usrah (Family Rehabilitation) Society in al-Bireh, which focused on distributing material for embroidery to village women. It likewise provided some medical assistance and vocational training. The main goal was to help women face their harsh conditions in the event of death, deportation, or imprisonment of the man. These services are doubtless important in the absence of a national authority. But by carrying out the PNF's directives and linking their work to the general struggle of women at a strictly "national" level, the charitable organizations were mobilizing women only sporadically and in a limited fashion.[21]

Although the PNF was progressively dismantled by Israel from 1974 to 1977, it fulfilled its function of directing and channeling protest activities. Several other factors also contributed to the mounting involvement of women in political resistance in the West Bank and Gaza Strip from 1975 to 1978:

1. Women were granted the right to vote for the first time in the 1976 municipal elections, through an Israeli military order amending the 1955 Jordanian electoral law, and enfranchising all people over twenty-one. Defense Minister Shimon Peres had made the mistaken calculation that Arab women would tend to vote conservatively. In fact, they voted heavily in favor of nationalist progressive candidates.[22]

   With this revolutionary transformation of two dozen town and city councils, bringing a younger and far more progressive leadership to the forefront, work with the masses assumed a new dimension. Various municipalities organized work camps (most notably in the Bethlehem–Jerusalem–Ramallah–Al-Bireh area) that became breeding grounds for women activists.

2. In the mid and late seventies, nine colleges and community colleges (four- and two-year undergraduate institutions) opened, heavily attended by young women (who made up from 35 to 55 percent of various student bodies).

3. The election in 1977 of the Likud government of Begin–Shamir–Sharon led immediately to a significant escalation in repressive measures taken against the Occupied Territories and their inhabitants.

As might have been expected, this palpably heightened repression led to greater determination and resistance, not least among women, many activists among whom were placed under house arrest. In the case of the charitable associations, the new Likud policy did some damage, since decision making was restricted to a few members, and their detention at home or in prison tended to paralyse the working of the organization. But student organizations, which included women among their cadres, elected their leadership democratically and in a decentralized manner. They and the new women's organizations were able to escape some of the effects of the repression. The role of charitable organizations in relation to student and women's organizations therefore began to decline.

4. Some of the cultural activities of the mid-1970s dealt increasingly with women's issues. This was true of theatrical performances, magazine articles, and even entire books.

This sequence of interrelated developments throughout the 1970s finally resulted in the birth in 1978 of a new women's vanguard within the Palestinian national movement in the Occupied Territories.

The emergence of a vanguard for the Palestinian women's movement, 1978

The experiences of the Palestinian National Front, and the National Guidance Committee had shown the importance of public efforts to organize the masses. The mass organizations were associated with PLO factions; each one sought to strengthen its following. Labor unions, voluntary work organizations, and women's organizations were all duly factionalized. And while it is true that a single organization would have sufficed in each case, this partisanship did have the advantage of increasing the numbers of people organized, by appealing to the partisans of all the political groups. It was also much harder to destroy these new organizations than the old ones.

First attempts

For these reasons, and against the background of the intensity of national resistance in 1976, International Women's Day, March 8, 1978, was especially important. Some activist women held a meeting which resulted in the creation of the Women's Work Committee. It was largely made up of that generation of women who worked in political organizations and were not welcomed in the existing women's charitable associations. Despite their minor political role, the charitable organizations were concerned with preserving their position and power. The Women's Work

Committee included the cadre of women who had emerged from various voluntary work camps, which proliferated especially after the 1976 municipal elections.

Although the Women's Work Committee was initially made up of active cadres without regard to political affiliation, soon enough a partisan power struggle emerged within its ranks. The only solution found was for each faction to establish its own women's mass organization, as was happening in other sectors, notably the trade unions. One therefore witnessed the successive creation of the Union of Palestinian Working Women's Committees (March 1980), the Palestinian Women's Committee (later the Union of Palestinian Women's Committees [March 1981]), and the Women's Committee for Social Work (June 1982). The division of the women's movement, which continues to the present, does not reflect differences in the agenda and goals of the different groups. Everybody's first goal is to involve the greatest possible number of women in the national movement. The achievement of this goal required flexible conditions of membership, such as attending meetings, the adoption of the organization's goal, and participation in decision making. This flexibility (contrary to the membership conditions of the charitable organizations) enabled women from different social classes to participate; thus, the women's movement was not restricted to middle-class women as in the past.[23]

The first goal of all these organizations is political. However, "emancipating Palestinian women" is an item in the agendas of all the organizations, specifically the left-oriented ones. Several demands are made in the quest for women's emancipation, such as equality with men in the form of equal pay for equal work, and various types of social protection for working women. What is meant by "women's social issues," then, takes the form of equality in general, dealing with union skills and qualifications. Accordingly, in the women's publications we find no mention of the laws that govern woman's status in society, or of the traditional values that still reinforce the tribal and patriarchal culture, especially for rural women. Many issues concerning gender are avoided.

The organizations have avoided such a discussion either because they actually believe it is not a priority in the period of national struggle or because they are afraid to open an internal front at a crucial time demanding the unity of all efforts to end the occupation.

In any event, there is a common and strong belief within the women's vanguard that the rising generation of Palestinian leaders cannot ignore the role of Palestinian women in resistance and that women are going to be liberated through a change in the laws. The leadership of the independent Palestinian state will, it is hoped, change the laws that govern women's status in society and thus liberate them.

The methods adopted by the women's groups do not differ in form from the charitable organization's methods. Some of these are establishing nurseries, training prograins, literacy centers, workshops, and cooperatives. The major difference between the former and the latter lies in the people who supervise such projects and their awareness. Their level of political consciousness helps in transforming that of the participants and in giving them self-confidence through shared decision making, taking decisions by vote, holding elections, deciding on agendas in common, and so on. All projects undertaken by the women's organizations provide a permanent pool for various national or women's activities, whether in the village, refugee camp, or city. The project here is not a goal in itself but a means to achieve a future goal. Sometimes, especially during intense factional conflict, the increase in the number of these projects is taken as a measure of the strength of a given political faction. In spite of all these overlapping efforts, the number of organized women is still low, not exceeding 3 percent of the population.[24]

The Palestinian women's movement and the *intifada*

Palestinian women have played a major role in the *intifada* since its beginning.[25] Many observers were surprised at this massive role. It was not new, however, for Palestinian women to take on a political role in society, especially in emergencies, as seen above. What was new, as will be discussed, was the scope and various manifestations of this role.

From the start, women of all ages and social classes took part in the demonstrations that broke out on December 9, 1987, throwing stones, burning tires, transporting and preparing stones, building roadblocks, raising Palestinian flags, and preventing soldiers from arresting people. These activities were most intense in poor neighborhoods in the towns, in villages, and in refugee camps. Women's actions were sometimes violent, and they were often involved in serious confrontations with the army.[26]

The role of women was duly acknowledged in leaflets distributed in Gaza in December 1987, which urged them to continue. With the spread of the *intifada* to the villages, towns, and cities of the West Bank and with the publication of the communiqués of the United National Leadership of the Uprising, women, like other sectors of society, were called upon to participate in different protest activities: "Oh people of martyrs. ... Oh revolutionary giants. ... Men and students. ... Our workers, peasants and women ... the land shall be burned under the feet of the occupiers." The language of such appeals differs from that of the appeals issued by the National Committees or the Arab Higher

Committee in the 1936–39 Palestinian revolt. The 1936–39 leaflets read, "Youngsters of Palestine, men, elderly people," without mentioning women. This evolution in the language reflects the importance of the present political role of women.[27] In contrast, the four women's organizations distributed a political leaflet on October 1, 1988, to protest the deportation of nine activists and addressed to "the heroic masses of our Palestinian people, the heroes of the great *intifada* ... " without mentioning women except in the sentence "heroic masses of our people, your *intifada* has reached the whole world ... and Palestinian women have thrilled with joy."[28]

Before March 8, 1988 (International Women's Day), the women's organizations did not have a clear agenda specifying the forms women's participation should take. It was left for the UNLU to call upon women as well as other sectors. Thus, each women's organization separately, or all four together, organized the activities called for by the UNLU, such as demonstrating and holding marches and sit-ins. The weekly average of women's demonstrations in the West Bank and Gaza Strip – as recorded through March 8, 1988 – was 115 demonstrations, during which 16 women from different places were killed.[29]

The first comprehensive program

The first leaflet containing a comprehensive program and addressing women was distributed on March 8, 1988, by the four women's organizations and the charitable associations, signed "Palestinian Women in the Occupied Territories." The leaflet reads:

Our heroic women, mothers of martyrs, the imprisoned and the injured, their wives, sisters and girls. To all the Palestinian women in camps, villages and cities, who are united in their struggle and their political confrontation with repression and terrorism ... to all our sisters in the battle where all hostile theories have been burnt ... let our activists participate extensively in the popular committees in neighborhoods, cities, villages and camps. Let them participate in making programs to promote the intifada and support our steadfast people. Let us send representatives to collect donations and expose the various occupation practices. Let our working women participate in the unions and organize as workers; and step by step we'll achieve victory. Oh working women, join your fellow workers in boycotting work on strike days for you mostly suffer from racism and continuous oppression. Oh heroic teachers, our children's future is important; the occupying authorities have closed down all our educational institutions. Therefore, unite and confront the policy

259

of closing the educational institutions, whose purpose is to produce an illiterate generation.

Mothers, in camps, villages and cities, continue confronting soldiers and settlers. Let each woman consider the wounded and imprisoned her own children. In the name of the great uprising, we ask you all to develop the concept of home economy by producing all food and clothes locally. This is a step in boycotting Israeli goods and paralysing their economy. We can achieve this goal by going to the land, the source of goodness and happiness.

Two demands set forth by this program need to be discussed in detail: setting up popular committees and engaging in home economy.

The popular committees were seen by some as alternative institutions and by others as the infrastructure of the future independent state. And they helped to unite people, including women, who were to varying degrees active in the five principal ones: agriculture, education, food storage, medical, and guarding committees. In the towns women participated actively from the beginning, with variations based on qualifications and age. The one committee reserved for urban males, and young ones at that, was the neighborhood guarding committee, whose activities were especially required at night. In camps and villages, on the other hand, older and less educated women assumed an active role in the guarding committees.

Women were relatively most active (in some neighborhoods to the exclusion of men) in the education committees. For much of the spring and summer of 1988, they bore the brunt of organizing and carrying out neighborhood popular schooling, made necessary by months of military-ordered closures of West Bank schools. In this respect, of course, women were in fact continuing traditional practice, since they are largely entrusted with childcare and are in the majority at all levels of pre-university education. Housewives were likewise most assiduous among the population in attending committee-organized lectures given in homes, notably on health matters (especially first aid) but on a variety of other subjects as well. Young women in the cities also took an active part in the distribution of leaflets and added a cooperative and enthusiastic tone to work in general.

From these indicators, one can infer the extent, but also the limitations, of women's involvement in the popular committees, in the urban setting at least. But there is no indication from these elements that women's participation in decision making increased through the experience of the popular committees.

A preliminary conclusion regarding the urban popular committees is, therefore, that they were used more as means for maximizing the number of organized people than as instruments of social change. This explains why the committees were essentially limited to those who organized them.[30]

The participation of village and refugee camp women in popular committees took a different course from that of urban women from the start. In the camps, committees actually carried out the activities called for in UNLU communiqués more spontaneously than in the towns. Usually, however, meetings were held in a coffee shop or in the mosque, places where women rarely go. Despite the massive participation of refugee camp women in demonstrations, their involvement in committees was rare and indirect.

In the villages, committees similar in structure and function to those of the camps were formed. But there only men took part. Women and girls did not participate, although here too women took an active part in such mass activities as marches, demonstrations, and martyrs' funeral processions. Here too there was coordination with women's organizations, but mixed popular committees like those found in the cities were never formed.[31]

Overall, it may be concluded that a variety of popular committees played an important role in the *intifada* during the year 1988. But they were not new instruments through which the status of women was transformed. Their essential goal was to find new members for the mass organizations of each faction. Women's role in the popular committees became an extension of what it traditionally had been in the society: teaching and rendering services. In this respect it was difficult to distinguish between committees controlled by the leftist organizations (PFLP, DFLP, Communist party) and those controlled by the centrist Fateh. A woman's participation in decision making was the result of political affiliation and remained within the confines of the existing political balance. By the beginning of 1989, however, the four major women's committees joined together to form the Higher Women's Council. The council became the nucleus for coordination among its participant groups.

Home economy

The second important demand made of the Palestinian people during the *intifada* requiring women's participation was the strengthening of home economy. The general connotation of the concept was self-reliance in the production of food and clothing and the return to the land. In implementing the demand, women's organizations in various cities worked directly or through popular committees to hold lectures on home economy. They also distributed publications discussing food storage and preservation and caring for plants and animals.

There is, if one looks at UNLU Communiqués No. 8 and 9 as well as publications of women's groups, some confusion as to the exact definition of home economy. In one instance it means taking steps toward boycotting Israeli goods,[32] in another measures to achieve "the highest levels of self-sufficiency in the face of the economic blockade imposed by the occupation forces."[33] In yet another context it is described as "the gradual return to the family farm, an economy of self-sufficiency led mainly by women."[34]

The UNLU entrusted to women responsibility for the success of the home economy movement. And various popular and women's committees endeavored to further one aspect or another of home economy.

The question then arises as to whether this particular woman's activity has a qualitatively new content, or whether it maintains her in her traditional social, economic, and familial role. In other words, is there, through the home economy movement, a new division of labor among the sexes, or is the role of women conceived according to the traditional and still prevailing gender division of labor, in which women's work is seen as unproductive?[35]

Two main types of cooperatives were established.[36] The first involves women in productive and income-generating projects outside the home. These cooperatives are run democratically, with women in control of production, management, and marketing. A second type encourages a variety of women to produce food at home, while the women's organizations market products and pass profits on to the women. The first type is qualitatively more advanced than the second, since its functioning is more truly cooperative and less oriented toward individual profit, and it helps bring women out of their homes. But one should not, as is sometimes done, take a mechanistic attitude regarding the virtues of women's work outside the house. Thus we read that "although women's work in the cooperatives [in Beitillo and Sa'ir, respectively Ramallah and Hebron area villages] has added new responsibilities for women, coming in addition to their housework, child-rearing etc., it has played an important role in transforming men's appraisal of women's work in general and housework in particular. . . . [Women's contribution to the family income] led to change in the traditional gender-based division of labor."[37] The fact of the matter is that such changes in the traditional division of labor, where they have occurred, have not been accompanied by a public critique of existing rural values. Setting up a women's production cooperative in the countryside does not automatically lead to changes in the gender-based division of labor, nor to an upward reevaluation by men of women's work. Political activists, although they are working women married to politically progressive men, continue to suffer from the existing division of labor. There is no congruity between their political or productive work and housework, which continues to be divided among women according to age and class, and not among men and women.[38] The theoretically highly developed political and productive role of women is not reflected in their social status.

A clear illustration of this gap is provided by events during the *intifada*, which gave great responsibilities to women activists. These required them to devote much time to physically and psychologically exhausting activities. In this context, women activists stood up and, for the first time in the history of the Palestinian women's movement, publicly criticized its long negligence of social issues.

It is difficult to argue that implementing home economy projects plays a progressive role in changing the status of women, unless it is associated with a change in existing values built on the gender division of labor. The present concept of implementing home economy is a qualitatively advanced one only through its connection to the *intifada*. It has value as a national demand, but there has been no attempt to imbue it with progressive social content.

Other questions

Other demands on the March 8 agenda were restricted to women only.[39] One was that of gathering to prevent men from being arrested. Despite the continuity of this role from the outset, it had not previously been an organized activity. Women's teams were formed to prevent arrests. But an accurate assessment of this phenomenon would have to describe it as the momentary reflex of women who know the fate that awaits prisoners: the process begins with kicking and ends with death. Women, unlike men, are not targeted when they gather in the streets, even if they represent a target during demonstrations and confrontations.

One can thus trace an evolution in the image of "ideal women" from "ladies" at the beginning of the women's movement, to "men's sisters" with the emergence of the Palestinian resistance in the 1960s, to "martyrs' mothers" or "factories for men" in the 1970s. This last image is still popular, unlike the first. Emerging images of the ideal woman are in fact positive, related to the struggle, and no longer limited to "cries of joy" of the martyrs' mothers. We are here speaking of popular concepts, those of the poor in villages, refugee camps, and city neighborhoods.

The women's organizations likewise worked actively to involve women in demonstrations, tire burnings, and martyrs' processions in camps and villages. Clearly, Palestinian women played a key role in activating the street and in encouraging men to participate. It became difficult to go out in a demonstration without seeing women in the front lines. During all of 1988, continuous demonstrations would break out from the mosques on Fridays and from the churches on Sundays. Women would start the demonstrations, which became serious confrontations with the soldiers. Different female sectors of society participated, including students, workers, housewives, girls, and employees.

The political role of women in the demonstrations helped in weakening the concept of "women's honor." Often, when soldiers broke into homes in villages and camps, they tried to strip the women, cursed using foul sexual language, exposed their own or attempted to expose women's sexual organs, or threatened to rape the women in an attempt to humiliate them. There were even some individual cases of attempted rape.[40] The new and unexpected women's response, instead of the traditional covering of the face, was to hurl back the identical curses unabashedly at the soldiers. Many stories of this nature (not all of them necessarily true) circulated and became part of the *intifada* heritage, reflecting new values concerning women. Women occupied leading positions in decision-making bodies for the first time. In addition to a certain political vacuum due to imprisonments and the enormity of the task at hand, the length of the *intifada* and the continuously acquired experience in politics facilitated the new role of women. Still, there were some political activities of women that can only be seen as an extension of the traditional political role. These took the form of solidarity visits to the camps and villages, consolation visits to the families of the martyrs, collecting donations, or distribution of food to suffering families. Also the *intifada* brought about a greater degree of coordination among activist women in the form of the Higher Women's Council.

Conclusion

In this discussion of the role of women in the *intifada* we have seen that politically experienced people led the masses of women into becoming involved in resistance. Most women's organizations, as has been shown, have programs that call for a linking of national issues (ending the occupation) with women's liberation. At the same time, most discussions within the women's movement focus on gaining rights for working women and giving women skills so that they can be active and productive members of the society. There is even some discussion of daring issues such as divorce, guaranteeing women's income, and raising women's status in the family.[41] And yet there has been no "agenda" for the women's movement until now. This fact endangers the few rights obtained by women through their involvement in politics and the relative advancement of their role. It is all the more risky since the tendency is to postpone the setting of such an agenda until after independence has been achieved.[42] The assumption is that women will legally obtain their rights along with national independence.

Unfortunately, a study of the Palestinian national movement does little to justify that assumption, for a variety of reasons. First, the women's movement stemmed from the Palestinian national movement. Women's political participation is therefore dependent on the national movement, that is to say, on development – positive or negative – at the level of the leadership. The women's movement is divided into four organizations following the leadership of the national movement. The absence of social critique in the national movement, especially on the part of Fateh, which is its backbone, adds to the danger facing the women's movement.

A second inhibiting factor is the emergence of the Islamic forces, which strongly affect Palestinian political life in the West Bank and Gaza Strip, as has clearly been shown in the *intifada*. What is women's position in society in the programs of the Islamic forces? Women's position is in the home, in reproduction, and in the improvement of the quality of life, although women's education is not prohibited. We read in a document of the Islamic resistance group Hamas under the title "The Roles of Muslim Women": "In the resistance, the role of the Muslim woman is equal to the man's. She is a factory of men, and she has a great role in raising and educating the generations."[43]

Because of the general strength of the Islamic movement in the area of social life, it is not going to be easy to change laws affecting women and family life in the event of independence, and it would be wrong to rely on a Palestinian government to change laws in recognition of the role of women in the resistance. The very fact that trust is placed in a future independent government is itself linked to the weak feminist consciousness of most women, raised to believe that gender division of labor is their natural duty.

Because of its roots in the national movement, the Palestinian women's movement was from the start characterized by its political work, that is to say, its concentration on national resistance while ignoring or avoiding issues of social change. The establishment of the women's organizations from 1978 on represented a qualitative step forward, since they devoted themselves to organizing women and encouraging them to be politically active. Bent on reaching large numbers of women, these organizations differed radically from the earlier charitable organizations.

Some of the leaders of these organizations, through their work in political organizations, had become aware of social issues; but they have not, in general, in their publications and speeches, focused on them. They believe that during the national liberation struggle they should focus on resistance and not open secondary fronts. Discussions nonetheless took place among members, making it difficult for them to adapt to obsolete values, notably marriage practices.

Then came the *intifada*, a supreme manifestation of popular resistance to the occupation due to its continuity and the participation of most classes, sectors of society, and ages, and of both genders. Spontaneously, women went out to participate courageously in resistance activities. Women's organizations, assuming their vanguard role within the Palestinian women's movement, organized and directed women's participation with an agenda of several points.

The program was popular, though imprecise. And the existing gender division of labor continues to place women at the lower end of the family hierarchy, even when they work inside and outside their homes. This reflects the continued low level of feminist consciousness within women's organizations and on the part of the UNLU.

Nonetheless, women play a crucial political role, even if it is a motherly one of saving demonstrators from soldiers. The point has been reached where it has become dangerous for men to participate in demonstrations or marches in the absence of women.

This in turn has led to the emergence of a new ideal of women as saviors rather than weak creatures needing protection. It has weakened traditional values and given women strength, self-confidence, and fearlessness in the face of killing, beating, arrest, and the threat of sexual assault. The new climate has helped the women's vanguard publicly to criticize restrictions placed on women's social life.

Will this trend be reflected in a new social agenda for the women's organizations? Or will the process be reversed if and when the confrontations diminish or come to an end? The answer to this question depends on women's awareness itself, an awareness that has penetrated the vanguard, where it continues to progress. It depends, ultimately, on whether that vanguard manages to formulate an appropriate agenda and communicate it to the masses of women.

NOTES

1 "The Women's Movement," in *Palestine Encyclopedia* (Damascus: Palestine Encyclopedia Committee, 1984), p. 212 (in Arabic).
2 Ibid., p. 211.
3 Union of Arab Women, *The Golden Jubilee* (Jerusalem: Union of Arab Women, 1980) (in Arabic).
4 Ibid.
5 Nahla Abu-Zu'bi *Family, Women and Social Change in the Middle East: The Palestinian Case* (Toronto: Scholar's Press, 1987), p. 21.
6 On May 14, 1936, 600 women students participated in a demonstration and called for the boycotting of Zionist goods. Ibid., p. 22.
7 Ghazi al-Khalili, *The Palestinian Women and the Revolution* (Akka: Dar al-Aswar, 1981).
8 Pamela Ann Smith, *Palestine and the Palestinians, 1876–1983* (London: Croom Helm, 1994), p. 137.
9 Ibid., p. 175.
10 Khadija Abu-Ali, *Introduction to Women's Reality and Their Experience in the*

Palestinian Revolution (Beirut: General Union of Palestinian Women, 1975), pp. 44, 54–55 (in Arabic).

11 *Woman and Her Role in the United Arab Movement* (Beirut: United Arab Studies Center, 1982), pp. 216–17.

12 Ziad Abu-Amr, *Origins of the Political Movement in Gaza* (Akka: Dar al-Aswar, 1987) (in Arabic).

13 League of Arab States, *Women's Associations and Committees in the West Bank and Gaza Strip* (Tunis: League of Arab States, 1984) (in Arabic).

14 Maysoon al-Weidy, *Palestinian Women and the Israeli Occupation* (Jerusalem: Arab Studies Society, 1986), pp. 8–9 (in Arabic).

15 Interview with 'Isam Abdul-Hadi, chair, GUPW executive committee, *Revue d'Etudes Palestiniennes* 1 (1981): 82.

16 Al-Khalili, *The Palestinian Women*, p. 113.

17 Interviews with women leaders in the movement, December 1988. For detailed figures on women prisoners and martyrs during that period, see ibid., and al-Weidy, *Palestinian Women*.

18 Raymonda Hawa-Tawil, *My Home, My Prison* (London: Zed Press, 1983), p. 131.

19 Sonya Antonius, "Femmes prisonnières pour la Palestine," *Revue d'Etudes Palestiniennes* 1 (1981): 76. A majority of women prisoners were from left-wing organizations, while the largest group of male prisoners belonged to Fateh.

20 Moshe Ma'oz, *Palestinian Leadership on the West Bank* (London: Frank Cass, 1984), pp. 116–17.

21 Conclusions drawn from the analysis of annual reports of charitable organizations in the Jerusalem, al-Bireh, and Bethlehem areas covering the period in question.

22 Ma'oz, *Palestinian Leadership*, pp. 134–36. Four candidates for municipal office (out of 577) were women.

23 See Lisa Taraki, "Mass Organizations in the West Bank," in Naseer Aruri, ed., *Occupation: Israel over Palestine*, 2nd ed. (Belmont, Mass.: AAUG Press, 1989).

24 Union of Women's Work Committees, *The Development of the Palestinian Women's Movement* (Jerusalem: Union of Women's Work Committees, n.d.) (in Arabic).

25 Often deaths resulted. For example, two female martyrs fell in Balata camp near Nablus on December 11, 1987: Suheila Ka'ibi, seventy-five years old, with a bullet in the heart; and Sahar al-Jarmi, seventeen years old, with a bullet in the heart.

26 During the funeral on December 9, 1987, of the *intifada*'s first martyr, Hatem al-Sisi, a woman grabbed a soldier's gun and threw it to the ground.

27 Which nonetheless, and notably in the Gaza Strip, has to deal with deeply ingrained conservative values concerning women's activities. Cf. Susan Rockwell, "Palestinian Women Workers in the Israeli-Occupied Gaza Strip," *Journal of Palestine Studies* 14, no. 2 (Winter 1985): 130.

28 Their first joint statement.

29 Data based on *Towards a State of Independence: The Palestinian Uprising, December 1987–August 1988* (Jerusalem: Facts Information Committee, 1988). It is significant that the four women's organizations were the first mass organizations to form a permanent coordination committee, even before the *intifada*, in March 1987. This shows that partisan conflict among women's organizations is less intense than among the male-dominated ones.

30 See *The Conscience of the Intifada* (Popular Resistance Committees in the Occupied Territories), no. 4 (November 1988) (in Arabic).
31 Interviews with women and girls from villages, as well as village activists in women's organizations.
32 Statement on March 8, 1988, signed "Palestinian Women in the Occupied Territories."
33 UNLU Communiqué No. 12, April 2, 1988.
34 Adel Samara and Odeh Shehadeh, *The Economy of the West Bank and Gaza*: *From Restricted Development to Popular Protection* (Akka: Dar al-Aswar, 1988), pp. 59–61 (in Arabic).
35 The concept of home economy in fact predates the *intifada*. See, for example, Muharram Barghouti, "Tanmiat al-Mafhoum Mutakhallif" (Developing the Concept of Backward), *al-Katib*, no. 78 (December 1986).
36 Seminar conducted by the four women's groups at Ramallah offices of Bir Zeit University (the campus has been shut by military order since January 1988). See also Union of Palestinian Women's Committees, *The Intifada Continues*, special issue (March 1988) (in Arabic).
37 Eileen Kuttab and Khalida al-Ratrout, "The Women's Cooperative Experience – The Beitillo and Sa'ir Cooperatives," *Shu'un Tanmawiyya* (Development Issues) 3 (1988): 24–26.
38 "In other words, the woman outside is a leader, but not inside [the home]." Roundtable: "The Palestinian Woman's Struggle – Obstacles and Ambitions," *Shu'un Tanmawiyya* 3 (1988): 10–11.
39 See Union of Palestinian Working Women's Committees, *Women of the Intifada* (Jerusalem: UPWWC, March 1988); Union of Palestinian Women's Work Committees Newsletter (Jerusalem), March 8, 1988, and June 1988.
40 Soldiers attempted to rape Samia Ibrahim Shir'a, eighteen years of age, in Jabalia camp on January 26, 1988. See National Information Committee, Gaza Strip, *Newsletter*, no. 6 (n.d.).
41 *Shu'un Filistiniyya* (Nicosia: Palestinian Research Center), no. 189 (December 1988).
42 See various publications by the women's committees over the years.
43 See, for example, the statement by the representative of the Palestinian Federation of Women's Action Committees at the debate on the Palestinian women's movement held at the offices of Bir Zeit University, January 1989.

INDEX